Globalization and State Power

Globalization and State Power

A Reader

JOEL KRIEGER
WELLESLEY COLLEGE

PEARSON
Longman

New York   San Francisco   Boston
London   Toronto   Sydney   Tokyo   Singapore   Madrid
Mexico City   Munich   Paris   Cape Town   Hong Kong   Montreal

Executive Editor:	Eric Stano
Senior Marketing Manager:	Elizabeth Fogarty
Production Manager:	Denise Phillip
Project Coordination, Text Design, and Electronic Page Makeup:	WestWords, Inc.
Cover Designer/Manager:	John Callaham
Cover Image:	Courtesy of Getty Images, Inc.
Senior Manufacturing Buyer:	Alfred C. Dorsey
Printer and Binder:	R.R. Donnelley & Sons
Cover Printer:	Phoenix Color Corporation

For permission to use copyrighted material, grateful acknowledgment is made to the copyright holders on pp. 353–354, which are hereby made part of this copyright page.

Library of Congress Cataloging-in-Publication Data

Globalization and state power: a reader / [edited by] Joel Krieger.
    p. cm.
ISBN 0-321-24522-9
    1. Globalization. 2. Power (Social sciences) 3. United States
—Relations—Foreign countries. 4. International relations.
I. Krieger, Joel, 1951– .
JZ1318.G579162 2006
327'.09'0511—dc22   2005015357

Please visit our website at http://www.ablongman.com

ISBN 0-321-24522-9

1 2 3 4 5 6 7 8 9 10—DOC—08 07 06 05

Contents

Chapter 3
STATE POWER IN THE ERA OF GLOBALIZATION: CASE STUDIES
109

✣

Chapter 4
POST–9/11: TERROR, WAR, AND EMPIRE

Preface

The shelves of bookstores are jam-packed with scholarly books and more than a few readers about globalization. But there are surprisingly few volumes that focus specifically on globalization and state power and there is no easy way for instructors to compile and make readily available a suitable range of top-notch offerings in this fast-paced field of study.

PURPOSE OF THE BOOK

Globalization and State Power A Reader aims to satisfy this need. The reader provides a balanced and carefully selected set of lively and informative contributions by premier scholars, political observers, and policy-makers who have shaped the public debate on two critical and interlocking questions:

1. How does globalization transform the role and functions of states and shape the exercise of state power?
2. How does unrivaled American power shape both the geopolitical order and the capacity of other states to exercise power?

The selections provide a range of insightful and informative answers to these and related questions about the global challenges of economic competitiveness, the battles for geopolitical influence, and the struggles for security from terror attacks. A compilation of twenty-six of the most powerful treatments of globalization and state power, the volume is designed to serve both as a stand alone reader, intended above all for use in undergraduate courses, and as a complement to the companion text, *Globalization and State Power.*

STRUCTURE OF THE BOOK

Divided into four chapters, the reader provides students with a complex and timely understanding of globalization and how it shapes the behavior and the capacity of states in this daunting contemporary era:

- **Chapter 1** reprises the "great globalization debate," engaging students with some of the most compelling and widely discussed alternative paradigms for understanding globalization and state power.

- **Chapter 2** focuses attention on the changing contours of state power—the erosion of traditional sovereignty expressed in autonomous control within territorial boundaries and the emergence of an increasingly refined new pattern of state power described by overlapping sovereignties and multi-level governance.
- **Chapter 3** brings front and center a comparative politics approach to global studies with the presentation of three case studies: the United States and its exercise of hegemonic power; the struggle by EU Europe (and, in particular, Britain, France, and Germany) to preserve distinctive economic and social models in the face of competitive pressures and American power; and the changing scope and exercise of state power in selected East Asian countries before, during, and after the economic and financial crisis in the late 1990s.
- **Chapter 4** shifts the book's focus to terror, war, and empire, with a set of contributions from a variety of hard-hitting and hotly contested perspectives. These readings will inspire reflection and spark classroom debate about national security, humanitarian intervention, and American foreign policy in the post–9/11, post-war in Iraq era.

PRINCIPLES OF SELECTION
AND PEDAGOGY

Having for several years taught a course on the themes of globalization and state power, I have observed the frustration of students who prefer sustained arguments that retain the voice, style, and depth of the original article or book to shorter heavily edited contributions. At the same time, I recognize that students also enjoy short pieces and, whatever the length, they appreciate clear lively argument. Hence *Globalization and State Power A Reader* contains pieces of varying lengths and formats that conform as closely as possible to the original texts. The contributions are quite accessible and suitable for a wide range of undergraduates.

In addition, to further encourage effective teaching, the reader includes introductions to each chapter and selection. Study and Discussion Questions help situate the selections and draw attention to key themes and interpretations.

The selections are provocative, engaging, and also present a rich menu of alternative arguments and interpretations. I believe deeply that the more controversial a subject matter, the more important it is to provide students with compelling alternatives so that everyone can find ammunition to support favorite arguments and, at the same time, discover less familiar perspectives that challenge assumptions and encourage new thinking.

The selections in *Globalization and State Power A Reader* will amply satisfy these guiding principles and promise to inspire students—and other readers—to enter the debate about globalization and state power themselves, fully informed about the issues and mindful of what is at stake in the debate.

ACKNOWLEDGMENTS

I wish to thank Anna Azaryeva for her superb research assistance. In addition, I greatly appreciate the efforts of those who reviewed the manuscript and offered very helpful feedback: Shaheen Ayubi, Rutgers University—Camden; Christopher L. Ball, Iowa State University; Linda Bishai, Towson University; Richard W. Chadwick, University of Hawaii; Stephen Crowley, Oberlin College; Michael Deaver, Sierra College; Thomas P. Dolan, Columbus State University; Geoffrey L. Herrera, Temple University; and Michaela Mihailescu, University of Minnesota. I am also very grateful to my editor Eric Stano at Longman, and to Jared Sterzer and Janel Anderson for their help throughout the production phase.

General Introduction

In February 2005, President George W. Bush toured Europe. He hoped to patch-up European-American relations, which had been battered by disagreements over the war in Iraq. In addition, he was determined to place his efforts to advance liberty and democracy at the center of global politics.

Despite determined diplomatic efforts on all sides to turn the page on arguments over Iraq, the role of multilateral institutions, and the use of force versus diplomacy in international disputes, the trip exposed some critical differences between America and its allies. Although the Germans made it clear that they appreciated the increased sense of cooperation with the United States, they insisted that the European Union rather than the U.S.-dominated NATO should be the primary institutional anchor for European security and geopolitical strategy. Similarly, France signaled that it could work together with the United States in Afghanistan and in a joint initiative to remove Syrian troops and influence from Lebanon. But the French left no doubt that the looming crisis concerning Iran's nuclear program should be resolved by European diplomacy, not the American threat to use military force.

Finally, despite all the diplomatic efforts to smooth over differences, a significant new dispute erupted—one that reveals the tension between the economic and geopolitical dimensions of globalization and lends focus to a critical question. When push comes to shove, does America's exercise of hegemonic power constrain all other states from exercising their power? Bush was horrified to learn that the EU was determined to lift the embargo on high-end arms sales to China. The Europeans seemed to have the collective political cohesion and power—and they certainly had the commercial incentives—to determine their own trade policies over the vigorous objections of the United States. America fumed over European intransigence and worried about the military and security implications in the Taiwan Straits—and globally—of China going on an extremely expensive military buying spree. *The Economist* wittily captured this flap on its cover, depicting the world-weary American president boarding Air Force One for his trip home, alongside the caption: "Merci, y'all (But why the heck are you selling arms to China?)". By June the EU's plan to lift the China arms ban was in tatters.

If anyone still doubted the agenda-setting force of America as the unrivaled superpower, the president's trip—and the instant flurry of activities in Syria and Lebanon and throughout the Middle East to advance his vision of democracy and liberty—removed more than a few of those doubts. If anyone questioned the fact that complex rivalries and crosscutting agendas drive global politics—

and can drive a wedge between great powers all jockeying for position and advantage—the trip also answered those questions. In addition, Bush's European tour provided some powerful lessons about the complex intrigues and multiform challenges that link globalization and the exercise of state power in this extremely challenging historical period.

Before September 11, 2001, the economic aspects of globalization and the growing development gap were at the top of the world's global agenda. Since the attacks of September 11, 2001, concern about the "clash of civilizations" between the West and the Arab and Muslim world, the problem of security against terror, and questions about how American power will set global agendas and redefine alliances have partially refocused our thinking about globalization.

The challenges of development and competitiveness, intensifying security threats, and the incessant demands for military and humanitarian intervention, have heightened the problems faced by all states, even the most powerful. As if that were not enough, this piling on of challenges is occurring in tandem with the unrelenting processes of globalization—from economic competition to multi-level governance—that compromise the ability of even the most powerful states to satisfy restive constituencies and achieve desirable policy outcomes.

Hence, we are challenged as never before to develop a more complex understanding of globalization and how it shapes the behavior and the capacity of states throughout the world. Are states being constrained more by economic and technological imperatives or by U.S. hegemony? Which is a more compelling characterization of the contemporary world—the one defined by increasing economic globalization or the one defined by the post–9/11 focus on terrorism, the exercise of U.S. power, and the transformed geopolitical dimension of globalization? How will unrivaled American power affect the capacities of states to sustain diverse economic and social models and secure desirable geopolitical outcomes?

This reader is motivated by the premise that globalization represents an historic political juncture. Globalization reframes both the role and function of states in the global order and how we understand their role and function. The selections in this reader analyze how globalization recasts state power in a world in which the United States exerts preeminent power and hence largely shapes the institutions and sets the agenda of global politics.

WHAT IS GLOBALIZATION?

Before introducing the thematic framework of this volume and further explaining the purpose of this collection of readings, it is necessary to clarify the frame of reference. Globalization is the watchword of our era. But what does the term mean and what phenomena can it be applied to profitably for analytical purposes?

For better or worse, globalization is an elastic concept: the scope and meaning of globalization can be stretched to apply broadly to "the process of increasing interconnectedness between societies such that events in one part of the world have effects on peoples and societies far away."[1] The concept is also rather eclectic. Globalization has come to be associated with any or all of a host of developments: the creation of a single world society or colonization or spatial reorganization or the compression of time and space through the application of new information technologies or Americanization or deterritorialization or the liberalization of markets. In addition, the term globalization is applied in a wide variety of academic disciplines from comparative politics and international relations, broadly defined, to sociology, economics, anthropology, and cultural studies.

The definition of globalization has become a hotly contested battlefield in the great globalization debate of the last decade. Our definition here recognizes the diversity of contending views and the scope of the phenomena associated with globalization, but focuses the definition explicitly on the politics of globalization.

1. Scope. Globalization refers to the increasing scale, extent, variety, speed, and magnitude of cross-border social, economic, military, political, and cultural interactions.
2. Definitional funnel. As broad in scope as the bundle of phenomena associated with globalization may be, in the *Globalization and State Power A Reader* the definition will be narrowed in focus to encompass primarily the political, political-economic, and geopolitical domain.*

In addition, most (although not all) of the contributors to this reader accept a third element of a definition of globalization that involves an empirical claim about the pattern of outcomes and distributional consequences.

3. Empirical proposition. Both the benefits and costs of globalization are unevenly distributed. Globalization therefore tends to produce paradoxical results. It fosters both growing interconnectedness and intensified animosities, driven by the prospect of expanding economic opportunities for some, yet exclusion and marginalization for others. Hence globalization is a contradictory phenomenon, one often experienced by ordinary citizens (and also by governments, grassroots activists, and officials in international organizations) as unsettling and full of risk.[2]

With this definition in place, the design of the reader comes into clear focus.

---

*This definitional focus will be widened selectively to consider the role of cultural identity in global politics—and in the key debates that have framed our understanding of globalization and state power. Culture and identity will be considered, for example, in discussing Samuel Huntington's "clash of civilizations" argument.

THE PLAN OF THE BOOK AND
PRINCIPLES OF SELECTION

Globalization has spawned a very active cottage industry, which has pro-duced many books and collections of essays, but there are surprisingly few focused efforts to analyze globalization and state power. This reader (which emerged as a companion volume to *Globalization and State Power: Who Wins When America Rules?*) is intended to play a distinctive role in exposing students and other interested readers to a sampling of the most influential, provocative, and insightful writings on the immensely important themes of globalization and state power.

Any reader requires selectivity from a huge literature of relevant contribu-tions. In this case, the emphasis has been placed on depth and focus. *GSP A Reader* is not designed to provide a comprehensive sampling of contributions that cover the full scope of globalization or support a multi-disciplinary intro-duction to global studies that would integrate the contributions of diverse disci-plinary approaches. Instead, in thematic and disciplinary terms, this reader is concerned, first and foremost, with how globalization shapes the role and func-tion of states—and how states, in turn, can (and cannot) act to bend the external political environment to their advantage. It focuses on national economic and social models, key geopolitical intrigues, and the daunting security challenges of the post-9/11 global order. It is also limited in geographical scope: core case stud-ies are limited to the United States, EU Europe, and East Asia (with particular emphasis on the response of the Asian Tigers to the economic crisis of 1997).

The contributions to the reader were selected because they make very impor-tant contributions to our understanding of two critical and interlocking ques-tions about globalization and state power:

1. How does globalization (and in particular, the global challenges of eco-nomic competitiveness, geopolitical influence, and security from terror attacks) affect state power understood as the capacity of states to secure desirable outcomes and influence the behavior of other states, transna-tional actors and international organizations?
2. What are the consequences of America's exercise of hegemonic power— for the capacity of other states to exercise power, for the shape of the geopolitical order, and for the United States itself?

The daunting challenges of the post–9/11 era endow these core questions (and a set of subsidiary questions identified below) with particular urgency. The reader is intended to provide a very readable and engaging set of answers within a clear organization and format.

Chapter 1 includes selections from some of the most influential writers who have inspired the academic and public debate about how globalization shapes state power. The sampling of the most compelling voices in the "great globalization debate" sets the frame of reference for everything that follows. It provides a rich intellectual template for considering whether economic competitiveness still drives globalization—or whether the security imperatives of the post–9/11 era combined with American hegemony have fundamentally redefined globalization. Which dimension of globalization—the economic or geopolitical—plays the biggest role in shaping the exercise of state power? In Chapter 2, contributors reveal the changing contours of state power, as traditional sovereignty understood as the autonomous control over a given territory gives way to complex, overlapping, negotiated authority and multi-level governance. This chapter examines the most distinctive and far-reaching political-institutional changes inspired by globalization. Chapter 3 includes a set of three case studies that capture the interactive effects of globalization and state power. They discuss and analyze, in turn, the exercise of hegemonic power by the United States, the challenges faced by Europe in preserving distinctive social and economic models in the face of global competitiveness and American dominance, and the role of the state power in East Asia, explored through the lens of the economic crisis of the late 1990s. Hence this chapter provides the most focused and sustained treatment of the political-economic dimension of globalization. Finally, Chapter 4 captures the urgent unfolding debate about security in the face of terror and the "new American Empire" set against the backdrop of 9/11, the war in Iraq, and its violent and thus far indeterminate aftermath.

GLOBALIZATION AND STATE POWER: BEFORE AND AFTER 9/11

Until the terror attacks of September 11, 2001, the theme that promised to dominate the political agenda of the early twenty-first century was whether globalization would promote increased human development spread more evenly across the globe or reinforce the comparative advantages of the North against the South, undermine local cultures, and intensify regional conflicts. Since 9/11, while none of these issues have been resolved, other questions have taken on new urgency. How can America and the world—as they must—meet the security threats posed by terror networks and the states that harbor them? What are the implications of a new geopolitical order shaped by the hard power of what many are considering a new American empire? *Globalization and State Power A Reader* analyzes this transformed global agenda and includes a sampling of the most significant writings available anywhere to examine how—and how successfully—states manage and absorb the repercussions of the immensely complex and inevitably destabilizing processes of globalization in its political, political-economic, and geopolitical dimensions.

The reader is dedicated to a careful investigation of the interactive effects of globalization and state power and is designed to provide a range of compelling alternative answers to urgent questions. It is hoped that the engagement with these powerful competing perspectives will inspire readers to enter the debate—with the experts and with each other—better informed about the issues and more cognizant about what is at stake in the arguments they advance.

Notes

[1]John Baylis and Steve Smith, eds., *The Globalization of World Politics*, 2nd ed. (Oxford: Oxford University Press, 2001), p. 7.

[2]This core definition of globalization draws on the extensive and influential work of David Held and his colleagues. See, for example: David Held, et al., *Global Transformations: Politics, Economics, and Culture* (Stanford, Ca.: Stanford University Press, 1999), pp. 27–28; David Held and Anthony McGrew, *Globalization/Anti-Globalization* (Cambridge: Polity Press, 2002), p. 1.

CHAPTER 1

Globalization and State Power: Competing Paradigms

During the Cold War, whether or not we liked it we understood the world, but the revolutions of 1989 in Eastern and Central Europe changed all that. When the Berlin Wall, which divided East and West was pulled down brick by brick in November 1989, the architecture of Europe—and with it the world political order—was transformed. Within a year Germany was unified. By the end of 1991, the Soviet Union had splintered into fifteen wary and troubled republics. For better or worse, the geopolitical order lost its grim predictability and, with the demise of the Cold War, the consensus about a conceptual framework and terminology for defining the era evaporated.

The search is on for a new paradigm that will capture the logic of today's international order as vividly and comprehensively as the term Cold War did for the period from the end of World War II to the start of the 1990s. In many ways, the debates about globalization and state power have become the terrain on which these architectonic battles for defining the contemporary era are fought.

Does globalization inevitably lead to the declining authority of states and a "one size fits all" style of neoliberal politics (welfare retrenchment, free trade, and minimal state interference in the economy)? Or has global politics been reconfigured along cultural fault lines? Is globalization best understood by an analysis of the key institutions of political and economic governance—and the role of state power most productively revealed in the way states manipulate institutional outcomes? Or perhaps we are seeing fewer real changes in the international arena than globalization theorists suppose and the old realist paradigm, in which the relentless pursuit of power and interests shapes the international system, remains the name of the game of great power politics. How does a feminist critique recast our understanding of globalization?

Once the Berlin Wall was taken apart piece by piece, the Cold War paradigm came tumbling down too. But what—if anything—has replaced it? Chapter 1 captures the debate about the reconfiguration of state power and the logic of global politics that has riveted the attention of citizens, students, and policy makers alike, as everyone tries to come to terms with the political challenges and consequences of globalization.

STUDY AND DISCUSSION QUESTIONS

1. Drawing critically on the insights of at least two of the contributors in this "great globalization debate," how would you define globalization?
2. Which model presents the most convincing account of how globalization affects the function of states and their exercise of power?
3. Does globalization really define a new international order—or is the geopolitical order better understood as it always has been, as the competition for power and influence by great powers?

1

The New System

Thomas L. Friedman

In principle, wrote Friedman in The Lexus and the Olive Tree, *the defining challenge of this era for individuals as for countries is to find a healthy balance between the sense of identity grounded in your local community (the olive tree) and doing what it takes to thrive in the "globalization system" that has replaced the Cold War. In practice, as Friedman explains in this selection, the pressures of imperious free-market capitalism (the Lexus) are paramount. The policies needed to establish market confidence in any government or national economy (such as balanced budgets, privatization, relatively low taxes, and minimal government regulation of markets) are the key to success in the era of globalization. Defy the logic of the global market and you risk*

*getting trampled by "the Electronic Herd" of investors who can make
or break governments at the click of a mouse.*

What was it that Forrest Gump's mama liked to say? Life is like a box of chocolates: you never know what you're going to get inside. For me, an inveterate traveler and foreign correspondent, life is like room service—you never know what you're going to find outside your door.

Take for instance the evening of December 31, 1994, when I began my assignment as the foreign affairs columnist for *The New York Times.* I started the column by writing from Tokyo, and when I arrived at the Okura Hotel after a long transpacific flight, I called room service with one simple request: "Could you please send me up four oranges." I am addicted to citrus and I needed a fix. It seemed to me a simple enough order when I telephoned it in, and the person on the other end seemed to understand. About twenty minutes later there was a knock at my door. A room service waiter was standing there in his perfectly creased uniform. In front of him was a cart covered by a starched white table-cloth. On the tablecloth were four tall glasses of fresh-squeezed orange juice, each glass set regally in a small silver bowl of ice.

"No, no," I said to the waiter, "I want oranges, oranges—not orange juice." I then pretended to bite into something like an orange.

"Ahhhh," the waiter said, nodding his head. "O-ranges, o-ranges."

I retreated into my room and went back to work. Twenty minutes later there was another knock at my door. Same waiter. Same linen-covered room service trolley. But this time, on it were four plates and on each plate was an orange that had been peeled and diced into perfect little sections that were fanned out on a plate like sushi, as only the Japanese can do.

"No, no," I said, shaking my head again. "I want the whole orange." I made a ball shape with my hands. "I want to keep them in my room and eat them for snacks. I can't eat four oranges all cut up like that. I can't store them in my mini-bar. I want the whole orange."

Again, I did my best exaggerated imitation of someone eating an orange.

"Ahhhh," the waiter said, nodding his head. "O-range, o-range. You want whole o-range."

Another twenty minutes went by. Again there was a knock on my door. Same waiter. Same trolley, only this time he had four bright oranges, each one on its own dinner plate, with a fork, knife and linen napkin next to it. That was progress.

"That's right," I said, signing the bill. "That's just what I wanted."

As he left the room, I looked down at the room service bill. The four oranges were $22. How am I going to explain that to my publisher?

But my citrus adventures were not over. Two weeks later I was in Hanoi, having dinner by myself in the dining room of the Metropole Hotel. It was the tangerine season in Vietnam, and vendors were selling pyramids of the most delicious, bright orange tangerines on every street corner. Each morning I had a few tangerines for breakfast. When the waiter came to get my dessert order I told him all I wanted was a tangerine.

He went away and came back a few minutes later.

"Sorry," he said, "no tangerines."

"But how can that be?" I asked in exasperation. "You have a table full of them at breakfast every morning! Surely there must be a tangerine somewhere back in the kitchen?"

"Sorry." He shook his head. "Maybe you like watermelon?"

"O.K.," I said, "bring me some watermelon."

Five minutes later the waiter returned with a plate bearing three peeled tangerines on it.

"I found the tangerines," he said. "No watermelon."

Had I known then what I know now I would have taken it all as a harbinger. For I too would find a lot of things on my plate and outside my door that I wasn't planning to find as I traveled the globe for the *Times*.

Being the foreign affairs columnist for *The New York Times* is actually the best job in the world. I mean, someone has to have the best job, right? Well, I've got it. The reason it is such a great job is that I get to be a tourist with an attitude. I get to go anywhere, anytime, and have attitudes about what I see and hear. But the question for me as I embarked on this odyssey was: Which attitudes? What would be the lens, the perspective, the organizing system—the superstory—through which I would look at the world, make sense of events, prioritize them, opine upon them and help readers understand them?

In some ways my predecessors had it a little easier. They each had a very obvious superstory and international system in place when they were writing. I am the fifth foreign affairs columnist in the history of the *Times*. "Foreign Affairs" is actually the paper's oldest column. It was begun in 1937 by a remarkable woman, Anne O'Hare McCormick, and was originally called "In Europe," because in those days, "in Europe" was foreign affairs for most Americans, and it seemed perfectly natural that the paper's one overseas columnist would be located on the European continent. Mrs. McCormick's 1954 obituary in the *Times* said she got her start in foreign reporting "as the wife of Mr. McCormick, a Dayton engineer whom she accompanied on frequent buying trips to Europe." (*New York Times* obits have become considerably more politically correct since then.) The international system which she covered was the disintegration of balance-of-power Versailles Europe and the beginnings of World War II.

As America emerged from World War II, standing astride the world as the preeminent superpower, with global responsibilities and engaged in a global power struggle with the Soviet Union, the title of the column changed in 1954 to "Foreign Affairs." Suddenly the whole world was America's playing field and the whole world mattered, because every corner was being contested with the Soviet Union. The Cold War international system, with its competition for influence and supremacy between the capitalist West and the communist East, between Washington, Moscow and Beijing, became the superstory within which the next three foreign affairs columnists organized their opinions.

By the time I started the column at the beginning of 1995, though, the Cold War was over. The Berlin Wall had crumbled and the Soviet Union was history. I had the good fortune to witness, in the Kremlin, one of the last gasps of the Soviet Union. The day was December 16, 1991. Secretary of State James A. Baker III was visiting Moscow, just as Boris Yeltsin was easing Mikhail Gorbachev out of power. Whenever Baker had met Gorbachev previously, they had held their talks in the Kremlin's gold-gilded St. Catherine Hall. There was always a very orchestrated entry scene for the press. Mr. Baker and his entourage would wait behind two huge wooden double doors on one end of the long Kremlin hall, with Gorbachev and his team behind the doors on the other end. And then, by some signal, the doors would simultaneously open and each man would stride out and they would shake hands in front of the cameras in the middle of the room. Well, on this day Baker arrived for his meeting at the appointed hour, the doors swung open and Boris Yeltsin walked out, instead of Gorbachev. Guess who's coming to dinner! "Welcome to Russian soil and this Russian building," Yeltsin said to Baker. Baker did meet Gorbachev later in the day, but it was clear that power had shifted. We State Department reporters who were there to chronicle the event ended up spending that whole day in the Kremlin. It snowed heavily while we were inside, and when we finally walked out after sunset we found the Kremlin grounds covered in a white snow blanket. As we trudged to the Kremlin's Spassky Gate, our shoes crunching fresh tracks in the snow, I noticed that the red Soviet hammer and sickle was still flying atop the Kremlin flagpole, illuminated by a spotlight as it had been for some seventy years. I said to myself, "That is probably the last time I'll ever see that flag flying there." In a few weeks it was indeed gone, and with it went the Cold War system and superstory.

But what wasn't clear to me as I embarked upon my column assignment a few years later was what had replaced the Cold War system as the dominant organizing framework for international affairs. So I actually began my column as a tourist without an attitude—just an open mind. For several years, I, like everyone else, just referred to "the post–Cold War world." We knew some new system was aborning that constituted a different framework for international relations, but we couldn't define what it was, so we defined it by what it wasn't. It wasn't the Cold War. So we called it the post–Cold War world.

The more I traveled, though, the more it became apparent to me that we were not just in some messy, incoherent, indefinable post–Cold War world.

Rather, we were in a new international system. This new system had its own unique logic, rules, pressures and incentives and it deserved its own name: "globalization." Globalization is not just some economic fad, and it is not just a passing trend. It is an international system—the dominant international system that replaced the Cold War system after the fall of the Berlin Wall. We need to understand it a such. If there can be a statute of limitations on crimes, then surely there must be a statute of limitations on foreign policy clichés. With that in mind, the "post–Cold War world" should be declared over. We are now in the new international system of globalization.

When I say that globalization has replaced the Cold War as the defining international system, what exactly do I mean?

I mean that, as an international system, the Cold War had its own structure of power: the balance between the United States and the U.S.S.R. The Cold War had its own rules: in foreign affairs, neither superpower would encroach on the other's sphere of influence; in economics, less developed countries would focus on nurturing their own national industries, developing countries on export-led growth, communist countries on autarky and Western economies on regulated trade. The Cold War had its own dominant ideas: the clash between communism and capitalism, as well as detente, nonalignment and perestroika. The Cold War had its own demographic trends: the movement of people from east to west was largely frozen by the Iron Curtain, but the movement from south to north was a more steady flow. The Cold War had its own perspective on the globe: the world was a space divided into the communist camp, the Western camp, and the neutral camp, and everyone's country was in one of them. The Cold War had its own defining technologies: nuclear weapons and the second Industrial Revolution were dominant, but for many people in developing countries the hammer and sickle were still relevant tools. The Cold War had its own defining measurement: the throw weight of nuclear missiles. And lastly, the Cold War had its own defining anxiety: nuclear annihilation. When taken all together the elements of this Cold War system influenced the domestic politics, commerce and foreign relations of virtually every country in the world. The Cold War system didn't shape everything, but it shaped many things.

Today's era of globalization is a similar international system, with its own unique attributes, which contrast sharply with those of the Cold War. To begin with the Cold War system was characterized by one overarching feature—division. The world was a divided-up, chopped-up place and both your threats and opportunities in the Cold War system tended to grow out of who you were divided from. Appropriately, this Cold War system was symbolized by a single word: the *wall*—the Berlin Wall. One of my favorite descriptions of that world was provided by Jack Nicholson in the movie *A Few Good Men*. Nicholson plays a Marine colonel who is the commander of the U.S. base in Cuba, at Guantánamo Bay. In the climactic scene of the movie, Nicholson is pressed by Tom Cruise to explain how a certain weak soldier under Nicholson's command, Santiago, was beaten to death by his own fellow Marines: "You want answers?" shouts Nicholson. "You want answers?" I want the truth, retorts Cruise. "You can't handle the truth," says Nicholson. "Son, we live in a world that has walls and those walls have to be guarded by men with guns. Who's gonna do it? You? You, Lieutenant Weinberg? I have a greater responsibility than you can possibly fathom. You weep for Santiago and you curse the Marines. You have that luxury. You have the luxury of not knowing what I know—that Santiago's death, while tragic, probably saved lives. And my existence, while grotesque and incomprehensible to you, saves lives. You don't want the truth because deep down in places you don't talk about at parties, you want me on that wall. You need me on that wall."

The globalization system is a bit different. It also has one overarching feature—integration. The world has become an increasingly interwoven place, and today, whether you are a company or a country, your threats and opportunities increasingly derive from who you are connected to. This globalization system is also characterized by a single word: the *Web*. So in the broadest sense we have gone from a system built around division and walls to a system increasingly built around integration and webs. In the Cold War we reached for the "hotline," which was a symbol that we were all divided but at least two people were in charge—the United States and the Soviet Union—and in the globalization system we reach for the Internet, which is a symbol that we are all increasingly connected and nobody is quite in charge.

This leads to many other differences between the globalization system and the Cold War system. The globalization system, unlike the Cold War system, is not frozen, but a dynamic ongoing process. That's why I define globalization this way: it is the inexorable integration of markets, nation-states and technologies to a degree never witnessed before—in a way that is enabling individuals, corporations and nation-states to reach around the world farther, faster, deeper and cheaper than ever before, and in a way that is enabling the world to reach into individuals, corporations and nation-states farther, faster, deeper, cheaper than ever before. This process of globalization is also producing a powerful backlash from those brutalized or left behind by this new system.

The driving idea behind globalization is free-market capitalism—the more you let market forces rule and the more you open your economy to free trade and competition, the more efficient and flourishing your economy will be. Globalization means the spread of free-market capitalism to virtually every country in the world. Therefore, globalization also has its own set of economic rules—rules that revolve around opening, deregulating and privatizing your economy, in order to make it more competitive and attractive to foreign investment. In 1975, at the height of the Cold War, only 8 percent of countries worldwide had liberal, free-market capital regimes, and foreign direct investment at the time totaled only

$23 billion, according to the World Bank. By 1997, the number of countries with liberal economic regimes constituted 28 percent, and foreign investment totaled $644 billion.

Unlike the Cold War system, globalization has its own dominant culture, which is why it tends to be homogenizing to a certain degree. In previous eras this sort of cultural homogenization happened on a regional scale—the Romanization of Western Europe and the Mediterranean world, the Islamification of Central Asia, North Africa, Europe and the Middle East by the Arabs and later the Ottomans, or the Russification of Eastern and Central Europe and parts of Eurasia under the Soviets. Culturally speaking, globalization has tended to involve the spread (for better and for worse) of Americanization—from Big Macs to iMacs to Mickey Mouse.

Globalization has its own defining technologies: computerization, miniaturization, digitization, satellite communications, fiber optics and the Internet, which reinforce its defining perspective of integration. Once a country makes the leap into the system of globalization, its elites begin to internalize this perspective of integration, and always try to locate themselves in a global context. I was visiting Amman, Jordan, in the summer of 1998 and having coffee at the Inter-Continental Hotel with my friend Rami Khouri, the leading political columnist in Jordan. We sat down and I asked him what was new. The first thing he said to me was: "Jordan was just added to CNN's worldwide weather highlights." What Rami was saying was that it is important for Jordan to know that those institutions which think globally believe it is now worth knowing what the weather is like in Amman. It makes Jordanians feel more important and holds out the hope that they will be enriched by having more tourists or global investors visiting. The day after seeing Rami I happened to go to Israel and meet with Jacob Frenkel, governor of Israel's Central Bank and a University of Chicago-trained economist. Frenkel remarked that he too was going through a perspective change: "Before, when we talked about macroeconomics, we started by looking at the local markets, local financial systems and the interrelationship between them, and then, as an afterthought, we looked at the international economy. There was a feeling that what we do is primarily our own business and then there are some outlets where we will sell abroad. Now we reverse the perspective. Let's not ask what markets we should export to, after having decided what to produce; rather let's first study the global framework within which we operate and then decide what to produce. It changes your whole perspective."

While the defining measurement of the Cold War was weight—particularly the throw weight of missiles—the defining measurement of the globalization system is speed—speed of commerce, travel, communication and innovation. The Cold War was about Einstein's mass-energy equation, $e = mc^2$. Globalization tends to revolve around Moore's Law, which states that the computing power of silicon chips will double every eighteen to twenty-four months, while the price will halve. In the Cold War, the most frequently asked question was: "Whose side are you on?" In globalization, the most frequently asked question is: "To what extent are you connected to everyone?" In the Cold War, the second most frequently asked question was: "How big is your missile?" In globalization, the second most frequently asked question is: "How fast is your modem?" The defining document of the Cold War system was "The Treaty." The defining document of globalization is "The Deal." The Cold War system even had its own style. In 1961, according to *Foreign Policy* magazine, Cuban President Fidel Castro, wearing his usual olive drab military uniform, made his famous declaration "I shall be a Marxist-Leninist for the rest of my life." In January 1999, Castro put on a business suit for a conference on globalization in Havana, to which financier George Soros and free-market economist Milton Friedman were both invited.

If the defining economists of the Cold War system were Karl Marx and John Maynard Keynes, who each in his own way wanted to tame capitalism, the defining economists of the globalization system are Joseph Schumpeter and Intel chairman Andy Grove, who prefer to unleash capitalism. Schumpeter, a former Austrian Minister of Finance and Harvard Business School professor, expressed the view in his classic work *Capitalism, Socialism and Democracy* that the essence of capitalism is the process of "creative destruction"—the perpetual cycle of destroying the old and less efficient product or service and replacing it with new, more efficient ones. Andy Grove took Schumpeter's insight that "only the paranoid survive" for the title of his book on life in Silicon Valley, and made it in many ways the business model of globalization capitalism. Grove helped to popularize the view that dramatic, industry-transforming innovations are taking place today faster and faster. Thanks to these technological breakthroughs, the speed by which your latest invention can be made obsolete or turned into a commodity is now lightning quick. Therefore, only the paranoid, only those who are constantly looking over their shoulders to see who is creating something new that will destroy them and then staying just one step ahead of them, will survive. Those countries that are most willing to let capitalism quickly destroy inefficient companies, so that money can be freed up and directed to more innovative ones, will thrive in the era of globalization. Those which rely on their governments to protect them from such creative destruction will fall behind in this era.

James Surowiecki, the business columnist for *Slate* magazine, reviewing Grove's book, neatly summarized what Schumpeter and Grove have in common, which is the essence of globalization economics. It is the notion that: "Innovation replaces tradition. The present—or perhaps the future—replaces the past. Nothing matters so much as what will come next, and what will come next can only arrive if what is here now gets overturned. While this makes the system a terrific place for innovation, it makes it a difficult place to live, since most people prefer some measure of security about the future to a life lived in almost constant uncertainty . . . We are not forced to re-create our relationships with those closest to us on a regular basis. And yet that's precisely what Schumpeter, and Grove after him, suggest is necessary to prosper [today]."

Indeed, if the Cold War were a sport, it would be sumo wrestling, says Johns Hopkins University foreign affairs professor Michael Mandelbaum. "It would be two big fat guys in a ring, with all sorts of posturing and rituals and stomping of feet, but actually very little contact, until the end of the match, when there is a brief moment of shoving and the loser gets pushed out of the ring, but nobody gets killed."

By contrast, if globalization were a sport, it would be the 100-meter dash, over and over and over. And no matter how many times you win, you have to race again the next day. And if you lose by just one hundredth of a second it can be as if you lost by an hour. (Just ask French multinationals. In 1999, French labor laws were changed, requiring—*requiring*—every employer to implement a four-hour reduction in the legal workweek, from 39 hours to 35 hours, with no cut in pay. Many French firms were fighting the move because of the impact it would have on their productivity in a global market. Henri Thierry, human resources director for Thomson-CSF Communications, a high-tech firm in the suburbs of Paris, told *The Washington Post*: "We are in a worldwide competition. If we lose one point of productivity, we lose orders. If we're obliged to go to 35 hours it would be like requiring French athletes to run the 100 meters wearing flippers. They wouldn't have much of a chance winning a medal.")

To paraphrase German political theorist Carl Schmitt, the Cold War was a world of "friends" and "enemies." The globalization world, by contrast, tends to turn all friends and enemies into "competitors."

If the defining anxiety of the Cold War was fear of annihilation from an enemy you knew all too well in a world struggle that was fixed and stable, the defining anxiety in globalization is fear of rapid change from an enemy you can't see, touch or feel—a sense that your job, community or workplace can be changed at any moment by anonymous economic and technological forces that are anything but stable. The defining defense system of the Cold War was radar—to expose the threats coming from the other side of the wall. The defining defense system of the globalization era is the X-ray machine—to expose the threats coming from within.

Globalization also has its own demographic pattern—a rapid acceleration of the movement of people from rural areas and agricultural lifestyles to urban areas and urban lifestyles more intimately linked with global fashion, food, markets and entertainment trends.

Last, and most important, globalization has its own defining structure of power, which is much more complex than the Cold War structure. The Cold War system was built exclusively around nation-states. You acted on the world in that system through your state. The Cold War was primarily a drama of states confronting states, balancing states and aligning with states. And, as a system, the Cold War was balanced at the center by two superstates: the United States and the Soviet Union.

The globalization system, by contrast, is built around three balances, which overlap and affect one another. The first is the traditional balance between nation-states. In the globalization system, the United States is now the sole and dominant superpower and all other nations are subordinate to it to one degree or another. The balance of power between the United States and the other states, though, still matters for the stability of this system. And it can still explain a lot of the news you read on the front page of the papers, whether it is the containment of Iraq in the Middle East or the expansion of NATO against Russia in Central Europe.

The second balance in the globalization system is between nation-states and global markets. These global markets are made up of millions of investors moving money around the world with the click of a mouse. I call them "the Electronic Herd," and this herd gathers in key global financial centers, such as Wall Street, Hong Kong, London and Frankfurt, which I call "the Supermarkets." The attitudes and actions of the Electronic Herd and the Supermarkets can have a huge impact on nation-states today, even to the point of triggering the downfall of governments. Who ousted Suharto in Indonesia in 1998? It wasn't another state, it was the Supermarkets, by withdrawing their support for, and confidence in, the Indonesian economy. You will not understand the front page of newspapers today unless you bring the Supermarkets into your analysis. Because the United States can destroy you by dropping bombs and the Supermarkets can destroy you by downgrading your bonds. In other words, the United States is the dominant player in maintaining the globalization gameboard, but it is not alone in influencing the moves on that gameboard. This globalization gameboard today is a lot like a Ouija board—sometimes pieces are moved around by the obvious hand of the superpower, and sometimes they are moved around by hidden hands of the Supermarkets.

The third balance that you have to pay attention to in the globalization system—the one that is really the newest of all—is the balance between individuals and nation-states. Because globalization has brought down many of the walls that limited the movement and reach of people, and because it has simultaneously wired the world into networks, it gives more power to individuals to influence both markets and nation-states than at any time in history. Individuals can increasingly act on the world stage directly—unmediated by a state. So you have today not only a superpower, not only Supermarkets, but, . . . you now have Super-empowered individuals. Some of these Super-empowered individuals are quite angry, some of them quite wonderful—but all of them are now able to act directly on the world stage.

Without the knowledge of the U.S. government, Long-Term Capital Management—a few guys with a hedge fund in Greenwich, Connecticut— amassed more financial bets around the world than all the foreign reserves of China. Osama bin Laden, a Saudi millionaire with his own global network, declared war on the United States in the late 1990s, and the U.S. Air Force retaliated with a cruise missile attack on him (where he resided in Afghanistan) as though he were another nation-state. Think about that. The United States fired 75 cruise missiles, at $1 million apiece, at a person! That was a superpower against a Super-empowered angry man. Jody Williams won the Nobel Peace Prize in 1997 for her contribution to the international ban on landmines. She achieved that ban not only without much government help, but in the face of opposition from all the major powers. And what did she say was her secret weapon for organizing 1,000 different human rights and arms control groups on six continents? "E-mail."

Nation-states, and the American superpower in particular, are still hugely important today, but so too now are Supermarkets and Super-empowered individuals. You will never understand the globalization system, or the front page of the morning paper, unless you see it as a complex interaction between all three of these actors: states bumping up against states, states bumping up against Supermarkets, and Supermarkets and states bumping up against Super-empowered individuals.

Unfortunately, . . . the system of globalization has come upon us far faster than our ability to retrain ourselves to see and comprehend it. Think about just this one fact: Most people had never even heard of the Internet in 1990, and very few people had an E-mail address then. That was just ten years ago! But today the Internet, cell phones and E-mail have become essential tools that many people, and not only in developed countries, cannot imagine living without. It was no different, I am sure, at the start of the Cold War, with the first appearance of nuclear arsenals and deterrence theories. It took a long time for leaders and analysts of that era to fully grasp the real nature and dimensions of the Cold War system. They emerged from World War II thinking that this great war had produced a certain kind of world, but they soon discovered it had laid the foundations for a world very different from the one they anticipated. Much of what came to be seen as great Cold War architecture and strategizing were responses on the fly to changing events and evolving threats. Bit by bit, these Cold War strategists built the institutions, the perceptions and the reflexes that came to be known as the Cold War system.

It will be no different with the globalization system, except that it may take us even longer to get our minds around it, because it requires so much retraining just to see this new system and because it is built not just around superpowers but also around Supermarkets and Super-empowered individuals. I would say that in 2000 we understand as much about how today's system of globalization is going to work as we understood about how the Cold War system was going to work in 1946—the year Winston Churchill gave his speech warning that an "Iron Curtain" was coming down, cutting off the Soviet zone of influence from Western Europe. We barely understood how the Cold War system was going to play out thirty years after Churchill's speech! That was when Routledge published a collection of essays by some of the top Sovietologists, entitled *Soviet Economy Towards the Year 2000*. It was a good seller when it came out. It never occurred at that time to any of the authors that there wouldn't be a Soviet economy in the year 2000.

If you want to appreciate how few people understand exactly how this system works, think about one amusing fact. The two key economists who were advising Long-Term Capital Management, Robert C. Merton and Myron S. Scholes, shared the Nobel Prize for economics in 1997, roughly one year before LTCM so misunderstood the nature of risk in today's highly integrated global marketplace that it racked up the biggest losses in hedge fund history. And what did LTCM's two economists win their Nobel Prize for? For their studies on how complex financial instruments, known as derivatives, can be used by global investors to offset risk! In 1997 they won the Nobel Prize for managing risk. In 1998 they won the booby prize for creating risk. Same guys, same market—new world.

STUDY AND DISCUSSION QUESTIONS

1. How does Friedman define globalization? How significant is it that he characterizes globalization as an international system?
2. Why—and how—does globalization change the balance between nation-states? Between individuals and nation-states?
3. Why does "the Electronic Herd" feature so prominently in Friedman's account?

2

The New Era in World Politics

Samuel P. Huntington

For Harvard University's Samuel Huntington in The Clash of Civilizations and the Remaking of World Order, *the years since the end of the Cold War have witnessed a fundamental paradigm shift. As this selection explains, global politics has been reconfigured along cultural lines. Deep-seated cultural differences are the root causes of today's fundamental disparities in political and economic development. In an argument that has captured enormous attention—and generated considerable controversy—in the aftermath of 9/11, Huntington contends that Muslim culture largely determines the failure of democracy in much of the Islamic world, while the West represents the culture of modernization, industrialization, innovation, and the "American Creed."*

INTRODUCTION: FLAGS AND CULTURAL IDENTITY

On January 3, 1992, a meeting of Russian and American scholars took place in the auditorium of a government building in Moscow. Two weeks earlier the Soviet Union had ceased to exist and the Russian Federation had become an independent country. As a result, the statue of Lenin which previously graced the stage of the auditorium had disappeared and instead the flag of the Russian Federation was now displayed on the front wall. The only problem, one American observed, was that the flag had been hung upside down. After this was pointed out to the Russian hosts, they quickly and quietly corrected the error during the first intermission.

The years after the Cold War witnessed the beginnings of dramatic changes in peoples' identities and the symbols of those identities. Global politics began to be reconfigured along cultural lines. Upside-down flags were a sign of the transition, but more and more the flags are flying high and true, and Russians and other peoples are mobilizing and marching behind these and other symbols of their new cultural identities.

On April 18, 1994, two thousand people rallied in Sarajevo waving the flags of Saudi Arabia and Turkey. By flying those banners, instead of U.N., NATO, or American flags, these Sarajevans identified themselves with their fellow Muslims and told the world who were their real and not-so-real friends.

On October 16, 1994, in Los Angeles 70,000 people marched beneath "a sea of Mexican flags" protesting Proposition 187, a referendum measure which would deny many state benefits to illegal immigrants and their children. Why are they "walking down the street with a Mexican flag and demanding that this country give them a free education?" observers asked. "They should be waving the American flag." Two weeks later more protestors did march down the street carrying an American flag—upside down. These flag displays ensured victory for Proposition 187, which was approved by 59 percent of California voters.

In the post–Cold War world flags count and so do other symbols of cultural identity, including crosses, crescents, and even head coverings because culture counts, and cultural identity is what is most meaningful to most people. People are discovering new but often old identities and marching under new but often old flags which lead to wars with new but often old enemies.

One grim *Weltanschauung* for this new era was well expressed by the Venetian nationalist demagogue in Michael Dibdin's novel, *Dead Lagoon:* "There can be no true friends without true enemies. Unless we hate what we are not, we cannot love what we are. These are the old truths we are painfully rediscovering after a century and more of sentimental cant. Those who deny them deny their family, their heritage, their culture, their birthright, their very selves! They will not lightly be forgiven." The unfortunate truth in these old truths cannot be ignored by statesmen and scholars. For peoples seeking identity and reinventing ethnicity, enemies are essential, and the potentially most dangerous enmities occur across the fault lines between the world's major civilizations.

The central theme of this [selection] is that culture and cultural identities, which at the broadest level are civilization identities, are shaping the patterns of cohesion, disintegration, and conflict in the post–Cold War world. . . .

- . . . For the first time in history global politics is both multipolar and multicivilizational; modernization is distinct from Westernization and is producing neither a universal civilization in any meaningful sense nor the Westernization of non-Western societies.
- . . . The balance of power among civilizations is shifting: the West is declining in relative influence; Asian civilizations are expanding their economic, military, and political strength; Islam is exploding demographically with destabilizing consequences for Muslim countries and their neighbors;

and non-Western civilizations generally are reaffirming the value of their own cultures.

- . . . A civilization-based world order is emerging: societies sharing cultural affinities cooperate with each other; efforts to shift societies from one civilization to another are unsuccessful; and countries group themselves around the lead or core states of their civilization.
- . . . The West's universalist pretensions increasingly bring it into conflict with other civilizations, most seriously with Islam and China; at the local level fault line wars, largely between Muslims and non-Muslims, generate "kin-country rallying," the threat of broader escalation, and hence efforts by core states to halt these wars.
- . . . The survival of the West depends on Americans reaffirming their Western identity and Westerners accepting their civilization as unique not universal and uniting to renew and preserve it against challenges from non-Western societies. Avoidance of a global war of civilizations depends on world leaders accepting and cooperating to maintain the multicivilizational character of global politics.

A MULTIPOLAR, MULTICIVILIZATIONAL WORLD

In the post–Cold War world, for the first time in history, global politics has become multipolar *and* multicivilizational. During most of human existence, contacts between civilizations were intermittent or nonexistent. Then, with the beginning of the modern era, about A.D. 1500, global politics assumed two dimensions. For over four hundred years, the nation states of the West—Britain, France, Spain, Austria, Prussia, Germany, the United States, and others—constituted a multipolar international system within Western civilization and interacted, competed, and fought wars with each other. At the same time, Western nations also expanded, conquered, colonized, or decisively influenced every other civilization. During the Cold War global politics became bipolar and the world was divided into three parts. A group of mostly wealthy and democratic societies, led by the United States, was engaged in a pervasive ideological, political, economic, and, at times, military competition with a group of somewhat poorer communist societies associated with and led by the Soviet Union. Much of this conflict occurred in the Third World outside these two camps, composed of countries which often were poor, lacked political stability, were recently independent, and claimed to be nonaligned.

In the late 1980s the communist world collapsed, and the Cold War international system became history. In the post–Cold War world, the most important distinctions among peoples are not ideological, political, or economic. They are cultural. Peoples and nations are attempting to answer the most basic question humans can face: Who are we? And they are answering that question in the traditional way human beings have answered it, by reference to the things that mean most to them. People define themselves in terms of ancestry, religion, language, history, values, customs, and institutions. They identify with cultural groups: tribes, ethnic groups, religious communities, nations, and, at the broadest level, civilizations. People use politics not just to advance their interests but also to define their identity. We know who we are only when we know who we are not and often only when we know whom we are against.

Nation states remain the principal actors in world affairs. Their behavior is shaped as in the past by the pursuit of power and wealth, but it is also shaped by cultural preferences, commonalities, and differences. The most important groupings of states are no longer the three blocs of the Cold War but rather the world's seven or eight major civilizations. Non-Western societies, particularly in East Asia, are developing their economic wealth and creating the basis for enhanced military power and political influence. As their power and self-confidence increase, non-Western societies increasingly assert their own cultural values and reject those "imposed" on them by the West. The "international system of the twenty-first century," Henry Kissinger has noted, ". . . will contain at least six major powers—the United States, Europe, China, Japan, Russia, and probably India—as well as a multiplicity of medium-sized and smaller countries."[1] Kissinger's six major powers belong to five very different civilizations, and in addition there are important Islamic states whose strategic locations, large populations, and/or oil resources make them influential in world affairs. In this new world, local politics is the politics of ethnicity; global politics is the politics of civilizations. The rivalry of the superpowers is replaced by the clash of civilizations.

In this new world the most pervasive, important, and dangerous conflicts will not be between social classes, rich and poor, or other economically defined groups, but between peoples belonging to different cultural entities. Tribal wars and ethnic conflicts will occur within civilizations. Violence between states and groups from different civilizations, however, carries with it the potential for escalation as other states and groups from these civilizations rally to the support of their "kin countries."[2] The bloody clash of clans in Somalia poses no threat of broader conflict. The bloody clash of tribes in Rwanda has consequences for Uganda, Zaire, and Burundi but not much further. The bloody clashes of civilizations in Bosnia, the Caucasus, Central Asia, or Kashmir could become bigger wars. In the Yugoslav conflicts, Russia provided diplomatic support to the Serbs, and Saudi Arabia, Turkey, Iran, and Libya provided funds and arms to the Bosnians, not for reasons of ideology or power politics or economic interest but because of cultural kinship. "Cultural conflicts," Vaclav Havel has observed, "are increasing and are more dangerous today than at any time in history," and Jacques Delors agreed that "future conflicts will be sparked by cultural factors rather than economics or ideology."[3] And the most dangerous cultural conflicts are those along the fault lines between civilizations.

In the post–Cold War world, culture is both a divisive and a unifying force. People separated by ideology but united by culture come together, as the two Germanys did and as the two Koreas and the several Chinas are beginning to. Societies united by ideology or historical circumstance but divided by civilization either come apart, as did the Soviet Union, Yugoslavia, and Bosnia, or are subjected to intense strain, as is the case with Ukraine, Nigeria, Sudan, India, Sri Lanka, and many others. Countries with cultural affinities cooperate economically and politically. International organizations based on states with cultural commonality, such as the European Union, are far more successful than those that attempt to transcend cultures. For forty-five years the Iron Curtain was the central dividing line in Europe. That line has moved several hundred miles east. It is now the line separating the peoples of Western Christianity, on the one hand, from Muslim and Orthodox peoples on the other.

The philosophical assumptions, underlying values, social relations, customs, and overall outlooks on life differ significantly among civilizations. The revitalization of religion throughout much of the world is reinforcing these cultural differences. Cultures can change, and the nature of their impact on politics and economics can vary from one period to another. Yet the major differences in political and economic development among civilizations are clearly rooted in their different cultures. East Asian economic success has its source in East Asian culture, as do the difficulties East Asian societies have had in achieving stable democratic political systems. Islamic culture explains in large part the failure of democracy to emerge in much of the Muslim world. Developments in the post-communist societies of Eastern Europe and the former Soviet Union are shaped by their civilizational identities. Those with Western Christian heritages are making progress toward economic development and democratic politics; the prospects for economic and political development in the Orthodox countries are uncertain; the prospects in the Muslim republics are bleak.

The West is and will remain for years to come the most powerful civilization. Yet its power relative to that of other civilizations is declining. As the West attempts to assert its values and to protect its interests, non-Western societies confront a choice. Some attempt to emulate the West and to join or to "bandwagon" with the West. Other Confucian and Islamic societies attempt to expand their own economic and military power to resist and to "balance" against the West. A central axis of post–Cold War world politics is thus the interaction of Western power and culture with the power and culture of non-Western civilizations.

In sum, the post–Cold War world is a world of seven or eight major civilizations. Cultural commonalities and differences shape the interests, antagonisms, and associations of states. The most important countries in the world come overwhelmingly from different civilizations. The local conflicts most likely to escalate into broader wars are those between groups and states from different civilizations. The predominant patterns of political and economic development differ from civilization to civilization. The key issues on the international agenda involve differences among civilizations. Power is shifting from the long predominant West to non-Western civilizations. Global politics has become multipolar and multicivilizational.

OTHER WORLDS?

Maps and Paradigms.   This picture of post–Cold War world politics shaped by cultural factors and involving interactions among states and groups from different civilizations is highly simplified. It omits many things, distorts some things, and obscures others. Yet if we are to think seriously about the world, and act effectively in it, some sort of simplified map of reality, some theory, concept, model, paradigm, is necessary. Without such intellectual constructs, there is, as William James said, only "a bloomin' buzzin' confusion." Intellectual and scientific advance, Thomas Kuhn showed in his classic *The Structure of Scientific Revolutions,* consists of the displacement of one paradigm, which has become increasingly incapable of explaining new or newly discovered facts, by a new paradigm, which does account for those facts in a more satisfactory fashion. "To be accepted as a paradigm," Kuhn wrote, "a theory must seem better than its competitors, but it need not, and in fact never does, explain all the facts with which it can be confronted."[4] Finding one's way through unfamiliar terrain," John Lewis Gaddis also wisely observed, "generally requires a map of some sort. Cartography, like cognition itself, is a necessary simplification that allows us to see where we are, and where we may be going." The Cold War image of superpower competition was, as he points out, such a model, articulated first by Harry Truman, as "an exercise in geopolitical cartography that depicted the international landscape in terms everyone could understand, and so doing prepared the way for the sophisticated strategy of containment that was soon to follow." World views and causal theories are indispensable guides to international politics.[5]

For forty years students and practitioners of international relations thought and acted in terms of the highly simplified but very useful Cold War paradigm of world affairs. This paradigm could not account for everything that went on in world politics. There were many anomalies, to use Kuhn's term, and at times the paradigm blinded scholars and statesmen to major developments, such as the Sino-Soviet split. Yet as a simple model of global politics, it accounted for more important phenomena than any of its rivals, it was an essential starting point for thinking about international affairs, it came to be almost universally accepted, and it shaped thinking about world politics for two generations.

Simplified paradigms or maps are indispensable for human thought and action. On the one hand, we may explicitly formulate theories or models and consciously use them to guide our behavior. Alternatively, we may deny the need for such guides and assume that we will act only in terms of specific "objective" facts, dealing with each case "on its merits." If we assume this, however, we delude ourselves. For in the back of our minds are hidden assumptions, biases, and prejudices that determine how we perceive reality, what facts we look at, and how we judge their importance and merits. We need explicit or implicit models so as to be able to:

1. order and generalize about reality;
2. understand causal relationships among phenomena;
3. anticipate and, if we are lucky, predict future developments;
4. distinguish what is important from what is unimportant; and
5. show us what paths we should take to achieve our goals.

Every model or map is an abstraction and will be more useful for some purposes than for others. A road map shows us how to drive from A to B, but will not be very useful if we are piloting a plane, in which case we will want a map highlighting airfields, radio beacons, flight paths, and topography. With no map, however, we will be lost. The more detailed a map is the more fully it will reflect reality. An extremely detailed map, however, will not be useful for many purposes. If we wish to get from one big city to another on a major expressway, we do not need and may find confusing a map which includes much information unrelated to automotive transportation and in which the major highways are lost in a complex mass of secondary roads. A map, on the other hand, which had only one expressway on it would eliminate much reality and limit our ability to find alternative routes if the expressway were blocked by a major accident. In short, we need a map that both portrays reality and simplifies reality in a way that best serves our purposes. Several maps or paradigms of world politics were advanced at the end of the Cold War.

One World: Euphoria and Harmony. One widely articulated paradigm was based on the assumption that the end of the Cold War meant the end of significant conflict in global politics and the emergence of one relatively harmonious world. The most widely discussed formulation of this model was the "end of history" thesis advanced by Francis Fukuyama. "We may be witnessing," Fukuyama argued, ". . . the end of history as such: that is, the end point of mankind's ideological evolution and the universalization of Western liberal democracy as the final form of human government." To be sure, he said, some conflicts may happen in places in the Third World, but the global conflict is over, and not just in Europe. "It is precisely in the non-European world" that the big changes have occurred, particularly in China and the Soviet Union. The war of ideas is at an end. Believers in Marxist-Leninism may still exist "in places like

Managua, Pyongyang, and Cambridge, Massachusetts," but overall liberal democracy has triumphed. The future will be devoted not to great exhilarating struggles over ideas but rather to resolving mundane economic and technical problems. And, he concluded rather sadly, it will all be rather boring.[6]

The expectation of harmony was widely shared. Political and intellectual leaders elaborated similar views. The Berlin wall had come down, communist regimes had collapsed, the United Nations was to assume a new importance, the former Cold War rivals would engage in "partnership" and a "grand bargain," peacekeeping and peacemaking would be the order of the day. The President of the world's leading country proclaimed the "new world order"; the president of, arguably, the world's leading university vetoed appointment of a professor of security studies because the need had disappeared: "Hallelujah! We study war no more because war is no more."

The moment of euphoria at the end of the Cold War generated an illusion of harmony, which was soon revealed to be exactly that. The world became different in the early 1990s, but not necessarily more peaceful. Change was inevitable; progress was not. Similar illusions of harmony flourished, briefly, at the end of each of the twentieth century's other major conflicts. World War I was the "war to end wars" and to make the world safe for democracy. World War II, as Franklin Roosevelt put it, would "end the system of unilateral action, the exclusive alliances, the balances of power, and all the other expedients that have been tried for centuries—and have always failed." Instead we will have "a universal organization" of "peace-loving Nations" and the beginnings of a "permanent structure of peace."[7] World War I, however, generated communism, fascism, and the reversal of a century-old trend toward democracy. World War II produced a Cold War that was truly global. The illusion of harmony at the end of that Cold War was soon dissipated by the multiplication of ethnic conflicts and "ethnic cleansing," the breakdown of law and order, the emergence of new patterns of alliance and conflict among states, the resurgence of neo-communist and neo-fascist movements, intensification of religious fundamentalism, the end of the "diplomacy of smiles" and "policy of yes" in Russia's relations with the West, the inability of the United Nations and the United States to suppress bloody local conflicts, and the increasing assertiveness of a rising China. In the five years after the Berlin wall came down, the word "genocide" was heard far more often than in any five years of the Cold War. The one harmonious world paradigm is clearly far too divorced from reality to be a useful guide to the post–Cold War world.

Two Worlds: Us and Them. While one-world expectations appear at the end of major conflicts, the tendency to think in terms of two worlds recurs throughout human history. People are always tempted to divide people into us and them, the in-group and the other, our civilization and those barbarians. Scholars have analyzed the world in terms of the Orient and the Occident, North and South, center and periphery. Muslims have traditionally divided the world into *Dar al-Islam* and *Dar al-Harb,* the abode of peace and the abode of war. This distinction was reflected, and in a sense reversed, at the end of the Cold War by American scholars who divided the world into "zones of peace" and "zones of turmoil." The former included the West and Japan with about 15 percent of the world's population, the latter everyone else.

Depending upon how the parts are defined, a two-part world picture may in some measure correspond with reality. The most common division, which appears under various names, is between rich (modern, developed) countries and poor (traditional, undeveloped or developing) countries. Historically correlating with this economic division is the cultural division between West and East, where the emphasis is less on differences in economic well-being and more on differences in underlying philosophy, values, and way of life. Each of these images reflects some elements of reality yet also suffers limitations. Rich modern countries share characteristics which differentiate them from poor traditional countries, which also share characteristics. Differences in wealth may lead to conflicts between societies, but the evidence suggests that this happens primarily when rich and more powerful societies attempt to conquer and colonize poor and more traditional societies. The West did this for four hundred years, and then some of the colonies rebelled and waged wars of liberation against the colonial powers, who may well have lost the will to empire. In the current world, decolonization has occurred and colonial wars of liberation have been replaced by conflicts among the liberated peoples.

At a more general level, conflicts between rich and poor are unlikely because, except in special circumstances, the poor countries lack the political unity, economic power, and military capability to challenge the rich countries. Economic development in Asia and Latin America is blurring the simple dichotomy of haves and have-nots. Rich states may fight trade wars with each other; poor states may fight violent wars with each other; but an international class war between the poor South and the wealthy North is almost as far from reality as one happy harmonious world.

The cultural bifurcation of the world division is still less useful. At some level, the West is an entity. What, however, do non-Western societies have in common other than the fact that they are non-Western? Japanese, Chinese, Hindu, Muslim, and African civilizations share little in terms of religion, social structure, institutions, and prevailing values. The unity of the non-West and the East-West dichotomy are myths created by the West. These myths suffer the defects of the Orientalism which Edward Said appropriately criticized for promoting "the difference between the familiar (Europe, the West, 'us') and the strange (the Orient, the East, 'them')" and for assuming the inherent superiority of the former to the latter.[8] During the Cold War the world was, in considerable measure, polarized along an ideological spectrum. There is, however, no single cultural spectrum. The polarization of "East" and "West" culturally is in part another consequence of the universal but unfortunate practice of calling European civilization Western civilization. Instead of "East and West," it is more appropriate to speak of "the West and the rest," which at least implies the existence of many non-Wests. The world is too complex to be usefully envisioned for most purposes as simply divided economically between North and South or culturally between East and West.

184 States, More or Less. A third map of the post–Cold War world derives from what is often called the "realist" theory of international relations. According to this theory states are the primary, indeed, the only important actors in world affairs, the relation among states is one of anarchy, and hence to insure their survival and security, states invariably attempt to maximize their power. If one state sees another state increasing its power and thereby becoming a potential threat, it attempts to protect its own security by strengthening its power and/or by allying itself with other states. The interests and actions of the more or less 184 states of the post–Cold War world can be predicted from these assumptions.

This "realist" picture of the world is a highly useful starting point for analyzing international affairs and explains much state behavior. States are and will remain the dominant entities in world affairs. They maintain armies, conduct diplomacy, negotiate treaties, fight wars, control international organizations, influence and in considerable measure shape production and commerce. The governments of states give priority to insuring the external security of their states (although they often may give higher priority to insuring their security as a government against internal threats). Overall this statist paradigm does provide a more realistic picture of and guide to global politics than the one- or two-world paradigms.

It also, however, suffers severe limitations.

It assumes all states perceive their interests in the same way and act in the same way. Its simple assumption that power is all is a starting point for understanding state behavior but does not get one very far. States define their interests in terms of power but also in terms of much else besides. States often, of course, attempt to balance power, but if that is all they did, Western European countries would have coalesced with the Soviet Union against the United States in the late 1940s. States respond primarily to perceived threats, and the Western European states then saw a political, ideological, and military threat from the East. They saw their interests in a way which would not have been predicted by classic realist theory. Values, culture, and institutions pervasively influence how states define their interests. The interests of states are also shaped not only by their domestic values and institutions but by international norms and institutions. Above and beyond their primal concern with security, different types of states define their interests in different ways. States with similar cultures and institutions will see common interest. Democratic states have commonalities with other democratic states and hence do not fight each other. Canada does not have to ally with another power to deter invasion by the United States.

At a basic level the assumptions of the statist paradigm have been true throughout history. They thus do not help us to understand how global politics after the Cold War will differ from global politics during and before the Cold War. Yet clearly there are differences, and states pursue their interests differently from one historical period to another. In the post–Cold War world, states increasingly define their interests in civilizational terms. They cooperate with and ally themselves with states with similar or common culture and are more often in conflict with countries of different culture. States define threats in terms of the intentions of other states, and those intentions and how they are perceived are powerfully shaped by cultural considerations. Publics and statesmen are less likely to see threats emerging from people they feel they understand and can trust because of shared language, religion, values, institutions, and culture. They are much more likely to see threats coming from states whose societies have different cultures and hence which they do not understand and feel they cannot trust. Now that a Marxist-Leninist Soviet Union no longer poses a threat to the Free World and the United States no longer poses a countering threat to the communist world, countries in both worlds increasingly see threats coming from societies which are culturally different.

While states remain the primary actors in world affairs, they also are suffering losses in sovereignty, functions, and power. International institutions now assert the right to judge and to constrain what states do in their own territory. In some cases, most notably in Europe, international institutions have assumed important functions previously performed by states, and powerful international bureaucracies have been created which operate directly on individual citizens. Globally there has been a trend for state governments to lose power also through devolution to substate, regional, provincial, and local political entities. In many states, including those in the developed world, regional movements exist promoting substantial autonomy or secession. State governments have in considerable measure lost the ability to control the flow of money in and out of their country and are having increasing difficulty controlling the flows of ideas, technology, goods, and people. State borders, in short, have become increasingly permeable. All these developments have led many to see the gradual end of the hard, "billiard ball" state, which purportedly has been the norm since the Treaty of Westphalia in 1648, and the emergence of a varied, complex, multilayered international order more closely resembling that of medieval times.

Sheer Chaos. The weakening of states and the appearance of "failed states" contribute to a fourth image of a world in anarchy. This paradigm stresses: the breakdown of governmental authority; the breakup of states; the intensification of tribal, ethnic, and religious conflict; the emergence of international criminal mafias; refugees multiplying into the tens of millions; the proliferation of nuclear and other weapons of mass destruction; the spread of terrorism; the prevalence of massacres and ethnic cleansing. . . .

Like the states paradigm, the chaos paradigm is close to reality. It provides a graphic and accurate picture of much of what is going on in the world, and unlike the states paradigm, it highlights the significant changes in world politics that have occurred with the end of the Cold War. As of early 1993, for instance, an estimated 48 ethnic wars were occurring throughout the world, and 164 "territorial-ethnic claims and conflicts concerning borders" existed in the former Soviet Union, of which 30 had involved some form of armed conflict.[9] Yet it suffers even more than the states paradigm in being too close to reality. The world may be chaos but it is not totally without order. An image of universal and undifferentiated anarchy provides few clues for understanding the world, for ordering events and evaluating their importance, for predicting trends in the anarchy, for distinguishing among types of chaos and their possibly different causes and consequences, and for developing guidelines for governmental policy makers.

COMPARING WORLDS: REALISM, PARSIMONY, AND PREDICTIONS

Each of these four paradigms offers a somewhat different combination of realism and parsimony. Each also has its deficiencies and limitations. Conceivably these could be countered by combining paradigms, and positing, for instance, that the world is engaged in simultaneous processes of fragmentation and integration. Both trends indeed exist, and a more complex model will more closely approximate reality than a simpler one. Yet this sacrifices parsimony for realism and, if pursued very far, leads to the rejection of all paradigms or theories. In addition, by embracing two simultaneous opposing trends, the fragmentation-integration model fails to set forth under what circumstances one trend will prevail and under what circumstances the other will. The challenge is to develop a paradigm that accounts for more crucial events and provides a better understanding of trends than other paradigms at a similar level of intellectual abstraction.

These four paradigms are also incompatible with each other. The world cannot be both one and fundamentally divided between East and West or North and South. Nor can the nation state be the base rock of international affairs if it is fragmenting and torn by proliferating civil strife. The world is either one, or two, or 184 states, or potentially an almost infinite number of tribes, ethnic groups, and nationalities.

Viewing the world in terms of seven or eight civilizations avoids many of these difficulties. It does not sacrifice reality to parsimony as do the one- and two-world paradigms; yet it also does not sacrifice parsimony to reality as the statist and chaos paradigms do. It provides an easily grasped and intelligible framework for understanding the world, distinguishing what is important from what is unimportant among the multiplying conflicts, predicting future developments, and providing guidelines for policy makers. It also builds on and incorporates elements of the other paradigms. It is more compatible with them than they are with each other. A civilizational approach, for instance, holds that:

- The forces of integration in the world are real and are precisely what are generating counterforces of cultural assertion and civilizational consciousness.
- The world is in some sense two, but the central distinction is between the West as the hitherto dominant civilization and all the others, which, however, have little if anything in common among them. The world, in short, is divided between a Western one and a non-Western many.
- Nation states are and will remain the most important actors in world affairs, but their interests, associations, and conflicts are increasingly shaped by cultural and civilizational factors.
- The world is indeed anarchical, rife with tribal and nationality conflicts, but the conflicts that pose the greatest dangers for stability are those between states or groups from different civilizations.

A civilizational paradigm thus sets forth a relatively simple but not too simple map for understanding what is going on in the world as the twentieth century ends. No paradigm, however, is good forever. The Cold War model of world politics was useful and relevant for forty years but became obsolete in the late 1980s, and at some point the civilizational paradigm will suffer a similar fate. For the contemporary period, however, it provides a useful guide for distinguishing what is more important from what is less important. Slightly less than half of the forty-eight ethnic conflicts in the world in early 1993, for example, were between groups from different civilizations. The civilizational perspective would lead the U.N. Secretary-General and the U.S. Secretary of State to concentrate their peacemaking efforts on these conflicts which have much greater potential than others to escalate into broader wars.

Paradigms also generate predictions, and a crucial test of a paradigm's validity and usefulness is the extent to which the predictions derived from it turn out to be more accurate than those from alternative paradigms. A statist paradigm, for instance, leads John Mearsheimer to predict that "the situation between Ukraine and Russia is ripe for the outbreak of security competition between them. Great powers that share a long and unprotected common border, like that between Russia and Ukraine, often lapse into competition driven by security fears. Russia and Ukraine might overcome this dynamic and learn to live together in harmony, but it would be unusual if they do."[10] A civilizational approach, on the other hand, emphasizes the close cultural, personal, and historical links between Russia and Ukraine and the intermingling of Russians and

Ukrainians in both countries, and focuses instead on the civilizational fault line that divides Orthodox eastern Ukraine from Uniate western Ukraine, a central historical fact of long standing which, in keeping with the "realist" concept of states as unified and self identified entities, Mearsheimer totally ignores. While a statist approach highlights the possibility of a Russian-Ukrainian war, a civilizational approach minimizes that and instead highlights the possibility of Ukraine splitting in half, a separation which cultural factors would lead one to predict might be more violent than that of Czechoslovakia but far less bloody than that of Yugoslavia. These different predictions, in turn, give rise to different policy priorities. Mearsheimer's statist prediction of possible war and Russian conquest of Ukraine leads him to support Ukraine's having nuclear weapons. A civilizational approach would encourage cooperation between Russia and Ukraine, urge Ukraine to give up its nuclear weapons, promote substantial economic assistance and other measures to help maintain Ukrainian unity and independence, and sponsor contingency planning for the possible breakup of Ukraine.

Many important developments after the end of the Cold War were compatible with the civilizational paradigm and could have been predicted from it. These include: the breakup of the Soviet Union and Yugoslavia; the wars going on in their former territories; the rise of religious fundamentalism throughout the world; the struggles within Russia, Turkey, and Mexico over their identity; the intensity of the trade conflicts between the United States and Japan; the resistance of Islamic states to Western pressure on Iraq and Libya; the efforts of Islamic and Confucian states to acquire nuclear weapons and the means to deliver them; China's continuing role as an "outsider" great power; the consolidation of new democratic regimes in some countries and not in others; and the developing arms competition in East Asia.

The relevance of the civilizational paradigm to the emerging world is illustrated by the events fitting that paradigm which occurred during a six-month period in 1993:

- the continuation and intensification of the fighting among Croats, Muslims, and Serbs in the former Yugoslavia;
- the failure of the West to provide meaningful support to the Bosnian Muslims or to denounce Croat atrocities in the same way Serb atrocities were denounced;
- the unwillingness of Russia to join other U.N. Security Council members in getting the Serbs in Croatia to make peace with the Croatian government, and the offer of Iran and other Muslim nations to provide 18,000 troops to protect Bosnian Muslims;
- the intensification of the war between Armenians and Azeris, Turkish and Iranian demands that the Armenians surrender their conquests, the deployment of Turkish troops to and Iranian troops across the Azerbaijan border,

and Russia's warning that the Iranian action contributes to "escalation of the conflict" and "pushes it to dangerous limits of internationalization";

- the continued fighting in central Asia between Russian troops and *mujahedeen* guerrillas;
- the confrontation at the Vienna Human Rights Conference between the West, led by U.S. Secretary of State Warren Christopher, denouncing "cultural relativism," and a coalition of Islamic and Confucian states rejecting "Western universalism";
- the refocusing in parallel fashion of Russian and NATO military planners on "the threat from the South";
- the voting, apparently almost entirely along civilizational lines, that gave the 2000 Olympics to Sydney rather than Beijing;
- the sale of missile components from China to Pakistan, the resulting imposition of U.S. sanctions against China, and the confrontation between China and the United States over the alleged shipment of nuclear technology to Iran;
- the breaking of the moratorium and the testing of a nuclear weapon by China, despite vigorous U.S. protests, and North Korea's refusal to participate further in talks on its own nuclear weapons program;
- the revelation that the U.S. State Department was following a "dual containment" policy directed at both Iran and Iraq;
- the announcement by the U.S. Defense Department of a new strategy of preparing for two "major regional conflicts," one against North Korea, the other against Iran or Iraq;
- the call by Iran's president for alliances with China and India so that "we can have the last word on international events";
- the new German legislation drastically curtailing the admission of refugees;
- the agreement between Russian President Boris Yeltsin and Ukrainian President Leonid Kravchuk on the disposition of the Black Sea fleet and other issues;
- the bombing of Baghdad by the United States, its virtually unanimous support by Western governments, and its condemnation by almost all Muslim governments as another example of the West's "double standard";
- the United States' listing Sudan as a terrorist state and indicting Egyptian Sheik Omar Abdel Rahman and his followers for conspiring "to levy a war of urban terrorism against the United States";
- the improved prospects for the eventual admission of Poland, Hungary, the Czech Republic, and Slovakia into NATO;
- the 1993 Russian parliamentary election which demonstrated that Russia was indeed a "torn" country with its population and elites uncertain whether they should join or challenge the West.

A comparable list of events demonstrating the relevance of the civilization paradigm could be compiled for almost any other six-month period in the early 1990s.

In the early years of the Cold War, the Canadian statesman Lester Pearson presciently pointed to the resurgence and vitality of non-Western societies. "It would be absurd," he warned, "to imagine that these new political societies coming to birth in the East will be replicas of those with which we in the West are familiar. The revival of these ancient civilizations will take new forms." Pointing out that international relations "for several centuries" had been the relations among the states of Europe, he argued that "the most far-reaching problems arise no longer between nations within a single civilization but between civilizations themselves."[11] The prolonged bipolarity of the Cold War delayed the developments which Pearson saw coming. The end of the Cold War released the cultural and civilizational forces which he identified in the 1950s, and a wide range of scholars and observers have recognized and highlighted the new role of these factors in global politics. "[A]s far as anyone interested in the contemporary world is concerned," Fernand Braudel has sagely warned, "and even more so with regard to anyone wishing to act within it, it 'pays' to know how to make out, on a map of the world, which civilizations exist today, to be able to define their borders, their centers and peripheries, their provinces and the air one breathes there, the general and particular 'forms' existing and associating within them. Otherwise, what catastrophic blunders of perspective could ensue!"[12]

Notes

[1]Henry A. Kissinger, *Diplomacy* (New York: Simon & Schuster, 1994), pp. 23–24.

[2]H. D. S. Greenway's phrase, *Boston Globe,* 3 December 1992, p. 19.

[3]Vaclav Havel, "The New Measure of Man," *New York Times,* 8 July 1994, p. A27; Jacques Delors, "Questions Concerning European Security," Address, International Institute for Strategic Studies, Brussels, 10 September 1993, p. 2.

[4]Thomas S. Kuhn, *The Structure of Scientific Revolutions* (Chicago: University of Chicago Press, 1962), pp. 17–18.

[5]John Lewis Gaddis, "Toward the Post–Cold War World," *Foreign Affairs,* 70 (Spring 1991), 101; Judith Goldstein and Robert O. Keohane, "Ideas and Foreign Policy: An Analytical Framework," in Goldstein and Keohane, eds., *Ideas and Foreign Policy: Beliefs, Institutions, and Political Change* (Ithaca: Cornell University Press, 1993), pp. 8–17.

[6]Francis Fukuyama, "The End of History," *The National Interest,* 16 (Summer 1989), 4, 18.

[7]"Address to the Congress Reporting on the Yalta Conference," 1 March 1945, in Samuel I. Rosenman, ed., *Public Papers and Addresses of Franklin D. Roosevelt* (New York: Russell and Russell, 1969), XIII, 586.

[8]Edward W. Said, *Orientalism* (New York: Pantheon Books, 1978), pp. 43–44.

[9]See *New York Times,* 7 February 1993, pp. 1, 14; and Gabriel Schoenfeld, "Outer Limits," *Post-Soviet Prospects,* 17 (Jan. 1993), 3, citing figures from the Russian Ministry of Defense.

[10]John J. Mearsheimer, "The Case for a Nuclear Deterrent," *Foreign Affairs*, 72 (Summer 1993), 54.

[11]Lester B. Pearson, *Democracy in World Politics* (Princeton: Princeton University Press, 1955), pp. 82–83.

[12]Fernand Brudel, *On History* (Chicago: University of Chicago Press, 1980), pp. 210–211.

STUDY AND DISCUSSION QUESTIONS

1. Why, according to Huntington, do the "most dangerous enmities occur at the fault lines between the world's major civilizations"?
2. What "severe limitations" does Huntington see in the realist paradigm that focuses on states as the dominant players in the international system?
3. How well does Huntington's "clash of civilizations" model explain the war in Iraq, the broader conflict in the Middle East, and the tentative steps toward democracy in the region?

3

Broken Promises

Joseph E. Stiglitz

In this selection Joseph E. Stiglitz, a Nobel Prize winning economist, who has served as the chairman of the Council of Economic Advisers and chief economist of the World Bank, offers an uncompromising critique of the institutions that govern globalization, such as the World Bank, the World Trade Organization (WTO), and especially the International Monetary Fund (IMF). Stiglitz argues that the most powerful states— the key industrial counties and, in particular, the United States—have hijacked the IMF and steered it towards one-size-fits-all policies that fail to address the specific problems faced by developing states. Stiglitz concludes that policies intended to reduce expenditures on education, health care, and infrastructure and increase interest rates lead only to a contraction in the economy, and increased misery and insecurity.

On my first day, February 13, 1997, as chief economist and senior vice president of the World Bank, as I walked into its gigantic, modern, gleaming main building on 19th Street in Washington, DC, the institution's motto was the first thing that caught my eye: *Our dream is a world without poverty*. In the center of the thirteen-story atrium there is a statue of a young boy leading an old blind man, a memorial to the eradication of river blindness (*onchocerciasis*). Before the World Bank, the World Health Organization, and others pooled their efforts, thousands were blinded annually in Africa from this preventable disease. Across the street stands another gleaming monument to public wealth, the headquarters of the International Monetary Fund. The marble atrium inside, graced with abundant flora, serves to remind visiting finance ministers from countries around the world that the IMF represents the centers of wealth and power.

These two institutions, often confused in the public mind, present marked contrasts that underline the differences in their cultures, styles, and missions: one is devoted to eradicating poverty, one to maintaining global stability. While both have teams of economists flying into developing countries for three-week missions, the World Bank has worked hard to make sure that a substantial fraction of its staff live permanently in the country they are trying to assist; the IMF generally has only a single "resident representative," whose powers are limited. IMF programs are typically dictated from Washington, and shaped by the short missions during which its staff members pore over numbers in the finance ministries and central banks and make themselves comfortable in five-star hotels in the capitals. There is more than symbolism in this difference: one cannot come to learn about, and love, a nation unless one gets out to the countryside. One should not see unemployment as just a statistic, an economic "body count," the unintended casualties in the fight against inflation or to ensure that Western banks get repaid. The unemployed are people, with families, whose lives are affected—sometimes devastated—by the economic policies that outsiders recommend, and, in the case of the IMF, effectively impose. Modern high-tech warfare is designed to remove physical contact: dropping bombs from 50,000 feet ensures that one does not "feel" what one does. Modern economic management is similar: from one's luxury hotel, one can callously impose policies about which one would think twice if one knew the people whose lives one was destroying.

Statistics bear out what those who travel outside the capital see in the villages of Africa, Nepal, Mindanao, or Ethiopia; the gap between the poor and the rich has been growing, and even the number in absolutely poverty—living on less than a dollar a day—has increased. Even where river blindness has been eliminated, poverty endures—this despite all the good intentions and promises made by the developed nations to the developing nations, most of which were once the colonial possessions of the developed nations.

Mind-sets are not changed overnight, and this is as true in the developed as in the developing countries. Giving developing countries their freedom (generally

after little preparation for autonomy) often did not change the view of their former colonial masters, who continued to feel that they knew best. The colonial
mentality—the "white man's burden" and the presumption that they knew what
was best for the developing countries—persisted. America, which came to dominate the global economic scene, had much less of a colonial heritage, yet America's credentials too had been tarred, not so much by its "Manifest Destiny"
expansionism as by the cold war, in which principles of democracy were compromised or ignored, in the all-encompassing struggle against communism.

The night before I started at the Bank, I held my last press conference as chairman
of the President's Council of Economic Advisers. With the domestic economy so
well under control, I felt that the greatest challenges for an economist now lay in
the growing problem of world poverty. What could we do about the 1.2 billion
people around the world living on less than a dollar a day, or the 2.8 billion people living on less than $2 a day—more than 45 percent of the world's population?
What could I do to bring to reality the dream of a world without poverty? How
could I embark on the more modest dream of a world with less poverty? I saw
my task as threefold: thinking through what strategies might be most effective in
promoting growth and reducing poverty; working with governments in the
developing countries to put these strategies in place; and doing everything I could
within the developed countries to advance the interests and concerns of the
developing world, whether it was pushing for opening up their markets or providing more effective assistance. I knew the tasks were difficult, but I never
dreamed that one of the major obstacles the developing countries faced was man-
made, totally unnecessary, and lay right across the street—at my "sister" institution, the IMF. I had expected that not everyone in the international financial
institutions or in the governments that supported them was committed to the
goal of eliminating poverty; but I thought there would be an open debate about
strategies—strategies which in so many areas seem to be failing, and especially
failing the poor. In this, I was to be disappointed.

ETHIOPIA AND THE STRUGGLE BETWEEN
POWER POLITICS AND POVERTY

After four years in Washington, I had become used to the strange world of
bureaucracies and politicians. But it was not until I traveled to Ethiopia, one of
the poorest countries in the world, in March 1997, barely a month into the
World Bank job, that I became fully immersed in the astonishing world of IMF
politics and arithmetic. Ethiopia's per capita income was $110 a year and the
country had suffered from successive droughts and famines that had killed 2 million people. I went to meet Prime Minister Meles Zenawi, a man who had led a
seventeen-year guerrilla war against the bloody Marxist regime of Mengistu

Haile Mariam. Meles's forces won in 1991 and then the government began the hard work of rebuilding the country. A doctor by training, Meles had formally studied economics because he knew that to bring his country out of centuries of poverty would require nothing less than economic transformation, and he demonstrated a knowledge of economics—and indeed a creativity—that would have put him at the head of any of my university classes. He showed a deeper understanding of economic principles—and certainly a greater knowledge of the circumstances in his country—than many of the international economic bureaucrats that I had to deal with in the succeeding three years.

Meles combined these intellectual attributes with personal integrity: no one doubted his honesty and there were few accusations of corruption within his government. His political opponents came mostly from the long-dominant groups around the capital who had lost political power with his accession, and they raised questions about his commitment to democratic principles. However, he was not an old-fashioned autocrat. Both he and the government were generally committed to a process of decentralization, bringing government closer to the people and ensuring that the center did not lose touch with the separate regions. The new constitution even gave each region the right to vote democratically to secede, ensuring that the political elites in the capital city, whoever they might be, could not risk ignoring the concerns of ordinary citizens in every part of the country, or that one part of the country could not impose its views on the rest. The government actually lived up to its commitment, when Eritrea declared its independence in 1993. (Subsequent events—such as the government's occupation of the university in Addis Ababa in the spring of 2000, with the imprisonment of some students and professors—show the precariousness, in Ethiopia as elsewhere, of basic democratic rights.)

When I arrived in 1997, Meles was engaged in a heated dispute with the IMF, and the Fund had suspended its lending program. Ethiopia's macroeconomic "results"—upon which the Fund was supposed to focus—could not have been better. There was no inflation; in fact, prices were falling. Output had been growing steadily since he had succeeded in ousting Mengistu. Meles showed that, with the right policies in place, even a poor African country could experience sustained economic growth. After years of war and rebuilding, international assistance was beginning to return to the country. But Meles was having problems with the IMF. What was at stake was not just $127 million of IMF money provided through its so-called Enhanced Structural Adjustment Facility (ESAF) program (a lending program at highly subsidized rates to help very poor countries), but World Bank monies as well.

The IMF has a distinct role in international assistance. It is supposed to review each recipient's macroeconomic situation and make sure that the country is living within its means. If it is not, there is inevitably trouble down the road. In the short run, a country can live beyond its means by borrowing, but eventually a day of reckoning comes, and there is a crisis. The IMF is particularly concerned about inflation. Countries whose governments spend more than they take in in taxes and foreign aid often will face inflation, especially if they finance their deficits by printing money. Of course, there are other dimensions to good macroeconomic policy besides inflation. The term *macro* refers to the *aggregate* behavior, the overall levels of growth, unemployment, and inflation, and a country can have low inflation but no growth and high unemployment. To most economists, such a country would rate as having a disastrous macroeconomic framework. To most economists, inflation is not so much an end in itself, but a means to an end: it is because *excessively* high inflation often leads to low growth, and low growth leads to high unemployment, that inflation is so frowned upon. But the IMF often seems to confuse means with ends, thereby losing sight of what is ultimately of concern. A country like Argentina can get an "A" grade, even if it has double-digit unemployment for years, so long as its budget seems in balance and its inflation seems in control!

If a country does not come up to certain minimum standards, the IMF suspends assistance; and typically, when it does, so do other donors. Understandably, the World Bank and the IMF don't lend to countries unless they have a good macroframework in place. If countries have huge deficits and soaring inflation, there is a risk that money will not be well spent. Governments that fail to manage their overall economy generally typically do a poor job managing foreign aid. But if the macroeconomic indicators—inflation and growth—are solid, as they were in Ethiopia, surely the underlying macroeconomic framework must be good. Not only did Ethiopia have a sound macroeconomic framework but the World Bank had direct evidence of the competence of the government and its commitment to the poor. Ethiopia had formulated a rural development strategy, focusing its attention on the poor, and especially the 85 percent of the population living in the rural sector. It had dramatically cut back on military expenditures— remarkable for a government which had come to power through military means— because it knew that funds spent on weapons were funds that could not be spent on fighting poverty. Surely, this was precisely the kind of government to which the international community should have been giving assistance. But the IMF had suspended its program with Ethiopia, in spite of the good macroeconomic performance, saying it was worried about Ethiopia's budgetary position.

The Ethiopian government had two revenue sources, taxes and foreign assistance. A government's budget is in balance so long as its revenue sources equal its expenditures. Ethiopia, like many developing countries, derived much of its revenues from foreign assistance. The IMF worried that if this aid dried up, Ethiopia would be in trouble. Hence it argued that Ethiopia's budgetary position could only be judged solid if expenditures were limited to the taxes it collected.

The obvious problem with the IMF's logic is that it implies no poor country can ever spend money on anything it gets aid for. If Sweden, say, gives money to

Ethiopia to build schools, this logic dictates that Ethiopia should instead put the money into its reserves. (All countries have, or should have, reserve accounts that hold funds for the proverbial rainy day. Gold is the traditional reserve, but today it has been replaced by hard currency and its interest-bearing relatives. The most common way to hold reserves is in U.S. Treasury bills.) But this is not why international donors give aid. In Ethiopia, the donors, who were working independently and not beholden to the IMF, wanted to see new schools and health clinics built, and so did Ethiopia. Meles put the matter more forcefully: He told me that he had not fought so hard for seventeen years to be instructed by some international bureaucrat that he could not build schools and clinics for his people once he had succeeded in convincing donors to pay for them.

. . .

There were other sticking points in IMF-Ethiopia relations, concerning Ethiopian financial market liberalization. Good capital markets are the hallmark of capitalism, but nowhere is the disparity between developed and less developed countries greater than in their capital markets. Ethiopia's entire banking system (measured, for instance, by the size of its assets) is somewhat smaller than that of Bethesda, Maryland, a suburb on the outskirts of Washington with a population of 55,277. The IMF wanted Ethiopia not only to open up its financial markets to Western competition but also to divide its largest bank into several pieces. In a world in which U.S. megafinancial institutions like Citibank and Travelers, or Manufacturers Hanover and Chemical, say they have to merge to compete effectively, a bank the size of North East Bethesda National Bank really has no way to compete against a global giant like Citibank. When global financial institutions enter a country, they can squelch the domestic competition. And as they attract depositors away from the local banks in a country like Ethiopia, they may be far more attentive and generous when it comes to making loans to large multinational corporations than they will to providing credit to small businesses and farmers.

The IMF wanted to do more than just open up the banking system to foreign competition. It wanted to "strengthen" the financial system by creating an auction market for Ethiopia's government Treasury bills—a reform, as desirable as it might be in many countries, which was completely out of tune with that country's state of development. It also wanted Ethiopia to "liberalize" its financial market, that is, allow interest rates to be freely determined by market forces—something the United States and Western Europe did not do until after 1970, when their markets, and the requisite regulatory apparatus, were far more developed. The IMF was confusing ends with means. One of the prime objectives of a good banking system is to provide credit at good terms to those who will repay. In a largely rural country like Ethiopia, it is especially important for farmers to be able to obtain credit at reasonable terms to buy seed and fertilizer. The task of providing such credit is not easy; even in the United States, at critical stages of its development when agriculture was more important, the government took a crucial role in providing needed credit. The Ethiopian banking system was at least seemingly quite efficient, the difference between borrowing and lending rates being far lower than those in other developing countries that had followed the IMF's advice. Still, the Fund was unhappy, simply because it believed interest rates should be freely determined by international market forces, whether those markets were or were not competitive. To the Fund, a liberalized financial system was an end in itself. Its naive faith in markets made it confident that a liberalized financial system would lower interest rates paid on loans and thereby make more funds available. The IMF was so certain about the correctness of its dogmatic position that it had little interest in looking at actual experiences.

Ethiopia resisted the IMF's demand that it "open" its banking system, for good reason. It had seen what happened when one of its East African neighbors gave in to IMF demands. The IMF had insisted on financial market liberalization, believing that competition among banks would lead to lower interest rates. The results were disastrous: the move was followed by the very rapid growth of local and indigenous commercial banks, at a time when the banking legislation and bank supervision were inadequate, with the predictable results—fourteen banking failures in Kenya in 1993 and 1994 alone. In the end, interest rates increased, not decreased. Understandably, the government of Ethiopia was wary. Committed to improving the living standards of its citizens in the rural sector, it feared that liberalization would have a devastating effect on its economy. Those farmers who had previously managed to obtain credit would find themselves unable to buy seed or fertilizer because they would be unable to get cheap credit or would be forced to pay higher interest rates which they could ill afford. This is a country wracked by droughts which result in massive starvation. Its leaders did not want to make matters worse. The Ethiopians worried that the IMF's advice would cause farmers' incomes to fall, exacerbating an already dismal situation.

Faced with Ethiopian reluctance to accede to its demands, the IMF suggested the government was not serious about reform and, as I have said, suspended its program. Happily, other economists in the World Bank and I managed to persuade the Bank management that lending more money to Ethiopia made good sense: it was a country desperately in need, with a first-rate economic framework and a government committed to improving the plight of its poor. . . .

The tussle over lending to Ethiopia taught me a lot about how the IMF works. There was clear evidence the IMF was wrong about financial market liberalization and Ethiopia's macroeconomic position, but the IMF had to have its way. It seemingly would not listen to others, no matter how well informed, no matter how disinterested. Matters of substance became subsidiary to matters of process. . . . Financial market liberalization—how best this should be done in a country at Ethiopia's stage of development—was a matter of substance and experts could have been asked for their opinion. The fact that outside experts were not called in to help arbitrate what was clearly a contentious issue is consonant with the style of the IMF, in which the Fund casts itself as the monopoly supplier of "sound" advice. . . .

But to the IMF the lack of detailed knowledge is of less moment, because it tends to take a "one-size-fits-all" approach. The problems of this approach become particularly acute when facing the challenges of the developing and transition economies. The institution does not really claim expertise in development—its original mandate is supporting global economic stability, as I have said, not reducing poverty in developing countries—yet it does not hesitate to weigh in, and weigh in heavily, on development issues. Development issues are complicated; in many ways developing countries present far greater difficulties than more developed countries. This is because in developing nations, markets are often absent, and when present, often work imperfectly. Information problems abound, and cultural mores may significantly affect economic behavior.

Unfortunately, too often the training of the macroeconomists does not prepare them well for the problems that they have to confront in developing countries. In some of the universities from which the IMF hires regularly, the core curricula involve models in which there is never any unemployment. After all, in the standard competitive model—the model that underlies the IMF's market fundamentalism—demand always equals supply. If the demand for labor equals supply, there is never any *involuntary* unemployment. Someone who is not working has evidently chosen not to work. In this interpretation, unemployment in the Great Depression, when one out of four people was out of work, would be the result of a sudden increase in the desire for more leisure. It might be of some interest to psychologists why there was this sudden change in the desire for leisure, or why those who were supposed to be enjoying this leisure seemed so unhappy, but according to the standard model these questions go beyond the scope of economics. While these models might provide some amusement within academia, they seemed particularly ill suited to understanding the problems of a country like South Africa, which has been plagued with unemployment rates in excess of 25 percent since apartheid was dismantled.

The IMF economists could not, of course, ignore the existence of unemployment. Because under market fundamentalism—in which, *by assumption,* markets work perfectly and demand must equal supply for labor as for every other good or factor—there cannot be unemployment, the problem cannot lie with markets. It must lie elsewhere—with greedy unions and politicians interfering with the workings of free markets, by demanding—and getting—excessively high wages. There is an obvious policy implication—if there is unemployment, wages should be reduced.

But even if the training of the typical IMF macroeconomist had been better suited to the problems of developing countries, it's unlikely that an IMF mission, on a three-week trip to Addis Ababa, Ethiopia's capital, or the capital of any other developing country, could really develop policies appropriate for that country. Such policies are far more likely to be crafted by highly educated, first-rate economists already in the country, deeply knowledgeable about it and working daily on solving that country's problems. Outsiders can play a role, in sharing the experiences of other countries, and in offering alternative interpretations of the economic forces at play. But the IMF did not want to take on the mere role of an adviser, competing with others who might be offering their ideas. It wanted a more central role in shaping policy. And it could do this because its position was based on an ideology—market fundamentalism—that required little, if any, consideration of a country's particular circumstances and immediate problems. IMF economists could ignore the short-term effects their policies might have on the country, content in the belief that *in the long run* the country would be better off; any adverse short-run impacts would be merely pain that was necessary as part of the process. Soaring interest rates might, today, lead to starvation, but market efficiency requires free markets, and eventually, efficiency leads to growth, and growth benefits all. Suffering and pain became part of the process of redemption, evidence that a country was on the right track. To me, sometimes pain *is* necessary, but it is not a virtue in its own right. Well-designed policies can often avoid much of the pain; and some forms of pain—the misery caused by abrupt cuts in food subsidies, for example, which leads to rioting, urban violence, and the dissolution of the social fabric—are counter-productive.

The IMF has done a good job of persuading many that its ideologically driven policies were necessary if countries are to succeed in the long run. Economists always focus on the importance of scarcity and the IMF often says it is simply the messenger of scarcity: countries cannot persistently live beyond their means. One doesn't, of course, need a sophisticated financial institution staffed by Ph.D. economists to tell a country to limit expenditures to revenues. But IMF reform programs go well beyond simply ensuring that countries live within their means.

· · ·

The IMF, of course, claims that it never dictates but always negotiates the terms of any loan agreement with the borrowing country. But these are one-sided negotiations in which all the power is in the hands of the IMF, largely because many countries seeking IMF help are in desperate need of funds. Although I had seen this so clearly in Ethiopia and the other developing countries with which I was involved, it was brought home again to me during my visit to South Korea in December 1997, as the East Asia crisis was unfolding. South Korea's economists knew that the policies being pushed on their country by the IMF would be disastrous. While, in retrospect, even the IMF agreed that it imposed excessive fiscal stringency, in prospect, few economists (outside the IMF) thought the policy made sense. Yet Korea's economic officials remained silent. I wondered why they had kept this silence, but did not get an answer from officials inside the government until a subsequent visit two years later, when the Korean economy had recovered. The answer was what, given past experience, I had suspected all along. Korean officials reluctantly explained that they had been scared to disagree openly. The IMF could not only cut off its own funds, but could use its bully pulpit to discourage investments from private market funds by telling private sector financial institutions of the doubts the IMF had about Korea's economy. So Korea had no choice. Even implied criticism by Korea of the IMF program could have a disastrous effect: to the IMF, it would suggest that the government didn't fully understand "IMF economics," that it had reservations, making it less likely that it would actually carry out the program. (The IMF has a special phrase for describing such situations: the country has gone "off track." There is one "right" way, and any deviation is a sign of an impending derailment.) A public announcement by the IMF that negotiations had broken off, or even been postponed, would send a highly negative signal to the markets. This signal would at best lead to higher interest rates and at worst a total cutoff from private funds. Even more serious for some of the poorest countries, which have in any case little access to private funds, is that other donors (the World Bank, the European Union, and many other countries) make access to their funds contingent on IMF approval. Recent initiatives for debt relief have effectively given the IMF even more power, because unless the IMF approves the country's economic policy, there will be no debt relief. This gives the IMF enormous leverage, as the IMF well knows.

The imbalance of power between the IMF and the "client" countries inevitably creates tension between the two, but the IMF's own behavior in negotiations exacerbates an already difficult situation. In dictating the terms of the agreements, the IMF effectively stifles any discussions within a client government—let alone more broadly within the country—about alternative economic policies. In times of crises, the IMF would defend its stance by saying there simply wasn't time. But its behavior was little different in or out of crisis. The IMF's view was simple: questions, particularly when raised vociferously and openly, would be viewed as a challenge to the inviolate orthodoxy. If accepted, they might even undermine its authority and credibility. Government leaders knew this and took the cue: they might argue in private, but not in public. The chance of modifying the Fund's views was tiny, while the chance of annoying Fund leaders and provoking them to take a tougher position on other issues was far greater. And if they were angry or annoyed, the IMF could postpone its loans—a scary prospect for a country facing a crisis. But the fact that the government officials *seemed* to go along with the IMF's recommendation did not mean that they really agreed. And the IMF knew it.

Even a casual reading of the terms of the typical agreements between the IMF and the developing countries showed the lack of trust between the Fund and its recipients. The IMF staff monitored progress, not just on the relevant indicators for sound macromanagement—inflation, growth, and unemployment—but on intermediate variables, such as the money supply, often only loosely connected to the variables of ultimate concern. Countries were put on strict targets—what would be accomplished in thirty days, in sixty days, in ninety days. In some cases the agreements stipulated what laws the country's Parliament would have to pass to meet IMF requirements or "targets"—and by when.

These requirements are referred to as "conditions," and "conditionality" is a hotly debated topic in the development world. Every loan document specifies basic conditions, of course. At a minimum, a loan agreement says the loan goes out on the condition that it will be repaid, usually with a schedule attached. Many loans impose conditions designed to increase the likelihood that they will be repaid. "Conditionality" refers to more forceful conditions, ones that often turn the loan into a policy tool. If the IMF wanted a nation to liberalize its financial markets, for instance, it might pay out the loan in installments, tying subsequent installments to verifiable steps toward liberalization. I personally believe that conditionality, at least in the manner and extent to which it has been used by the IMF, is a bad idea; there is little evidence that it leads to improved economic policy, but it does have adverse political effects because countries resent having conditions imposed on them. Some defend conditionality by saying that any banker imposes conditions on borrowers, to make it more likely that the loan will be repaid. But the conditionality imposed by the IMF and the World Bank was very different. In some cases, it even *reduced* the likelihood of repayment.

For instance, conditions that might weaken the economy in the short run, whatever their merits in the long, run the risk of exacerbating the downturn and thus making it more difficult for the country to repay the short-term IMF loans. Eliminating trade barriers, monopolies, and tax distortions may enhance long-run growth, but the disturbances to the economy, as it strives to adjust, may only deepen its downturn.

While the conditionalities could not be justified in terms of the Fund's fiduciary responsibility, they might be justified in terms of what it might have perceived as its moral responsibility, its obligation to do everything it could to strengthen the economy of the countries that had turned to it for help. But the danger was that even when well intentioned, the myriad of conditions—in some cases over a hundred, each with its own rigid timetable—detracted from the country's ability to address the central pressing problems.

The conditions went beyond economics into areas that properly belong in the realm of politics. In the case of Korea, for instance, the loans included a change in the charter of the Central Bank, to make it more independent of the political process, though there was scant evidence that countries with more independent central banks grow faster or have fewer or shallower fluctuations. There is a widespread feeling that Europe's independent Central Bank exacerbated Europe's economic slowdown in 2001, as, like a child, it responded peevishly to the natural political concerns over the growing unemployment. Just to show that it was independent, it refused to allow interest rates to fall, and there was nothing anyone could do about it. The problems partly arose because the European Central Bank has a mandate to focus on inflation, a policy which the IMF has advocated around the world but one that can stifle growth or exacerbate an economic downturn. In the midst of Korea's crisis, the Korean Central Bank was told not only to be more independent but to focus exclusively on inflation, although Korea had not had a problem with inflation, and there was no reason to believe that mismanaged monetary policy had anything to do with the crisis. The IMF simply used the opportunity that the crisis gave it to push its political agenda. When, in Seoul, I asked the IMF team why they were doing this, I found the answer shocking (though by then it should not have come as a surprise): We always insist that countries have an independent central bank focusing on inflation. This was an issue on which I felt strongly. When I had been the president's chief economic adviser, we beat back an attempt by Senator Connie Mack of Florida to change the charter of the U.S. Federal Reserve Bank to focus exclusively on inflation. The Fed, America's central bank, has a mandate to focus not just on inflation but also on employment and growth. The president opposed the change, and we knew that, if anything, the American people thought the Fed already focused *too much* on inflation. The president made it clear that this was an issue he would fight, and as soon as this was made clear, the proponents backed off. Yet here was the IMF—partially under the influence of the U.S. Treasury—imposing a political condition on Korea that most Americans would have found unacceptable for themselves.

Sometimes, the conditions seemed little more than a simple exercise of power: in its 1997 lending agreement to Korea, the IMF insisted on moving up the date of opening Korea's markets to certain Japanese goods although this could not possibly help Korea address the problems of the crisis. To some, these actions represented "seizing the window of opportunity," using the crisis to leverage in changes that the IMF and World Bank had long been pushing; but to others, these were simply acts of pure political might, extracting a concession, of limited value, simply as a demonstration of who was running the show.

While conditionality did engender resentment, it did not succeed in engendering development. Studies at the World Bank and elsewhere showed not just that conditionality did not *ensure* that money was well spent and that countries would grow faster but that there was little evidence it worked at all. Good policies cannot be bought.

. . .

I should be clear: all of these criticisms of how the IMF operates do not mean the IMF's money and time is always wasted. Sometimes money has gone to governments with good policies in place—but not necessarily because the IMF recommended these policies. Then, the money did make a difference for the good. Sometimes, conditionality shifted the debate inside the country in ways that led to better policies. The rigid timetables that the IMF imposed grew partly from a multitude of experiences in which governments promised to make certain reforms, but once they had the money, the reforms were not forthcoming; sometimes, the rigid timetables helped force the pace of change. But all too often, the conditionality did not ensure either that the money was well used or that meaningful, deep, and long-lasting policy changes occurred. Sometimes, conditionality was even counterproductive, either because the policies were not well suited to the country or because the way they were imposed engendered hostility to the reform process. Sometimes, the IMF program left the country just as impoverished but with more debt and an even richer ruling elite.

. . .

STUDY AND DISCUSSION QUESTIONS

1. What is the core mission of the IMF?
2. What lessons about the effectiveness of the IMF—and how it works—does Stiglitz take away from his experience in Ethiopia?
3. Why is Stiglitz so critical of conditionality, especially without consultation?

4

Anarchy and the Struggle for Power

John J. Mearsheimer

In this excerpt from The Tragedy of Great Power Politics, *John Mearsheimer, a political scientist at the University of Chicago, argues that states inhabit a zero-sum world of competition over power, which is intense, dangerous, and unforgiving. Advancing the realist approach to understanding international relations systems and great power politics, Mearsheimer makes one of the most compelling cases for the globalization skeptics who argue that globalization does not define a new era of international politics. In this selection, Mearsheimer presents his theory about why states pursue hegemony and compete for power—and why they always have, long before the concept of globalization inspired such wide-ranging debate about state power. The theory—which he calls* offensive realism—*suggests that states want more power than they possess, to protect themselves and to advance their interests.*

Great powers, I argue, are always searching for opportunities to gain power over their rivals, with hegemony as their final goal. This perspective does not allow for status quo powers, except for the unusual state that achieves preponderance. Instead, the system is populated with great powers that have revisionist intentions at their core. This [selection] presents a theory that explains this competition for power. Specifically, I attempt to show that there is a compelling logic behind my claim that great powers seek to maximize their share of world power. . . .

WHY STATES PURSUE POWER

My explanation for why great powers vie with each other for power and strive for hegemony is derived from five assumptions about the international system. None of these assumptions alone mandates that states behave competitively.

Taken together, however, they depict a world in which states have considerable reason to think and sometimes behave aggressively. In particular, the system encourages states to look for opportunities to maximize their power vis-à-vis other states.

How important is it that these assumptions be realistic? Some social scientists argue that the assumptions that underpin a theory need not conform to reality. Indeed, the economist Milton Friedman maintains that the best theories "will be found to have assumptions that are wildly inaccurate descriptive representations of reality, and, in general, the more significant the theory, the more unrealistic the assumptions."[1] According to this view, the explanatory power of a theory is all that matters. If unrealistic assumptions lead to a theory that tells us a lot about how the world works, it is of no importance whether the underlying assumptions are realistic or not.

I reject this view. Although I agree that explanatory power is the ultimate criterion for assessing theories, I also believe that a theory based on unrealistic or false assumptions will not explain much about how the world works. Sound theories are based on sound assumptions. Accordingly, each of these five assumptions is a reasonably accurate representation of an important aspect of life in the international system.

BEDROCK ASSUMPTIONS

The first assumption is that the international system is anarchic, which does not mean that it is chaotic or riven by disorder. It is easy to draw that conclusion, since realism depicts a world characterized by security competition and war. By itself, however, the realist notion of anarchy has nothing to do with conflict; it is an ordering principle, which says that the system comprises independent states that have no central authority above them. Sovereignty, in other words, inheres in states because there is no higher ruling body in the international system. There is no "government over governments."[2]

The second assumption is that great powers inherently possess some offensive military capability, which gives them the wherewithal to hurt and possibly destroy each other. States are potentially dangerous to each other, although some states have more military might than others and are therefore more dangerous. A state's military power is usually identified with the particular weaponry at its disposal, although even if there were no weapons, the individuals in those states could still use their feet and hands to attack the population of another state. After all, for every neck, there are two hands to choke it.

The third assumption is that states can never be certain about other states' intentions. Specifically, no state can be sure that another state will not use its offensive military capability to attack the first state. This is not to say that states necessarily have hostile intentions. Indeed, all of the states in the system may be reliably benign, but it is impossible to be sure of that judgment because intentions are impossible to divine with 100 percent certainty. There are many possible causes of aggression, and no state can be sure that another state is not motivated by one of them. Furthermore, intentions can change quickly, so a state's intentions can be benign one day and hostile the next. Uncertainty about intentions is unavoidable, which means that states can never be sure that other states do not have offensive intentions to go along with their offensive capabilities.

The fourth assumption is that survival is the primary goal of great powers. Specifically, states seek to maintain their territorial integrity and the autonomy of their domestic political order. Survival dominates other motives because, once a state is conquered, it is unlikely to be in a position to pursue other aims. Soviet leader Josef Stalin put the point well during a war scare in 1927: "We can and must build socialism in the [Soviet Union]. But in order to do so we first of all have to exist."[3] States can and do pursue other goals, of course, but security is their most important objective.

The fifth assumption is that great powers are rational actors. They are aware of their external environment and they think strategically about how to survive in it. In particular, they consider the preferences of other states and how their own behavior is likely to affect the behavior of those other states, and how the behavior of those other states is likely to affect their own strategy for survival. Moreover, states pay attention to the long term as well as the immediate consequences of their actions.

As emphasized, none of these assumptions alone dictates that great powers as a general rule *should* behave aggressively toward each other. There is surely the possibility that some state might have hostile intentions, but the only assumption dealing with a specific motive that is common to all states says that their principal objective is to survive, which by itself is a rather harmless goal. Nevertheless, when the five assumptions are married together, they create powerful incentives for great powers to think and act offensively with regard to each other. In particular, three general patterns of behavior result: fear, self-help, and power maximization.

STATE BEHAVIOR

Great powers fear each other. They regard each other with suspicion, and they worry that war might be in the offing. They anticipate danger. There is little room for trust among states. For sure, the level of fear varies across time and space, but it cannot be reduced to a trivial level. From the perspective of any one great power, all other great powers are potential enemies. This point is illustrated by the reaction of the United Kingdom and France to German reunification at the end of the Cold War. Despite the fact that these three states had been close allies for almost forty-five years, both the United Kingdom and France immediately began worrying about the potential dangers of a united Germany.

The basis of this fear is that in a world where great powers have the capability to attack each other and might have the motive to do so, any state bent on survival must be at least suspicious of other states and reluctant to trust them. Add to this the "911" problem—the absence of a central authority to which a threatened state can turn for help—and states have even greater incentive to fear each other. Moreover, there is no mechanism, other than the possible self-interest of third parties, for punishing an aggressor. Because it is sometimes difficult to deter potential aggressors, states have ample reason not to trust other states and to be prepared for war with them.

The possible consequences of falling victim to aggression further amplify the importance of fear as a motivating force in world politics. Great powers do not compete with each other as if international politics were merely an economic marketplace. Political competition among states is a much more dangerous business than mere economic intercourse; the former can lead to war, and war often means mass killing on the battlefield as well as mass murder of civilians. In extreme cases, war can even lead to the destruction of states. The horrible consequences of war sometimes cause states to view each other not just as competitors, but as potentially deadly enemies. Political antagonism, in short, tends to be intense, because the stakes are great.

States in the international system also aim to guarantee their own survival. Because other states are potential threats, and because there is no higher authority to come to their rescue when they dial 911, states cannot depend on others for their own security. Each state tends to see itself as vulnerable and alone, and therefore it aims to provide for its own survival. In international politics, God helps those who help themselves. This emphasis on self-help does not preclude states from forming alliances. But alliances are only temporary marriages of convenience: today's alliance partner might be tomorrow's enemy, and today's enemy might be tomorrow's alliance partner. For example, the United States fought with China and the Soviet Union against Germany and Japan in World War II, but soon thereafter flip-flopped enemies and partners and allied with West Germany and Japan against China and the Soviet Union during the Cold War.

States operating in a self-help world almost always act according to their own self-interest and do not subordinate their interests to the interests of other states, or to the interests of the so-called international community. The reason is simple: it pays to be selfish in a self-help world: This is true in the short term as well as in the long term, because if a state loses in the short run, it might not be around for the long haul.

Apprehensive about the ultimate intentions of other states, and aware that they operate in a self-help system, states quickly understand that the best way to ensure their survival is to be the most powerful state in the system. The stronger a state is relative to its potential rivals, the less likely it is that any of those rivals will attack it and threaten its survival. Weaker states will be reluctant to pick fights with more powerful states because the weaker states are likely to suffer military defeat. Indeed, the bigger the gap in power between any two states, the less likely it is that the weaker will attack the stronger. Neither Canada nor Mexico, for example, would countenance attacking the United States, which is far more powerful than its neighbors. The ideal situation is to be the hegemon in the system. As Immanuel Kant said, "It is the desire of every state, or of its ruler, to arrive at a condition of perpetual peace by conquering the whole world, if that were possible."[4] Survival would then be almost guaranteed.

Consequently, states pay close attention to how power is distributed among them, and they make a special effort to maximize their share of world power. Specifically, they look for opportunities to alter the balance of power by acquiring additional increments of power at the expense of potential rivals. States employ a variety of means—economic, diplomatic, and military—to shift the balance of power in their favor, even if doing so makes other states suspicious or even hostile. Because one state's gain in power is another state's loss, great powers tend to have a zero-sum mentality when dealing with each other. The trick, of course, is to be the winner in this competition and to dominate the other states in the system. Thus, the claim that states maximize relative power is tantamount to arguing that states are disposed to think offensively toward other states, even though their ultimate motive is simply to survive. In short, great powers have aggressive intentions.

Even when a great power achieves a distinct military advantage over its rivals, it continues looking for chances to gain more power. The pursuit of power stops only when hegemony is achieved. The idea that a great power might feel secure without dominating the system, provided it has an "appropriate amount" of power, is not persuasive, for two reasons. First, it is difficult to assess how much relative power one state must have over its rivals before it is secure. Is twice as much power an appropriate threshold? Or is three times as much power the magic number? The root of the problem is that power calculations alone do not determine which side wins a war. Clever strategies, for example, sometimes allow less powerful states to defeat more powerful foes.

Second, determining how much power is enough becomes even more complicated when great powers contemplate how power will be distributed among them ten or twenty years down the road. The capabilities of individual states vary over time, sometimes markedly, and it is often difficult to predict the direction and scope of change in the balance of power. Remember, few in the West anticipated the collapse of the Soviet Union before it happened. In fact, during the first half of the Cold War, many in the West feared that the Soviet economy would eventually generate greater wealth than the American economy, which would cause a marked power shift against the United States and its allies. What the future holds for China and Russia and what the balance of power will look like in 2020 is difficult to foresee.

Given the difficulty of determining how much power is enough for today and tomorrow, great powers recognize that the best way to ensure their security is to achieve hegemony now, thus eliminating any possibility of a challenge by another great power. Only a misguided state would pass up an opportunity to be the hegemon in the system because it thought it already had sufficient power to survive. But even if a great power does not have the wherewithal to achieve hegemony (and that is usually the case), it will still act offensively to amass as much power as it can, because states are almost always better off with more rather than less power. In short, states do not become status quo powers until they completely dominate the system.

All states are influenced by this logic, which means that not only do they look for opportunities to take advantage of one another, they also work to ensure that other states do not take advantage of them. After all, rival states are driven by the same logic, and most states are likely to recognize their own motives at play in the actions of other states. In short, states ultimately pay attention to defense as well as offense. They think about conquest themselves, and they work to check aggressor states from gaining power at their expense. This inexorably leads to a world of constant security competition, where states are willing to lie, cheat, and use brute force if it helps them gain advantage over their rivals. Peace, if one defines that concept as a state of tranquility or mutual concord, is not likely to break out in this world.

The "security dilemma," which is one of the most well-known concepts in the international relations literature, reflects the basic logic of offensive realism. The essence of the dilemma is that the measures a state takes to increase its own security usually decrease the security of other states. Thus, it is difficult for a state to increase its own chances of survival without threatening the survival of other states. John Herz first introduced the security dilemma in a 1950 article in the journal *World Politics*.[5] After discussing the anarchic nature of international politics, he writes, "Striving to attain security from . . . attack, [states] are driven to acquire more and more power in order to escape the impact of the power of others. This, in turn, renders the others more insecure and compels them to prepare for the worst. Since none can ever feel entirely secure in such a world of competing units, power competition ensues, and the vicious circle of security and power accumulation is on."[6] The implication of Herz's analysis is clear: the best way for a state to survive in anarchy is to take advantage of other states and gain power at their expense. The best defense is a good offense. Since this message is widely understood, ceaseless security competition ensues. Unfortunately, little can be done to ameliorate the security dilemma as long as states operate in anarchy.

It should be apparent from this discussion that saying that states are power maximizers is tantamount to saying that they care about relative power, not absolute power. There is an important distinction here, because states concerned about relative power behave differently than do states interested in absolute power. States that maximize relative power are concerned primarily with the distribution of material capabilities. In particular, they try to gain as large a power advantage as possible over potential rivals, because power is the best means to survival in a dangerous world. Thus, states motivated by relative power concerns are likely to forgo large gains in their own power, if such gains give rival states even greater power, for smaller national gains that nevertheless provide them with a power advantage over their rivals. States that maximize absolute power, on the other hand, care only about the size of their own gains, not those of other states. They are not motivated by balance-of-power logic but instead are concerned with amassing power without regard to how much power other states control. They would jump at the opportunity for large gains, even if a rival gained more in the deal. Power, according to this logic, is not a means to an end (survival), but an end in itself.

CALCULATED AGGRESSION

There is obviously little room for status quo powers in a world where states are inclined to look for opportunities to gain more power. Nevertheless, great powers cannot always act on their offensive intentions, because behavior is influenced not only by what states want, but also by their capacity to realize these desires. Every state might want to be king of the hill, but not every state has the wherewithal to compete for that lofty position, much less achieve it. Much depends on how military might is distributed among the great powers. A great power that has a marked power advantage over its rivals is likely to behave more aggressively, because it has the capability as well as the incentive to do so.

By contrast, great powers facing powerful opponents will be less inclined to consider offensive action and more concerned with defending the existing balance of power from threats by their more powerful opponents. Let there be an opportunity for those weaker states to revise the balance in their own favor, however, and they will take advantage of it. Stalin put the point well at the end of World War II: "Everyone imposes his own system as far as his army can reach. It cannot be otherwise."[7] States might also have the capability to gain advantage over a rival power but nevertheless decide that the perceived costs of offense are too high and do not justify the expected benefits.

In short, great powers are not mindless aggressors so bent on gaining power that they charge headlong into losing wars or pursue Pyrrhic victories. On the contrary, before great powers take offensive actions, they think carefully about the balance of power and about how other states will react to their moves. They weigh the costs and risks of offense against the likely benefits. If the benefits do not outweigh the risks, they sit tight and wait for a more propitious moment. Nor do states start arms races that are unlikely to improve their overall position. . . . [S]tates sometimes limit defense spending either because spending more would bring no strategic advantage or because spending more would weaken the economy and undermine the state's power in the long run. To paraphrase Clint Eastwood, a state has to know its limitations to survive in the international system.

Nevertheless, great powers miscalculate from time to time because they invariably make important decisions on the basis of imperfect information. States hardly ever have complete information about any situation they confront. There are two dimensions to this problem. Potential adversaries have incentives to misrepresent their own strength or weakness, and to conceal their true aims. For example, a weaker state trying to deter a stronger state is likely to exaggerate its own power to discourage the potential aggressor from attacking. On the other hand, a state bent on aggression is likely to emphasize its peaceful goals while exaggerating its military weakness, so that the potential victim does not build up its own arms and thus leaves itself vulnerable to attack. Probably no national leader was better at practicing this kind of deception than Adolf Hitler.

But even if disinformation was not a problem, great powers are often unsure about how their own military forces, as well as the adversary's, will perform on the battlefield. For example, it is sometimes difficult to determine in advance how new weapons and untested combat units will perform in the face of enemy fire. Peacetime maneuvers and war games are helpful but imperfect indicators of what is likely to happen in actual combat. Fighting wars is a complicated business in which it is often difficult to predict outcomes. Remember that although the United States and its allies scored a stunning and remarkably easy victory against Iraq in early 1991, most experts at the time believed that Iraq's military would be a formidable foe and put up stubborn resistance before finally succumbing to American military might.

Great powers are also sometimes unsure about the resolve of opposing states as well as allies. For example, Germany believed that if it went to war against France and Russia in the summer of 1914, the United Kingdom would probably stay out of the fight. Saddam Hussein expected the United States to stand aside when he invaded Kuwait in August 1990. Both aggressors guessed wrong, but each had good reason to think that its initial judgment was correct. In the 1930s, Adolf Hitler believed that his great-power rivals would be easy to exploit and isolate because each had little interest in fighting Germany and instead was determined to get someone else to assume that burden. He guessed right. In short, great powers constantly find themselves confronting situations in which they have to make important decisions with incomplete information. Not surprisingly, they sometimes make faulty judgments and end up doing themselves serious harm.

Some defensive realists go so far as to suggest that the constraints of the international system are so powerful that offense rarely succeeds, and that aggressive great powers invariably end up being punished. As noted, they emphasize that 1) threatened states balance against aggressors and ultimately crush them, and 2) there is an offense-defense balance that is usually heavily tilted toward the defense, thus making conquest especially difficult. Great powers, therefore, should be content with the existing balance of power and not try to change it by force. After all, it makes little sense for a state to initiate a war that it is likely to lose; that would be self-defeating behavior. It is better to concentrate instead on preserving the balance of power. Moreover, because aggressors seldom succeed, states should understand that security is abundant, and thus there is no good strategic reason for wanting more power in the first place. In a world where conquest seldom pays, states should have relatively benign intentions toward each other. If they do not, these defensive realists argue, the reason is probably poisonous domestic politics, not smart calculations about how to guarantee one's security in an anarchic world.

There is no question that systemic factors constrain aggression, especially balancing by threatened states. But defensive realists exaggerate those restraining forces. Indeed, the historical record provides little support for their claim that offense rarely succeeds. One study estimates that there were 63 wars between 1815 and 1980, and the initiator won 39 times, which translates into about a 60 percent success rate. Turning to specific cases, Otto von Bismarck unified Germany by winning military victories against Denmark in 1864, Austria in 1866, and France in 1870, and the United States as we know it today was created in good part by conquest in the nineteenth century. Conquest certainly paid big dividends in these cases. Nazi Germany won wars against Poland in 1939 and France in 1940, but lost to the Soviet Union between 1941 and 1945. Conquest ultimately did not pay for the Third Reich, but if Hitler had restrained himself after the fall of France and had not invaded the Soviet Union, conquest probably would have paid handsomely for the Nazis. In short, the historical record shows that offense sometimes succeeds and sometimes does not. The trick for a sophisticated power maximizer is to figure out when to raise and when to fold.

HEGEMONY'S LIMITS

Great powers, as I have emphasized, strive to gain power over their rivals and hopefully become hegemons. Once a state achieves that exalted position, it becomes a status quo power. More needs to be said, however, about the meaning of hegemony.

A hegemon is a state that is so powerful that it dominates all the other states in the system. No other state has the military wherewithal to put up a serious fight against it. In essence, a hegemon is the only great power in the system. A state that is substantially more powerful than the other great powers in the system is not a hegemon, because it faces, by definition, other great powers. The United Kingdom in the mid-nineteenth century, for example, is sometimes called a hegemon. But it was not a hegemon, because there were four other great powers in Europe at the time—Austria, France, Prussia, and Russia—and the United Kingdom did not dominate them in any meaningful way. In fact, during that period, the United Kingdom considered France to be a serious threat to the balance of power. Europe in the nineteenth century was multipolar, not unipolar.

Hegemony means domination of the system, which is usually interpreted to mean the entire world. It is possible, however, to apply the concept of a system more narrowly and use it to describe particular regions, such as Europe, Northeast Asia, and the Western Hemisphere. Thus, one can distinguish between *global hegemons,* which dominate the world, and *regional hegemons,* which dominate distinct geographical areas. The United States has been a regional hegemon in the Western Hemisphere for at least the past one hundred years. No other state in the Americas has sufficient military might to challenge it, which is why the United States is widely recognized as the only great power in its region.

My argument is that except for the unlikely event wherein one state achieves clear-cut nuclear superiority, it is virtually impossible for any state to achieve global hegemony. The principal impediment to world domination is the difficulty of projecting power across the world's oceans onto the territory of a rival great power. The United States, for example, is the most powerful state on the planet today. But it does not dominate Europe and Northeast Asia the way it does the Western Hemisphere, and it has no intention of trying to conquer and control those distant regions, mainly because of the stopping power of water. Indeed, there is reason to think that the American military commitment to Europe and Northeast Asia might wither away over the next decade. In short, there has never been a global hegemon, and there is not likely to be one anytime soon.

The best outcome a great power can hope for is to be a regional hegemon and possibly control another region that is nearby and accessible over land. The United States is the only regional hegemon in modern history, although other states have fought major wars in pursuit of regional hegemony: imperial Japan in Northeast Asia, and Napoleonic France, Wilhelmine Germany, and Nazi Germany in Europe. But none succeeded. The Soviet Union, which is located in Europe and Northeast Asia, threatened to dominate both of those regions during the Cold War. The Soviet Union might also have attempted to conquer the oil-rich Persian Gulf region, with which it shared a border. But even if Moscow had been able to dominate Europe, Northeast Asia, and the Persian Gulf, which it never came close to doing, it still would have been unable to conquer the Western Hemisphere and become a true global hegemon.

States that achieve regional hegemony seek to prevent great powers in other regions from duplicating their feat. Regional hegemons, in other words, do not want peers. Thus the United States, for example, played a key role in preventing imperial Japan, Wilhelmine Germany, Nazi Germany, and the Soviet Union from gaining regional supremacy. Regional hegemons attempt to check aspiring hegemons in other regions because they fear that a rival great power that dominates its own region will be an especially powerful foe that is essentially free to cause trouble in the fearful great power's backyard. Regional hegemons prefer that there be at least two great powers located together in other regions, because their proximity will force them to concentrate their attention on each other rather than on the distant hegemon.

Furthermore, if a potential hegemon emerges among them, the other great powers in that region might be able to contain it by themselves, allowing the distant hegemon to remain safely on the sidelines. Of course, if the local great powers were unable to do the job, the distant hegemon would take the appropriate measures to deal with the threatening state. The United States, as noted, has assumed that burden on four separate occasions in the twentieth century, which is why it is commonly referred to as an "offshore balancer."

In sum, the ideal situation for any great power is to be the only regional hegemon in the world. That state would be a status quo power, and it would go to considerable lengths to preserve the existing distribution of power. The United States is in that enviable position today; it dominates the Western Hemisphere and there is no hegemon in any other area of the world. But if a regional hegemon is confronted with a peer competitor, it would no longer be a status quo power. Indeed, it would go to considerable lengths to weaken and maybe even destroy its distant rival. Of course, both regional hegemons would be motivated by that logic, which would make for a fierce security competition between them.

. . .

CONCLUSION

In sum, my argument is that the structure of the international system, not the particular characteristics of individual great powers, causes them to think and act offensively and to seek hegemony. I do not adopt Morgenthau's claim that states invariably behave aggressively because they have a will to power hardwired into them. Instead, I assume that the principal motive behind great-power behavior is survival. In anarchy, however, the desire to survive encourages states to behave aggressively. Nor does my theory classify states as more or less aggressive on the basis of their economic or political systems. Offensive realism makes only a handful of assumptions about great powers, and these assumptions apply equally to all great powers. Except for differences in how much power each state controls, the theory treats all states alike.

I have now laid out the logic explaining why states seek to gain as much power as possible over their rivals. . . .

Notes

[1] Milton Friedman, *Essays in Positive Economics* (Chicago: University of Chicago Press, 1953), p. 14. Also see Kenneth N. Waltz, *Theory of International Politics* (Reading, MA: Addison-Wesley, 1979), pp. 5–6, 91, 119.

[2] Inis L. Claude, Jr., *Swords into Plowshares: The Problems and Progress of International Organization,* 4th ed. (New York: Random House, 1971), p. 14.

[3] Quoted in Jon Jacobson, *When the Soviet Union Entered World Politics* (Berkeley: University of California Press, 1994), p. 271.

[4]Quoted in Martin Wight, *Power Politics* (London: Royal Institute of International Affairs, 1946), p. 40.

[5]John H. Herz, "Idealist Internationalism and the Security Dilemma," *World Politics* 2, No. 2 (January 1950), pp. 157–80. Although Dickinson did not use the term "security dilemma," its logic is clearly articulated in *European Anarchy*, pp. 20, 88.

[6]Herz, "Idealist Internationalism," p. 157.

[7]Quoted in Marc Trachtenberg, *A Constructed Peace: The Making of the European Settlement, 1945–1963* (Princeton, NJ: Princeton University Press, 1999), p. 36.

STUDY AND DISCUSSION QUESTIONS

1. According to Mearsheimer, how do great powers behave? How should they behave?
2. How is hegemony defined? Why—or why not—is the United States a global hegemon?
3. What are the prospects for a stable international order?

5

Global Cities and Survival Circuits

Saskia Sassen

In this selection, Saskia Sassen offers a powerful feminist critique of globalization, challenging what she calls the "dominant narrative" that focuses on high-technology and high-flyers. Sassen examines globalization from the perspective of poor women who are compelled to become the agents of globalization as they cross borders, moving from poorer to richer countries, to seek employment as domestics, nannies, sex workers, secretaries, and janitors.

Sassen contends that "place" matters in the politics of globalization as "global cities" such as New York, London, Berlin, and Tokyo operate increasingly as key nodes in a global network, and become increasingly reliant on migrant and immigrant women to provide essential services. Sassen concludes that the incorporation of low-paid women service workers into strategic economic sectors describes an important—and far-reaching—alternative narrative about globalization.

When today's media, policy, and economic analysts define globalization, they emphasize hypermobility, international communication, and the neutralization of distance and place. This account of globalization is by far the dominant one. Central to it are the global information economy, instant communication, and electronic markets—all realms within which place no longer makes a difference, and where the only type of worker who matters is the highly educated professional. Globalization thus conceived privileges global transmission over the material infrastructure that makes it possible; information over the workers who produce it, whether these be specialists or secretaries; and the new transnational corporate culture over the other jobs upon which it rests, including many of those held by immigrants. In brief, the dominant narrative of globalization concerns itself with the upper circuits of global capital, not the lower ones, and with the hypermobility of capital rather than with capital that is bound to place.

The migration of maids, nannies, nurses, sex workers, and contract brides has little to do with globalization by these lights. Migrant women are just individuals making a go of it, after all, and the migration of workers from poor countries to wealthier ones long predates the current phase of economic globalization. And yet it seems reasonable to assume that there are significant links between globalization and women's migration, whether voluntary or forced, for jobs that used to be part of the First World woman's domestic role. Might the dynamics of globalization alter the course or even reinscribe the history of the migration and exploitation of Third World laborers? There are two distinct issues here. One is whether globalization has enabled formerly national or regional processes to go global. The other is whether globalization has produced a new kind of migration, with new conditions and dynamics of its own.

GLOBAL CITIES AND SURVIVAL CIRCUITS

When today's women migrate from south to north for work as nannies, domestics, or sex workers, they participate in two sets of dynamic configurations. One of these is the global city. The other consists of survival circuits that have emerged in response to the deepening misery of the global south.

Global cities concentrate some of the global economy's key functions and resources. There, activities implicated in the management and coordination of the global economy have expanded, producing a sharp growth in the demand for highly paid professionals. Both this sector's firms and the lifestyles of its professional workers in turn generate a demand for low-paid service workers. In this way, global cities have become places where large numbers of low-paid women and immigrants get incorporated into strategic economic sectors. Some are incorporated directly as low-wage clerical and service workers, such as janitors and repairmen. For others, the process is less direct, operating instead through the consumption practices of high-income professionals, who employ maids and nannies and who patronize expensive restaurants and shops staffed by low-wage workers. Traditionally, employment in growth sectors has been a source of workers' empowerment; this new pattern undermines that linkage, producing a class of workers who are isolated, dispersed, and effectively invisible.

Meanwhile, as Third World economies on the periphery of the global system struggle against debt and poverty, they increasingly build survival circuits on the backs of women—whether these be trafficked low-wage workers and prostitutes or migrant workers sending remittances back home. Through their work and remittances, these women contribute to the revenue of deeply indebted countries. "Entrepreneurs" who have seen other opportunities vanish as global firms entered their countries see profit-making potential in the trafficking of women; so, too, do longtime criminals who have seized the opportunity to operate their illegal trade globally. These survival circuits are often complex; multiple locations and sets of actors constitute increasingly far-reaching chains of traders and "workers."

Through their work in both global cities and survival circuits, women, so often discounted as valueless economic actors, are crucial to building new economies and expanding existing ones. Globalization serves a double purpose here, helping to forge links between sending and receiving countries, and enabling local and regional practices to assume a global scale. On the one hand, the dynamics that converge in the global city produce a strong demand for low-wage workers, while the dynamics that mobilize women into survival circuits produce an expanding supply of migrants who can be pushed—or sold—into such jobs. On the other hand, the very technological infrastructure and transnationalism that characterize global industries also enable other types of actors to expand onto the global stage, whether these be money launderers or people traffickers. It seems, then, that in order to understand the extraction from the Third World of services that used to define women's domestic role in the First, we must depart from the mainstream view of globalization.

TOWARD AN ALTERNATIVE NARRATIVE ABOUT GLOBALIZATION

The spatial dispersal of economic activities and the neutralization of place constitute half of the globalization story. The other half involves the territorial centralization of top-level management, control operations, and the most advanced specialized services. Markets, whether national or global, and companies, many of which have gone global, require central locations where their most complex tasks are accomplished. Furthermore, the information industry rests on a vast physical infrastructure, which includes strategic nodes where facilities are densely concentrated. Even the most advanced sectors of the information industry employ many different types of workplaces and workers.

If we expand our analysis of globalization to include this production process, we can see that secretaries belong to the global economy, as do the people who clean professionals' offices and homes. An economic configuration very different from the one suggested by the concept of an "information economy" emerges— and it is one that includes material conditions, production sites, and activities bounded by place.

The mainstream account of globalization tends to take for granted the existence of a global economic system, viewing it as a function of the power of transnational corporations and communications. But if the new information technologies and transnational corporations can be operated, coordinated, and controlled globally, it's because that capacity has been produced. By focusing on its production, we shift our emphasis to the *practices* that constitute economic globalization: the work of producing and reproducing the organization and management of a global production system and a global marketplace for finance.

This focus on practices draws the categories of place and work process into the analysis of economic globalization. In so broadening our analysis, we do not deny the importance of hypermobility and power. Rather, we acknowledge that many of the resources necessary for global economic activities are not hypermobile and are, on the contrary, deeply embedded in place, including such sites as global cities and export processing zones. Global processes are structured by local constraints, including the work culture, political culture, and composition of the workforce within a particular nation state.

If we recapture the geography behind globalization, we might also recapture its workers, communities, and work cultures (not just the corporate ones). By focusing on the global city, for instance, we can study how global processes become localized in specific arrangements, from the high-income gentrified urban neighborhoods of the transnational professional class to the work lives of the foreign nannies and maids in those same neighborhoods.

WOMEN IN THE GLOBAL CITY

Globalization has greatly increased the demand in global cities for low-wage workers to fill jobs that offer few advancement possibilities. The same cities have seen an explosion of wealth and power, as high-income jobs and high-priced urban space have noticeably expanded. How, then, can workers be hired at low wages and with few benefits even when there is high demand and the jobs belong to high-growth sectors? The answer, it seems, has involved tapping into a growing new labor supply—women and immigrants—and in so doing, breaking the historical nexus that would have empowered workers under these conditions. The fact that these workers tend to be women and immigrants also lends cultural legitimacy to their nonempowerment. In global cities, then, a majority of today's resident workers are women, and many of these are women of color, both native and immigrant.

At the same time, global cities have seen a gathering trend toward the informalization of an expanding range of activities, as low-profit employers attempt to escape the costs and constraints of the formal economy's regulatory apparatus. They do so by locating commercial or manufacturing operations in areas zoned exclusively for residential use, for example, or in buildings that violate fire and health standards; they also do so by assigning individual workers industrial homework. This allows them to remain in these cities. At its best, informalization reintroduces the community and the household as important economic spaces in global cities. It is in many ways a low-cost (and often feminized) equivalent to deregulation at the top of the system. As with deregulation (for example, financial deregulation), informalization introduces flexibility, reduces the "burdens" of regulation, and lowers costs, in this case of labor. In the cities of the global north—including New York, London, Paris, and Berlin—informalization serves to downgrade a variety of activities for which there is often a growing local demand. Immigrant women, in the end, bear some of the costs.

As the demand for high-level professional workers has skyrocketed, more and more women have found work in corporate professional jobs. These jobs place heavy demands on women's time, requiring long work hours and intense engagement. Single professionals and two-career households therefore tend to prefer urban to suburban residence. The result is an expansion of high-income residential areas in global cities and a return of family life to urban centers. Urban professionals want it all, including dogs and children, whether or not they have the time to care for them. The usual modes of handling household tasks often prove inadequate. We can call this type of household a "professional household without a 'wife,'" regardless of whether its adult couple consists of a man and a woman, two men, or two women. A growing share of its domestic tasks are relocated to the market: they are bought directly as goods and services or indirectly through hired labor. As a consequence, we see the return of the so-called serving classes in all of the world's global cities, and these classes are largely made up of immigrant and migrant women.

This dynamic produces a sort of double movement: a shift to the labor market of functions that used to be part of household work, but also a shift of what used to be labor market functions in standardized workplaces to the household and, in the case of informalization, to the immigrant community. This reconfiguration of economic spaces has had different impacts on women and men, on male-typed and female-typed work cultures, and on male- and female-centered forms of power and empowerment.

For women, such transformations contain the potential, however limited, for autonomy and empowerment. Might informalization, for example, reconfigure certain economic relationships between men and women? With informalization, the neighborhood and the household reemerge as sites for economic activity, creating "opportunities" for low-income women and thereby reordering some of the hierarchies in which women find themselves. This becomes particularly clear in the case of immigrant women, who often come from countries with traditionally male-centered cultures.

A substantial number of studies now show that regular wage work and improved access to other public realms has an impact on gender relations in the lives of immigrant women. Women gain greater personal autonomy and independence, while men lose ground. More control over budgeting and other domestic decisions devolves to women, and they have greater leverage in requesting help from men in domestic chores. Access to public services and other public resources also allows women to incorporate themselves into the mainstream society; in fact, women often mediate this process for their households. Some women likely benefit more than others from these circumstances, and with more research we could establish the impact of class, education, and income. But even aside from relative empowerment in the household, paid work holds out another significant possibility for women: their greater participation in the public sphere and their emergence as public actors.

Immigrant women tend to be active in two arenas: institutions for public and private assistance, and the immigrant or ethnic community. The more women are involved with the migration process, the more likely it is that migrants will settle in their new residences and participate in their communities. And when immigrant women assume active public and social roles, they further reinforce their status in the household and the settlement process. Positioned differently from men in relation to the economy and state, women tend to be more involved in community building and community activism. They are the ones who will likely handle their families' legal vulnerabilities as they seek public and social services. These trends suggest that women may emerge as more forceful and visible actors in the labor market as well.

And so two distinct dynamics converge in the lives of immigrant women in global cities. On the one hand, these women make up an invisible and disempowered class of workers in the service of the global economy's strategic sectors. Their invisibility keeps immigrant women from emerging as the strong proletariat that followed earlier forms of economic organization, when workers' positions in leading sectors had the effect of empowering them. On the other hand, the access to wages and salaries, however low; the growing feminization of the job supply; and the growing feminization of business opportunities thanks to informalization, all alter the gender hierarchies in which these women find themselves.

NEW EMPLOYMENT REGIMES IN CITIES

Most analysts of postindustrial society and advanced economies report a massive growth in the need for highly educated workers but little demand for the type of labor that a majority of immigrants, perhaps especially immigrant women, have tended to supply over the last two or three decades. But detailed empirical studies of major cities in highly developed countries contradict this conventional view of the postindustrial economy. Instead, they show an ongoing demand for immigrant workers and a significant supply of old and new low-wage jobs that require little education.

Three processes of change in economic and spatial organization help explain the ongoing, indeed growing, demand for immigrant workers, especially immigrant women. One is the consolidation of advanced services and corporate head-quarters in the urban economic core, especially in global cities. While the corporate headquarters-and-services complex may not account for the majority of jobs in these cities, it establishes a new regime of economic activity, which in turn produces the spatial and social transformations evident in major cities. Another relevant process is the downgrading of the manufacturing sector, as some manufacturing industries become incorporated into the postindustrial economy. Downgrading is a response to competition from cheap imports, and to the modest profit potential of manufacturing compared to telecommunications, finance, and other corporate services. The third process is informalization, a notable example of which is the rise of the sweatshop. Firms often take recourse to informalized arrangements when they have an effective local demand for their goods and services but they cannot compete with cheap imports, or cannot compete for space and other business needs with the new high-profit firms of the advanced corporate service economy.

In brief, that major cities have seen changes in their job supplies can be chalked up both to the emergence of new sectors and to the reorganization of work in sectors new and old. The shift from a manufacturing to a service-dominated economy, particularly evident in cities, destabilizes older relationships between jobs and economic sectors. Today, much more than twenty years ago, we see an expansion of low-wage jobs associated with growing sectors rather than with declining ones. At the same time, a vast array of activities that once took place under standardized work arrangements have become increasingly informalized, as some manufacturing relocates from unionized factories to sweatshops and private homes. If we distinguish the characteristics of jobs from those of the sectors in which they are located, we can see that highly dynamic, technologically advanced growth sectors may well contain low-wage, dead-end jobs. Similarly, backward sectors like downgraded manufacturing can reflect the major growth trends in a highly developed economy.

It seems, then, that we need to rethink two assumptions: that the post-industrial economy primarily requires highly educated workers, and that informalization and downgrading are just Third World imports or anachronistic holdovers. Service-dominated urban economies do indeed create low-wage jobs with minimal education requirements, few advancement opportunities, and low pay for demanding work. For workers raised in an ideological context that emphasizes success, wealth, and career, these are not attractive positions; hence the growing demand for immigrant workers. But given the provenance of the jobs these immigrant workers take, we must resist assuming that they are located in the backward sectors of the economy.

THE OTHER WORKERS IN THE
ADVANCED CORPORATE ECONOMY

Low-wage workers accomplish a sizable portion of the day-to-day work in global cities' leading sectors. After all, advanced professionals require clerical, cleaning, and repair workers for their state-of-the-art offices, and they require truckers to bring them their software and their toilet paper. In my research on New York and other cities, I have found that between 30 and 50 percent of workers in the leading sectors are actually low-wage workers.

The similarly state-of-the-art lifestyles of professionals in these sectors have created a whole new demand for household workers, particularly maids and nannies, as well as for service workers to cater to those professionals' high-income consumption habits. Expensive restaurants, luxury housing, luxury hotels, gourmet shops, boutiques, French hand laundries, and special cleaning services, for example, are more labor-intensive than their lower-priced equivalents. To an extent not seen in a very long time, we are witnessing the reemergence of a "serving class" in contemporary high-income households and neighborhoods. The image of the immigrant woman serving the white middle-class professional woman has replaced that of the black female servant working for the white master in centuries past. The result is a sharp tendency toward social polarization in today's global cities.

We are beginning to see how the global labor markets at the top and at the bottom of the economic system are formed. The bottom is mostly staffed through the efforts of individual workers, though an expanding network of organizations has begun to get involved. Kelly Services, a Fortune 500 global staffing company that operates in twenty-five countries, recently added a home-care division that is geared toward people who need assistance with daily living but that also offers services that in the past would have been taken care of by the mother or wife figure in a household. A growing range of smaller global staffing organizations offer day care, including dropping off and picking up school-children, as well as completion of in-house tasks from child care to cleaning and cooking. One international agency for nannies and au pairs (EF Au Pair Corporate Program) advertises directly to corporations, urging them to include the service in their offers to potential hires.

Meanwhile, at the top of the system, several global Fortune 500 staffing companies help firms fill high-level professional and technical jobs. In 2001, the largest of these was the Swiss multinational Adecco, with offices in fifty-eight countries; in 2000 it provided firms worldwide with 3 million workers. Manpower, with offices in fifty-nine different countries, provided 2 million workers. Kelly Services provided 750,000 employees in 2000.

The top and the bottom of the occupational distribution are becoming internationalized and so are their labor suppliers. Although midlevel occupations are increasingly staffed through temporary employment agencies, these companies have not internationalized their efforts. Occupations at the top and at the bottom are, in very different but parallel ways, sensitive. Firms need reliable and hopefully talented professionals, and they need them specialized but standardized so that they can use them globally. Professionals seek the same qualities in the workers they employ in their homes. The fact that staffing organizations have moved into providing domestic services signals both that a global labor market has emerged in this area and that there is an effort afoot to standardize the services maids, nannies, and home-care nurses deliver.

· · · ·

CONCLUSION

Globalization is not only about the hypermobility of capital and the ascendance of information economies. It is also about specific types of places and work processes. In order to understand how economic globalization relates to the extraction of services from the Third World to fulfill what was once the First World woman's domestic role, we must look at globalization in a way that emphasizes some of these concrete conditions.

The growing immiserization of governments and economies in the global south is one such condition, insofar as it enables and even promotes the migration and trafficking of women as a strategy for survival. The same infrastructure designed to facilitate cross-border flows of capital, information, and trade also makes possible a range of unintended cross-border flows, as growing numbers of traffickers, smugglers, and even governments now make money off the backs of women. Through their work and remittances, women infuse cash into the economies of deeply indebted countries, and into the pockets of "entrepreneurs" who have seen other opportunities vanish. These survival circuits are often complex, involving multiple locations and sets of actors, which altogether constitute increasingly global chains of traders and "workers."

But globalization has also produced new labor demand dynamics that center on the global cities of the north. From these places, global economic processes are managed and coordinated by increasing numbers of highly paid professionals. Both the firms and the lifestyles of these professionals are maintained by low-paid service workers, who are in growing demand. Large numbers of low-wage women and immigrants thus find themselves incorporated into strategic economic sectors in global cities. This incorporation happens directly, as in the case of low-wage clerical and blue collar workers, such as janitors and repair workers. And it happens indirectly, through the consumption practices of high-income professionals, which generate a demand for maids and nannies as well as low-wage workers in expensive restaurants and shops. Low-wage workers are then incorporated into the leading sectors, but under conditions that render them invisible.

Both in global cities and in survival circuits, women emerge as crucial economic actors. It is partly through them that key components of new economies have been built. Globalization allows links to be forged between countries that send migrants and countries that receive them; it also enables local and regional practices to go global. The dynamics that come together in the global city produce a strong demand for migrant workers, while the dynamics that mobilize women into survival circuits produce an expanding supply of workers who can be pushed or sold into those types of jobs. The technical infrastructure and transnationalism that underlie the key globalized industries also allow other types of activities, including money-laundering and trafficking, to assume a global scale.

STUDY AND DISCUSSION QUESTIONS

1. How do women who migrate from poorer to wealthier countries to find low-paid service jobs function as "survival circuits" for Third World economies?
2. Are women empowered or further marginalized by their experiences in Sassen's global cities?
3. Does Sassen's account change your understanding of globalization in a significant way? If so, how?

CHAPTER 2

From Autonomy to Multi-level Governance

As globalization intensifies the scale, extent, variety, speed and significance of cross-border social, economic, political, cultural, and military interactions, the sovereignty of states has been fundamentally recast—in part by voluntary participation in international organizations that pool authority and policy-making and in part by the uncontrollable cross-border incursions associated with globalization. In the end, globalization has transformed the exercise of state power as well as our understanding of it. Sovereignty is neither the exclusive property of the state, nor an effective tool for achieving desirable outcomes through the autonomous exercise of state power.

Left to their own devises, states cannot protect their citizens from either want or attack. They must operate in the radically changed context of pooled and overlapping sovereignty where no state or international organization, even the most powerful, can control outcomes alone. Thus multi-level governance (MLG) is the characteristic framework for politics today. Even more than the intensification of world trade or investment, this emerging framework of overlapping, incomplete, and competing sovereignties captures the defining feature of the contemporary global age. In the world today, we can observe a growing tension between sovereignty defined by bounded territory and authority and the dynamics of globalization that make all borders porous and every attempt to exert control over a territory seem anachronistic—or even counterproductive.

The readings in Chapter 2 deepen our understanding of the reconfiguration of sovereignty and the compromises and negotiations involved in the exercise of power, once states are bound up in complex institutionalized interdependencies on many fronts.

STUDY AND DISCUSSION QUESTIONS

1. Is multi-level governance a contemporary elaboration of federalism—or a fundamental transformation of the decision-making process driven by globalization?
2. Does MLG mean that state sovereignty has become an historical artifact?
3. Is MLG a stabilizing or a destabilizing force?

6

Sovereignty and Its Discontents

Stephen D. Krasner

For centuries, our understanding of state power was framed by a taken-for-granted assumption of sovereignty, *understood as effective governmental or state control over policy-making processes. A country's domestic politics was nestled within an interstate system that has been called the* Westphalian model *(referring to the Peace of Westphalia of 1648 which ended the German phase of the Thirty Years War). The model assumes a world of autonomous sovereign states, operating by national interest, with diplomatic relations and recourse to force, but with minimal cooperation. Above all, explains Stephen Krasner in this selection, the Westphalian model asserts two principles—territoriality and autonomy, defined by the exclusion of external actors from exercising authority or effective control within the borders of a given state. Krasner traces the diverse ways the term* sovereignty *has been applied, and the confusion that has arisen from the conflicting application of definitions, practices, and institutional arrangements. He concludes that the resulting muddle of mutually inconsistent and weakly institutionalized norms has turned sovereignty into little more than organized hypocrisy.*

Some analysts have argued that sovereignty is being eroded by one aspect of the contemporary international system, globalization, and others that it is being sustained, even in states whose governments have only the most limited resources, by another aspect of the system, the mutual recognition and shared expectations generated by international society. Some have pointed out that the scope of state authority has increased over time, and others that the ability of the state to exercise effective control is eroding. Some have suggested that new norms, such as universal human rights, represent a fundamental break with the past, while others see these values as merely a manifestation of the preferences of the powerful. Some students of international politics take sovereignty as an analytic assumption, others as a description of the practice of actors, and still others as a generative grammar.

This muddle in part reflects the fact that the term "sovereignty" has been used in different ways, and in part it reveals the failure to recognize that the norms and rules of any international institutional system, including the sovereign state system, will have limited influence and always be subject to challenge because of logical contradictions (nonintervention versus promoting democracy, for instance), the absence of any institutional arrangement for authoritatively resolving conflicts (the definition of an international system), power asymmetries among principal actors, notably states, and the differing incentives confronting individual rulers. In the international environment actions will not tightly conform with any given set of norms regardless of which set is chosen. The justification for challenging specific norms may change over time but the challenge will be persistent.

The term sovereignty has been used in four different ways—international legal sovereignty, Westphalian sovereignty, domestic sovereignty, and interdependence sovereignty. International legal sovereignty refers to the practices associated with mutual recognition, usually between territorial entities that have formal juridical independence. Westphalian sovereignty refers to political organization based on the exclusion of external actors from authority structures within a given territory. Domestic sovereignty refers to the formal organization of political authority within the state and the ability of public authorities to exercise effective control within the borders of their own polity. Finally, interdependence sovereignty refers to the ability of public authorities to regulate the flow of information, ideas, goods, people, pollutants, or capital across the borders of their state.

International legal sovereignty and Westphalian sovereignty involve issues of authority and legitimacy, but not control. They both have distinct rules or logics of appropriateness. The rule for international legal sovereignty is that recognition is extended to territorial entities that have formal juridical independence. The rule for Westphalian sovereignty is the exclusion of external actors, whether de facto or de jure, from the territory of a state. Domestic sovereignty involves both authority and control, both the specification of legitimate authority within a polity and the extent to which that authority can be effectively exercised. Inter-dependence sovereignty is exclusively concerned with control and not authority, with the capacity of a state to regulate movements across its borders.

The various kinds of sovereignty do not necessarily covary. A state can have one but not the other. The exercise of one kind of sovereignty—for instance, international legal sovereignty—can undermine another kind of sovereignty, such as Westphalian sovereignty, if the rulers of a state enter into an agreement that recognizes external authority structures, as has been the case for the members of the European Union. A state such as Taiwan can have Westphalian sovereignty, but not international legal sovereignty. A state can have international legal sover-eignty, be recognized by other states, but have only the most limited domestic sovereignty either in the sense of an established structure of authority or the abil-ity of its rulers to exercise control over what is going on within their own terri-tory. In the 1990s some failed states in Africa, such as Somalia, served as unfortunate examples. A state can have international legal, Westphalian, and established domestic authority structures and still have very limited ability to reg-ulate cross-border flows and their consequent domestic impacts, a situation that many contemporary observers conceive of as a result of globalization.

This study focuses primarily on Westphalian sovereignty and, to a lesser extent, on international legal sovereignty. Domestic authority and control and the regulation of transborder movements are examined only insofar as they impinge on questions associated with recognition and the exclusion of external actors from domestic authority structures.

This study does not attempt to explain the evolution or development of the international system over the millennia. I offer no explanation for the displace-ment of other institutional forms, such as the Holy Roman Empire, the Chinese tributary system, or the Hanseatic League by an international system in which states are the most prevalent organizational unit. Rather, this study is an effort to understand what sovereign statehood has meant in actual practice with regard to international legal and Westphalian sovereignty.

All political and social environments are characterized by two logics of actions, what James March and Johan Olsen have called logics of expected conse-quences and logics of appropriateness. Logics of consequences see political action and outcomes, including institutions, as the product of rational calculating behav-ior designed to maximize a given set of unexplained preferences. Classical game theory and neoclassical economics are well-known examples. Logics of appropri-ateness understand political action as a product of rules, roles, and identities that stipulate appropriate behavior in given situations. The question is not how can I maximize my self-interest but rather, given who or what I am, how should I act in this particular circumstance. Various sociological approaches offer examples.

These two logics are not mutually incompatible but their importance varies across environments. If a logic of appropriateness is unambiguous and the consequences of alternative courses of action unclear, the behavior of actors (primarily rulers for this study) is likely to be determined by their roles. If actors find themselves in a situation in which they have multiple and contradictory roles and rules, or no rules at all, but the results of different courses of action are obvious, a logic of consequences will prevail. In a well-established domestic polity a logic of appropriateness will weigh heavily, although within the confines imposed by specific roles (president, general, senator, voter) actors will also calculate the course of action that will maximize their interests. Even in very well settled situations, such as Swedish local governments, which Nils Brunsson uses to motivate his study of what he has ingeniously termed the organization of hypocrisy, actors never fully conform with the logic of appropriateness associated with their specific roles; they also engage in purely instrumental behavior generated by a logic of expected consequences.

The basic contention of this study is that the international system is an environment in which the logics of consequences dominate the logics of appropriateness. Actors embody multiple roles, such as head of state, diplomatic representative, government leader, party organizer, ethnic representative, revolutionary avatar, or religious prophet, that imply conflicting rules for action. International rules can be contradictory—nonintervention as opposed to the protection of human rights, for example—and there is no authority structure to adjudicate such controversies. In most cases domestic roles will be more compelling than international ones, because domestic rather than international logics of appropriateness are most likely to dominate the self-conceptualization of any political leader. Moreover, the international system is characterized by power asymmetries. Stronger actors can, in some cases, conquer weaker ones, eliminating the existence of a particular state, although not necessarily challenging the general principles associated with Westphalian or international legal sovereignty. Conquest simply changes borders. But rulers might also choose to reconfigure domestic authority structures in other states, accepting their juridical independence but compromising their de facto autonomy, a policy that does violate Westphalian sovereignty. Stronger states can pick and choose among different rules selecting the one that best suits their instrumental objectives, as the European powers did during the era of colonialism when they "resuscitated pre-Westphalian forms of divided sovereignty" such as protectorates and subordinate states.[1] In the international environment roles and rules are not irrelevant. Rulers do have to give reasons for their actions, but their audiences are usually domestic. Norms in the international system will be less constraining than would be the case in other political settings because of conflicting logics of appropriateness, the absence of mechanisms for deciding among competing rules, and power asymmetries among states.

The prevailing approaches to international politics in the United States, neo-realism and neoliberalism, properly deploy a logic of consequences, although their ontology, states conceived of as unified rational autonomous actors, is not suitable for understanding some elements of sovereignty, especially the extent to which the domestic autonomy of states has been compromised. Various efforts to employ a logic of appropriateness, reflected most prominently in the English school and more recent constructivist treatments, understate the importance of power and interest and overemphasize the impact of international, as opposed to domestic, roles and rules.

Both international legal sovereignty and Westphalian sovereignty can be defined by clear rules or logics of appropriateness: recognize juridically indepen-dent territorial entities; exclude external authority structures from the territory of the state. Yet both of these logics have been violated, more frequently for West-phalian sovereignty than international legal sovereignty, because logics of conse-quences can be so compelling in the international environment. Rulers have found that it is in their interest to break the rules. Violations of international legal sover-eignty have taken place through mutual agreement, since recognition depends on the voluntary acceptance of other states. Violations of Westphalian sovereignty have occurred through both voluntary agreements and the use of coercion.

The starting point for this study, the ontological givens, are rulers, specific policy makers, usually but not always the executive head of state. Rulers, not states—and not the international system—make choices about policies, rules, and institu-tions. Whether international legal sovereignty and Westphalian sovereignty are honored depends on the decisions of rulers. There is no hierarchical structure to prevent rulers from violating the logics of appropriateness associated with mutual recognition or the exclusion of external authority. Rulers can recognize another state or not; they can recognize entities that lack juridical independence or territory. They can intervene in the internal affairs of other states or voluntar-ily compromise the autonomy of their own polity.

Any actor-oriented approach must start with simple assumptions about the underlying preferences of actors. These preferences must be applicable to all actors across space and time. If the preferences, the underlying interests of actors, are problematic, then the preferences become something to be explained rather than something that can do the explaining. The assumption of this study is that rulers want to stay in power and, being in power, they want to promote the secu-rity, prosperity, and values of their constituents. The ways in which they accom-plish these objectives will vary from one state to another. Some rulers need to cultivate their military; others seek a majority of votes. Some will enhance their position by embracing universal human rights; others succeed by endorsing exclusionary nationalism. Some are highly dependent on external actors for their financial support; others rely almost exclusively on domestic sources.

International legal sovereignty has been almost universally desired by rulers, including rulers who have lacked juridical independence and even a territory. Recognition provides benefits and does not impose costs. Recognition facilitates treaty making, establishes diplomatic immunity, and offers a shield against legal actions taken in other states. International legal sovereignty can indicate to domestic actors that a particular ruler is more likely to remain in power if only because that ruler can more easily secure external resources.

The basic rule of international legal sovereignty, that mutual recognition be extended among formally independent territorial entities, has never been universally honored. The fact that rulers want recognition does not mean that they will always get it. Nonrecognition has been used as an instrument of policy. Rulers with territory and juridical and de facto autonomy, such as the Chinese Communist regime from 1949 to the 1970s, have not been recognized. At the same time rulers have recognized entities lacking in formal juridical autonomy—Byelorussia and the Ukraine were members of the United Nations. Even entities without territory have been recognized. The Iranian mullahs had a better chance of staying in power in 1979 by violating diplomatic immunity (a long-standing rule associated with international legal sovereignty) than by honoring it. These departures from the standard norm have not, however, generated alternative logics of appropriateness.

While almost all states in the international system have enjoyed international recognition (even if other kinds of entities are sometimes recognized as well), many fewer states have enjoyed Westphalian sovereignty. Rulers have frequently departed from the principle that external actors should be excluded from authority structures within the territory of their own or other states. Westphalian sovereignty can be violated through both intervention and invitation. More powerful states have engaged in intervention, coercing public authorities in weaker states to accept externally dictated authority structures. Rulers have also issued invitations, voluntary policies that compromise the autonomy of their own polity, such as signing human rights accords that establish supranational judicial structures, or entering into international loan agreements that give the lender the right not just to be paid back but also to influence domestic policies and institutions. The norm of autonomy, the core of Westphalian sovereignty, has been challenged by alternatives including human rights, minority rights, fiscal responsibility, and the maintenance of international stability. Moreover, in the international system principled claims have sometimes merely been a rationalization for exploiting the opportunities presented by power asymmetries.

The logic of appropriateness of Westphalian sovereignty, the exclusion of external actors from internal authority arrangements, has been widely recognized but also frequently violated. The multiple pressures on rulers have led to a decoupling between the norm of autonomy and actual practice. Talk and action do not coincide. Rulers might consistently pledge their commitment to nonintervention but at the same time attempt to alter the domestic institutional structures of other states, and justify this practice by alternative norms such as human rights or opposition to capitalism. Rulers must speak to and secure the support of different constituencies making inconsistent demands. Nationalist groups agitate for an end to external influence; the International Monetary Fund (IMF) insists on a legitimated role in domestic policy formation. Rulers might talk nonintervention to the former, while accepting the conditionality terms of the latter. For rulers making choices in an anarchic environment in which there are many demands, multiple norms, power asymmetries, and no authoritative decision-making structures, adhering to Westphalian sovereignty might, or might not, maximize their utility.

Outcomes in the international system are determined by rulers whose violation of, or adherence to, international principles or rules is based on calculations of material and ideational interests, not taken-for-granted practices derived from some overarching institutional structures or deeply embedded generative grammars. Organized hypocrisy is the normal state of affairs.

Violations of the basic rule of Westphalian sovereignty have occurred more frequently than violations of the basic rule of international legal sovereignty and have been more explicitly justified by alternative principles. Departures from the logic of appropriateness associated with international legal sovereignty have often been unproblematic because they involve agreements among rulers that are mutually beneficial; everyone is better off and no one needs to be convinced. In contrast, coercive violations of the logic of appropriateness associated with Westphalian sovereignty can leave some actors worse off; justifications in the form of alternative principles or rules have been offered, sometimes to convince targets and sometimes to insure support from domestic constituents in those states engaged in coercion.

FOUR MEANINGS OF SOVEREIGNTY

The term sovereignty has been commonly used in at least four different ways: domestic sovereignty, referring to the organization of public authority within a state and to the level of effective control exercised by those holding authority; interdependence sovereignty, referring to the ability of public authorities to control transborder movements; international legal sovereignty, referring to the mutual recognition of states or other entities; and Westphalian sovereignty, referring to the exclusion of external actors from domestic authority configurations. These four meanings of sovereignty are not logically coupled, nor have they covaried in practice.

Embedded in these four usages of the term is a fundamental distinction between authority and control. Authority involves a mutually recognized right for an actor to engage in specific kinds of activities. If authority is effective, force or compulsion would never have to be exercised. Authority would be coterminous with control. But control can be achieved simply through the use of brute force with no mutual recognition of authority at all. In practice, the boundary between control and authority can by hazy. A loss of control over a period of time could lead to a loss of authority. The effective exercise of control, or the acceptance of a rule for purely instrumental reasons, could generate new systems of authority. If a practice works, individuals might come to regard it as normatively binding, not just instrumentally efficacious; conversely, if a mutually accepted rule fails to control behavior, its authority might be rejected over time. In many social and political situations both a logic of consequences, in which control is the key issue, and a logic of appropriateness, associated with authority, can both affect the behavior of actors.

Westphalian sovereignty and international legal sovereignty exclusively refer to issues of authority: does the state have the right to exclude external actors, and is a state recognized as having the authority to engage in international agreements? Interdependence sovereignty exclusively refers to control: can a state control movements across its own borders? Domestic sovereignty is used in ways that refer to both authority and control: what authority structures are recognized within a state, and how effective is their level of control? A loss of interdependence sovereignty (control over transborder flows) would almost certainly imply a loss of domestic sovereignty in the sense of domestic control but would not necessarily imply that the state had lost domestic authority.

Domestic Sovereignty   The intellectual history of the term sovereignty is most closely associated with domestic sovereignty. How is public authority organized within the state? How effectively is it exercised? Bodin and Hobbes, the two most important early theorists of sovereignty, were both driven by a desire to provide an intellectual rationale for the legitimacy of some one final source of authority within the state. Both were anxious to weaken support for the religious wars that tore France and Britain apart by demonstrating that revolt against the sovereign could never be legitimate. Strayer, in his study of the early state, suggests that "For those who were skeptical about the divine right of monarchs there was the theory that the state was absolutely necessary for human welfare, and that the concentration of power which we call sovereignty was essential for the existence of the state."[2] F. H. Hinsley writes, "at the beginning, at any rate, the idea of sovereignty was the idea that there is a final and absolute political authority in the political community; and everything that needs to be added to complete the definition is added if this statement is continued in the following words: 'and no final and absolute authority exists elsewhere,'".[3] Later theorists from Locke, to Mill, to Marx, to Dahl have challenged the notion that there has to be some one final source of authority, but the work of all of these writers is concerned primarily with the organization of authority within the state.

Polities can be organized in many different ways without raising any issues for either international legal or Westphalian sovereignty. Authority may be concentrated in the hands of one individual, as Bodin and Hobbes advocated, or divided among different institutions, as is the case in the United States. There can be federal or unitary structures. The one point at which the organization of domestic authority could affect international legal sovereignty occurs in the case of confederations in which the individual units of the state have some ability to conduct external relations.

The effectiveness of political authorities within their own borders may also vary without empirically or logically influencing international legal or Westphalian sovereignty. Whether operating in a parliamentary or presidential, monarchical or republican, or authoritarian or democratic polity, political leaders might, or might not, be able to control developments within their own territory. They might, or might not, be able to maintain order, collect taxes, regulate pornography, repress drug use, prevent abortion, minimize corruption, or control crime. A state with very limited effective domestic control could still have complete international legal sovereignty. It could still be recognized as a juridical equal by other states, and its representatives could still exercise their full voting rights in international organizations. The Westphalian sovereignty of an ineffective state would not necessarily be compromised. Domestic leaders might continue to exclude external actors, especially if these actors were not much interested in local developments. Domestic sovereignty, the organization and effectiveness of political authority, is the single most important question for political analysis, but the organization of authority within a state and the level of control enjoyed by the state are not necessarily related to international legal or Westphalian sovereignty.

Interdependence Sovereignty

In contemporary discourse it has become commonplace for observers to note that state sovereignty is being eroded by globalization. Such analysts are concerned fundamentally with questions of control, not authority. The inability to regulate the flow of goods, persons, pollutants, diseases, and ideas across territorial boundaries has been described as a loss of sovereignty. In his classic study, *The Economics of Interdependence,* Richard Cooper argued that in a world of large open capital markets smaller states would not be able to control their own monetary policy because they could not control the transborder movements of capital. James Rosenau suggests in *Turbulence in World Politics* that the basic nature of the international system is changing. The scope of activities over which states can effectively exercise control is declining. New issues have emerged such as "atmospheric pollution, terrorism, the drug trade, currency crises, and AIDs," which are a product of interdependence or new technologies and which are transnational rather than national. States cannot provide solutions to these and other issues.[4]

While a loss of interdependence sovereignty does not necessarily imply anything about domestic sovereignty understood as the organization of authoritative decision making, it does undermine domestic sovereignty comprehended simply as control. If a state cannot regulate what passes across its borders, it will not be able to control what happens within them.

It is nowhere near as self-evident as many observers have suggested that the international environment at the end of the twentieth century has reached unprecedented levels of openness that are placing new and unique strains on states. By some measures international capital markets were more open before the First World War than they are now. The importance of international trade has followed a similar trajectory, growing during the last half of the nineteenth century, then falling from the first to the fifth decades of the twentieth century, then growing after 1950 to unprecedented levels for most but not all states. International labor movements were more open in the nineteenth century than they are now. Some areas have become more deeply enmeshed in the international environment, especially East Asia; others, notably most of Africa, remain much more isolated. Regardless of the conclusions that are reached about changes in international flows, there have still been considerable variations in national political responses. Increases in transnational flows have not made states impotent with regard to pursuing national policy agendas; increasing transnational flows have not necessarily undermined state control. Indeed, the level of government spending for developed countries has increased along with various measures of globalization since 1950.

Interdependence sovereignty, or the lack thereof, is not practically or logically related to international legal or Westphalian sovereignty. A state can be recognized as a juridical equal by other states and still be unable to control movements across its own borders. Unregulated transborder movements do not imply that a state is subject to external structures of authority, which would be a violation of Westphalian sovereignty. Rulers can lose control of transborder flows and still be recognized and be able to exclude external actors.

In practice, however, a loss of interdependence sovereignty might lead rulers to compromise their Westphalian sovereignty. Indeed, neoliberal institutionalism suggests that technological changes, which have reduced the costs of transportation and communication, have led to a loss of interdependence sovereignty, which, in turn, has prompted states to enter into agreements (an exercise of international legal sovereignty) to create international institutions, some of which have compromised their Westphalian sovereignty by establishing external authority structures.

Thus the first two meanings of sovereignty, interdependence sovereignty and domestic sovereignty, are logically distinct from the basic concerns of this study—international legal sovereignty and Westphalian sovereignty. The structure of domestic political authority and the extent of control over activities within and across territorial boundaries are not necessarily related to international recognition or the exclusion of external actors, although behaviorally the erosion of domestic or interdependence sovereignty can lead rulers to compromise their Westphalian sovereignty.

International Legal Sovereignty

The third meaning of sovereignty, international legal sovereignty, has been concerned with establishing the status of a political entity in the international system. Is a state recognized by other states? Is it accepted as a juridical equal? Are its representatives entitled to diplomatic immunity? Can it be a member of international organizations? Can its representatives enter into agreements with other entities? This is the concept used most frequently in international legal scholarship, but it has been employed by scholars and practitioners of international relations more generally.

The classic model of international law is a replication of the liberal theory of the state. The state is treated at the international level as analogous to the individual at the national level. Sovereignty, independence, and consent are comparable with the position that the individual has in the liberal theory of the state. States are equal in the same way that individuals are equal. The concept of the equality of states was introduced into international law by Vattel in *Le droit de gens,* first published 1758. Vattel reasoned from the logic of the state of nature. If men were equal in the state of nature, then states were also free and equal and living in a state of nature. For Vattel a small republic was no less a sovereign state than was a powerful kingdom.

The basic rule for international legal sovereignty is that recognition is extended to entities, states, with territory and formal juridical autonomy. This has been the common, although as we shall see, not exclusive, practice. There have also been additional criteria applied to the recognition of specific governments rather than states: the Communist government in China, for instance, as opposed to the state of China. These additional rules, which have varied over time, have included the ability to defend and protect a defined territory, the existence of an established government, and the presence of a population.

The supplementary rules for recognizing specific governments, as opposed to states, have never been consistently applied. The decision to recognize or withhold recognition can be a political act that can support or weaken a target government. Weaker states have sometimes argued that the recognition of governments should be automatic, but stronger states, who might choose to use recognition as a political instrument, have rejected this principle. States have recognized other governments even when they did not have effective control over their claimed territory, such as the German and Italian recognition of the Franco regime in 1936, and the American recognition of the Lon Nol government in Cambodia in 1970. States have continued to recognize governments that have lost power, including

Mexican recognition of the Spanish republican regime until 1977, and recognition of the Chinese Nationalist regime by all of the major Western powers until the 1970s. States have refused to recognize new governments even when they have established effective control, such as the British refusal in the nineteenth century to recognize the newly independent Latin American states until a decade after they had established effective control, the Russian refusal to recognize the July monarchy in France until 1832, and the U.S. refusal to recognize the Soviet regime until 1934. The frequency and effectiveness of the use of recognition or nonrecognition as a political instrument have depended both upon the distribution of power (conflicting policies by major powers reduce the impact of recognition policies) and the degree of ideological conflict.

More interesting from the perspective of this study is not the fact that specific governments have been denied or given recognition, but rather that even entities, as opposed to specific governments, that do not conform with the basic norm of appropriateness associated with international legal sovereignty have been recognized. Entities that lack either formal juridical autonomy or territory have also been recognized. India was a member of the League of Nations and a signatory of the Versailles settlements even though it was a colony of Britain. The British Dominions were signatories at Versailles and members of the league even though their juridical independence from Britain was unclear. India and the Philippines were founding members of the United Nations even though they did not become formally independent until 1946 and 1947 respectively. The Palestinian Liberation Organization (PLO) was given observer status in the United Nations in 1974 and this status was changed to that of a mission in 1988 coincident with the declaration of Palestinian independence even though the PLO did not have any independent control over territory. Byelorussia and the Ukraine were members of the United Nations even though they were part of the Soviet Union. Andorra became a member of the United Nations in 1993 even though France and Spain have control over its security affairs and retain the right to appoint two of the four members of its Constitutional Tribunal. Hong Kong, a British colony and then part of China, became a founding member of the World Trade Organization even though China was not. The Order of Malta is recognized as a sovereign person by more than sixty states even though it lost control of Malta in 1798 and holds no territory other than some buildings in Rome.

The uncertainty surrounding the recognition of specific governments, and even the violations of the principle that recognition should be limited to territorial entities that are juridically independent, have not reduced the attractiveness of international legal sovereignty for rulers or created an environment in which basic institutional arrangements have been challenged.

Almost all rulers have sought international legal sovereignty, the recognition of other states, because it provides them with both material and normative resources. Sovereignty can be conceived of as "a ticket of general admission to the international arena."[5] All recognized states have juridical equality. International law is based on the consent of states. Recognized states can enter into treaties with each other, and these treaties will generally be operative even if the government changes. Dependent or subordinate territories do not generally have the right to conclude international agreements (although, as with everything else in the international system, there are exceptions), giving the central or recognized authority a monopoly over formal arrangements with other states.

Even though the differences in treatment can be blurred, it is better to be recognized than not. Nonrecognition is not a bar to the conduct of commercial and even diplomatic discourse, but it can introduce an element of uncertainty into the calculations of actors. Ex ante they may not be able to predict how particular governments or national court systems will respond to an unrecognized government. Multinational firms might be more reluctant to invest.

By facilitating accords, international legal sovereignty offers the possibility for rulers to secure external resources that can enhance their ability to stay in power and to promote the security, economic, and ideational interests of their constituents. The rulers of internationally recognized states can sit at the table. Entering into certain kinds of contracts, such as alliances, can enhance security by reducing uncertainty about the commitment of other actors. Membership in international financial institutions opens the possibility, although not the assurance, of securing foreign capital. Even if rulers have entered into accords that have far-reaching effects on their domestic autonomy, such as the European Union, they have nothing to lose by retaining their international legal sovereignty, including their formal right to withdraw from any international agreements.

Recognition also provides a state, and by implication its rulers, with a more secure status in the courts of other states. The act of state doctrine holds, in the words of one U.S. Supreme Court decision, that "Every sovereign State is bound to respect the independence of every other sovereign State, and the courts of one country will not sit in judgment on the acts of the government of another done within its own territory."[6] In British and American courts recognition is consequential because the sovereign or public acts of a recognized state, as opposed to its private or commercial acts, cannot be challenged, and the property of a recognized state is immune from seizure. Traditionally only the citizens of recognized states have been able to appear as parties to litigation in the United States. If a government or state is not recognized either de jure or de facto, then American and British courts need not consider its legislation valid—for instance, in deciding whether a piece of property has been legally transferred.

Recognition also provides immunity for diplomatic representatives from both civil and criminal actions. Representatives are not subject to any form of arrest or detention, although the host country can refuse to receive, or can expel, specific individuals. Diplomatic premises can not be entered by representatives of the host country. Diplomatic bags can not be opened.

The attractiveness of international legal sovereignty can also be understood from a more sociological or cognitive perspective. Recognition as a state is a widely, almost universally understood construct in the contemporary world. A ruler attempting to strengthen his own position by creating or reinforcing a particular national identity is more likely to be successful if his state or his government enjoys international recognition. Recognition gives the ruler the opportunity to play on the international stage; even if it is only a bit part, parading at the United Nations or shaking hands with the president of the United States or the chancellor of Germany, can enhance the standing of a ruler among his or her own followers. In an uncertain domestic political situation (a situation in which domestic sovereignty is problematic), international recognition can reinforce the position of rulers by signaling to constituents that a ruler may have access to international resources, including alliances and sovereign lending. Hence, international legal sovereignty can promote the interests of rulers by making it easier for them to generate domestic political support not just because they are in a better position to promote the interests of their constituents but also because recognition is a signal about the viability of a political regime and its leaders.

Like other institutional arrangements in the international environment, however, international recognition is not a constitutive act in the sense that the absence of recognition precludes the kinds of activities that recognition itself facilitates. Governments have maintained administrative contacts and signed agreements with governments they have not recognized; they have exchanged trade missions, registered trademarks, accepted consular missions, and concluded arrangements for the exchange of prisoners of war. Representatives of one state have had contacts with representatives of other states that they have not recognized; for instance, the United States sent a personal representative to the Holy See when the Vatican was not recognized by the United States; U.S. and mainland Chinese officials met in Geneva in 1954; the Vietnam peace negotiations in Paris from 1970 to 1973 took place when the United States did not recognize the North Vietnamese government; President Nixon went on an official visit to China in 1971 when the two countries did not recognize each other. National court systems have increasingly been given discretion by their own governments to decide whether the actions of nonrecognized governments will be given special legal standing. The U.S. Protection of Diplomats Act of 1971 provides for the protection of diplomats even if their governments have not been recognized by the United States. When the United States recognized the People's Republic of China as the legitimate government of China in 1979 and withdrew recognition from the Republic of China (ROC), it established a special status for Taiwan. The Taiwan Relations Act stipulated that the legal standing of the ROC in American courts would not be affected, that Taiwan would continue to be a member of international financial institutions, and that the American Institute in Taiwan, a nongovernmental agency, would be created, in effect, to conduct the functions of an embassy.

As the following chapters demonstrate, whatever international recognition has meant, it has not led rulers to eschew efforts to alter the domestic authority structures, policies, or even personnel of other states, or to enter into contractual relationships that compromise the autonomy of their own state. International legal sovereignty does not mean Westphalian sovereignty. Moreover, it does not guarantee that legitimate domestic authorities will be able to monitor and regulate developments within the territory of their state or flows across their borders; that is, it does not guarantee either domestic sovereignty or interdependence sovereignty.

Indeed, international legal sovereignty is the necessary condition for rulers to compromise voluntarily aspects of their Westphalian sovereignty. Nowhere is this more apparent than in the European Union. In an interview shortly before the opening of the April 1996 European Union conference on governance in Turin, Jacques Chirac, the president of France, stated that "In order for Europe to be widened it must in the first instance be deepened, but the sovereignty of each state must be respected."[7] Chirac was arguing that the member states of the European Union must retain their international legal sovereignty, even while they were entering into agreements that compromised their Westphalian, interdependence, and domestic sovereignty since the European Union can regulate transborder movements; the European Court exercises transnational authority; and some European Union decisions can be taken by a majority vote of the member states.

Finally, it should be obvious that international legal sovereignty does not guarantee the territorial integrity of any state or even the existence of a state. Recognized states have been dismembered and even absorbed. The conquest of any particular state extinguishes the sovereignty of that state (domestic, Westphalian, interdependence, and usually international legal), but conquest is not a challenge to Westphalian and international legal sovereignty as institutional forms. It reconfigures borders but does not create new principles and norms.

Westphalian Sovereignty

Finally, sovereignty has been understood as the Westphalian model, an institutional arrangement for organizing political life that is based on two principles: territoriality and the exclusion of external actors from domestic authority structures. Rulers may be constrained, sometimes severely, by the external environment, but they are still free to choose the institutions and policies they regard as optimal. Westphalian sovereignty is violated when external actors influence or determine domestic authority structures.

Domestic authority structures can be infiltrated through both coercive and voluntary actions, through intervention and invitation. Foreign actors, usually the rulers of other states, can use their material capabilities to dictate or coerce changes in the authority structures of a target; they can violate the rule of nonintervention in the internal affairs of other states. Rulers may also themselves establish supranational or extranational authority structures that constrain their own domestic autonomy; they can extend invitations, sometimes inadvertent, that result in compromises of their own Westphalian sovereignty. While coercion, intervention, is inconsistent with international legal as well as Westphalian sovereignty, voluntary actions by rulers, invitations, do not violate international legal sovereignty although they do transgress Westphalian sovereignty.

The norm of nonintervention in internal affairs had virtually nothing to do with the Peace of Westphalia, which was signed in 1648. It was not clearly articulated until the end of the eighteenth century. Nevertheless, the common terminology is used here because the Westphalian model has so much entered into common usage, even if it is historically inaccurate.

The fundamental norm of Westphalian sovereignty is that states exist in specific territories, within which domestic political authorities are the sole arbiters of legitimate behavior. While autonomy can be compromised as a result of both intervention and invitation, the former has gotten much more attention. For many observers, the rule of nonintervention—which is always violated through coercion or imposition, as opposed to voluntary invitation—is the key element of sovereign statehood. Robert Jackson writes that: "The *grundnorm* of such a political arrangement (sovereign statehood) is the basic prohibition against foreign intervention which simultaneously imposes a duty of forbearance and confers a right of independence on all statesmen. Since states are profoundly unequal in power the rule is obviously far more constraining for powerful states and far more liberating for weak states."[8]

The principle of nonintervention was first explicitly articulated by Wolff and Vattel during the last half of the eighteenth century. Wolff wrote in the 1760s that "To interfere in the government of another, in whatever way indeed that may be done is opposed to the natural liberty of nations, by virtue of which one is altogether independent of the will of other nations in its action."[9] Vattel argued that no state had the right to intervene in the internal affairs of other states. He applied this argument to non-European as well as European states, claiming that "The Spaniards violated all rules when they set themselves up as judges of the Inca Athualpa. If that prince had violated the law of nations with respect to them, they would have had a right to punish him. But they accused him of having put some of his subjects to death, of having had several wives, &c—things, for which he was not at all accountable to them; and, to fill up the measure of their extravagant injustice, they condemned him by the laws of Spain."[10]

Weaker states have always been the strongest supporters of the rule of nonintervention. During the nineteenth century the Latin American states endorsed this rule at international meetings in 1826 and 1848. In 1868 the Argentine jurist Carlos Calvo published a treatise in which he condemned intervention by foreign powers to enforce contractual obligations of private parties. The foreign minister of Argentina, Luis Drago, argued in a note to the American government in 1902 that intervention to enforce the collection of public debts was illegitimate. The Calvo and Drago doctrines became recognized claims in international law. At the sixth International Conference of American States held in Havana in 1928, the Commission of Jurists recommended adoption of the principle that "No state has a right to interfere in the internal affairs of another." This proposal, however, was rejected, in large part because of the opposition of the United States. The United States had engaged in several interventions in Central America and the Caribbean. The American secretary of state, Charles Evans Hughes, argued that the United States had a right to intervene to protect the lives of its nationals should order break down in another country. At the seventh International Conference of American States held in 1933, the United States finally accepted the principle of nonintervention. The wording that "no state has the right to intervene in the internal or external affairs of another" was included in the Convention on Rights and Duties of States and accepted by the United States. The Charter of the Organization of American States (OAS) stipulates that "No State or group of States has the right to intervene, directly or indirectly, for any reason whatever, in the internal or external affairs of any other State. The foregoing principle prohibits not only armed force but also any other form of interference or attempted threat against the personality of the State or against its political, economic, and cultural elements."[11] In the latter part of the twentieth century nonintervention has been routinely endorsed in major international agreements such as the United Nations Charter and the 1975 Helsinki agreement, albeit often along with other principles such as human rights that are in tension with nonintervention.

While Westphalian sovereignty can be compromised through invitation as well as intervention, invitation has received less notice in the literature because observers have confounded international legal and Westphalian sovereignty. Intervention violates both. Invitation violates only Westphalian sovereignty. Invitation occurs when a ruler voluntarily compromises the domestic autonomy of his or her own polity. Free choices are never inconsistent with international legal sovereignty.

Invitations can, however, infringe domestic autonomy. Rulers may issue invitations for a variety of reasons, including tying the hands of their successors, securing external financial resources, and strengthening domestic support for values that they, themselves, embrace. Invitations may sometimes be inadvertent; rulers might not realize that entering into an agreement may alter their own domestic institutional arrangements. Regardless of the motivation or the perspicacity of rulers, invitations violate Westphalian sovereignty by subjecting internal authority structures to external constraints. The rulings of the European Court of Justice, for instance, have legitimacy in the judicial systems of the member states of the European Union. IMF conditionality agreements, which may include stipulations requiring changes in domestic structures, carry weight not only because they are attached to the provision of funding but also because the IMF has legitimacy for some actors in borrowing countries derived from its claims to technical expertise. Human rights conventions can provide focal points that alter conceptions of legitimacy among groups in civil society and precipitate possibly unanticipated changes in the institutional arrangements of signatory states.

Violations of Westphalian sovereignty can arise in a sovereign state system because the absence of a formal hierarchical system of authority, the defining characteristic of any international system, does not mean that the authority structures in any given political entity will be free of external influence. Wendt and Friedheim have defined informal empires as "transnational structures of de facto political authority in which members are juridically sovereign states."[12] Formal constitutional independence does not guarantee de facto autonomy. A recognized international legal sovereign will not necessarily be a Westphalian sovereign.

In recent years a number of analysts have used the Westphalian model as a bench mark to assert that the character of the international system is changing in some fundamental ways. Writing of the pre–1950s world, James Rosenau contends that "In that system, legitimate authority was concentrated in the policy-making institutions of states, which interacted with each other on the basis of equality and accepted principles of diplomacy and international law. Their embassies remained inviolable and so did their domestic affairs. Intrusion into such matters were met with protests of violated sovereignty and, not infrequently, with preparations for war. For all practical purposes, the line between domestic and foreign affairs was preserved and clearly understood by all. The norms of the Western state system lodged control over external ties in the state and these were rarely defied and even more rarely revised." Philip Windsor states that "It is fashionable, at present, to suggest that the old Westphalian system of a world of non-interventionist states is on the decline, and that the dangers of growing intervention by different powers in the affairs of other states have been on the increase. The Westphalian system represented some remarkable achievements: the absolute sovereignty of a state rested on a dual basis whereby internal authority was matched by freedom from external interference; and in this way the principle of *cuius regio, eius religio,* codified in the Religious Peace of Augsburg, laid the foundation of the modern states system."[13]

The way in which some analysts have understood sovereignty in terms of the Westphalian model is brought out clearly by authors who have studied minority or human rights, because claims about such rights are seen as a contradiction of sovereignty. In one of the most important studies of minority rights in the interwar period C. A. Macartney writes, "The doctrine of state sovereignty does not admit that the domestic policy of any state—the policy which it follows towards its own citizens—can be any concern of any other state." In a more recent study of human rights Forsythe suggests that "The most fundamental point about human rights law is that it establishes a set of rules for all states and all people. It thus seeks to increase world unity and to counteract national separateness (but not necessarily national distinctions). In this sense, the international law of human rights is revolutionary because it contradicts the notion of national sovereignty— that is, that a state can do as it pleases in its own jurisdiction." Writing in the 1990s about the status of minority groups Kay Hailbronner claims that "Modern public international law seems to have broken through the armour of sovereignty." Similarly Brian Hehir has asserted that "In the Westphalian order both state sovereignty and the rule of nonintervention are treated as absolute norms." He then goes on to suggest that this Westphalian system is under an unprecedented level of assault.[14]

Despite these claims about unparalleled change, the most important empirical conclusion of the present study is that the principles associated with both Westphalian and international legal sovereignty have always been violated. Neither Westphalian nor international legal sovereignty has ever been a stable equilibrium from which rulers had no incentives to deviate. Rather, Westphalian and international legal sovereignty are best understood as examples of organized hypocrisy. At times rulers adhere to conventional norms or rules because it provides them with resources and support (both material and ideational). At other times, rulers have violated the norms, and for the same reasons. If rulers want to stay in power and to promote the security, material, and ideational interests of their constituents, following the conventional practices of Westphalian and international legal sovereignty might or might not be an optimal policy. After the Second World War it was preferable for the rulers of western Europe to sign the European Human Rights Convention, which compromised their Westphalian sovereignty, than to insist that the domestic autonomy of their polities be unconstrained. In the late 1990s it was better for the rulers of China and other states to allow Hong Kong, which did not have juridical independence after its return to China, to enjoy international recognition; Hong Kong continued its participation or joined international organizations, including the World Trade Organization, whose members denied China itself the right to become a founding member.

In sum, analysts and practitioners have used the term sovereignty in four different and distinct ways. The absence or loss of one kind of sovereignty does not logically imply an erosion of others, even though they may be empirically associated with each other. A state can be recognized, but its authority structures can be de facto subject to external authority or control. It can lose control of transborder movements but still be autonomous.

Rulers have almost universally desired international legal sovereignty, but this has not meant that they have universally followed the rule of recognizing only juridically autonomous territorial entities. Rulers have recognized entities that lack formal juridical autonomy or even territory, and they have denied recognition to governments that have exercised effective control over the territory of a recognized state. Recognition can be a political act, one designed to support a specific government or legitimate the claims to territorial autonomy of particular rulers, and adherence to the basic principle of international legal sovereignty might, or might not, enhance these purposes.

The tensions between the conventional rule and actual practice have been more severe for Westphalian than international legal sovereignty. Rulers have sometimes invited external actors to compromise the autonomy of their own state. Westphalian sovereignty has also been violated through intervention; more powerful states have coerced their weaker counterparts into altering the domestic institutional arrangements of their polities. Following the rule of Westphalian sovereignty—preserving the de facto autonomy of a territorial political entity—might, or might not, further the interests of rulers.

The international system is complex. Information is imperfect. There are no universal structures that can authoritatively resolve conflicts. Principles and rules can be logically contradictory. Power asymmetries can be high. Widely recognized and endorsed principles will not always promote the interests of rulers. Logics of consequences can trump logics of appropriateness. Westphalian and international legal sovereignty, the major concerns of this study, are examples of organized hypocrisy. They are both defined by widely understood rules. Yet, these rules have been comprised, more frequently in the case of Westphalian than international legal sovereignty.

. . .

CONCLUSIONS

The term sovereignty has been used in four different ways: domestic sovereignty, interdependence sovereignty, international legal sovereignty, and Westphalian sovereignty. The latter two, and most particularly Westphalian sovereignty, are the subject of this study. Both international legal and Westphalian sovereignty are best conceptualized as examples of organized hypocrisy. Both have clear logics of appropriateness, but these logics are sometimes inconsistent with a logic of consequences. Given the absence of authoritative institutions and power asymmetries, rulers can follow a logic of consequences and reject a logic of appropriateness. Principles have been enduring but violated.

For Westphalian sovereignty the violations have taken place through conventions, contracting, coercion, and imposition. Conventions and contracting are voluntary; rulers have invited violations of the de facto autonomy of their own polities because it leaves them better off than in the status quo ante. Coercion leaves one of the parties worse off; the target must alter its domestic policies or institutions or accept the costs of sanctions. Imposition occurs when the target is so weak that it has no choice but to comply either because the ruler or would-be ruler is faced with military force or because the failure to secure international legal sovereignty, recognition, would threaten the very existence of the state. Coercion and imposition are examples of violations of Westphalian sovereignty through intervention rather than invitation.

For international legal sovereignty violations have primarily been the result of contracting and conventions. Rulers have recognized entities that lacked formal juridical autonomy or, in the case of the Knights of Malta, even territory. Rulers have also refused to recognize governments that have demonstrated domestic sovereignty, and extended recognition to governments that have not exercised effective control over their own territory. These have often been unilateral actions that have not been contingent on the policies of other states.

The logic of appropriateness that is associated with the Westphalian norm of autonomy has mattered in the calculations of rulers, but so have alternatives such as human rights, minority rights, international stability, and fiscal responsibility. Rulers have different constituencies. They respond primarily to domestic supporters who hold different values in different states. The material interests of states often clash. Power is asymmetrical. There is no hierarchical authority. Logics of consequences have trumped Westphalian logics of appropriateness.

The basic rule of international legal sovereignty has been more robust and more widely adhered to. Once rulers have recognition, they hardly ever want to give it up. International legal sovereignty provides an array of benefits, including reducing the transaction costs of entering into agreements with other entities, facilitating participation in international organizations, extending diplomatic immunity, and establishing special legal protections. Because international legal sovereignty is a widely accepted and recognized script, it makes it easier to organize support from internal as well as external sources. Especially in polities with weak domestic sovereignty, international legal sovereignty, international recognition, can provide a signal to constituents that a regime and its rulers are more likely to survive and thereby make it more likely that these constituents would support the regime.

Nevertheless, international legal sovereignty like Westphalian sovereignty is not a Nash equilibrium, nor is it taken for granted. Rulers have had reasons to deviate from the rule and have invented other institutional forms when it has suited their purpose. The British Commonwealth, with its high commissioners rather than ambassadors, was an alternative to international legal sovereignty. Meetings of the major industrialized states include not only the representatives of international legal sovereigns—the presidents, premiers, and prime ministers of this and that country—but also the commissioner of the European Union. The consequences for Taiwan of losing its international legal sovereignty in the 1970s have been mitigated by the fact that some countries, notably the United States, have invented alternative arrangements that provide the functional equivalent of recognition.

Of all the social environments within which human beings operate, the international system is one of the most complex and weakly institutionalized. It lacks authoritative hierarchies. Rulers are likely to be more responsive to domestic material and ideational incentives than international ones. Norms are sometimes mutually inconsistent. Power is asymmetrical. No rule or set of rules can cover all circumstances. Logics of consequences can be compelling. Organized hypocrisy is the norm.

References

Damrosch, Lori. 1993. Changing Conceptions of Intervention in International Law. In *Emerging Norms of Justified Intervention: A Collection of Essays from a Project of the American Academy of Arts and Sciences,* edited by Laura W. Reed and Carl Kaysen, 91–110. Cambridge, Mass.: American Academy of Arts and Sciences.

Forsythe, David P. 1983. *Human Rights and World Politics.* Lincoln: University of Nebraska Press.

Fowler, Michael Ross, and Julie Marie Bunck. 1995. *Law, Power, and the Sovereign State: The Evolution and Application of the Concept of Sovereignty.* University Park: Pennsylvania State University Press.

Hailbronner, Kay. 1992. The Legal Status of Population Groups in a Multinational State under Public International Law. In *The Protection of Minorities and Human Rights,* edited by Yoram Dinstein and Mala Tabory, 117–44. Dordrecht: Martinus Nijhoff.

Hehir, J. Brian. 1995. Intervention: From Theories to Cases. *Ethics and International Affairs* 9: 1–14.

Hinsley, F. H. 1986. *Sovereignty.* 2nd ed. Cambridge: Cambridge University Press.

Jackson, Robert H. 1990. *Quasi-States: Sovereignty, International Relations and the Third World.* Cambridge: Cambridge University Press.

Macartney, Carlile Aylmer. 1934. *National States and National Minorities.* Oxford: Oxford University Press.

Oppenheim, L. 1992. *Oppenheim's International Law.* Edited by Robert Jennings and Arthur Watts. 9th ed. Harlow, Essex: Longman.

Rosenau, James. 1990. *Turbulence in World Politics: A Theory of Change and Continuity.* Princeton, N.J.: Princeton University Press.

Strang, David. 1996. Contested Sovereignty: The Social Constuction of Colonial Imperialism. In *State Sovereignty as a Social Construct,* edited by Thomas Biersteker and Cynthia Weber, 22–49. Cambridge: Cambridge University Press.

Strayer, Joseph R. 1970. *On the Medieval Origins of the Modern State.* Princeton, N.J.: Princeton University Press.

Thomas, Ann, and A. J. Thomas. 1956. *Non Intervention: The Law and Its Import in the Americas.* Dallas: Southern Methodist University Press.

Vattel, Emer de. 1852. *The Law of Nations; or, Principles of the Law of Nature, applied to the Conduct and Affairs of Nations and Sovereigns.* From the new edition Translated by Joseph Chitty. Philadelphia: T. & J. W. Johnson, Law Booksellers.

Wendt, Alexander, and Daniel Friedheim. 1996. Hierarchy under Anarchy: Informal Empire and the East German State. In *State Sovereignty as a Social Construct,* edited by Thomas J. Biersteker and Cynthia Weber, 240–72. Cambridge: Cambridge University Press.

Windsor, Philip. 1984. Superpower Intervention. In *Intervention in World Politics,* edited by Hedley Bull, 45–65. Oxford: Clarendon Press.

Notes

1. Strang 1996, 24.
2. Strayer 1970, 108.
3. Hinsley 1986, 25–26.
4. Rosenau 1990, 13.
5. Fowler and Bunck 1995, 12.
6. The case is *Underhill vs. Hernandez,* quoted in Oppenheim 1992, 365–67.
7. *Frankfurter Allgemeine Zeitung,* March 26, 1996, 1, translated by the author.
8. Jackson 1990, 6.
9. Quoted in A. Thomas and Thomas 1956, 5.
10. Vattel 1852, 155.
11. Quoted in Damrosch 1993.
12. Wendt and Friedheim 1996, 245.
13. Rosenau 1990, 109; Windsor 1984, 45.
14. Macartney 1934, 296; Forsythe 1983, 4; Hailbronner 1992, 117; Hehir 1995, 6.

STUDY AND DISCUSSION QUESTIONS

1. What are the four distinct ways that analysts and practitioners have used the term sovereignty?
2. How can one form of sovereignty (for example, international legal sovereignty) undermine another form of sovereignty (for example, Wetphalian sovereignty)?
3. Why, according to Krasner, does sovereignty amount to little more than "organized hypocrisy" today?

7

Political Globalization

David Held

With the conceptual clarity and comprehensive empirical grasp that have established David Held as one of the leading contributors to the "great globalization debate," this selection captures the new context and organization of politics as it has been reshaped by the processes of globalization. The state today is "criss-crossed by a vast array of networks and organizations" that are intended to manage and regulate finance, trade, communications, to name a few policy domains no longer subject to narrow territorial control. As states are increasingly enmeshed in webs of global and regional interconnections, they are less able to control outcomes by themselves. The result is a distinctive new form of political activity and decision-making, which muddies the distinctions between domestic politics and geopolitical affairs and blurs the line between state power and the influence wielded by international non-governmental organizations (INGOs) and a variety of hybrid organizations like the EU. As a result, the international order can no longer be understood as a realm controlled by inter-state relations. Rather, as Held concludes, politics operates at multiple levels and through a variety of networks and power centers in which an expanding range of actors are involved in shaping outcomes, with uncertain institutional and normative challenges.

Economic globalization has not occurred in a static political system; there has been a shift in the nature and form of political organization as well. A distinctive aspect of this is the emergence of 'global politics' (McGrew, 1992). Political events in one part of the world can rapidly acquire worldwide ramifications. Spatially focused political activity, whether in a city or subnational region, can become embedded in extensive networks of political interaction. As a result, developments at the local level—whether economic, social or environmental—can acquire almost instantaneous global consequences and vice versa.

THE NEW CONTEXT OF POLITICS

Nations, peoples and social movements are linked by many new forms of communication. Over the last few decades a wave of new technological innovations, along with the transformation of older technologies, has generated global communication and transportation infrastructures. These have opened up a massive series of communication channels that cross national borders, increasing the range and type of communications to and from all the world's regions. In addition, contemporary patterns of communication have created a far greater intensity of concepts, symbols and images, moving with far greater extensity and at a far greater velocity, than in earlier periods. This process is compounded by the fact that new global communication systems are used for business and commercial purposes. While there remain significant differences in information density and velocity in different parts of the globe, it is becoming increasingly difficult for people to live in any place isolated from the wider world.

These developments have engendered fundamental changes in the organization of political life. The close connection between 'physical setting', 'social situation' and politics which distinguished most political associations from premodern to modern times has been ruptured; the new communication systems create new experiences, new modes of understanding and new frames of political reference independently of direct contact with particular peoples, issues or events. The speed with which the events of 9/11 reverberated across the world and made mass terrorism a global issue is one poignant example.

The idea of global politics calls into question the traditional demarcations between the domestic and the foreign, and between the territorial and the non-territorial, found in modern conceptions of 'the political'. These categories shaped not only modern political thought but also institution building, as a clear division was established between great ministries of state founded to focus on domestic matters and those created to pursue geopolitical questions. Global problems highlight the richness and complexity of the interconnections that now transcend states and societies in the global order. Moreover, global politics is anchored today not just in traditional geopolitical concerns—trade, power, security—but in a large diversity of social and ecological questions. Pollution, water supply, genetically engineered food and drugs are among an increasing number of policy issues which cut across territorial jurisdictions and existing political alignments, and which require international cooperation for their satisfactory resolution. In many parts of the world the notion of global politics corresponds much more closely to the character of politics than do images of politics as simply state and interstate relations. There are now multiple spheres of politics and authority.

In charting political globalization, it is important to explore the way in which the sovereign state is now criss-crossed by a vast array of networks and organizations that have been established to regulate and manage diverse areas of international and transnational activity—trade, communications, crime and so on. The rapid growth of transnational issues and challenges has generated a multicentric system of governance both within and across political borders. It has been marked by the transformation of aspects of territorially based political decision-making, the development of regional and global organizations and, in many places, the increased importance of regional and international law. There is nothing inevitable, it should be stressed, about these developments. While they form highly significant trends, they are contingent upon many factors, and could be halted or reversed by protracted global conflicts or cataclysmic events.

MULTICENTRIC GOVERNANCE

In the first instance, where once states were the main actors, and multilateral international conventions, negotiated over many years, were the primary expression of interstate cooperation, today this constitutes too narrow a view of international politics. For the primary actors in the international order are no longer just heads of states and foreign ministries, but administrative agencies, courts and legislatures as well. The unitary state has given way to the 'disaggregated state' and the rise of government networks. While these networks take many forms and perform a variety of different functions, they herald 'a new era of transgovernmental regulatory co-operation' and define transgovernmentalism 'as a distinctive mode of global governance: horizontal rather than vertical, composed of national government officials rather than international bureaucrats, decentralized and informal rather than organized and rigid.' Influential examples include the networks formed by financial regulators, including central bankers, securities regulators, insurance supervisors and anti-trust officials. Regulatory networks are a key medium for adjusting and responding to the fast moving challenges of the information age; and through them political power is recast—not simply eroded or undermined.

The end of the Cold War and of the division of the world by two superpowers marks a new distribution of power among states, markets and civil society. New information technologies have helped drive the expansion of networks of businesses, citizens, trade unions, IGOs and INGOs (international non-governmental organizations) which now share aspects of power with governments. The hierarchical organization of governments is increasingly ill-equipped to manage and regulate the new divisions of economic, social and cultural resources. Although it is not easy to imagine political entities that could compete with 'the emotional attachment of a shared landscape, national history, language, flag, and currency', new geographic and functional entities are emerging which challenge the state's hegemony in these areas. The development of global cities, such as London, Barcelona and Los Angeles, substate regions (Catalonia, Scotland, Quebec) and new political formations like the EU, alongside the explosive growth of INGOs and social movements, creates new forms of hybrid organization and allegiances. These networks of business, INGOs and IGOs solve problems, from economic management to environmental tasks, that governments cannot resolve alone. Despite the resurgence of US power and unilateralist politics since 9/11, this underlying transformation of power is likely to continue.

The development of new forms of political and regulatory bodies can be illustrated by a number of phenomena, including, most obviously, the rapid emergence of multilateral organizations and transnational agencies. New forms of multilateral and global politics have been established involving governments, IGOs, INGOs, and a wide variety of pressure groups and other non-governmental organizations (NGOs). At the start of the twentieth century there were just a handful of IGOs and INGOs; by 1996 there were 4,667 active IGOs and 25,260 active INGOs. Membership in organizations of this sort has increased across all income country categories, even though, not surprisingly, the nature and extent of membership varies considerably across such categories and by region. In addition, there has been a very substantial development in the number of international treaties in force, as well as in the number of international regimes, formal and informal, altering the political and legal context in which states operate.

To this dense web of political interconnectedness can be added the routine pattern of meetings and activities of the key international policy-making fora, including the UN, G7, IMF, World Bank and WTO. A century and a half ago there were just one or two interstate conferences or congresses per annum; today the number totals over 9,000 annually. National government is increasingly locked into an array of governance systems at diverse levels—and can barely monitor them all, let alone stay in command. Foreign and domestic policies have become chronically intermeshed, making the coordination and control of government policy increasingly complex.

A thickening web of multilateral agreements, institutions, regimes and transgovernmental policy networks has evolved over the last five decades, intervening in and regulating many aspects of national and transnational life, from finance to flora and fauna. This evolving global governance complex is, of course, far from constituting a world government, with ultimate legal authority and coercive powers, but it is much more than a system of limited intergovernmental cooperation. With the UN as its institutional core, it comprises a vast range of formal suprastate bodies and regional organizations, as well as regimes and transnational policy networks embracing government officials, technocrats, corporate representatives, pressure groups and non-governmental organizations. Although

these bodies and networks lack the kind of centralized, coordinated political programme that is associated with national government, few would dismiss out of
hand the expanding jurisdiction or scope of global policy-making, most especially the vast range of issues it touches on and its growing intrusion into the
domestic affairs of states—illustrated, for example, by the rulings of the WTO's
trade dispute panels. Whatever its limits and faults, the current system of global
governance is a significant arena 'in which struggles over wealth, power and
knowledge are taking place' (see Murphy, 2000).

Global governance today is a *multilayered, multidimensional* and *multi-
actor* system. It is multilayered in so far as the development and implementation of global policies involve a process of political coordination between
suprastate, transnational, national and often substate agencies. Attempts to
combat AIDS/HIV, for instance, require the coordinated efforts of global,
regional, national and local agencies. It is multidimensional in so far as the
engagement and configuration of agencies often differs from sector to sector and
issue to issue, giving rise to significantly differentiated political patterns. The
politics of, for example, global financial regulation is different in interesting
ways from the politics of global trade regulation. Further, many of the agencies
of, and participants in, the global governance complex are no longer purely
intergovernmental bodies. There is involvement by representatives of transnational civil society—from Greenpeace to Jubilee 2000 and an array of NGOs;
the corporate sector—from Monsanto to the International Chamber of Commerce and other trade or industrial associations; and mixed public–private organizations, such as the International Organization of Security Commissions
(IOSCO). Accordingly, global governance is a multi-actor complex in which
diverse agencies participate in the development of global public policy. Of
course, this essentially pluralistic conception of global governance does not presume that all states or interests have an equal voice in, let alone an equal influence over, its agenda or programmes—not at all.

An important feature of the formulation and implementation of global public
policy is that it occurs within an expanding array of different kinds of networks—
transgovernmental networks (such as the Financial Action Task Force (FATF)),
trisectoral networks (such as the World Commission on Dams Forum), involving
public, corporate and NGO groups, and transnational networks (such as the
International Accounting Standards Board (IASB)). These networks—which can
be ad hoc or institutional—have become increasingly important in coordinating
the work of experts and functionaries within governments, international organizations and the corporate and the NGO sectors. They function to set policy agendas, disseminate information, formulate rules and establish and implement policy
programmes—from the money-laundering measures of the FATF to global initiatives to counter AIDS. While many of these networks have a clear bureaucratic
function, they have also become mechanisms through which civil society and cor-

porate interests are embedded in the global policy process (examples include the Global Water Partnership and the Global Alliance for Vaccines and Immunization). In part, the growth of these networks is a response to the overload and politicization of multilateral bodies, but it is also an outcome of the growing technical complexity of global policy issues and the communications revolution.

Another notable trend is the growing enmeshment of public and private agencies in the making of rules, the setting of codes and the establishment of standards. Many new sites of rulemaking and lawmaking have emerged, creating a multitude of 'decentred lawmaking processes' in various sectors of the global order (Teubner, 1997, p. xiii). Many of these have come into existence through processes of self-validation in relation to technical standardization, professional rule production and transnational regulation of multinational corporations, and through business contracting, arbitration and other elements of *lex mercatoria* (the global framework of commercial law) (see Teubner, 1997). A new transnational legal order is developing, 'globalizing a corpus of commercial law and practice that derives from increasingly diverse and multiple local, regional, and global locations involving both state and nonstate authorities' (Cutler, 2003, p. 3). Global public policy networks are reshaping the basis on which national and international rules are made and regulatory systems operate; and the results cannot easily be fitted into traditional legal distinctions. There is no longer a strict separation between public and private, domestic and international legal procedures and mechanisms; models of lawmaking and enforcement no longer simply follow the form and logic of the states system.

To this complex pattern of global governance and rule-making can be added the new configurations of regional governance. The EU has, in remarkably little time, taken Europe from the edge of catastrophe in two world wars to a world in which sovereignty is pooled across a growing number of areas of common concern. For all its flaws, it is, judged in the context of the history of states, a remarkable political formation. In addition, there has been a significant acceleration in regional relations beyond Europe: in the Americas, in Asia-Pacific and, to a lesser degree, in Africa. While the form taken by this type of regionalism is very different from the model of the EU, it has nonetheless had significant consequences for political power, particularly in the Asia-Pacific, which has seen the formation of ASEAN, APEC, ARF, PBEC, and many other groupings. Furthermore, as regionalism has deepened, so interregional diplomacy has intensified as old and new regional groups seek to consolidate their relations with each other. In this respect, regionalism, as noted earlier, has not been a barrier to globalization; it has been a building block for it.

Interlaced with these political and legal transformations are changes in the world military order; a key consideration for the argument being made here. Few states, except for the US and China, can now realistically contemplate unilateralism or neutrality as a credible defence strategy. Global and regional security institutions have become more significant as the collectivization of national security has evolved. But it is not just the institutions of defence that have become multinational. The way military hardware is manufactured has also changed. The age of 'national champions' has been superseded by a sharp increase in licensing co-production agreements, joint ventures, corporate alliances and sub-contracting. This means that few countries—not even the United States—can claim to have a wholly autonomous military production capacity. Such a point can be highlighted in connection with key civil technologies, such as electronics, which are vital to advanced weapons systems, and which are themselves the products of highly globalized industries.

The paradox and novelty of the globalization of organized violence is that security today is increasingly a collective or multilateral affair. The war against Iraq in 2003 occupies an interesting place in this regard. While the dominant military position of the US allows it to act unilaterally—indeed, two weeks before the start of the war, the US Secretary of Defense, Donald Rumsfeld, made it clear to the British government that the US was willing and able to act alone—it has been unable to protect its soldiers after the formal declaration of the end of hostilities, and unable to win the peace. At the time of writing, the US is searching for multilateral support (from India, Japan and other countries) in the form of both military and financial assistance; and it is hoping that a new resolution in the UN (resolution 1511, 16 October 2003) will help restore legitimacy to its control of Iraq and release further international resources. While the war dramatized the military power of the US and its willingness to deploy this massive capability, it also highlighted how complex security challenges and threats cannot be managed satisfactorily by states acting alone, or even in small alliances.

Moreover, states no longer have a monopoly of force, as the growth of transnational terrorism and the events of postwar Iraq all too clearly demonstrate. Private armies and the private provision of security also play a significant role in many regions of the globe. Thus, for the first time in history, the one thing that did most to give modern nation-states a focus and a purpose, that is, national security, and that has been at the very heart of modern statehood as understood from Hobbes onwards, can now be realized effectively only if nation-states come together and pool resources, technology, intelligence, power and authority.

THE RECONFIGURATION
OF POLITICAL POWER

Political communities can no longer be considered (if they ever could with any validity) as simply 'discrete worlds'; they are enmeshed in complex structures of overlapping forces, relations and networks. Clearly, these are structured by inequality and hierarchy. However, even the most powerful among them—

including the most powerful states—do not remain unaffected by the changing conditions and processes of regional and global entrenchment.

At the core of these developments is the reconfiguration of political power. While many states retain the ultimate legal claim to effective supremacy over what occurs within their own territories, this should be juxtaposed with, and understood in relation to, the expanding jurisdiction of institutions of global and regional governance and the constraints of, as well as the obligations derived from, new and changing forms of international regulation. This is especially evident in the European Union, where sovereign power is divided between international, national and local authorities, but it is also evident in the operation of IGOs such as the WTO. However, even where sovereignty still appears intact, states do not retain sole command of what transpires within their own territorial boundaries. Complex global systems, from the financial to the ecological, connect the fate of communities in one locale to the fate of communities in distant regions of the world. Globalization, in other words, is associated with a transformation or an 'unbundling' of the relationship between sovereignty, territoriality and political power.

This unbundling involves a plurality of actors, a variety of political processes, and diverse levels of coordination and operation. Specifically, it includes:

- Different forms of intergovernmental arrangements embodying various levels of legalization, types of instruments utilized and degrees of responsiveness to stakeholders.
- An increasing number of public agencies—such as central bankers—maintaining links with similar agencies in other countries and thus forming transgovernmental networks for the management of various global issues.
- Diverse business actors—for instance, firms, their associations and organizations such as international chambers of commerce—establishing their own transnational regulatory mechanisms to manage issues of common concern.
- Non-governmental organizations and transnational advocacy networks—that is, leading actors in global civil society—playing a role in various domains of global governance and at various stages of the global public policy-making process.
- Public bodies, business actors and NGOs collaborating in many issue areas in order to provide novel approaches to social problems through multistakeholder networks.

While many people—politicians, political activists and academics—link contemporary globalization with new constraints on politics, it is more accurately associated with the expansion of the terms of political activity. Not only has contemporary globalization triggered or reinforced the significant politicization of a growing array of issue areas, it has been accompanied by an extraordinary growth of institutionalized arenas and networks of political mobilization, decision-making and regulatory activity which transcend national political jurisdictions. This has expanded the capacity for, and scope of, political activity and the exercise of political authority. In principle, globalization is not beyond regulation and control. Yet it is hard to overlook the profound institutional and normative challenges it presents to the existing organization of political communities.

References

Cutler, A. C. (2003) *Private Power and Global Authority*. Cambridge: Cambridge University Press.

McGrew, A. G. (1992) Conceptualizing global politics. In A. G. McGrew et al., *Global Politics*. Cambridge: Polity.

Mathews, J. (2003) Power shift. In D. Held and A. McGrew (eds), *The Global Transformation Reader*. Cambridge: Polity.

Murphy, C. N. (2000) Global governance: poorly done and poorly understood. *International Affairs*, 76(4).

Slaughter, A.-M. (2003b) Governing the global economy through government networks. In D. Held and A. G. McGrew (eds), *The Global Transformations Reader*. Cambridge: Polity.

Teubner, G. (ed.) (1997) *Global Law without a State*. Aldershot: Dartmouth.

STUDY AND DISCUSSION QUESTIONS

1. What does Held mean when he says that global governance today is a multidimensional, multilayered, multi-actor system?

2. Held acknowledges that the changed context and organization of global political power does *not* mean that all states, interests, or actors equally influence outcomes. Do you think that, despite all the changes in governance that limit the power of governments, the most powerful states still control most outcomes—or that globalization has fundamentally changed the equation of state power?

3. Think about the war against terrorism and the war in Iraq. How convincing is Held's claim that security is increasingly collective and multilateral?

8

Briefing Paper: Multi-level Governance

❖

Paul Carmichael

Prepared as part of a wide-ranging review of public administration in Northern Ireland, this contribution provides an unusually lucid and revealing account of multi-level governance. Told from the UK perspective, the selection nonetheless has far-reaching implications for emerging patterns of multi-level governance (MLG) more broadly and, in particular, for the European Union. As Paul Carmichael explains, MLG is a descriptive term intended to identify the growing complexity of policy-making, implementation, and accountability in a political and organizational context framed by overlapping functional responsibilities at the supranational, national, regional, and local level. MLG also speaks to the proliferation in the number and diversity of political actors including formal governmental officials and agencies, quasi-governmental bodies (non-elected bodies outside of government that have significant influence over public policy such as judicial ethics commissions or Amtrak in the United States), as well as private actors. As Carmichael explains, MLG is most highly developed in the European Union, where the European Commission (the supranational executive), national governments, and regional and local authorities share responsibility throughout the decision-making process, but are formally autonomous.

There has never been a time when the nation-state has stood alone, totally free to determine its own fate. Other states, as well as international, transnational and multi-national bodies, have always been important. Until recently, the influence of such external forces was modelled largely in terms of nation-states engaged with intergovernmental relations with other nation-states. Changing conditions, chiefly, the growing role and influence of these extra-national actors have occasioned a revision of our understanding, however. Transnational bodies have developed a growing regulatory role in steering national governments. Thus, the term multi-level governance (MLG) was devised for use in conceptualizing the emerging system of governance within the EU.

Essentially, MLG is a descriptive rather than prescriptive concept that primarily serves to describe the new realities of governance. It is not usually referred to as a desired or preferred state of affairs, although those who tend to employ the term to depict reality frequently endorse the new dispensation as fulfilling their pluralist aspirations. Marquand's (1998) sentiments convey the point neatly: "power, like muck, is no use unless it be spread" (p. 10). As such, MLG stresses the complexity of policy-making, implementation and accountability relationships between a variety of state and societal actors at the levels of supranational activity (EU), central government, devolved administration, local authorities and quasi-government.

Tommel (1998) has contended that MLG has emerged as a result of the decline of classical authoritative or even coercive decision-making, these having been replaced by indirect market-led steering instruments and 'soft' forms of decision-making. Thus, there has been a shift from a hierarchical territorial modes of government based on the dominant position of the nation-state to a more non-hierarchically, functionally based system. The nation-state has been 'hollowed out', a process that "opens up a wide space of autonomous action to lower-level tiers and external actors" (Tommel, 1998, p.55). Additionally, "private and non-governmental actors will increasingly be involved in public decision and policy-making, particularly at regional and local level, in exchange for a more direct representation of their interests within government" (p.56). The net result is to have created what has been dubbed 'Maze Europe'.

Being descriptive rather than prescriptive, MLG carries no pre-judgments about the hierarchical order of institutions: global patterns of governance can hook up with local institutions just as local or regional coalitions of actors can bypass the nation-state level and pursue their interests in international arenas. MLG denotes a highly fluid and potential unstable institutional and policy matrix in which the powers and responsibilities of different actors and tiers of government are in flux. Increasingly, too, the new governance encompasses a wide variety of actors and processes beyond the state in which the relationships between state and non-state actors become less hierarchical and more interactive and the essential business of government is the regulation of public activities rather than the redistribution of resources.

. . .

In short, MLG means not only are there more levels of government but also the number and diversity of players involved has risen to include quasi-governmental and even private actors. Government has shifted from being state-centric to a more variegated and multi-faceted process of governance. The resulting increasing tension between a static 'territorial space' and dynamic 'functional space' causes many governance problems in terms of legitimacy and public accountability. Thus, the challenge is to accommodate and, if necessary adapt, the traditional systems of representative democracy associated 'old' government within these systems of 'new' and multi-level governance.

MULTI-LEVEL GOVERNANCE: THE EUROPEAN DIMENSION

Regionalism and European integration have steadily transformed the nature of national state and territorial politics across the members of the EU. The world's economic order has changed radically through the combined effects of globalisation in capital flows, the muscle of multinational corporations, and extensive technology transfer. The collapse of the Iron Curtain following the Velvet Revolutions in Eastern Europe unleashed unsavoury elements of nationalism while in Western Europe, regionalism, nationalism and separatism have been given a fillip. Concurrently, intergovernmental relations between EU members have been strengthened considerably with the creation of the Single Market and Euro, not least because their implementation and consequences demand concerted action by, and impose restrictions on, national governments. Together, these developments have fashioned a distinctive European political space, meriting being styled MLG.

Although not a theory to explain European integration, MLG is a highly descriptive conceptual model useful for explaining Europe's new governmental architecture. Thus, for many commentators, the situation within the EU illustrates MLG in practice. Marks G. et al (1996) contended that EU policy is produced by a complex web of interconnected institutions at the supranational, national subnational levels of government and that the locus of political control within states has shifted. A variety of channels and interconnections exist between different levels of government—supra, national and sub. No longer is there an unambiguous separation of domestic and international policies. Territorial and functional constituencies are overlapping and variable. Underpinning the outplay of MLG in the EU is the rather elusive principle of 'subsidiarity', essentially, that decisions made at the lowest possible level consistent/commensurate with them being effective. However, operationalising the term subsidiarity is not straightforward and, in truth, MLG is entrenched within EU policy making. The previously dyadic relationship between European institutions and national governments has been transformed into a triadic one among regions, national states and European actors. That said, there is not a homogenous tier of regions across Europe. That is, size, functions, and powers of regions vary from country to country and, indeed, within individual states, all of which serves to add to the growing complexity.

In terms of Member State to EU relations, Member State sovereignty has been diluted by both collective decision-making in the EU using qualified majority voting as well as the autonomous decisions of supranational EU institutions. The Centre within each Member State remains important but each has lost its respective national monopoly position. Thus, MLG conceives the EU as a post-national embryonic polity in its own right, in which power and influence are exercised at multiple levels of governance. . . .

Undeniably, the EU is more than just an additional vertical tier. It involves the transformation of European governance into a more federal and pluralist form. . . . For example, in the EU budgeting process, "the delivery system developed for the structural funds is characterised by MLG, i.e., the European Commission, national governments and regional and local authorities are formally autonomous, but there is a high level of shared responsibility at each stage of the decision-making process. The relationship between these is, accordingly, one of partnership and negotiation, rather than being a hierarchical one (Keating and Hooghe, 2001). Moreover, EU decision-making is not only by national governments but also by EU institutions and actors at other levels. Acting autonomously, the European Commission, the European Court of Justice and the European Parliament exert independent influence on EU policy process/outcomes. All told, Brussels is exercising an increasingly strong centrifugal force within the policy networks of the member states.

Similarly, *within* each Member State, sub-national units increasingly seek to advance their interests in EU using consultants, agents or formal representation—paradiplomacy, with some having become very accomplished actors (for instance, Spain's Catalonia and Germany's Baden-Würtemburg). Of course, such subnational activity should not be confused with influence. Nonetheless, subnational governments engage in activities not (wholly) controllable by national governments as well as in relationships with other subnational actors both with and beyond the borders of the home state. Indeed, the proliferation of networks between local authorities is foreshadowing a transformation of the existing power relations between local authorities, regional administrations, national governments and the European Commission.

Although there is no homogenous region model, the variety of sub-national governmental arrangements varies enormously across the different EU states. That said, Europeanisation has encouraged the erosion of the longstanding divide between federal and unitary states in the EU. In its place, a continuum has emerged. At one end of the spectrum are federal states such as Austria and Germany. Then there are 'regionalised' states such as Spain, Italy, and Belgium that exhibit federal characteristics but without fully fledged federal constitutions. Unitary states have become equally differentiated. Those with looser more decentralised systems include Finland, the Netherlands and Sweden while those remaining highly centralised include Greece and Portugal. The UK, so long one of Europe's most centralised unitary states has witnessed a progressive if rather uneven form of decentralisation since the late 1990s. . . .

Irrespective of its desirability or otherwise, as a depiction of the reality of contemporary governance in Europe, MLG is here to stay. British membership of the EU appears irrevocable, withdrawal inconceivable. Indeed, the UK has been drawn ever deeper into the EU thanks to the Single European Act (1986) and Maastricht Treaty on European Union (1992) which pooled collective decision-making of the Member States and diluted it through the extended use of majority voting as well as the sharing of EU legislative capacity with the European Parliament. The picture is complicated further by the fact that some states, brandishing the threat of using their veto on Treaty changes, have been granted leave to 'opt out' of some developments. Opting in and opting out has created a multi-track/speed Europe of variable geometry in its institutional architecture and policy transmission process. Political-juridical problems ensue such as representation, accountability and the legitimacy of decision-making. In effect, therefore, the EU offers an emerging menu that is increasingly *a la carte* rather than a uniform *table d'hote*. Thus, even having chosen to remain outside the Euro zone for the present, the UK remains nonetheless locked into a web of European governance. Progressive federalization seems inevitable given the inescapable logic of ever-closer union although it is a novel form of federalism that is emerging, quite distinct to current working models such as the USA (see Elazar, 1996).

. . .

Bibliography

Elazar D. (1996) 'From Statism to Federalism—A Paradigm Shift,' *International Political Science Review* Vol. 17 No. 4 pp. 417–29.

Keating M. and Hooghe L. (2001) Regions and the EU Policy Process, in Richardson J. (ed.) *European Union,* London: Routledge.

Marquand D (1998) *Must Labour Win?,* London: Fabian Society.

Marks G., Hooghe L., and Blank K. (1996) European Integration from the 1980s: State-Centric v. Multi-Level Governance, *Journal of Common Market Studies* Vol. 34 No. 3 pp. 341–378.

Tommel I. (1998) 'Transformation of Governance: The European Commission's Strategy for Creating a "Europe of the Regions,"' *Regional and Federal Studies* Vol. 8 No. 2 pp. 52–80.

STUDY AND DISCUSSION QUESTIONS

1. Define multi-level governance. How is it different from—and how similar to—the federalism that characterizes the American or the German model of government?

2. Carmichael suggests that multi-level governance is a descriptive term that does not prejudge the virtues or faults of the model. But, in your judgment, is MLG more of a prescription for effective governance within a complex decision-making environment—or a prescription for gridlock and confusion?

3. What lessons should American policy-makers and citizens take away from Carmichael's description of MLG in the European Union?

CHAPTER 3

State Power in the Era of Globalization: Case Studies

Some observers have suggested that globalization has led inevitably to the declining authority of the state with heads of government the last to know that their power—defined as the effective capacity to control policy outcomes—has all but evaporated. The arguments expressed in the selections in this chapter point in a very different direction. They suggest that globalization has complicated the exercise of state power and that the exercise of hegemonic power by the United States circumscribes the exercise of effective power by other states. And yet, unmistakably, these case studies in state power make it very clear that states matter and state power still makes the political world go round.

As Peter Gourevitch has argued, although the international system shapes domestic politics, there are always alternatives. Domestic politics—institutional arrangements, ideological preferences, and partisan considerations—determine what choices are made.* At the same time, as several of the selections that follow demonstrate, the most powerful states, and particularly the United States, can exert enormous power in the way they shape the institutions of economic and global governance—from the World Trade Organization to the United Nations—to serve their national interests and advance their geopolitical agendas. In the end, as Alexander Wendt observed, "states still are at the center of the international system, and as such it makes no more sense to criticize a theory of international politics as 'state-centric' than it does to criticize a theory of forests for being 'tree-centric.'"[†]

*Peter Gourevitch, *Politics in Hard Times* (Ithaca and London: Cornell University Press, 1986), pp. 35–68.
[†]Alexander Wendt, *Social Theory of International Politics* (Cambridge: Cambridge University Press, 1999), p. 9.

The selections in Chapter 3 are state-centric in the best sense, applying the lens of globalization to an analysis of state power in three comparative case studies: the United States, EU Europe (especially Britain, Germany, and France), and East Asia (with particular emphasis on the response of the Asian Tigers to the economic crisis of 1997). Taken together, they analyze how globalization shapes the exercise of state power—and how state power, in turn, shapes the contours, defines the goals, and determines the agendas of key institutions of global economic and political governance.

STUDY AND DISCUSSION QUESTIONS

1. Recall the competing paradigms introduced in Chapter 1. Which paradigm would best explain the economic crisis in East Asia in 1997? Which would best explain the range of responses to the crisis by particular states?

2. How would Mearsheimer explain the evolution of EU-U.S. relations since the end of the Cold War?

3. Does the unrivaled power of the United States make it all but impossible for other states to pursue independent geopolitical strategies? Economic and social models?

Globalization and the Exercise of American Power

9

Liberal Hegemony and the Future of the American Postwar Order

G. John Ikenberry

In this selection, G. John Ikenberry argues that American hegemony was built on a pair of postwar settlements (or tacit agreements about the era's institutionalized arrangements) that articulated a compelling vision for liberal hegemony. The more sharply drawn and acutely focused of the two was the "containment order" that consecrated the Cold War: a wary balance of power backed by nuclear deterrence and animated by ideological and geopolitical competition. More sweeping, but also more diffuse, was the broader vision for a liberal democratic order. American policy makers succeeded because they were able to make the case that free trade, an open trading system, and a set of multilateral institutions were in the broader interests of Western democracies.

Ikenberry argues that it was a case that could be sold convincingly to Asian and European partners because the United States was satisfied to "lock in" the terms of these favorable settlements, preferring stability and predictability to the uncertainty of an unconstrained hegemonic order in which the United States might aggrandize even greater power. Ikenberry argues that the willingness of the United States to exercise "strategic restraint"—and persuade potential partners of their commitment to the principles of a non-coercive and multilateral postwar order—was essential to achieving a settlement that was mutually acceptable to a group of states with huge power asymmetries.

INTRODUCTION

A remarkable aspect of world politics at century's end is the utter dominance of the United States. Fifty years after it emerged hegemonic, the United States is still the dominant world power at the center of a relatively stable and expanding democratic capitalist order. This is surprising. Most observers have expected dramatic shifts in world politics after the Cold War—such as the disappearance of American hegemony, the return of great power balancing, the rise of competing regional blocs, and the decay of multilateralism. Yet despite expectations of great transformations and new world orders, the half-century-old American order is still the dominant reality in world politics today.

This durable American order is a puzzle. Its relative material power capabilities have declined to be sure, but its larger package of political institutions, economic assets, and far-flung relations makes it a resilient and singular world power. The durability of the wider democratic capitalist order is also a puzzle. The conventional view is that the Cold War was an essential "glue" that held the advanced industrial countries together, dampening conflict and facilitating cooperation. Yet even without the Soviet threat and Cold War bipolarity, the United States along with Japan and Western Europe have reaffirmed their alliance partnerships, contained political conflicts, expanded trade and investment between them, and avoided a return to strategic rivalry and great power balance.

The durability of American hegemony and Western order is a puzzle primarily because scholars of international relations have tended to rely on realist theories of balance and hegemony to explain it. Realist theories of balance argue that order and cohesion in the West are a result of cooperation to balance against an external threat, in this case the Soviet Union, and with the disappearance of the threat, alliance and cooperation will decline (Waltz 1979; Mearsheimer 1990). Realist theories of hegemony argue that order is a result of the concentration of material power capabilities in a single state, which uses its commanding position to create and maintain order. With the decline of hegemonic power, order will decay. To understand the continued primacy of the United States and the continued durability and cohesion of the advanced industrial world, we need to go beyond our existing theories of hegemony and balance.

In particular, I want to make three arguments. First, I argue that the basic logic of order among the Western states was set in place before the Cold War, and it was a logic that addressed problems internal to Western capitalism and industrial society. Economic openness, reciprocity, multilateral management—these were, and continue to be, the organizing arrangements of a distinctively liberal Western order. Although the Cold War reinforced this liberal order, it was not triggered by or ultimately dependent on the Cold War for its functioning and stability. The "containment order" ended along with the Cold War, but the much more deeply rooted Western liberal order lives on.

Second, I argued that in the wake of World War II, American hegemony was built around decidedly liberal features. Here the problem was how to build a durable and mutually acceptable order among a group of states with huge power asymmetries. The penetrated character of American hegemony, allowing for access by secondary states, and binding economic and security institutions, provided mechanisms to increase confidence that the participating states would remain within the order and operate according to its rules and institutions. Liberal hegemony involves institutions and practices that reduce the returns to power; that is, they reduce the long-term implications of asymmetries of power. Agreement results from a trade-off; the hegemonic state gets commitments by secondary states to participate within the hegemonic order, and in return the hegemon places limits on the exercise of its power. The weaker states are not as inclined to fear domination or abandonment and the leading state does not need to use its power assets to enforce order and compliance.

Third, I argue that the American hegemonic order has actually become more stable because the rules and institutions have become more firmly embedded in the wider structures of politics and society. This is an argument about the increasing returns to institution, in this case American and Western security and economic institutions. Over the decades, the core institutions of Western order have sunk their roots ever more deeply into the political and economic structures of the states that participate within the order. The result is that it is becoming increasingly difficult for "alternative institutions" or "alternative leadership" to seriously emerge. American hegemony has become institutionalized and path-dependent—that is, more and more people will have to disrupt their lives if the order is to radically change. This makes wholesale change less likely.

Overall, the durability of American liberal hegemony is built on two core logics. First, the constitution-like character of the institutions and practices of the order serves to reduce the "returns to power," which lowers the risks of participation by strong and weak states alike. This, in turn, makes a resort to balancing and relative gains competition less necessary. Second, the institutions also exhibit an "increasing returns" character, which makes it more and more difficult for would-be orders and would-be hegemonic powers to compete against and replace the existing order and leader.

The implication of this analysis is that the American hegemonic order is a relatively stable and expansive political order. This is not only because the United States is an unmatched economic and military power today, but also because it is uniquely capable of engaging in "strategic restraint," reassuring partners and facilitating cooperation. Because of its distinctively penetrated domestic political system, and because of the array of international institutions it has created to manage political conflict, the United States has been able to remain at the center of a large and expanding hegemonic order. Its capacity to win in specific struggles with others within the system may rise and fall, but the larger hegemonic order remains in place with little prospect of decline.

TWO POSTWAR SETTLEMENTS

World War II produced two postwar settlements. One was a reaction to deteriorating relations with the Soviet Union, and it culminated in the containment order. It was a settlement based on the balance of power, nuclear deterrence, and political and ideological competition. The other settlement was a reaction to the economic rivalry and political turmoil of the 1930s and the resulting world war, and it culminated in a wide range of new institutions and relations among the Western industrial democracies—a Western liberal order. This settlement was built around economic openness, political reciprocity, multilateral institutions, and joint management of relations.

The Cold War did play a role in reinforcing Western solidarity by dampening incentives to engage in relative gains competition. Cold War threats were also useful to American officials as they sought to convince an otherwise reluctant Congress to appropriate funds for postwar reconstruction and assistance. Cold War bipolarity also gave the United States added hegemonic leverage at critical moments in the management of Western order. But the two settlements had distinct political visions, intellectual rationales, political logics, and (as has become clear lately) historical trajectories.

The containment order is well known in the popular imagination. It is celebrated in our historical accounts of the early years after World War II, when intrepid American officials struggled to make sense of Soviet military power and geopolitical intentions. In these early years, a few "wise men" fashioned a coherent and reasoned response to the global challenge of Soviet communism. The doctrine of containment that emerged was the core concept that gave clarity and purpose to several decades of American foreign policy. In the decades that followed, sprawling bureaucratic and military organizations were built on the containment orientation. The bipolar division of the world, nuclear weapons of growing size and sophistication, the ongoing clash of two expansive ideologies—all these circumstances gave life to and reinforced the centrality of the containment order.

By comparison, the ideas and policies of Western liberal order were more diffuse and wide-ranging. It was less obvious that the liberal democratic agenda was a "grand strategy" designed to advance American security interests. As a result, during the Cold War it was inevitable that this agenda would be seen as secondary—a preoccupation of economists and American business. The policies and institutions that supported free trade and economic openness among the advanced industrial societies were quintessentially the stuff of "low politics." But this view is wrong. The liberal democratic agenda was built on a robust and sophisticated set of ideas about American security interests, the causes of war and depression, and the proper and desirable foundations of postwar political order. Indeed, although the containment order overshadowed it, the ideas behind postwar liberal democratic order were more deeply rooted in the American experience and a thoroughgoing understanding of history, economics, and the sources of political order.

The most basic conviction behind the postwar liberal agenda was that the closed autarkic regions that had contributed to world depression and split the world into competing blocs before the war must be broken up and replaced by an open and nondiscriminatory world economic system. Peace and security were impossible in a world of closed and exclusive economic regions. The challengers to liberal multilateralism occupied almost every corner of the advanced industrial world. Germany and Japan, of course, were the most overt and hostile challengers. Each had pursued a dangerous pathway into the modern industrial age that combined authoritarian capitalism with military dictatorship and coercive regional autarky. But the British Commonwealth and its imperial preference system was also a challenge to liberal multilateral order. The hastily drafted Atlantic Charter was at American effort to insure that Britain signed onto its liberal democratic war aims. The joint statement of principles affirmed free trade, equal access for countries to the raw materials of the world, and international collaboration in the economic field so as to advance labor standards, employment security, and social welfare. Roosevelt and Churchill insisted on telling the world that they had learned the lessons of the interwar years—and those lessons were fundamentally about the proper organization of the Western world economy. It was not just America's enemies, but also its friends and America itself, that had to be reformed and integrated.

This liberal "grand strategy" for building order within the Western world reflected a confluence of ideas and designs from a wide array of American officials and thinkers involved in making postwar policy. One group, located primarily at the State Department and inspired by Cordell Hull, was primarily interested in creating an open trading system after the war. They gave voice to the old liberal view that free trade and open economies would check tyranny and military aggression and reinforce peaceful international relations. Trade officials at the State Department saw liberal trade as a core American interest that reached back to the Open Door policy of the 1890s. Their argument was not just that free trade would advance American interests, but that an open trading system was an essential element of a stable world political order.

Another group of thinkers was concerned with creating political order among the democracies of the North Atlantic region. This vision was of a community or union between the United States, Britain, and the wider Atlantic world. Ideas of an Atlantic union can be traced to the turn of the century and a few British and American statesmen and thinkers, such as John Hay, British

Ambassador to Washington Lord Bryce, American Ambassador to London Walter Hines Page, Admiral Alfred T. Mahan, and Henry Adams. These ideas resurfaced during and after World War II, reflecting a variety of convictions and historical experiences: that the failure of the League of Nations revealed the virtues of a less universal security community; and that there was a pressing need to protect the shared democratic values and institutions that united the Atlantic world.

Another position on postwar order was animated more directly by considerations of American geopolitical interests and the Eurasian rimlands. This is where American strategic thinkers began their debates in the 1930s, as they witnessed the collapse of the world economy and the emergence of German and Japanese regional blocs. The question these thinkers pondered was whether the United States could remain as a great industrial power within the confines of the Western Hemisphere. What were the minimum geographical requirements for the country's economic and military viability? For all practical purposes this question was answered by the time the United States entered the war. An American hemispheric bloc would not be sufficient; the United States must have security of markets and raw materials in Asia and Europe. If the rimlands of Europe and Asia became dominated by one or several hostile imperial powers, the security implications for the United States would be catastrophic. To remain a great power, the United States could not allow itself "merely to be a buffer state between the mighty empires of Germany and Japan" (Spykman 1942: 195). It must seek openness, access, and balance in Europe and Asia.

Finally, a related view of postwar order was concerned with encouraging political and economic unity in Western Europe, creating in effect a European "third force." This view emerged as a strategic option as cooperation with the Soviet Union began to break down after the war. As officials in the State Department began to rethink relations with Western Europe and the Soviet Union, a new policy emphasis emerged concerned with the establishment of a strong and economically integrated Europe. The idea was to encourage a multipolar postwar system, with Europe as a relatively independent center of power. The policy shift was not to a bipolar or spheres-of-influence approach with a direct and ongoing American military and economic presence in Europe. Rather, the aim was to build Europe into an independent center of military and economic power.

These various positions on postwar order reflect the diversity of agendas and problems that officials sought to address—but they shared an underlying view that the major Western industrial powers must be united and interconnected in new and fundamental ways. Several additional conclusions follow. First, it is clear that sophisticated and well-developed sets of ideas and plans about postwar order predated the rise of bipolarity and containment. Indeed, it is remarkable how late and reluctant the United States was in organizing its foreign policy around a global balance of power.

Second, most of the ideas that were proposed and debated before containment and the breakdown of relations with the Soviet Union dealt with the reconstruction of relations within the West, particularly among the Atlantic countries. American officials were clearly preoccupied with how to stabilize Europe and integrate the Atlantic world into the core of a wider postwar order. Some postwar designs were more universal, such as those concerning free trade and global governance, but they also were to be anchored in a deepened set of relations and institutions among the Western democracies. Other ideas, such as the geopolitical arguments about access to the Eurasian rimlands, saw the stability and integration of the liberal capitalist world in essentially instrumental terms. But the goals and policies would have the same result. Likewise, many who supported NATO and containment did so not simply to build an alliance against the Soviet Union but also because these initiatives would feed back into the Western liberal democratic order. NATO was partly a structure designed to reintegrate Germany into the West—partly to counter Soviet power, but also to reconstruct and reintegrate Germany as a liberal capitalist country. It was both a means and an end.

Third, even many of the advocates of containment and the preservation of the European balance were also concerned with safeguarding and strengthening liberal democratic institutions in the West. One virtue that Kennan saw in a multipolar postwar order was that it would help to protect the liberal character of American politics and institutions. Kennan worried that if bipolar order emerged, the United States might find itself trying to impose political institutions on other states within its sphere and that would eventually threaten its domestic institutions. The encouragement of dispersed authority and power centers abroad would reinforce pluralism at home.

American postwar thinkers and planners did not wait until the Cold War clarified necessary principles and policies of American foreign policy. Those ideas and policies were already actively being formulated, debated, and implemented. The postwar liberal democratic settlement among the Western industrial countries reflected a synthesis of various intellectual, historical, and political strands of thinking and experience. But in this amalgam of ideas and agendas was a vision of America's basic postwar goal—to secure an open, stable, interconnected, legitimate, and jointly managed community of Western industrial democracies.

LIMITING THE RETURNS TO POWER

The United States had a postwar agenda to build a new structure of relations among the industrial Western powers. But how actually was agreement secured? How was it that American dominance was rendered acceptable to the Western Europeans and Japanese? Why was it that the Europeans and Japanese did not balance against American power, returning the industrial countries to a world of strategic rivalry, fragmentation, and estrangement? How were American hegemony and the great upheaval of the war turned into a widely acceptable political order?

The answer is that the United States engaged (through policy and structural circumstance) in "strategic restraint," thereby reassuring its would-be European and Asian partners that participation in the American postwar order would not entail coercive domination. In other words, the United States gained the acquiescence of secondary states by accepting limits on the exercise of its own hegemonic power. At the heart of the American hegemonic order is an ongoing trade-off: the United States agrees to operate within an institutionalized political process and, in return, its partners agree to be willing participants.

This logic is seen most clearly in the immediate aftermath of World War II, when the asymmetries in power relations between the United States and the other Western industrial countries were most extreme. At such moments, there are incentives for the victorious and suddenly hegemonic state to construct a postwar order that is legitimate and durable. That is, there are incentives for the leading state to convert its favorable postwar power position into a durable political order that commands the allegiance of the other states within it. To achieve a legitimate order means to secure agreement among the relevant states on the basic rules and principles of political order. A legitimate political order is one whose members willingly participate and agree with the overall orientation of the system. They abide by its rules and principles because they accept them as desirable—they embrace them as their own.

More specifically, the newly emerged hegemon has an incentive to move toward a "constitutional" settlement after the war—that is, to create basic institutions and operating principles that limit what the leading state can do with its power. In effect, constitutional agreements reduce the implications of "winning" in international relations, or, to put it more directly, they serve to reduce the returns to power. This is fundamentally what constitutions do within domestic orders. They set limits on what a state that gains disproportionately within the order can do with those gains, thereby reducing the stakes of uneven gains. This means that they reduce the possibilities that a state can turn short-term gains into a long-term power advantage. Taken together, constitutional agreements set limits on what actors can do with momentary advantages. Losers realize that their losses are limited and temporary—to accept those losses is not to risk everything nor will it give the winner a permanent advantage.

If agreements can be reached on constitutional arrangements after the war, the asymmetries in power are rendered more tolerable by secondary states. This is potentially an attractive outcome for weaker states for two reasons. First, if the actions of the hegemonic state are carried out (more or less) within an agreed upon and institutionalized political process, it means that competition over outcomes will not simply be determined by brute material power, which will always work to the advantage of the leading state. Second, the institutionalized settlement creates greater certainty over what the hegemonic state will do in the future. The possibility of indiscriminate and ruthless domination is mitigated. Just as importantly, the possibility of abandonment is also lessened. If the hegemonic state is rendered more predictable, this means that the secondary states do not need to spend as many resources on "risk premiums," which would otherwise be needed to prepare for either domination or abandonment.

But why would a newly hegemonic state want to restrict itself by agreeing to limits on the use of hegemonic power? The basic answer is that a constitutional settlement conserves hegemonic power, and this for two reasons. First, if the hegemonic state calculates that its overwhelming postwar power advantages are only momentary, an institutionalized order might "lock in" favorable arrangements that continue beyond the zenith of its power. In effect, the creation of basic ordering institutions is a form of hegemonic investment in the future. The hegemonic state gives up some freedom on the use of its power in exchange for a durable and predictable order that safeguards its interests in the future.

This investment motive rests on several assumptions. The hegemonic state must be convinced that its power position will ultimately decline. If it does, it should want to use its momentary position to get things that it wants accomplished. On the other hand, if the new hegemon calculates that its power position will remain preponderant into the foreseeable future, the incentive to conserve its power will disappear. Also, the hegemon must be convinced that the institutions it creates will persist beyond its own power capabilities—that is, it must calculate that these institutions have some independent ordering capacity. If institutions are seen as simply isomorphic with the distribution of power, the appeal of an institutional settlement will obviously decline.

The second reason why a hegemon might want to reach agreement on basic institutions, even if it means giving up some autonomy and short-term advantage, is that it can reduce the "enforcement costs" for maintaining order. The constant use of power capabilities to punish and reward secondary states and resolve conflicts is costly. It is far more effective over the long term to shape the interests and orientations of other states than to directly shape their actions through coercion and inducements. A constitutional settlement reduces the necessity of the costly expenditure of resources by the leading state on bargaining, monitoring, and enforcement.

Even if there are reasons why the leading and secondary states might favor a constitutional order, it is not obvious that they would accept the risks seemingly inherent in such an order. The leading state, in placing limits on its use of power, must be confident that it will not be exploited by secondary states, and secondary states must be confident that they are not opening themselves up to domination or abandonment by the leading state. In effect, each state agrees to forswear a range of actions that, in the absence of guarantees that the other state will also abide by the limits, it would be prudent to pursue. For self-regarding states to agree to pursue their interests within binding institutions, they must convey to each other a credible sense of commitment—an assurance that they will not abandon their mutual restraint and exploit momentary advantages.

There were a variety of ways in which the United States and its prospective partners were able to overcome these constraints and create reassurances and credible commitments—all of which reflect the remarkably liberal character of American hegemony. These include America's policy of "strategic restraint" over postwar order; the "penetrated" character of American hegemony, which provides opportunities for voice and reciprocity in hegemonic relations; and the use of "institutional binding" as a mechanism to mutually constrain the hegemon and secondary states. In each of these ways, the postwar order was established in a way that served to limit the returns to power.

The first way in which the United States provided reassurances to its partners was in its basic orientation toward postwar order—that it was a "reluctant hegemon" in many respects, and that it fundamentally sought agreement among the Western states on a mutually acceptable order, even if this meant extensive compromise. It is revealing that the initial and most forcefully presented American view on postwar order was the State Department's proposal for a postwar system of free trade. This proposal did not only reflect an American conviction about the virtues of open markets, but it also was a vision of order that would require very little direct American involvement or management. The system would be largely self-regulating, leaving the United States to operate within it, but without the burdens of direct and ongoing supervision.

This view on postwar trade reflected a more general American orientation as the war came to an end. It wanted a world order that would advance American interests, but it was not eager to actively organize and run that order. It is in this sense that the United States was a reluctant superpower. This general characteristic was not lost on Europeans, and it mattered as America's potential partners contemplated whether and how to cooperate with the United States. To the extent the United States could convey the sense that it did not seek to dominate the Europeans, it gave greater credibility to America's proposals for a constitutional settlement. It provided some reassurance that the United States would operate within limits and not use its overwhelming power position simply to dominate.

This orientation was reflected in the compromises that the United States made in accommodating European views about the postwar world economy. The British and the continental Europeans, worried about postwar depression and the protection of their fragile economies, were not eager to embrace America's stark proposals for an open world trading system, favoring a more regulated and compensatory system. The United States did attempt to use its material resources to pressure and induce Britain and the other European countries to abandon bilateral and regional preferential agreements and accept the principles of a postwar economy organized around a nondiscriminatory system of trade and payments. The United States knew it held a commanding position and sought to use its power to give the postwar order a distinctive shape. But it also prized agreement over deadlock, and it ultimately moved a great distance away from its original proposals in setting up the various postwar economic institutions.

A second major way that the United States projected reassurance was structural—its own liberal democratic polity. The open and decentralized character of the American political system provided opportunities for other states to exercise their "voice" in the operation of the American hegemonic order, thereby reassuring these states that their interests could be actively advanced and processes of conflict resolution would exist. In this sense, the American postwar order was a "penetrated hegemony," an extended system that blurred domestic and international politics as it created an elaborate transnational and transgovernmental political system with the United States at its center.

There are actually several ways in which America's penetrated hegemony serves to reinforce the credibility of the United States' commitment to operating within an institutionalized political order. The first is simply the transparency of the system, which reduces surprises and allays worries by partners that the United States might make abrupt changes in policy. This transparency comes from the fact that policy-making in a large, decentralized democracy involves many players and an extended and relatively visible political process. But not only is it an open and decentralized system, it is also one with competing political parties and an independent press—features that serve to expose the underlying integrity and viability of major policy commitments. The open and competitive process may produce mixed and ambiguous policies at times, but the transparency of the process at least allows other states to make more accurate calculations about the likely direction of American foreign policy, which lowers levels of uncertainty and provides a measure of reassurance—which, everything else being equal, provides greater opportunities to cooperate.

Another way in which the penetrated hegemonic order provides reassurances to partners is that the American system invites (or at least provides opportunities for) the participation of outsiders. The fragmented and penetrated American system allows and invites the proliferation of a vast network of transnational and transgovernmental relations with Europe, Japan, and other parts of the industrial world. Diffuse and dense networks of governmental, corporate, and private associations tie the system together. The United States is the primary site for the pulling and hauling of trans-Atlantic and trans-Pacific politics. Europeans and Japanese do not have elected officials in Washington—but they do have representatives. Although this access to the American political process is not fully reciprocated abroad, the openness and extensive decentralization of the American liberal system assures other states that they have routine access to the decision-making processes of the United States.

A final way in which reassurance was mutually conveyed was in the institutions themselves, which provided "lock in" and "binding" constraints on the United States and its partners, thereby mitigating fears of domination or abandonment. The Western countries made systematic efforts to anchor their joint commitments in principled and binding institutional mechanisms. Governments might ordinarily seek to preserve their options, to cooperate with other states but to leave open the option of disengaging. What the United States and the other Western states did after the war was exactly the opposite: they built long-term economic, political, and security commitments that were difficult to retract. They "locked in" their commitments and relationships, to the extent that this can be done by sovereign states.

The practice of institutional binding makes sense only if international institutions or regimes can have an independent ordering impact on the actions of states. The assumption is that institutions are sticky—that they can take on a life and logic of their own, shaping and constraining even the states that create them. When states employ institutional binding as a strategy, they are essentially agreeing to mutually constrain themselves. In effect, institutions specify what it is that states are expected to do and they make it difficult and costly for states to do otherwise. In the case of international institutions, examples of binding mechanisms include treaties, interlocking organizations, joint management responsibilities, agreed upon standards and principles of relations, and so forth. These mechanisms raise the "costs of exit" and create "voice opportunities," thereby providing mechanisms to mitigate or resolve the conflict.

The Bretton Woods economic and monetary accords exhibit the institutional binding logic. These were the first accords to establish a permanent international institutional and legal framework to ensure economic cooperation between states. They were constructed as elaborate systems of rules and obligations with quasi-judicial procedures for adjudicating disputes. In effect, the Western governments created an array of functionally organized transnational political systems. Moreover, the democratic character of the United States and the other Western countries facilitated the construction of these dense interstate connections. The permeability of domestic institutions provided congenial grounds for reciprocal and pluralistic "pulling and hauling" across the advanced industrial world.

It was here that the Cold War's security alliances provided additions institutional binding opportunities. The old saying that NATO was created to "keep the Russians out, the Germans down, and the Americans in" is a statement about the importance of the alliance structures for locking in long-term commitments and expectations. The American-Japanese security alliance also had a similar "dual containment" character. These institutions not only served as alliances in the ordinary sense as organized efforts to balance against external threats, they also provided mechanisms and venues to build political relations, conduct business, and regulate conflict.

The constitutional features of the Western order have been particularly important for Germany and Japan. Both countries were reintegrated into the advanced industrial world as "semi-sovereign" powers; that is, they accepted unprecedented constitutional limits on their military capacity and independence (Katzenstein 1987). As such, they became unusually dependent on the array of Western regional and multilateral economic and security institutions. The Western political order in which they were embedded was integral to their stability and functioning. The Christian Democrat Walther Leisler Kiep argued in 1972 that "the German-American alliance . . . is not merely one aspect of modern German history, but a decisive element as a result of its preeminent place in our politics. In effect, it provides a second constitution for our country" (Schwartz 1995: 555). Western economic and security institutions provide Germany and Japan with a political bulwark of stability that far transcends their more immediate and practical purposes.

Overall, American hegemony is reluctant, penetrated, and highly institutionalized. All these characteristics have helped to facilitate a rather stable and durable political order. American strategic restraint after the war left Europeans more worried about abandonment than domination, and they actively sought American institutionalized commitments to Europe. The American polity's transparency and permeability fostered an "extended" political order—reaching outward to the other industrial democracies—with most of its roads leading to Washington. Transnational and transgovernmental relations provide the channels. Multiple layers of economic, political, and security institutions bind these countries together in ways that reinforce the credibility of their mutual commitments. The United States remains the center of the system, but other states are highly integrated into it, and its legitimacy diminishes the need for the exercise of coercive power by the United States or for balancing responses from secondary states.

AMERICAN HEGEMONY AND INCREASING RETURNS

The bargains struck and institutions created at the early moments of American hegemony have not simply persisted for fifty years, but they have actually become more deeply rooted in the wider structures of politics and society of the countries that participate within the order. That is, more people and more of their activities are hooked into the institutions and operations of the American liberal hegemonic order. A wider array of individuals and groups, in more countries and more realms of activity, has a stake—or a vested interest—in the continuation of the system. The costs of disruption or change in this system have steadily grown over the decades. Together, this means that "competing orders" or "alternative institutions" are at a disadvantage. The system is increasingly hard to replace.

The reason institutions have a "lock in" effect is primarily because of the phenomenon of increasing returns. There are several aspects to increasing returns to institutions. First, there are large initial start-up costs to creating new institutions. Even when alternative institutions might be more efficient or accord more closely with the interests of powerful states, the gains from the new institutions must be overwhelmingly greater before they overcome the sunk costs of the existing institutions. Moreover, there tend to be learning effects that are achieved in the operation of the existing institution that give it advantages over a new start-up institution. Finally, institutions tend to create relations and commitments with other actors and institutions that serve to embed the institution and raise the costs of change. Taken together, as Douglass North concludes, "the interdependent web of an institutional matrix produces massive increasing returns" (North 1990: 95).

When institutions manifest increasing returns, it becomes very difficult for potential replacement institutions to compete and succeed. The logic is seen most clearly in regard to competing technologies. The history of the videocassette recorder is the classic example, where two formats, VHS and Beta, competed for standardization. The two formats were introduced at roughly the same time and initially had equal market share, but soon the VHS format, through luck and circumstances unrelated to efficiency, expanded its market share. Increasing returns on early gains tilted the competition toward VHS, allowing it to accumulate enough advantages to take over the market. Even if Beta was ultimately a superior technology, a very small market advantage by VHS at an early and critical moment allowed it to lower its production costs, and the accumulation of connecting technologies and products that require compatibility made it increasingly hard for the losing technology to compete. The costs of switching to the other technology rise as production costs are lowered, learning effects accumulate, and the technology gets embedded in a wider system of compatible and interdependent technologies.

American postwar hegemonic order has exhibited this phenomenon of increasing returns to its institutions. At the early moments after 1945, when the imperial, bilateral, and regional alternatives to America's postwar agenda were most imminent, the United States was able to use its unusual and momentary advantages to tilt the system in the direction it desired. The pathway to the present liberal hegemonic order began at a very narrow passage where really only Britain and the United States—and a few top officials—could shape decisively the basic orientation of the world political economy. But once the institutions, such as Bretton Woods and GATT, were established, it became increasingly hard for competing visions of postwar order to have any viability. America's great burst of institution-building after World War II fits a general pattern of international continuity and change: crisis or war opens up a moment of flux and opportunity, choices get made, and interstate relations get fixed or settled for a while.

The notion of increasing returns to institutions means that once a moment of institutional selection comes and goes, the cost of large-sale institutional change rises dramatically—even if potential institutions, when compared with existing ones, are more efficient and desirable. In terms of American hegemony, this means that, short of a major war or a global economic collapse, it is very difficult to envisage the type of historical breakpoint needed to replace the existing order. This would be true even if a new would-be hegemon or coalition of states had an interest in and agenda for an alternative set of global institutions—which they do not.

While the increasing returns to institutions can serve to perpetuate institutions of many sorts, American hegemonic institutions have characteristics that particularly lend themselves to increasing returns. First, the set of principles that infuses these institutions—particularly principles of multilateralism, openness, and reciprocity—are ones that command agreement because of their seeming fairness and legitimacy. Organized around principles that are easy for states to accept, regardless of their specific international power position, the institutional pattern is more robust and easy to expand. Moreover, the principled basis of hegemonic order also makes it more durable. This is Ruggie's argument about the multilateral organization of postwar international institutions: "all other things being equal, an arrangement based on generalized organizing principles should be more elastic than one based on particularistic interests and situational exigencies" (Ruggie 1993:32–3). Potential alternative institutional orders are at an added disadvantage because the principles of the current institutional order are adaptable, expandable, and easily accepted as legitimate.

Second, the open and permeable character of American hegemonic institutions also serves to facilitate increasing returns. One of the most important aspects of increasing returns is that once a particular institution is established, other institutions and relations tend to grow up around it and become interconnected and mutually dependent. A good analogy is computer software, where a software provider like Microsoft, after gaining an initial market advantage, encourages the proliferation of software applications and programs based on Microsoft's operating language. This, in turn, leads to a huge complex of providers and users who are heavily dependent on the Microsoft format. The result is an expanding market community of individuals and firms with an increasingly dense set of commitments to Microsoft—commitments that are not based on loyalty but on the growing reality that changing to another format would be more costly, even if it were more efficient.

The penetrated character of American hegemony encourages this sort of proliferation of connecting groups and institutions. A dense set of transnational and transgovernmental channels are woven into the trilateral regions of the advanced industrial world. A sort of layer cake of inter-governmental institutions spans outward from the United States across the Atlantic and Pacific. Global multilateral economic institutions, such as the IMF and WTO, are connected to more circumscribed governance institutions, such as the G7 and G10. Private groups, such as the Trilateral Commission and hundreds of business trade associations, are also connected in one way or another to individual governments and their joint management institutions. The steady rise of trade and investment across the advanced industrial world has made these countries more interdependent, which in turn has expanded the constituency within these countries for a perpetuation of an open, multilateral system.

What this means is that great shifts in the basic organization of the American hegemonic order are increasingly costly to a widening array of individuals and groups who make up the order. More and more people have a stake in the system, even if they have no particular loyalty or affinity for the United States and even if they might really prefer a different order. As the postwar era has worn on, the operating institutions of the American hegemonic order have expanded and deepened. More and more people would have their lives disrupted if the system were to be radically changed—which is another way of saying that the constituency for preserving the postwar political order among the major industrial countries is greater than ever before. It is in this sense that the American postwar order is stable and growing.

CONCLUSION

The twentieth century began as a world dominated by a handful of great powers, but it will end dominated by a single superpower. The character of that domination is as interesting and remarkable as the fact of its existence. American domination or hegemony is very unusual, and the larger political order that surrounds it is unique as well. Fundamentally, American hegemony is reluctant, penetrated, and highly institutionalized—or in a word, liberal. This is what makes it unusual, and it is also what makes it so stable and expansive.

Even with the end of the Cold War and the shifting global distribution of power, the relations between the United States and the other industrial countries of Europe and Asia remain remarkably stable and cooperative. This chapter offers two major reasons why American hegemony has endured and facilitated cooperation and integration among the major industrial countries rather than triggered balancing and estrangement. Both reasons underscore the importance of the liberal features of American hegemony.

First, the United States moved very quickly after the war to insure that relations among the liberal democracies would take place within an institutionalized political process. In effect, the United States offered the other countries a bargain: if the United States agreed to operate within mutually acceptable institutions, thereby muting the implications of power asymmetries, the other countries would agree to be willing participants as well. The United States got the acquiescence of the other Western states, and they in turn got the reassurance that the United States would neither dominate nor abandon them.

The stability of this bargain comes from its underlying logic: the postwar hegemonic order is infused with institutions and practices that reduce the returns to power. This means that the implications of winning and losing are minimized and contained. A state could "lose" in intra-Western relations and yet not worry that the winner will be able to use those winnings to permanently dominate. This is a central characteristic of domestic liberal constitutional orders. Parties that win elections must operate within well-defined limits. They cannot use their powers of incumbency to undermine or destroy the opposition party. They can press the advantage of office to the limits of the law, but there are limits and laws. This reassures the losing party; it can accept its loss and prepare for the next election. The features of the postwar order—and, importantly, the open and penetrated character of the American polity itself—have mechanisms to provide the same sort of assurances to America's European and Asian partners.

Secondly, the institutions of American hegemony also have a durability that comes from the phenomenon of increasing returns. The overall system—organized around principles of openness, reciprocity, and multilateralism—has become increasingly connected to the wider and deeper institutions of politics and society within the advanced industrial world. As the embeddedness of these institutions has grown, it has become increasingly difficult for potential rival states to introduce a competing set of principles and institutions. American hegemony has become highly institutionalized and path-dependent. Short of large-scale war or a global economic crisis, the American hegemonic order appears to be immune from would-be hegemonic challengers. Even if a large coalition of states had interests that favored an alternative type of order, to justify change, the benefits would have to be radically higher than are those that flow from the present system. But there is no potential hegemonic state (or coalition of states) and no set of rival principles and organizations even on the horizon. The world of the 1940s contained far more rival systems, ideologies, and interests than the world of the 1990s.

The phenomenon of increasing returns is really a type of positive feedback loop. If initial institutions are established successfully, where the United States and its partners have confidence in their credibility and functioning, this allows these states to make choices that serve to strengthen the binding character of these institutions.

The American hegemonic order fits this basic logic. Its open and penetrated character invites participation and creates assurances of steady commitment. Its institutionalized character also provides mechanisms for the resolution of conflicts and creates assurances of continuity. Within this liberal and institutionalized order, the fortunes of particular states will continue to rise and fall. The United States itself, while remaining at the center of the order, also continues to experience gains and losses. But the mix of winning and losing across the system is distributed widely enough to mitigate the interest that particular states might have in replacing it. In an order where the returns to power are low and the returns to institutions are high, stability will be its essential feature.

References

Mearsheimer, John 1990, "Why We Will Soon Miss the Cold War," *The Atlantic Monthly* 266: 35–50.

North, Douglass C. 1990, *Institutions, Institutional Change and Economic Performance,* New York: Cambridge University Press.

Ruggie, John G. 1993, "Multilateralism: The Anatomy of an Institution," in *Multilateralism Matters,* Ruggie (ed.), New York: Columbia University Press, pp. 3–47.

Schwartz, Thomas A. 1995, "The United States and Germany after 1945: Alliances, Transnational Relations, and the Legacy of the Cold War," *Diplomatic History* 19: 549–68.

Spykman, Nicholas 1942, *America's Strategy in the World,* New York: Harcourt, Brace.

Waltz, Kenneth 1979, *Theory of International Politics,* New York: Wiley.

Weber, Steve 1995, "Shaping the Postwar Balance of Power," in *Multilateralism Matters,* John Gerard Ruggie (ed.), New York: Columbia University Press, pp. 233–92.

STUDY AND DISCUSSION QUESTIONS

1. Why were the two postwar settlements described by Ikenberry so important for the stability of the post–World War II order? Are they still in place?
2. Does Ikenberry consider the consolidation of American hegemony the result of a grand strategy? Why—or why not?
3. Does the post–9/11 foreign policy of the United States mark a decisive break with the doctrine of strategic restraint?

10

America's Empire Rules an Unbalanced World

Robert Hunter Wade

Is American hegemony (and perhaps the "new American empire") the result of explicit bargains and grand designs—or simply a product of the institutionalized framework of the global financial and economic system? In this selection Robert Hunter Wade downplays the intentionality or grand vision associated with American hegemony. Instead, he emphasizes the powerful advantages of key "hand-wired" features of the international political economy that buttress the geopolitical and economic power of the United States. Wade contends that these structural features guarantee that globalization reinforces U.S. power by yielding disproportionate economic and geopolitical benefits.

Hence, argues Wade, the rest of the world is harnessed to the economic rhythms of the United States. Not only can the hegemonic power pull the levers to advance its interests with reference to financial markets and international trade. It can also use its dominance in military affairs and in the arenas of global governance to advance parochial policy aims, whether unilaterally or through multilateral institutions. In the end, argues Wade, the architectural design of American hegemony produces an unequal world order, inviting serious consideration of a fundamental redesign.

Suppose you are a modern-day Roman emperor, the leader of the most powerful country in a world of sovereign states and international markets. What sort of framework of international political economy arrangements do you create so that without having to throw your weight around more than occasionally, normal market forces bolster the economic preeminence of your country, allow your citizens to consume far more than they themselves produce, and keep challengers down?

You want autonomy to decide on your exchange rate and monetary policy in response only to your own national objectives, while having other countries depend on your support in managing their own economies. You want to be able to engineer volatility and economic crises in the rest of the world in order to hinder the growth of centers that might challenge your preeminence and in order to allow your vulture funds periodically to buy up their assets at fire-sale prices. You want intense competition between exporters in the rest of the world that gives you an inflow of imports at constantly decreasing prices relative to the price of your exports.

You want to invite the best brains in the rest of the world to come to your universities, companies and research institutes. You befriend the middle classes elsewhere and make sure they have good material reasons for supporting the framework. You make it unlikely that elites and masses should ever unite in nativistic reactions to your dominance or demand "nationalistic" development policies that nurture competitors to your industries.

What features do you hard-wire into the international political economy? First, free capital mobility. Second, free trade (excepting imports that threaten domestic industries important for your re-selection). Third, international investment free from any discriminatory favoring of national companies through protection, public procurement, public ownership or other devices, with special emphasis on the freedom of your companies to get the custom of national elites for the management of their financial assets, their private education, health care, pensions, and the like.

Fourth, your currency as the main reserve currency. Fifth, no constraint on your ability to create your currency at will (such as a dollar-gold link), so that you can finance unlimited trade deficits with the rest of the world. Sixth, international lending at variable interest rates denominated in your currency, which means that borrowing countries in crisis have to repay you more when their capacity to repay is less.

This combination allows your people to consume far more than they produce; it periodically produces financial instability and crises in the rest of the world, which hold back the crisis-affected countries and also cause other governments to hold more of your currency and therefore help to finance your deficits; and it allows your firms and your capital to enter and exit other markets quickly. You also need, of course, a bail-out mechanism that protects your creditors and displaces any losses from periodic panics onto the citizens of the borrowing country. To supervise the international framework you want international organizations that look like cooperatives of member states and carry the legitimacy of multilateralism, but are financed in a way that allows you to control them.

A Machiavellian interpretation of the U.S. role in the world economy since the end of the Bretton Woods regime around 1970? Certainly. In reality, America's engineering of its dominance has at times been for the general good, when it used its clout to "think for the world." But often its clout has been used solely in the interests of its richest citizens and most powerful corporations. This latter tendency has been dominant lately.

We see it in its new single-minded unilateralism in international relations, much exacerbated by the mixture of rage at Sept. 11th and gung-ho jubilation at "success" in Afghanistan. And we see it in what the United States is now ramming through the international supervisory organizations.

The United States has engineered the World Trade Organization to commit itself to negotiate a General Agreement on Trade in Services, which will facilitate a global market in private health care, welfare, pensions, education and water, supplied—naturally—by U.S. companies, and which will undermine political support for universal access to social services in developing countries.

And it has engineered the World Bank, through congressional conditions on the replenishment of IDA, the soft-loan facility, to launch its biggest refocusing in a decade—a "private sector development" agenda devoted to the same end of accelerating the private (and nongovernmental) provision of basic services on a commercial basis.

The World Bank has made no evaluation of its earlier efforts to support private participation in social sectors. Its new private sector development thrust, especially in the social sectors, owes everything to intense U.S. pressure.

These power relations and exercises of statecraft are obscured in the current talk about globalization. Far from being just a collapsing of distance and widening of opportunities for all, the increasing mobility of information, finance, goods and services frees the American government of constraints while more tightly constraining everyone else. Globalization and the global supervisory organizations enable the United States to harness the rest of the world to its own rhythms and structure.

Of course these arrangements do not produce terrorism in any direct way. But they are deeply implicated in the very slow economic growth in most of the developing world since 1980, and in the wide and widening world income inequality. (The average purchasing power of the bottom 10 percent of Americans is higher than that of two-thirds of the rest of the world's population.)

Slow economic growth and vast income disparities, when seen as such, breed cohorts of partly educated young people who grow up in anger and despair. Some try by legal or illegal means to migrate to the West; some join militant ethnic or religious movements directed at each other and their own rulers. But now the idea has spread among a few vengeful fundamentalists that the United States should be attacked directly.

The United States and its allies can stamp out specific groups by force and bribery. But in the longer run, the structural arrangements that replicate a grossly unequal world have to be redesigned, as we did at the Bretton Woods conference after World War II, so that markets working within the new framework produce more equitable results. Historians looking back a century from now will say that the time to have begun was now.

STUDY AND DISCUSSION QUESTIONS

1. What are the key "hard-wired" features of the international political economy—and how do they contribute to American dominance?
2. What role do international organizations play in assisting the United States in maintaining geopolitical leverage in a unipolar world?
3. Where would Ikenberry agree with Wade's analysis—and where would he disagree?

11

Redefining the National Interest

Joseph P. Nye

Hegemony in the twenty-first century, argues Joseph P. Nye, Dean of the Kennedy School of Government at Harvard, and Chairman of the National Intelligence Council and an Assistant Secretary of Defense in the Clinton administration, involves a mix of hard power and soft power. As important as the hard power of military capability and economic competitive strength continues to be for the United States, Nye argues that even in the post–9/11 era soft power is an essential—even an increasing—part of the mix.

In this selection from his extremely influential study of American power, Nye explains the continuing importance of soft power and why, in his view, it is vital to America's national interest. Soft power determines the capacity of the United States to set the geopolitical agenda, influence the behavior of individuals, nations, and states across the world, and lead by example. Soft power inspires others to emulate America because they admire its values. Hence, Nye concludes, as globalization weakens the capacity of states to control outcomes and makes

all states vulnerable to transnational issues—from the spread of AIDS,
to financial transactions, to the threat of terrorism—the role of soft
power grows commensurately. Nye cautions that it is imperative for
America's leaders to exercise hard power in a way that does not under-
cut soft power, a warning that seems especially prescient as American
leaders contemplate both the enduring consequences of the war in Iraq
for the exercise of power by the United States and potential showdowns
with Iran and North Korea.

How should the United States define its interests in this global information age? How shall we decide how much and when to join with others? What should we do with our unprecedented power? Isolationists who think we can avoid vulnerability to terrorism by drawing inward fail to understand the realities of a global information age. At the same time, the new unilateralists who urge us to unashamedly deploy it on behalf of self-defined global ends are offering a recipe for undermining our soft power and encouraging others to create the coalitions that will eventually limit our hard power. We must do better than that.

When Condoleezza Rice, now the [Secretary of State], wrote during the 2000 campaign that we should "proceed from the firm ground of the national interest and not from the interest of an illusory international community," what disturbed our European allies was "the assumption that a conflict between the pursuit of national interest and commitment to the interests of a far-from-illusory international community necessarily exists."[1] The ties that bind the international community may be weak, but they matter. Failure to pay proper respect to the opinion of others and to incorporate a broad conception of justice into our national interest will eventually come to hurt us. As our allies frequently remind us, even well-intentioned American champions of benign hegemony do not have all the answers. While our friends welcomed the multilateralism of the Bush administration's approach after September 2001, they remained concerned about a return to unilateralism.

Democratic leaders who fail to reflect their nation's interest are unlikely to be reelected, and it is in our interest to preserve our preeminent position. But global interests can be incorporated into a broad and farsighted concept of the national interest. After all, terrorism is a threat to all societies; international trade benefits us as well as others; global warming will raise sea levels along all our coasts as well as those of other countries; infectious diseases can arrive anywhere by ship or plane; and financial instability can hurt the whole world economy. In addition to such concrete interests, many Americans want global values incorporated into our national interest. There are strong indications that Americans' values operate in a highly global context—that our sphere of concern extends well beyond national boundaries. Seventy-three percent agreed with the poll statement "I regard myself as a citizen of the world as well as a citizen of the United States," and 44 percent agreed strongly.[2] We need a broad definition of our national interest that takes account of the interests of others, and it is the role of our leaders to bring this into popular discussions. An enlightened national interest need not be myopic—as September 2001 reminded us.

Traditionalists distinguish between a foreign policy based on values and a foreign policy based on interests. They describe as vital those interests that would directly affect our safety and thus merit the use of force—for example, to prevent attacks on the United States, to prevent the emergence of hostile hegemons in Asia or Europe, to prevent hostile powers on our borders or in control of the seas, and to ensure the survival of U.S. allies. Promoting human rights, encouraging democracy, or developing specific economic sectors is relegated to a lower priority.

I find this approach too narrow, as I believe that humanitarian interests are also important to our lives and our foreign policy. Certainly national strategic interests are vital and deserve priority, because if we fail to protect them, our very survival would be at stake. For example, today countering and suppressing catastrophic terrorism will deserve the priority that was devoted to containing Soviet power during the Cold War. Survival is the necessary condition of foreign policy, but it is not all there is to foreign policy. Moreover, the connection between some events (for example, Iraq's invasion of Kuwait, or a North Korean missile test) and a threat to our national survival may involve a long chain of causes. People can disagree about how probable any link in the chain is and thus about the degree of the threat to our survival. Consequently, reasonable people can disagree about how much "insurance" they want our foreign policy to provide against remote threats to a vital interest before we pursue other values such as human rights.

In my view, in a democracy, the national interest is simply what citizens, after proper deliberation, say it is. It is broader than vital strategic interests, though they are a crucial part. It can include values such as human rights and democracy, particularly if the American public feels that those values are so important to our identity or sense of who we are that people are willing to pay a price to promote them. Values are simply an intangible national interest. If the American people think that our long-term shared interests include certain values and their promotion abroad, then they become part of the national interest. Leaders and experts may point out the costs of indulging certain values, but if an informed public disagrees, experts cannot deny the legitimacy of their opinion.

Determining the national interest involves more than just poll results. It is opinion after public discussion and deliberation. That is why it is so important that our leaders do a better job of discussing a broad formulation of our national interest. Democratic debate is often messy and does not always come up with the "right" answers. Nonetheless, it is difficult to see a better way to decide on the national interest in a democracy. A better-informed political debate is the only way for our people to determine how broadly or narrowly to define our interests.

THE LIMITS OF AMERICAN POWER

Even when we agree that values matter, the hard job is figuring out how to bring them to bear in particular instances. Many Americans find Russia's war in Chechnya disturbing, but there are limits to what we can do because Russia remains a nuclear power and we seek its help on terrorism. As our parents reminded us, "Don't let your eyes get bigger than your stomach, and don't bite off more than you can chew." Given our size, the United States has more margin of choice than most countries do. But as we have seen in the earlier chapters, power is changing, and it is not always clear how much we can chew. The danger posed by the outright champions of hegemony is that their foreign policy is all accelerator and no brakes. Their focus on unipolarity and hegemony exaggerates the degree to which the United States is able to get the outcomes it wants in a changing world.

. . . [P]ower in a global information age is distributed like a three-dimensional chess game. The top military board is unipolar, with the United States far out-stripping all other states, but the middle economic board is multipolar, with the United States, Europe, and Japan accounting for two-thirds of world product, and the bottom board of transnational relations that cross borders outside the control of governments has a widely dispersed structure of power. While it is important not to ignore the continuing importance of military force for some purposes, particularly in relation to the preindustrial and industrial parts of the world, the hegemonists' focus on military power can blind us to the limits of our power. As we have seen, American power is not equally great in the economic and transnational dimensions. Not only are there new actors to consider in these domains, but many of the transnational issues—whether financial flows, the spread of AIDS, or terrorism—cannot be resolved without the cooperation of others. Where collective action is a necessary part of obtaining the outcomes we want, our power is by definition limited and the United States is bound to share.

We must also remember the growing role of soft power in this global infor-mation age. It matters that half a million foreign students want to study in the United States each year, that Europeans and Asians want to watch American films and TV, that American liberties are attractive in many parts of the world, and that others respect us and want to follow our lead when we are not too arro-gant. Our values are significant sources of soft power. Both hard and soft power are important, but in a global information age, soft power is becoming even more so than in the past. Massive flows of cheap information have expanded the number of transnational channels of contacts across national borders. As we also noted earlier, global markets and nongovernmental groups—including terrorists—play a larger role, and many possess soft power resources. States are more easily penetrated and less like the classic military model of sovereign billiard balls bouncing off each other.

The United States, with its open democratic society, will benefit from the rapidly developing global information age if we develop a better understanding of the nature and limits of our power. Our institutions will continue to be attractive to many and the openness of our society will continue to enhance our credibility. Thus as a country, we will be well placed to benefit from soft power. But since much of this soft power is the unintended by-product of social forces, the government will often find it difficult to manipulate.

The good news is that the social trends of the global information age are helping to shape a world that will be more congenial to American values in the long run. But the soft power that comes from being a shining "city upon a hill" (as the Puritan leader John Winthrop first put it) does not provide the coercive capability that hard power does. Soft power is crucial, but alone it is not sufficient. Both hard and soft power will be necessary for successful foreign policy in a global information age. Our leaders must make sure that they exercise our hard power in a manner that does not undercut our soft power.

GRAND STRATEGY AND GLOBAL PUBLIC GOODS

How should Americans set our priorities in a global information age? What grand strategy would allow us to steer between the "imperial overstretch" that would arise out of the role of global policeman while avoiding the mistake of thinking the country can be isolated in this global information age? The place to start is by understanding the relationship of American power to global public goods. On one hand, for reasons given above, American power is less effective than it might first appear. We cannot do everything. On the other hand, the United States is likely to remain the most powerful country well into this century, and this gives us an interest in maintaining a degree of international order. More concretely, there is a simple reason why Americans have a national interest beyond our borders. Events out there can hurt us, and we want to influence distant governments and organizations on a variety of issues such as proliferation of weapons of mass destruction, terrorism, drugs, trade, resources, and ecological damage, After the Cold War, we ignored Afghanistan, but we discovered that even a poor, remote country can harbor forces that can harm us.

To a large extent, international order is a public good—something everyone can consume without diminishing its availability to others. A small country can benefit from peace in its region, freedom of the seas, suppression of terrorism, open trade, control of infectious diseases, or stability in financial markets at the same time that the United States does without diminishing the benefits to the United States or others. Of course, pure public goods are rare. And sometimes things that look good in our eyes may look bad in the eyes of others. Too narrow an appeal to public goods can become a self-serving ideology for the powerful. But these caveats are a reminder to consult with others, not a reason to discard an important strategic principle that helps us set priorities and reconcile our national interests with a broader global perspective.

If the largest beneficiary of a public good (like the United States) does not take the lead in providing disproportionate resources toward its provision, the smaller beneficiaries are unlikely to be able to produce it because of the difficulties of organizing collective action when large numbers are involved. While this responsibility of the largest often lets others become "free riders," the alternative is that the collective bus does not move at all. (And our compensation is that the largest tends to have more control of the steering wheel.)

This puts a different twist on former secretary of state Madeleine Albright's frequent phrase that the United States is "the indispensable nation." We do not get a free ride. To play a leading role in producing public goods, the United States will need to invest in both hard power resources and the soft power resources of setting a good example. The latter will require more self-restraint on the part of Congress as well as putting our own house in order in economics, environment, criminal justice, and so forth. The rest of the world likes to see the United States lead by example, but when "America is seen, as with emission standards, to put narrow domestic interests before global needs, respect can easily turn to disappointment and contempt."[3]

Increasing hard power will require an investment of resources in the nonmilitary aspects of foreign affairs, including better intelligence, that Americans have recently been unwilling to make. While Congress has been willing to spend 16 percent of the national budget on defense, the percentage devoted to international affairs has shrunk from 4 percent in the 1960s to just 1 percent today. Our military strength is important, but it is not sixteen times more important than our diplomacy. Over a thousand people work on the staff of the smallest regional military command headquarters, far more than the total assigned to the Americas at the Departments of State, Commerce, Treasury, and Agriculture. The military rightly plays a role in our diplomacy, but we are investing in our hard power in overly militarized terms.

As Secretary of State Colin Powell . . . pleaded to Congress, we need to put more resources into the State Department, including its information services and the Agency for International Development (AID), if we are going to get our messages across. A bipartisan report on the situation of the State Department recently warned that "if the 'downward spiral' is not reversed, the prospect of relying on military force to protect U.S. national interests will increase because Washington will be less capable of avoiding, managing or resolving crises through the use of statecraft."[4] Moreover, the abolition of the United States Information Agency (which promoted American government views abroad) as a separate entity and its absorption into the State Department reduced the effectiveness of one of our government's important instruments of soft power. It is difficult to be a superpower on the cheap—or through military means alone.

In addition to better means, we need a strategy for their use. Our grand strategy must first ensure our survival, but then it must focus on providing *global* public goods. We gain doubly from such a strategy: from the public goods themselves, and from the way they legitimize our power in the eyes of others. That means we should give top priority to those aspects of the international system that, if not attended to properly, would have profound effects on the basic international order and therefore on the lives of large numbers of Americans as well as others. The United States can learn from the lesson of Great Britain in the nineteenth century, when it was also a preponderant power. Three public goods that Britain attended to were (1) maintaining the balance of power among the major states in Europe, (2) promoting an open international economic system, and (3) maintaining open international commons such as the freedom of the seas and the suppression of piracy.

All three translate relatively well to the current American situation. Maintaining regional balances of power and dampening local incentives to use force to change borders provides a public good for many (but not all) countries. The United States helps to "shape the environment" (in the words of the Pentagon's quadrennial defense review) in various regions, and that is why even in normal times we keep roughly a hundred thousand troops forward-based in Europe, the same number in Asia, and some twenty thousand near the Persian Gulf. The American role as a stabilizer and reassurance against aggression by aspiring hegemons in key regions is a blue chip issue. We should not abandon these regions, as some have recently suggested, though our presence in the Gulf could be handled more subtly.

Promoting an open international economic system is good for American economic growth and is good for other countries as well. . . . [O]penness of global markets is a necessary (though not sufficient) condition for alleviating poverty in poor countries even as it benefits the United States. In addition, in the long term, economic growth is also more likely to foster stable, democratic middle-class societies in other countries, though the time scale may be quite lengthy. To keep the system open, the United States must resist protectionism at home and support international economic institutions such as the World Trade Organization, the International Monetary Fund, and the Organization for Economic Cooperation and Development that provide a framework of rules for the world economy.

The United States, like nineteenth-century Britain, has an interest in keeping international commons, such the oceans, open to all. Here our record is mixed. It is good on traditional freedom of the seas. For example, in 1995, when Chinese claims to the Spratly Islands in the South China Sea sparked concern in Southeast Asia, the United States avoided the conflicting claims of various states to the islets and rocks, but issued a statement reaffirming that the sea should remain open to all countries. China then agreed to deal with the issue under the Law of the Seas Treaty. Today, however, the international commons include new issues such as global climate change, preservation of endangered species, and the uses of outer space, as well as the virtual commons of cyberspace. But on some issues, such as the global climate, the United States has taken less of a lead than is necessary. The establishment of rules that preserve access for all remains as much a public good today as in the nineteenth century, even though some of the issues are more complex and difficult than freedom of the seas.

These three classic public goods enjoy a reasonable consensus in American public opinion, and some can be provided in part through unilateral actions. But there are also three new dimensions of global public goods in today's world. First, the United States should help develop and maintain international regimes of laws and institutions that organize international action in various domains—not just trade and environment, but weapons proliferation, peacekeeping, human rights, terrorism, and other concerns. Terrorism is to the twenty-first century what piracy was to an earlier era. Some governments gave pirates and privateers safe harbor to earn revenues or to harass their enemies. As Britain became the dominant naval power in the nineteenth century, it suppressed piracy, and most countries benefited from that situation. Today, some states harbor terrorists in order to attack their enemies or because they are too weak to control powerful groups. If our current campaign against terrorism is seen as unilateral or biased, it is likely to fail, but if we continue to maintain broad coalitions to suppress terrorism, we have a good prospect of success. While our antiterrorism campaign will not be seen as a global public good by the groups that attack us, our objective should be to isolate them and diminish the minority of states that give them harbor.

We should also make international development a higher priority, for it is an important global public good as well. Much of the poor majority of the world is in turmoil, mired in vicious circles of disease, poverty, and political instability. Large-scale financial and scientific help from rich countries is important not only for humanitarian reasons but also, as Harvard economist Jeffrey Sachs has argued, "because even remote countries become outposts of disorder for the rest of the world."[5] Here our record is less impressive. Our foreign aid has shrunk to 0.1 percent of our GNP, roughly one-third of European levels, and our protectionist trade measures often hurt poor countries most. Foreign assistance is generally unpopular with the American public, in part (as polls show) because they think we spend fifteen to twenty times more on it than we do. If our political leaders appealed more directly to our humanitarian instinct as well as our interest in stability, our record might improve. As President Bush said in July 2001,

"This is a great moral challenge."[6] To be sure, aid is not sufficient for development, and opening our markets, strengthening accountable institutions, and discouraging corruption are even more important. Development will take a long time, and we need to explore better ways to make sure that our help actually reaches the poor, but both prudence and a concern for our soft power suggest that we should make development a higher priority.

As a preponderant power, the United States can provide an important public good by acting as a mediator. By using our good offices to mediate conflicts in places such as Northern Ireland, the Middle East, or the Aegean Sea, the United States can help in shaping international order in ways that are beneficial to us as well as to other nations. It is sometimes tempting to let intractable conflicts fester, and there are some situations where other countries can more effectively play the mediator's role. Even when we do not want to take the lead, our participation can be essential—witness our work with Europe to try to prevent civil war in Macedonia. But often the United States is the only country that can bring together mortal enemies as in the Middle East peace process. And when we are successful, we enhance our reputation and increase our soft power at the same time that we reduce a source of instability.

Table 3.1   *A Strategy Based on Global Public Goods*

1. Maintain the balance of power in important regions
2. Promote an open international economy
3. Preserve international commons
4. Maintain international rules and institutions
5. Assist economic development
6. Act as convenor of coalitions and mediator of disputes.

. . .

THE BATTLE BETWEEN UNILATERALISTS AND MULTILATERALISTS

How should we engage with other countries? There are three main approaches; isolation, unilateralism, and multilateralism. Isolationism persists in public opinion, but it is not a major strategic option for American foreign policy today. While some people responded to the September 2001 terrorist attacks by suggesting that we cut back on foreign involvements, the majority realized that such a policy would not curtail our vulnerability and could even exacerbate it. The main battle lines are drawn among internationalists, between those who advocate unilateralism and those who prefer multilateral tactics. In William Safire's phrase, "Uni- is not iso-. In our reluctance to appear imperious, we could all too quickly abdicate leadership by catering to the envious crowd."[7] Of course, the differences are a matter of degree, and there are few pure unilateralists or multilateralists. When the early actions of the Bush administration led to cries of outrage about unilateralism, the president disclaimed the label and State Department officials described the administration's posture as selective multilateralism. But the two ends of the spectrum anchor different views of the degree of choice that grows out of America's position in the world today. I will suggest below some rules for the middle ground.

Some unilateralists advocate an assertive damn-the-torpedoes approach to promoting American values. They see the danger as a flagging of our internal will and confusion of our goals, which should be to turn a unipolar moment "into a unipolar era." In this view, a principal aim of American foreign policy should be to bring about a change of regime in undemocratic countries such as Iraq, North Korea, and China.[8] Unilateralists believe that our intentions are good, American hegemony is benevolent, and that should end the discussion. Multilateralism would mean "submerging American will in a mush of collective decision-making—you have sentenced yourself to reacting to events or passing the buck to multilingual committees with fancy acronyms."[9] They argue that "the main issue of contention between the United States and those who express opposition to its hegemony is not American 'arrogance.' It is the inescapable reality of American power in its many forms. Those who suggest that these international resentments could somehow be eliminated by a more restrained American foreign policy are engaging in pleasant delusions."[10]

But Americans are not immune from hubris, nor do we have all the answers. Even if it happened to be true, it would be dangerous to act according to such an idea. "For if we were truly acting in the interests of others as well as our own, we would presumably accord to others a substantive role and, by doing so, end up embracing some form of multilateralism. Others, after all, must be supposed to know their interests better than we can know them."[11] As one sympathetic European correctly observed, "From the law of the seas to the Kyoto Protocol, from the biodiversity convention, from the extraterritorial application of the trade embargo against Cuba or Iran, from the brusk calls for reform of the World Bank and the International Monetary Fund to the International Criminal Court: American unilateralism appears as an omnipresent syndrome pervading world politics."[12] When Congress legislated heavy penalties on foreign companies that did business with countries that the United States did not like, the Canadian foreign minister complained, "This is bullying, but in America, you call it 'global leadership.'"[13]

Other unilateralists (sometimes called sovereigntists) focus less on the promotion of American values than on their protection, and they sometimes gain support from the significant minority of isolationist opinion that still exists in this country. As one put it, the strongest and richest country in the world can afford to safeguard its sovereignty. "An America that stands aloof from various international undertakings will not find that it is thereby shut out from the rest of the world. On the contrary, we have every reason to expect that other nations, eager for access to American markets and eager for other cooperative arrangements with the United States, will often adapt themselves to American preferences."[14] In this view, Americans should resist the encroachment of international law, especially claims of universal jurisdiction. Instead, "the United States should strongly espouse national sovereignty, the bedrock upon which democracy and self-government are built, as the fundamental organizing principle of the international system."[15] Or as Senator Jesse Helms warned, the United Nations can be a useful instrument for America's world role, but if it "aspires to establish itself as the central moral authority of a new international order . . . then it begs for confrontation and, more important, eventual U.S. withdrawal."[16]

This battle between multilateralists and unilateralists, often played out in a struggle between the president and Congress, has led to a somewhat schizophrenic American foreign policy. The United States played a prominent role in promoting such multilateral projects as the Law of the Seas Treaty, the Comprehensive Test Ban Treaty, the Land Mines Treaty, the International Criminal Court, the Kyoto Protocol on climate change, and others, but it has failed to follow through with congressional ratification. In some instances, the result has been what *The Economist* calls "parallel unilateralism—a willingness to go along with international accords, but only so far as they suit America, which is prepared to conduct policy outside their constraints."[17] For instance, the United States asserts the jurisdictional limits of the unratified Law of the Seas Treaty. It has pledged not to resume testing nuclear weapons, but because of the unilateral nature of the decision, it does not gain the benefits of verification and the ability to bind others. In other instances, such as antipersonnel land mines, the United States has argued that it needs them to defend against tanks in Korea, but it has undertaken research on a new type of mine that might allow it to join by 2006. In the case of the Kyoto Protocol, President Bush refused to negotiate and peremptorily pronounced it "dead." The result was a foreign reaction of frustration and anger that undermined our soft power.

During the 2000 political campaign, George W. Bush aptly described the situation: "Our nation stands alone right now in the world in terms of power. And that's why we've got to be humble and yet project strength in a way that promotes freedom. . . . If we are an arrogant nation, they'll view us that way, but if we're a humble nation, they'll respect us."[18] Yet our allies and other foreign nations considered the early actions of his administration arrogantly unilateral. Within a few months, America's European allies joined other countries in refusing for the first time to reelect the United States to the UN Human Rights Commission. The secretary of defense, Donald Rumsfeld, said that "gratitude is gone,"[19] and the secretary of state, Colin Powell, explained that "the 'sole superpower' charge is always out there and that may have influenced some."[20] In the less temperate words of television commentator Morton Kondracke, "We're the most powerful country in the world by far, and a lot of pipsqueak wannabes like France resent the hell out of it. . . . When they have a chance to stick it to us, they try."[21] The House of Representatives responded by voting to withhold funds from the UN. But the situation was more complicated than such responses acknowledged.

At the beginning of the last century, as America rose to world power, Teddy Roosevelt advised that we should speak softly but carry a big stick. Now that we have the stick, we need to pay more attention to the first part of his admonition. And we need not just to speak more softly but to listen more carefully. As Chris Patten, the EU commissioner for external affairs and former British Conservative leader, explained a year earlier, the United States is a staunch friend with much to admire, "but there are also many areas in which I think they have got it wrong, the UN, for example, environmental policy, and a pursuit of extraterritorial powers combined with a neuralgic hostility to any external authority over their own affairs."[22] In the words of one observer, at the start of his administration President Bush "contrived to prove his own theory that arrogance provokes resentment for a country that, long before his arrival, was already the world's most conspicuous and convenient target."[23]

The United States should aim to work with other nations on global problems in a multilateral manner whenever possible. I agree with the recent bipartisan commission on our national security, chaired by former senators Gary Hart and Warren Rudman, which concluded that "emerging powers—either singly or in coalition—will increasingly constrain U.S. options regionally and limit its strategic influence. As a result we will remain limited in our ability to impose our will, and we will be vulnerable to an increasing range of threats." Borders will become more porous, rapid advances in information and biotechnologies will create new vulnerabilities, the United States will become "increasingly vulnerable to hostile attack on the American homeland, and the U.S. military superiority will not entirely protect us."[24] This means we must develop multilateral laws and institutions that constrain others and provide a framework for cooperation. In the words of the Hart-Rudman Commission, "America cannot secure and advance its own interests in isolation."[25] As the terrorist attacks of September 11 showed, even a superpower needs friends.

Granted, multilateralism can be used as a strategy by smaller states to tie the United States down like Gulliver among the Lilliputians. It is no wonder that France prefers a multipolar and multilateral world, and less developed countries see multilateralism as in their interests, because it gives them some leverage on the United States. But this does not mean multilateralism is not generally in American interests as well. "By resting our actions on a legal basis (and accepting the correlative constraints), we can make the continued exercise of our disproportionate power easier for others to accept."[26]

Multilateralism involves costs, but in the larger picture, they are outweighed by the benefits. International rules bind the United States and limit our freedom of action in the short term, but they also serve our interest by binding others as well. Americans should use our power now to shape institutions that will serve our long-term national interest in promoting international order. "Since there is little reason for believing that the means of policy will be increased, we are left to rely on the greater cooperation of others. But the greater cooperation of others will mean that our freedom of action is narrowed."[27] It is not just that excessive unilateralism can hurt us; multilateralism is often the best way to achieve our long-run objectives.

Action to shape multilateralism now is a good investment for our future. Today, as we have seen, "worried states are making small adjustments, creating alternatives to alliance with the United States. These small steps may not look important today, but eventually the ground will shift and the U.S.-led postwar order will fragment and disappear."[28] These tendencies are countered by the very openness of the American system. The pluralistic and regularized way in which foreign policy is made reduces surprises. Opportunities for foreigners to raise their voice and influence the American political and governmental system not only are plentiful but constitute an important incentive for alliance. Ever since Athens transformed the Delian League into an empire, smaller allies have been torn between anxieties over abandonment or entrapment. The fact that American allies are able to voice their concerns helps to explain why American alliances have persisted so long after Cold War threats receded.

The other element of the American order that reduces worry about power asymmetries is our membership in a web of multilateral institutions ranging from the UN to NATO. Some call it an institutional bargain. The price for the United States was reduction in Washington's policy autonomy, in that institutional rules and joint decision making reduced U.S. unilateralist capacities. But what Washington got in return was worth the price. America's partners also had their autonomy constrained, but they were able to operate in a world where U.S. power was more restrained and reliable. Seen in the light of a constitutional bargain, the multilateralism of American preeminence is a key to its longevity, because it reduces the incentives for constructing alliances against us. And to the extent that the EU is the major potential challenger in terms of capacity, the idea of a loose constitutional framework between the United States and the societies with which we share the most values makes sense.

Of course, not all multilateral arrangements are good or in our interests, and the United States should occasionally use unilateral tactics in certain situations, which I will describe below. The presumption in favor of multilateralism that I recommend need not be a straitjacket. Richard Haass, the State Department's director of policy planning, says, "What you're going to get from this administration is 'à la carte multilateralism.' We'll look at each agreement and make a decision, rather than come out with a broad-based approach."[29] So how should Americans choose between unilateral and multilateral tactics? Here are seven tests to consider.

First, in cases that involve vital survival interests, we should not rule out unilateral action, though when possible we should seek international support for these actions. The starkest case in the last half century was the 1962 Cuban missile crisis. American leaders felt obliged to consider unilateral use of force, though it is important to note that President Kennedy also sought the legitimacy of opinion expressed in multilateral forums such as the United Nations and the Organization of American States. Strikes against terrorist camps and safe havens are a current example, but again, unilateral actions are best when buttressed by multilateral support.

Second, we should be cautious about multilateral arrangements that interfere with our ability to produce stable peace in volatile areas. Because of our global military role, the United States sometimes has interests and vulnerabilities that are different from those of smaller states with more limited interests—witness the role of land mines in preventing North Korean tanks crossing the demilitarized zone into South Korea. Thus the multilateral treaty banning land mines was easier for other countries to sign. As noted previously, the United States announced that it would work to develop new mines that might allow it to sign by 2006. Similarly, given the global role of American military forces, if the procedures of the International Criminal Court cannot be clarified to ensure protection of American troops from unjustified charges of war crimes, they might deter the United States from contributing to the public good of peacekeeping. The ICC procedures currently proposed give primary jurisdiction over alleged war crimes by American servicemen to the United States, but there is still a danger of overzealous prosecutors egged on by hostile NGOs in instances where the United States finds no case. We should seek further assurances such as clarifying declarations by the UN Security Council. While the ICC has problems, helping to shape its procedures would be a better policy than abetting the current trend toward national claims of universal legal jurisdiction that are evolving in ad hoc fashion beyond our control.

Third, unilateral tactics sometimes help lead others to compromises that advance multilateral interests. The multilateralism of free trade and the international gold standard in the nineteenth century were achieved not by multilateral means but by Britain's unilateral moves of opening its markets and maintaining the stability of its currency. America's relative openness after 1945 and, more recently, trade legislation that threatened unilateral sanctions if others did not negotiate helped create conditions that prodded other countries to move forward with the WTO dispute settlement mechanism. Sometimes the United States is big enough to set high standards and get away with it—witness our more stringent regulations for financial markets. Such actions can lead to the creation of higher international standards. The key is whether the unilateral action was designed to promote a global public good.

The Kyoto Protocol, which caused President Bush such trouble at the beginning of his presidency, could have been another case in point had it been handled differently. Many who accept the reality of global warming and support the Framework Convention on Climate Change (the Rio agreement signed by President George H. Bush and ratified by the Senate in 1992) believed that the Kyoto agreement was badly flawed because it did not include developing countries and because its target for emission cuts, according to *The Economist*, "could not be done except at ruinous cost, and perhaps not even then." A longer-term plan based on milder reductions at the start followed by more demanding targets farther out would provide time for capital stocks to adjust and market-based instruments such as tradable permits to lower the costs of emissions reductions. It would also reduce the trade-off with economic growth, which benefits a wide range of nations, including the poor. If, instead of resisting the science and abruptly pronouncing the protocol dead on grounds of domestic interest, the Bush administration had said, "We will work on a domestic energy policy that cuts emissions and at the same time negotiate with you for a better treaty," his initial unilateralism would arguably have advanced multilateral interests.[30]

Fourth, the United States should reject multilateral initiatives that are recipes for inaction, promote others' self-interest, or are contrary to our values. The New International Information Order proposed by the UN Educational, Scientific and Cultural Organization (UNESCO) in the 1970s would have helped authoritarian governments to restrict freedom of the press. Similarly, the New International Economic Order fostered by the General Assembly at the same time would have interfered with the public good of open markets. Sometimes multilateral procedures are obstructive—for example, Russia's and China's efforts to prevent Security Council authorization of intervention to stop the human rights violations in Kosovo in 1999. Ultimately the United States decided to go ahead without Security Council approval, but even then the American intervention was not purely unilateral but taken with strong support of our allies in NATO.

Fifth, multilateralism is essential on intrinsically cooperative issues that cannot be managed by the United States without the help of other countries. Climate change is a perfect example. Global warming will be costly to us, but it cannot be prevented by the United States alone cutting emissions of carbon dioxide, methane, and particulates. The United States is the largest source of such warming agents, but three-quarters of the sources originate outside our borders. Without cooperation, the problem is beyond our control. The same is true of a long list of items: the spread of infectious diseases, the stability of global financial markets, the international trade system, the proliferation of weapons of mass destruction, narcotics trafficking, international crime syndicates, transnational terrorism. All these problems have major effects on Americans, and their control ranks as an important national interest—but one that cannot be achieved except by multilateral means.

Sixth, multilateralism should be sought as a means to get others to share the burden and buy into the idea of providing public goods. Sharing helps foster commitment to common values. Even militarily, the United States should rarely intervene alone. Not only does this comport with the preferences of the American public, but it has practical implications. The United States pays a minority share of the cost of UN and NATO peacekeeping operations, and the legitimacy of a multilateral umbrella reduces collateral political costs to our soft power.

Seventh, in choosing between multilateral and unilateral tactics, we must consider the effects of the decision on our soft power. If we continue to define our power too heavily in military terms, we may fail to understand the need to invest in other instruments. As we have seen, soft power is becoming increasingly important, but soft power is fragile and can be destroyed by excessive unilateralism and arrogance. In balancing whether to use multilateral or unilateral tactics, or to adhere to or refuse to go along with particular multilateral initiatives, we have to consider how we explain it to others and what the effects will be on our soft power.

Table 3.2   *Checklist for Multilateral Versus Unilateral Tactics*

1. Survival interests at stake
2. Effect on military and peace
3. Leadership increases public goods
4. Consistency with our values
5. Intrinsically cooperative issues
6. Helps on burden sharing
7. Effects on our soft power

In short, American foreign policy in a global information age should have a general preference for multilateralism, but not all multilateralism. At times we will have to go it alone. When we do so in pursuit of public goods, the nature of our ends may substitute for the means in legitimizing our power in the eyes of others. If, on the other hand, the new unilateralists try to elevate unilateralism from an occasional temporary tactic to a full-fledged strategy, they are likely to fail.

. . .

PEERING INTO THE FUTURE

The September 2001 wake-up call means that Americans are unlikely to slip back into the complacency that marked the first decade after the Cold War. If we respond effectively, it is highly unlikely that terrorists could destroy American power, but the campaign against terrorism will require a long and sustained effort. At the same time, the United States is unlikely to face a challenge to its pre-eminence unless it acts so arrogantly that it helps other states to overcome their built-in limitations. The one entity with the capacity to challenge the United States in the near future is the European Union if it were to become a tight federa-tion with major military capabilities and if the relations across the Atlantic were allowed to sour. Such an outcome is possible but would require major changes in Europe and considerable ineptitude in American policy to bring it about. Nonetheless, even short of such a challenge, the diminished fungibility of military power in a global information age means that Europe is already well placed to balance the United States on the economic and transnational chessboards. Even short of a military balance of power, other countries may be driven to work together to take actions to complicate American objectives. Or, as the French critic Dominique Moisi puts it, "The global age has not changed the fact that nothing in the world can be done without the United States. And the multiplicity of new actors means that there is very little the United States can achieve alone."[31]

The United States can learn useful lessons about a strategy of providing pub-lic goods from the history of Pax Britannica. An Australian analyst may be right in her view that if the United States plays its cards well and acts not as a soloist but as the leader of a concert of nations, "the Pax Americana, in terms of its dura-tion, might . . . become more like the Pax Romana than the Pax Britannica."[32] If so, our soft power will play a major role. As Henry Kissinger has argued, the test of history for the United States will be whether we can turn our current predomi-nant power into international consensus and our own principles into widely accepted international norms. That was the greatness achieved by Rome and Britain in their times.[33]

Unlike Britain, Rome succumbed not to the rise of a new empire, but to inter-nal decay and a death of a thousand cuts from various barbarian groups. . . . [W]hile internal decay is always possible, none of the commonly cited trends seems to point strongly in that direction at this time. At the start of the century, terrorist threats notwithstanding, American attitudes are both positive and realis-tic. The initial response to September 2001 was encouraging. The public did not turn to isolationism and the Congress and administration curbed their unilateral-ism. The public is also realistic about the limits of American power and expresses a willingness to share. "While 28% say America will remain the major world power in the next 100 years, 61% believe the United States will share this status with a few other countries. (Fewer than one in 10 thinks the U.S. will no longer be a major power.)"[34] Large majorities oppose a purely unilateralist approach. "Upwards of two-thirds of the public oppose, in principle, the U.S. acting alone overseas without the support of other countries."[35] The American public seems to have an intuitive sense for soft power even if the term is unfamiliar.

On the other hand, it is harder to exclude the barbarians. The dramatically decreased cost of communication, the rise of transnational domains (including the Internet) that cut across borders, and the democratization of technology that puts massive destructive power (once the sole preserve of governments) into the hands of groups and individuals all suggest dimensions that are historically new. In the last century, men such as Hitler, Stalin, and Mao needed the power of the state to wreak great evil. "Such men and women in the twenty-first century will be less bound than those of the 20th by the limits of the state, and less obliged to gain industrial capabilities to wreak havoc. . . . Clearly the threshold for small groups or even individuals to inflict massive damage on those they take to be their enemies is falling dramatically"[36] Countering such terrorist groups must be a top priority. Homeland defense takes on a new importance and a new meaning and will require an intelligent combination of hard and soft power. If such groups were to produce a series of events involving even greater destruction and disruption of society than occurred in September 2001, American attitudes might change dramatically, though the direction of the change is difficult to predict. Isolationism might make a comeback, but greater engagement in world events is equally plausible.

Other things being equal, the United States is well placed to remain the leading power in world politics well into the twenty-first century or beyond. This prognosis depends upon assumptions that can be spelled out. For example, it assumes that the long-term productivity of the American economy will be sustained, that American society will not decay, that the United States will maintain its military strength but not become overmilitarized, that Americans will not become so unilateral and arrogant in their strength that they squander the nation's considerable fund of soft power, that there will not be some catastrophic series of events that profoundly transforms American attitudes in an isolationist direction, and that Americans will define their national interest in a broad and farsighted way that incorporates global interests. Each of these assumptions can be questioned, but they currently seem more plausible than their alternatives. If the assumptions hold, America will continue to be number one, but even so, in this global information age, number one ain't gonna be what it used to be. To succeed in such a world, America must not only maintain its hard power but understand its soft power and how to combine the two in the pursuit of national and global interests.

Notes

[1]Peter Ludlow, "Wanted: A Global Partner," *The Washington Quarterly,* summer 2001, 167.

[2]Program on International Policy Attitudes, "Americans on Globalization: A Study of US Public Attitudes," University of Maryland, 1999, 8.

[3]Philip Bowring, "Bush's America Is Developing an Image Problem," *International Herald Tribune,* May 31, 2001, 8.

[4]Robin Wright, "State Dept. Mismanaged, Report Says," *Los Angeles Times,* January 30, 2001, 10.

[5]Jeffrey Sachs, "What's Good for the Poor Is Good for America," *The Economist,* July 14, 2001, 32–33.

[6]"Bush Proposes Aid Shift to Grants for Poor Nations," *New York Times,* July 18, 2001, A1.

[7]William Safire, "The Purloined Treaty," *New York Times,* April 9, 2001, A21.

[8]Robert Kagan and William Kristol, "The Present Danger," *The National Interest,* spring 2000, 58, 64, 67.

[9]Charles Krauthammer, "The New Unilateralism," *Washington Post,* June 8, 2001, A29.

[10]Kagan and Kristol, "The Present Danger," 67.

[11]Robert W. Tucker in "American Power—For What? A Symposium," *Commentary,* January 2000, 46.

[12]Harald Muller quoted in Franz Nuscheler, "Multilateralism vs. Unilateralism," Development and Peace Foundation, Bonn, 2001, 5.

[13]Lloyd Axworthy quoted in Stewart Patrick, "Lead, Follow, or Get Out of the Way: America's Retreat from Multilateralism," *Current History,* December 2000, 433.

[14]Quoted in Peter Spiro, "The New Sovereigntist," *Foreign Affairs,* November-December 2000, 12–13.

[15]David B. Rivkin Jr. and Lee A. Casey, "The Rocky Shoals of International Law," *The National Interest,* winter 2000–1, 42.

[16]Jesse Helms, "American Sovereignty and the UN," *The National Interest,* winter 2000–1, 34.

[17]"Working Out the World," *The Economist,* March 31, 2001, 24.

[18]"2nd Presidential Debate Between Gov. Bush and Vice President Gore," *New York Times,* October 12, 2000, A20.

[19]Brian Knowlton, "Bush Aide Calls UN Vote an Outrage," *International Herald Tribune,* May 7, 2001 (http://www.iht.com/articles/19081.html).

[20]David Sanger, "House Threatens to Hold U.N. Dues in Loss of a Seat," *New York Times,* May 9, 2001, A1.

[21]Quoted in *The Hotline: National Journal's Daily Briefing on Politics,* May 8, 2001, 4.

[22]Barry James, "The EU Counterweight to American Influence," *International Herald Tribune,* June 16, 2000, 4.

[23]Roger Cohen, "Arrogant or Humble? Bush Encounters Europeans' Hostility," *International Herald Tribune,* May 8, 2001, 1.

[24]United States Commission on National Security in the Twenty-first Century, *New World Coming: American Security in the 21st Century* (Washington, D.C., 1999), 4.

[25]United States Commission on National Security in the Twenty-first Century, *Roadmap for National Security: Imperative for Change, Phase III Report* (Washington, D.C., 2001), 2, 5.

[26]Joshua Muravchik in "American Power—For What? A Symposium," *Commentary,* January 2000, 41.

[27]Robert W. Tucker in "American Power—For What? A Symposium," *Commentary,* January 2000, 46.

[28]G. John Ikenberry, "Getting Hegemony Right," *The National Interest,* spring 2001, 19.

[29]Thom Shanker, "White House Says the US Is Not a Loner, Just Choosy," *New York Times,* July 31, 2001, i.

[30]Andrew Revkin, "After Rejecting Climate Treaty, Bush Calls in Tutors to Give Courses and Help Set One," *New York Times,* April 28, 2001, A9.

[31]Dominique Moisi, "The Real Crisis over the Atlantic," *Foreign Affairs,* July-August 2001, 153.

[32]Coral Bell, "American Ascendancy—and the Pretense of Concert," *The National Interest,* fall 1999, 60.

[33]Henry Kissinger, "Our Nearsighted World Vision," *Washington Post,* January 10, 2000, A19.

[34]Albert R. Hunt, "Americans Look to 21st Century with Optimism and Confidence," *Wall Street Journal,* September 16, 1999, A9.

[35]Department of State, Opinion Analysis, "Sizable Majority of U.S. Public Supports Active, Cooperative Involvement Abroad," Washington, D.C., October 29, 1999.

[36]United States Commission on National Security in the Twenty-first Century, *New World Coming,* 4.

STUDY AND DISCUSSION QUESTIONS

1. How does Nye define soft power?
2. Does Nye consider soft power an alternative to the hard power of economic and military strength—or a complement to hard power?
3. Why does Nye think that soft power is becoming increasingly significant in this era of globalization? Do you agree or disagree?

12

The Bush Revolution

Ivo H. Daalder and James M. Lindsay

For more than a half-century, the leadership of the United States was entrenched in a rule-bound system of international law and global governance that limited the prerogatives of the powerful as well as the weak. Paradoxically, American strength and global influence was enhanced by its willingness to accept limits on the exercise of its hegemonic privileges.

In this selection, Ivo H. Daalder and James M. Lindsay argue that after the terror attacks of September 11, 2001, and with the emergence of the "Bush revolution" in foreign policy, America's rules of engagement with the rest of the world changed. The Bush revolution in foreign policy involved two fundamental changes that, at a stroke, abrogated the terms of the postwar settlements described by Ikenberry and ended 50 years of strategic restraint. It also set aside principles, argue Daalder and Lindsay, that have governed how the United States engaged the world from its inception.

First, because the nation faced terrible new dangers, the United States took the reasonable position that it could not rely on others to protect its people or safeguard its borders. This belief won very broad support at home and an extremely sympathetic hearing abroad. It went the more controversial step further of asserting that the United States could not afford to be constrained by multilateral institutions. What was even more revolutionary, argue Daalder and Lindsay, was the second belief enshrined in the Bush foreign policy doctrine that an America unconstrained by the preferences of allies or the conventions of multilateralism should use its power to change the status quo and reshape the world to advance American interests and values.

George W. Bush had reason to be pleased as he peered down at Baghdad from the window of Air Force One in early June 2003. He had just completed a successful visit to Europe and the Middle East. The trip began in Warsaw, where he had the opportunity to personally thank Poland for being one of just two European countries to contribute troops to the Iraq War effort. He then traveled to Russia to celebrate the three hundredth birthday of St. Petersburg and to sign the papers formally ratifying a treaty committing Moscow and Washington to slash their nuclear arsenals. He flew on to Évian, a city in the French Alps, to attend a summit meeting of the heads of the world's major economies. He next stopped in Sharm el-Sheik, Egypt, for a meeting with moderate Arab leaders, before heading to Aqaba, Jordan, on the shore of the Red Sea to discuss the road map for peace with the Israeli and Palestinian prime ministers. He made his final stop in Doha, Qatar, where troops at U.S. Central Command greeted him with thunderous applause. Now Bush looked down on the city that American troops had seized only weeks before. As he pointed out landmarks below to his advisers, the pilot dipped Air Force One's wings in a gesture of triumph.

Bush's seven-day, six-nation trip was in many ways a victory lap to celebrate America's win in the Iraq War—a war that many of the leaders Bush met on his trip had opposed. But in a larger sense he and his advisers saw it as a vindication of his leadership. The man from Midland had been mocked throughout the 2000 presidential campaign as a know-nothing. He had been denounced early in his presidency for turning his back on time-tested diplomatic practices and ignoring the advice of America's friends and allies. Yet here he was traveling through Europe and the Middle East, not as a penitent making amends but as a leader commanding respect.

As Air Force One flew over Iraq, Bush could say that he had become an extraordinarily effective foreign policy president. He had dominated the American political scene like few others. He had been the unquestioned master of his own administration. He had gained the confidence of the American people and persuaded them to follow his lead. He had demonstrated the courage of his convictions on a host of issues—abandoning cold-war treaties, fighting terrorism, overthrowing Saddam Hussein. He had spent rather than hoarded his considerable political capital, consistently confounding his critics with the audacity of his policy initiatives. He had been motivated by a determination to succeed, not paralyzed by a fear to fail. And while he had steadfastly pursued his goals in the face of sharp criticism, he had acted pragmatically when circumstances warranted.

In the process, Bush had set in motion a revolution in American foreign policy. It was not a revolution in America's goals abroad, but rather in how to achieve them. In his first thirty months in office, he discarded or redefined many of the key principles governing the way the United States should act overseas. He relied on the unilateral exercise of American power rather than on international law and institutions to get his way. He championed a proactive doctrine of preemption and de-emphasized the reactive strategies of deterrence and containment. He promoted forceful interdiction, preemptive strikes, and missile defenses as means to counter the proliferation of weapons of mass destruction, and he downplayed America's traditional support for treaty-based non-proliferation regimes. He preferred regime change to direct negotiations with countries and leaders that he loathed. He depended on ad hoc coalitions of the willing to gain support abroad and ignored permanent alliances. He retreated from America's decades-long policy of backing European integration and instead exploited Europe's internal divisions. And he tried to unite the great powers in the common cause of fighting terrorism and rejected a policy that sought to balance one power against another. By rewriting the rules of America's engagement in the world, the man who had been dismissed throughout his political career as a lightweight left an indelible mark on politics at home and abroad.

Nevertheless, good beginnings do not always come to good endings. Even as Bush peered out the window of Air Force One to look at Baghdad, there were troubling signs of things to come. American troops in Iraq found themselves embroiled in what had all the makings of guerrilla war. Anger had swelled over-seas at what was seen as an arrogant and hypocritical America. Several close allies spoke openly about how to constrain America rather than how best to work with it. As the president's plane flew home, Washington was beginning to confront a new question: Were the costs of the Bush revolution about to swamp the benefits?

The question of how the United States should engage the world is an old one in American history. The framers confronted the question only four years after rati-fying the Constitution when England went to war with France. President George Washington ultimately opted for neutrality, disappointing partisans on both sides. The hero of Valley Forge calculated that the small and fragile experiment in republican government would likely be crushed if it joined a battle between the world's two greatest powers.

America's relationship with Europe remained an issue throughout Washington's presidency. He discussed the topic at length in his magisterial address announcing his decision to retire to his beloved Mount Vernon. He encouraged his countrymen to pursue peace and commercial relations. "Harmony, liberal intercourse with all nations are recommended by policy, humanity, and interest." But he discouraged them from tying their political fate to the decisions of others. "It is our true policy," Washington counseled, "to steer clear of permanent alliances with any portion of the foreign world." His argument for keeping polit-ical ties to a minimum was simple: "Europe has a set of primary interests which to us have none or a very remote relation. Hence she must be engaged in frequent controversies, the causes of which are essentially foreign to our concerns."[1]

Washington concluded his Farewell Address by noting, "I dare not hope [that my advice] will make the strong and lasting impression I could wish."[2] He should not have feared. His vision of an America that traded happily with Europe but otherwise stood apart from it became the cornerstone of the new nation's foreign policy. John Quincy Adams eloquently summarized this sentiment and gave it an idealistic twist in an address he made before the House of Representatives on July 4, 1821. America applauds those who fight for liberty and independence, he argued, "but she goes not abroad, in search of monsters to destroy. She is the well-wisher to the freedom and independence of all. She is the champion and vindicator only of her own." America stuck to its own business not merely for pragmatic reasons, but because to do otherwise would repudiate its special moral claim. "The fundamental maxims of her policy would insensibly change from *liberty to force*," Adams warned. "She might become the dictatress of the world. She would be no longer the ruler of her own spirit."[3]

However, even liberal, democratic spirits can be tempted by changed circumstances. When Adams spoke, the United States was an inconsequential agrarian country of twenty-three states, only one of which—Louisiana—was west of the Mississippi. By the end of the nineteenth century, it was an industrial colossus that spanned a continent. Its new status as a leading economic power brought with it growing demands from within to pursue imperial ambitions. Intellectuals used the reigning theory of the day, Social Darwinism, to advocate territorial expansion as a demonstration of American superiority and the key to national survival. Church groups saw American imperialism as a means to spread Christianity to "primitive" areas of the world. Commercial interests hoped to reap financial gain by winning access to new markets for American goods. Anti-imperialists such as Andrew Carnegie and Mark Twain challenged these arguments for expansion with great passion, but they were fighting a losing battle. As William McKinley's secretary of state John Hay put it, "No man, no party, can fight with any chance of success against a cosmic tendency; no cleverness, no popularity avails against the spirit of the age."[4]

The opportunity that imperialists had waited for came with the Spanish-American War. The windfall from that "splendid little war," as its supporters took to calling it, was an empire that stretched from Puerto Rico in the Caribbean to the Philippines in the Pacific. With victory safely in hand, concerns that America would lose its soul if it went abroad quickly faded. Under Teddy Roosevelt's corollary to the Monroe Doctrine, which had been largely forgotten for seven decades after it was first issued, Washington assumed the role of policeman of the Western Hemisphere. The former Rough Rider denied that "the United States feels any land hunger or entertains any projects as regards the other nations of the Western Hemisphere." Nonetheless, he insisted that the United States could not stand idly by while Latin American nations mismanaged their economies and political affairs. Latin American nations needed to "realize that the right of such independence can not be separated from the responsibility of making good use of it."[5] In the view of Roosevelt and his successors, they failed to do that. Between 1904 and 1934, the United States sent eight expeditionary forces to Latin America, took over customs collections twice, and conducted five military occupations. The Caribbean was soon nicknamed Lake Monroe.

With the Spanish-American War and the Roosevelt corollary to the Monroe Doctrine, internationalists for the first time triumphed over isolationists in the struggle to define the national interest. However, the imperialist cause would soon begin to struggle. Part of the problem was the cost of empire. America's new subjects did not always take easily to Washington's rule. In the Philippines, the United States found itself bloodily suppressing a rebellion. American occupations of several Caribbean countries failed to produce the stability that Roosevelt had promised. By then, the imperialists were confronted by another, more serious challenge. This one came not from isolationists, but from within the internationalist camp itself.

Woodrow Wilson took office in 1913 determined to concentrate on domestic concerns. Shortly before taking the oath of office, he told an old colleague: "It would be the irony of fate if my administration had to deal chiefly with foreign affairs."[6] Yet fate had precisely that destiny for Wilson. His domestic policies are long forgotten; his foreign policy legacy is historic. Wilson's importance rests not on his achievements—he ultimately failed to see his proposal for a new world order enacted—but on his vision of America's role in the world. It was a vision that would dominate American politics after World War II.

Wilson shared with all his predecessors an unwavering belief in American exceptionalism. "It was as if in the Providence of God a continent had been kept unused and waiting for a peaceful people who loved liberty and the rights of men more than they loved anything else, to come and set up an unselfish commonwealth."[7] But whereas that claim had always been used to argue that America would lose its soul if it went abroad in search of monsters to destroy, Wilson turned it on its head. America would lose its soul if it did not go abroad. His liberal internationalism set forth a moral argument for broad American engagement in world affairs.

"We insist," Wilson told Congress in 1916, "upon security in prosecuting our self-chosen lines of national development. We do more than that. We demand it also for others. We do not confine our enthusiasm for individual liberty and free national development to the incidents and movements of affairs which affect only ourselves. We feel it wherever there is a people that tries to walk in these difficult paths of independence and right."[8] Not surprisingly, when Wilson requested a declaration of war against Germany—thereby doing the unthinkable, plunging the United States into a European war—he did not argue that war was necessary because Germany endangered American interests. Rather, the United States must fight because "the world must be made safe for democracy."[9]

Wilson's commitment to a world in which democracy could flourish was by itself revolutionary. Equally revolutionary was the second component of his vision—the belief that the key to creating that world lay in extending the reach of international law and building international institutions. The former college president—who ironically during his first term had enthusiastically used American military power to enforce the Roosevelt corollary to the Monroe Doctrine—called on the victorious powers to craft an international agreement that would provide "mutual guarantees of political independence and territorial integrity to great and small states alike."[10] He went to the Paris Peace Conference in December 1918 to push his idea on deeply skeptical European leaders. He was ultimately forced to compromise on many of the particulars of his plan. Nevertheless, in the end he prevailed on the core point. The Treaty of Versailles, signed in July 1919, established a League of Nations that would "respect and preserve as against external aggression the territorial integrity and existing political independence of all."[11] Wilson returned to the United States convinced that the idea of collective security—"one for all and all for one"—would prevent war and remake world politics.

The idea of the League of Nations was also revolutionary for American politics. Wilson was asking Americans to do more than just cast away their aversion to entangling alliances. The United States, after all, had fought World War I as an "associated" power and not an "allied" one in deference to the traditional reluctance to become tied militarily to other countries. He was asking them to spearhead an international organization that would seek to protect the security of its members, however far they might be from American shores. That would prove the rub.

The Senate's rejection of the Treaty of Versailles is usually recounted as a triumph of traditional isolationism. Isolationists certainly were the treaty's most vociferous critics. The "irreconcilables" and "bitterenders," as they were called, were led by Republican Senator William E. Borah of Idaho, a man who had a reputation as an expert on world affairs despite never having left American soil. The irreconcilables were traditional isolationists who vehemently opposed entangling the country in foreign alliances. Borah insisted that if he had his way the League of Nations would be "20,000 leagues under the sea" and he wanted "this treacherous and treasonable scheme" to be "buried in hell." Even "if the Savior of men would revisit the earth and declare for a League of Nations," he declared, "I would be opposed to it."[12]

Although Borah and his fellow irreconcilables lacked the votes to carry the day, many of the Senate's most ardent internationalists and imperialists also opposed the treaty. What bothered them was not that Wilson wanted to involve the United States in affairs beyond its borders. They were all for that. They simply opposed the way Wilson intended to engage the world. These anti-League internationalists, who included most Republicans and a few Democrats, believed that the United States had to preserve a free hand to act abroad, not tie its fate to the whims and interests of others. They charged that the League would trump the Constitution and usurp Congress's power to declare war. The leader of the anti-League internationalists, Republican Senator Henry Cabot Lodge of Massachusetts, went to the heart of the matter when he asked his colleagues: "Are you willing to put your soldiers and your sailors at the disposition of other nations?"[13]

The victory of the anti-treaty forces heralded for a time the continuation of the policy of the free hand that Lodge and others so loved. By the beginning of the 1930s, however, this unilateral internationalism began giving way to rising isolationist sentiment. As the country entered the Great Depression and war clouds gathered on the European horizon, Americans increasingly retreated to Fortress America. Some isolationists argued that war would not occur. In July 1939 Senator Borah confidently predicted, "We are not going to have a war. Germany isn't ready for it. . . . I have my own sources of information."[14] Others admitted war might occur and that it would be best for the United States to remain apart. Regardless of the reason, the German invasion of Poland, the Battle of Britain, and Germany's invasion of the Soviet Union came and went without convincing most Americans of the need to act. It took Pearl Harbor to do that.

The foreign policy questions Americans faced at the end of World War II had little to do with what the United States *could* do abroad. By every measure, America dominated the world as no nation had ever done before. All the other major powers, whether victor or vanquished, were devastated. The United States, in contrast, emerged from the war not only unscathed, but far stronger than it was when it entered the hostilities. Its economy was by far the world's largest. It possessed the world's strongest navy and most powerful air force. And it alone held the secret to the world's most terrifying weapon: the atomic bomb.

The foreign policy questions facing Americans dealt much more with what the United States *should* do abroad. Some Americans wanted to "bring the boys back home" from Europe and the Pacific and to return to a "normal" life. Others warned against a return to isolationism. But internationalists themselves disagreed on important questions. Should the United States define its interests regionally or globally? What were the threats to U.S. security? How should the United State respond to these threats?

The task of answering these questions fell to President Harry Truman, a man who in many ways was ill prepared for it. By his own admission he was "not a deep thinker."[15] A product of the Democratic political machine in Kansas City, he had cut his political teeth on domestic issues. He had served in the Senate for ten years with modest distinction before becoming Franklin Roosevelt's surprise choice in 1944 to be his running mate. When FDR died in April 1945, Truman had been vice president for less than three months and had not been included in the administration's foreign policy deliberations. Indeed, he did not learn that the United States was building an atomic bomb until *after* he was sworn in as president.

Whatever Truman lacked in experience he more than made up for with a commitment to pursuing Woodrow Wilson's aims without making his mistakes.

During his seven years as president, Truman remade American foreign policy. In March 1947 the former Kansas City haberdasher went before a joint session of Congress and declared what became known as the Truman Doctrine: "It must be the policy of the United States to support free peoples who are resisting attempted subjugation by armed minorities or by outside pressures."[16] Three months later his secretary of state, George C. Marshall, unveiled the Marshall Plan in a commencement address at Harvard, claiming a major role for the United States in rebuilding a war-torn Europe. Two years later Truman signed the treaty creating the North Atlantic Treaty Organization (NATO). With the stroke of his pen, he cast off America's traditional aversion to entangling alliances and formally declared that Washington saw its security interests as inextricably linked with those of Western Europe.

The hallmark of Truman's foreign policy revolution was its blend of power and cooperation. Truman was willing to exercise America's great power to remake world affairs, both to serve American interests and to advance American values. However, he and his advisers calculated that U.S. power could more easily be sustained, with less chance of engendering resentment, if it were embedded in multilateral institutions. During his presidency, Truman oversaw the creation of much of the infrastructure of the international order: the United Nations, the International Monetary Fund, the World Bank, the General Agreement on Tariffs and Trade, and the Organization of American States among other multilateral organizations. In creating these institutions, he set a precedent: Even though the United States had the power to act as it saw fit, it accepted, at least notionally, that its right to act should be constrained by international law. In marked contrast to the epic League of Nations debate, the Senate overwhelmingly endorsed this multilateral approach.

Nonetheless, Truman's foreign policy choices were not unanimously applauded. The challenge, however, did not come from isolationists. The smoke pouring from the USS *Arizona* had shown the vulnerability of Fortress America. The complaints instead came from hard-line conservatives who thought Truman's policy of containing the Soviet Union was too timid. These critics believed that the United States had a moral and strategic interest in working to liberate nations that had fallen under Soviet control. Truman rejected these calls for "rollback" because he judged the costs of the wars that would inevitably follow as too high.

Proponents of rollback thought they had found their leader in Truman's successor, Dwight Eisenhower. Ike campaigned in 1952 criticizing Truman's foreign policy and particularly his handling of Korea. The official Republican Party platform denounced containment as a "negative, futile, and immoral" policy that abandoned "countless human beings to a despotism and Godless terrorism."[17]

However, it is one thing to campaign, another to govern. Once Eisenhower was in office, his actions made clear, in the words of one historian, that Republican rhetoric about " 'liberation' had been aimed more at freeing the government in Washington from Democrats than at contesting Soviet influence in Eastern Europe."[18] In June 1953 the former Supreme Allied Commander stood by as Soviet troops crushed a revolt in East Germany. The following month he brought the Korean War to an end not by invading North Korea but by signing an armistice with Pyongyang. The next year he rebuffed a French appeal for U.S. military help to relieve the French forces trapped at Dien Bien Phu. Two years after that, Washington again did nothing when Soviet tanks rolled into Hungary, crushing yet another revolt against communist rule. Eisenhower's reason for inaction was not timidity but prudence. Any effort to liberate Eastern Europe by force of arms could have led to a nuclear war that turned American cities into smoking, radiating ruins. With the cost of being wrong so high, the appeal of rollback policies dimmed.

Eisenhower's embrace of Truman's foreign policy blueprint solidified America's basic approach to world affairs for the next half century. Even with the debacle in Vietnam, a basic foreign policy consensus held. The United States had extensive interests overseas that it must be prepared to defend. Washington actively cultivated friends and allies because in a world with a superpower adversary it was dangerous to be without them. International organizations, and especially military alliances, were a key instrument of foreign policy.

At the same time, however, the ever-present Soviet threat muffled the continuing disagreement between the intellectual descendants of Woodrow Wilson and those of Henry Cabot Lodge. Those in the Wilson school cherished the contribution of international law to world stability and prosperity. They took pride in the fact that Washington had championed the creation of international organizations such as NATO and the United Nations and that by doing so the United States was laying the groundwork for the gradual expansion of the rule of law in international affairs. Those in the Lodge school longed for the policy of the free hand but were comforted by the fact that America's great wealth and military might enabled it to dominate international organizations. In NATO, for example, the United States was not simply Italy with more people. It was the superpower that provided the alliance's ultimate security guarantee, and as a result it had a disproportionate say over alliance policy. When multilateral organizations refused to heed American wishes, the United States could—and frequently did—act alone.

As the cold war ground on and America's allies became less willing to follow Washington's lead, it became harder to paper over the differences between those who emphasized cooperation and those who stressed the free exercise of power. While the former saw new possibilities for building multilateral organizations, the latter decried the ineffectiveness of many international organizations and despaired at the constraints they placed on America's freedom to act. These differences flared into the open in the 1990s with the demise of the Soviet Union.

Suddenly those who emphasized international institutions and law lost the trump card they had long held over those who favored the unilateral exercise of American power—the prospect that going it alone might produce costs that were unbearably high.

The foreign-policy debates of the 1990s were at first mistakenly seen as a replay of the debates between isolationists and internationalists of the 1930s. True, some voices called for America to return home, but this was a distinctly minority view. Most Americans had little interest in disengaging from the world. They quite liked American predominance and saw it as costing them little. As a result, politicians such as Patrick Buchanan, who thought they could ride an isolationist tide to power, instead sank without leaving a ripple.

The real debate in the 1990s was not over *whether,* but *how* the United States should engage the world. Bill Clinton's presidency in most ways represented a continuation of the traditional Wilsonian approach of building a world order based on the rule of law. Clinton and his advisers argued that globalization was increasing economic, political, and social ties among nations and that this growing interconnectedness made fulfillment of Wilson's vision all the more important. In keeping with this thinking, the Clinton administration pursued traditional arms control agreements such as the Comprehensive Test Ban Treaty and a strengthening of the Biological Weapons Convention. It also sought to create new international arrangements such as the Kyoto Protocol and the International Criminal Court to deal with a new set of policy challenges.

Clinton's opponents criticized his decisions on numerous grounds, but one in particular stood out: He had failed to recognize that, with the demise of the Soviet Union, the United States now had the freedom to act as it saw fit. In their view, Clinton not only failed to assert American primacy; he also ensnared the country in multilateral frameworks that did not even serve broader international interests. As the columnist Charles Krauthammer put it, "An unprecedentedly dominant United States . . . is in the unique position of being able to fashion its own foreign policy. After a decade of Prometheus playing pygmy, the first task of the new [Bush] administration is precisely to reassert American freedom of action."[19] America, in short, could and should be unbound.

George W. Bush delivered the revolution that Krauthammer urged. It was not a revolution that started, as many later have suggested, on September 11, 2001. The worldview that drove it existed long before jet planes plowed into the Twin Towers and the Pentagon. Bush outlined its main ideas while he was on the campaign trail, and he began implementing parts of it as soon as he took the oath of office. What September 11 provided was the rationale and the opportunity to carry out his revolution.

But what precisely was the Bush revolution in foreign policy? At its broadest level, it rested on two beliefs. The first was that in a dangerous world the best—if not the only—way to ensure America's security was to shed the constraints imposed by friends, allies, and international institutions. Maximizing America's freedom to act was essential because the unique position of the United States made it the most likely target for any country or group hostile to the West. Americans could not count on others to protect them; countries inevitably ignored threats that did not involve them. Moreover, formal arrangements would inevitably constrain the ability of the United States to make the most of its primacy. Gulliver must shed the constraints that he helped the Lilliputians weave.

The second belief was that an America unbound should use its strength to change the status quo in the world. Bush's foreign policy did not propose that the United States keep its powder dry while it waited for dangers to gather. The Bush philosophy instead turned John Quincy Adams on his head and argued that the United States should aggressively go abroad searching for monsters to destroy. That was the logic behind the Iraq War, and it animated the administration's efforts to deal with other rogue states.

These fundamental beliefs had important consequences for the practice of American foreign policy. One was a decided preference for unilateral action. Unilateralism was appealing because it was often easier and more efficient, at least in the short term, than multilateralism. Contrast the Kosovo war, where Bush and his advisers believed that the task of coordinating the views of all NATO members greatly complicated the war effort, with the Afghanistan war, where Pentagon planners did not have to subject any of their decisions to foreign approval. This is not to say that Bush flatly ruled out working with others. Rather, his preferred form of multilateralism—to be indulged when unilateral action was impossible or unwise—involved building ad hoc coalitions of the willing, or what Richard Haass, an adviser to Colin Powell, called "a la carte multilateralism."[20]

Second, preemption was no longer a last resort of American foreign policy. In a world in which weapons of mass destruction were spreading and terrorists and rogue states were readying to attack in unconventional ways, Bush argued that "the United States can no longer solely rely on a reactive posture as we have in the past.... We cannot let our enemies strike first."[21] Indeed, the United States should be prepared to act not just preemptively against imminent threats, but also preventively against potential threats. Vice President Dick Cheney was emphatic on this point in justifying the overthrow of Saddam Hussein on the eve of the Iraq War. "There's no question about who is going to prevail if there is military action. And there's no question but what it is going to be cheaper and less costly to do now than it will be to wait a year or two years or three years until he's developed even more deadly weapons, perhaps nuclear weapons."[22]

Third, the United States should use its unprecedented power to produce regime change in rogue states. The idea of regime change was not new to American foreign policy. The Eisenhower administration engineered the overthrow of Iranian Prime Minister Mohammed Mossadegh; the CIA trained Cuban exiles in a botched bid to oust Fidel Castro; Ronald Reagan channeled aid to the Nicaraguan contras to overthrow the Sandinistas; and Bill Clinton helped Serb opposition forces get rid of Slobodan Milosevic. What was different in the Bush presidency was the willingness, even in the absence of a direct attack on the United States, to use U.S. military forces for the express purpose of toppling other governments. This was the gist of both the Afghanistan and the Iraq wars. Unlike proponents of rollback, who never succeeded in overcoming the argument that their policies would produce World War III, Bush based his policy on the belief that nobody could push back.

George W. Bush presided over a revolution in foreign policy, but was he responsible for it? Commentators across the political spectrum said no. They gave the credit (or blame) to neoconservatives within the administration, led by Deputy Secretary of Defense Paul Wolfowitz who they said were determined to use America's great power to transform despotic regimes into liberal democracies. One critic alleged that Bush was "the callow instrument of neoconservative ideologues."[23] Another saw a "neoconservative coup" in Washington and wondered if "George W fully understands the grand strategy that Wolfowitz and other aides are unfolding."[24] Pundits weren't the only ones to argue that the Bush revolution represented a neoconservative triumph. "Right now, the neoconservatives in this administration are winning," Democratic Senator Joseph Biden, the ranking member of the Senate Foreign Relations Committee, said in July 2003. "They seem to have captured the heart and mind of the President, and they're controlling the foreign policy agenda."[25]

This conventional wisdom was wrong on at least two counts. First, it fundamentally misunderstood the intellectual currents within the Bush administration and the Republican Party more generally. Neoconservatives—who might be better called democratic imperialists— were more prominent outside the administration, particularly on the pages of *Commentary* and the *Weekly Standard* and in the television studios of Fox News, than they were inside it. The bulk of Bush's advisers, including most notably Dick Cheney and Defense Secretary Donald Rumsfeld, were not neocons. Nor for that matter was Bush. They were instead assertive nationalists—traditional hard-line conservatives willing to use American military power to defeat threats to U.S. security but reluctant as a general rule to use American primacy to remake the world in its image.

Although neoconservatives and assertive nationalists differed on whether the United States should actively spread its values abroad, they shared a deep skepticism of traditional Wilsonianism's commitment to the rule of law and its belief in the relevance of international institutions. They placed their faith not in diplomacy and treaties, but in power and resolve. Agreement on this key point allowed neoconservatives and assertive nationalists to form a marriage of convenience in overthrowing the cold-war approach to foreign policy even as they disagreed about what kind of commitment the United States should make to rebuilding Iraq and remaking the rest of the world.

The second and more important flaw of the neoconservative coup theory was that it grossly underestimated George W. Bush. The man from Midland was not a figurehead in someone else's revolution. He may have entered the Oval Office not knowing which general ran Pakistan, but during his first thirty months in office he was the puppeteer, not the puppet. He governed as he said he would on the campaign trail. He actively solicited the counsel of his seasoned advisers, and he tolerated if not encouraged vigorous disagreement among them. When necessary, he overruled them. George W. Bush led his own revolution.

Notes

[1]*The Writings of George Washington,* vol. 35, ed. John C. Fitzpatrick (Government Printing Office, 1940), p. 234.

[2]Ibid., p. 236.

[3]John Quincy Adams, "Address of July 4, 1821," in Walter LaFeber, ed., *John Quincy Adams and American Continental Empire: Letters, Papers, and Speeches* (Chicago: Quadrangle Books, 1965), p. 45, emphasis in original.

[4]Quoted in Howard Jones, *Quest for Security: A History of U.S. Foreign Relations,* Volume I to 1913 (McGraw-Hill, 1996), p. 236.

[5]Theodore Roosevelt, "Annual Message to Congress," *Congressional Record,* December 6, 1904, p. 19.

[6]Quoted in Graham Evans, "The Vision Thing: In Search of the Clinton Doctrine," *World Today,* vol. 53 (August/September 1997), p. 216.

[7]*The Papers of Woodrow Wilson,* vol. 37, ed. Arthur S. Link (Princeton University Press, 1981), pp. 213–14.

[8]Woodrow Wilson, "Annual Address to Congress," *Congressional Record,* December 7, 1915, p. 96.

[9]Woodrow Wilson, "Address to Congress," *Congressional Record,* April 2, 1917, p. 120.

[10]Woodrow Wilson, "Address to Congress," *Congressional Record,* January 18, 1918, pp. 680–81.

[11]Quoted in C. Howard Ellis, *The Origin, Structure and Workings of the League of Nations* (London: George Allen & Unwin, 1928), p. 489.

[12]Quoted in Robert H. Ferrell, *American Diplomacy,* 3^d ed. (Norton, 1975), p. 496; and Jones, *Quest for Security,* vol. 2, p. 340.

[13]Quoted in Thomas G. Paterson, J. Garry Clifford, and Kenneth J. Hagan, *Amerian Foreign Relations: A History since 1895,* vol. 2, 4th ed. (Lexington, Mass,: D.C. Heath 1995), p. 112.

[14]Quoted in William L. Langer and S. Everett Gleason, *The Challenge of Isolation* (Harper and Bros., 1952), p. 144.

[15]Quoted in Paterson, Clifford, and Hagan, *American Foreign Relations,* p. 28.

[16]*Public Papers of the President of the United Sates: Harry S. Truman, 1947* (Government Printing Office, 1963), pp. 178–79.

[17]Quoted in Stephen E. Ambrose, *Rise to Globalism: American Foreign Policy since 1938*, 6th rev. ed. (Penguin, 1991), p. 133.

[18]John Lewis Gaddis, *Russia, the Soviet Union, and the United States: An Interpretive History*, 2[d] ed. (McGraw-Hill, 1990), p. 216.

[19]Charles Krauthammer, "The New Unilateralism," *Washington Post*, June 8, 2001, p. A29.

[20]Quoted in Thom Shanker, "White House Says the U.S. Is Not a Loner, Just Choosy," *New York Times*, July 31, 2001, p. A1.

[21]*The National Security Strategy of the United States*, Washington, D.C., September 2002 (www.whitehouse.gov/nsc.nss/pdf [accessed July 2003])

[22]Dick Cheney, NBC's *Meet the Press*, Washington D.C., March 16, 2003 (www.mtholyoke.edu/acad/intrel/bush/cheneymeetthepress.htm [accessed July 2003]).

[23]Jason Epstein, "Leviathan, " *New York Review of Books*, May 1, 2003, p. 13

[24]Michael Lind, "The Weird Men behind George W. Bush's War," *New Statesman*, April 7, 2003, p. 12.

[25]Joseph R. Biden Jr., "The National Dialogue on Iraq + One Year," Brookings Institution, Washington D.C., July 31, 2003 (www.brook.edu/comm/events/20030731.htm [accessed August 2003]).

STUDY AND DISCUSSION QUESTIONS

1. What are the core features of the Bush doctrine?
2. Are Daalder and Lindsay right to call the Bush foreign policy revolutionary? Or are they framing the question in a partisan manner?
3. How might Ikenberry characterize the Bush doctrine? How revolutionary would he consider it?

Globalization and European Integration

13

European Integration and Globalization

George Ross

For many, the EU represents more than anything else a collective regional response to the global challenges of economic interdependence. It also represents an effort to sustain a distinctive social and economic model promising extensive (and expensive) social insurance, income redistribution, and the public provision of health care, university education, and generous pensions. Do global competitive pressures make it all but impossible for the EU to sustain this model? Or will this most extensive experiment in pooled sovereignty—now extending to 25 states— prove that state power combined into a formidable regional bloc can harness the forces of globalization to achieve desirable goals?

In this selection, George Ross traces the complex interplay of stages of globalization and European integration. He argues that it is an oversimplification to view the Economic and Monetary Union (EMU) and the completion of the Single Market simply as a response to globalization. Ross explains, rather, that it is important to focus on the motivations of key national players and the interpretations of globalization that motivated their behavior. He worries that the EU's reading of globalization and the policy decisions that resulted are leading toward a convergence between the European and American social and economic models.

GLOBALIZATION AND THE BEGINNINGS
OF EUROPEAN INTEGRATION

A half century has passed since modern European integration began. In the aftermath of the Second World War, European nations sought workable formulas for new co-operation, and eventually six among them—Italy, France, West

Germany, Belgium, The Netherlands and tiny Luxembourg—agreed on the 1957 Treaty of Rome that established the European Economic Community (now the European Union, EU).[1] Much lay behind this search, including a genuine desire to prevent Europe from regressing to bloody warfare. Yet the origins of European integration may best be seen in the light of globalizing tendencies at work at the time, even if the word was not used at the time.

Three Globalizing Processes and the New Europe

Arguably the most important influence on the coming of European integration was the emergence of the United States as an economic superpower. Initially the Americans seemed more concerned with setting up a viable 'globalized' trading regime than with regional integration. US leadership thus reconstructed the capitalist world's financial operations in the Bretton Woods system, involving US commitment to make the dollar a global reserve currency backed by a fixed gold standard. It also was decisive in founding a World Bank and the International Monetary Fund to grant individual trading nations the financial leeway to run occasional international payments deficits and to police the system in the interests of balanced international accounts. The General Agreement on Tariffs and Trade (GATT), a multilateral organization to promote free trade, also came from this period.

The Europeans, flat broke after the war, needed to rebuild but they had little to trade and no money to pay for what they bought. The Americans very quickly got involved in the loan business. The coming of the Marshall Plan in 1947 formalized and elaborated the American role as financier of European recovery, making billions of dollars available for the reconstruction of European economies, provided mainly that the Europeans co-ordinated plans for putting the money to good use. Only Western Europeans signed on, however. The USSR and its satellite countries, who were invited, refused to participate. The Plan also prodded the Europeans to greater regional economic co-operation through the Organization for European Economic Cooperation (OEEC). In general, the Europeans used Marshall Plan aid in ways that suited their national goals. But America's globalizing purposes had to be heeded.

The outbreak of Cold War, the systematic confrontation between the United States and the Soviet Union, coincided with the Marshall Plan and involved a second, different process of 'globalizing', this one geo-strategic. Cold War mobilization and rearmament formed the background for European integration. The biggest step was taken by the USA itself when it committed huge new resources for the most massive peacetime military build-up in its history. The USA then promoted and largely paid for European nations to follow through the formation of the North Atlantic Alliance, founded in 1949. American troops and matériel were stationed strategically throughout Europe under a unified North Atlantic Treaty Organization (NATO) command structure. In essence, the security environment within which European integration began had become a global one dominated by superpower rivalry in general, and, from the point of view of future EU members, specifically by American power. Put another way, the bulk of European national military capacity was pooled into new transnational arrangements over which Europeans themselves had but minimal control, a loss of sovereignty that happened long before recent economic globalization.

The 1950 Schuman Plan, which led to the European Coal and Steel Community (ECSC), the first breakthrough to integration, was an indirect product of this new and globalizing economic, political and security setting. The immediate ideas came from the fertile brain of Jean Monnet, but the constraints which made producing such ideas necessary—American pressure to resolve outstanding postwar economic and political differences between the French and the Germans and thus normalize the new Germany and allow it to participate in European defence in the Cold War context—were global. In the immediate wake of ECSC success, advocates of integration decided to promote the 'Monnet method' of sectoral integration with supranational ambitions in other areas, failing in the beginning, most spectacularly with the European Defence Community (EDC). Energy returned quickly, however, under the leadership of the Belgian Paul-Henri Spaak, with Monnet in the background. The Spaak Report of April 1956 suggested 'a European common market . . . [leading to] a vast zone with a common economic policy.'

The two Treaties of Rome in 1957 officially founded the European Economic Community (EEC) and Euratom (the European Atomic Energy Authority). Underlying the success were deals between France and Germany, themselves undergirded by the logics of the Cold War. A common market was at the core of the new EU to remove barriers to trade and establish rules for promoting trading relationships among member states. It would also create a common commercial policy towards third countries and abolish 'obstacles to freedom of movement for persons, services and capital' among member states. Its other general objectives included common policies in agriculture, transport, a 'system ensuring that competition in the common market is not distorted,' and procedures for co-ordinating economic policy and controlling balance of payments disequilibria. There were also a European Social Fund and a European Investment Bank to promote the development of less developed regions and 'association of the overseas countries and territories.' Member states would be obligated to harmonize their legal systems on common market matters.

The initial period of implementation of the Rome Treaty revealed yet a third form of globalization, the transnational diffusion of an American model of consumerism and mass production. Europeans began to taste the joys of cars, household appliances, seaside vacations and television. [Mass] manufacturing was the driving force, usually in large 'national champion' companies. By the 1960s average growth in EU member states was an impressive 5+ per cent per year and trade among them grew even more rapidly than economic growth itself.

Paradoxical Globalization and National Specificity

This third form of globalization was paradoxical, however. For the period of the great post-war boom, from 1950 to 1974, the diffusion of the American model helped reconfigure European *national* developmental models, along with a solidification of democratic institutions, new commitments to social justice and the redistribution of wealth. Where did European integration fit, then? These national islands of new . . . [mass] consumerism were highly interdependent. Economically, each traded more and more with the others. Integration decisively helped increase such trade. Politically the Germans needed Europe to rebuild self-respect and credibility after the Nazi era. Others needed Europe to keep the Germans in place. Everyone needed the United States for military help in the context of Cold War, and the United States wanted the Europeans to co-ordinate.

This confluence of globalizing and nationalizing trends meant that European integration and national goals coexisted with difficulty. The EU's designers had clearly nourished hopes that the integrationist activists they were letting loose in Brussels, particularly at the European Commission, would rapidly 'Europeanize' more and more activities. They also counted on functional linkages between policy areas to create a snowball towards greater integration. National leaders, promoting their own national models, had little desire to see the EU's mandate enlarged, however. The problems crystallized as the new EU carried out the busy schedule of activities prescribed by the Rome Treaty. Constructing the customs union went well, the EU negotiated for its members in the General Agreement on Tariffs and Trade (GATT) and certain other processes were smooth. Dealing with matters which could interfere in the internal business of member states was more of a problem, however. In particular regulatory issues like competition policy, social protection and regional development presented challenges. Setting up the Common Agricultural Policy (CAP) was perhaps most complicated.

The treaties had proposed that after January 1966, the Council of Ministers would be able to decide certain matters by qualified majority, implying that a nation might be outvoted. This was anathema to President Charles de Gaulle of France, who forced everyone into the so-called 'Luxembourg Compromise' of January 1966. After this point unanimity became the EU decision-making rule for nearly two decades. De Gaulle spoke not only for France. Most member state governments were at the epicentre of national economic and social regulatory mechanisms and in a period when national trajectories in macroeconomic, industrial and social policy were successful there was little real demand for a major transfer of regulatory activities to a supranational level. EU institutional and policy development thus stalled after the mid-1960s at about the level which its member states needed. The Common Market became a handmaiden to continental

Europe's post-war boom, a useful tool for certain purposes, but unwelcome in other areas. The further Europeanization of economic processes that the Rome Treaty had originally proposed, the movement of capital, for example, was not on the cards, since it would have undercut the key components of the different national models.

In the early 1970s, after the first, 'Common Market' phase of implementing the Rome Treaty was completed, European idealism re-emerged. Leaders thus set out plans to 'widen' the EU by including the British, Danish, Irish and Norwegians and to 'deepen' it by giving the Community larger budgetary powers, foreign policy co-ordination and Economic and Monetary Union (EMU). The EU enlarged from six to nine members in 1973 (the Norwegians voted against in a national referendum). There were ambitious new plans in regional development (through the creation of the European Regional Development Fund) and social policy as well. The world around Europe was changing, however, leading to policy divergence between key member states. The French, still determined to minimize EU supranationality, disagreed with the Germans about Economic and Monetary Union. *Détente* in the Cold War renewed debate about foreign policy issues. Most importantly, enlargement to Britain was troublesome. The British quickly became chronic EU nay-sayers, particularly on budgetary matters. Monetary policy also became a troubling issue, traceable to a sea-change in the post-war order, the collapse of the American-administered Bretton Woods monetary system. The new financial world brought fluctuating, often volatile, exchange rates which made EU members more vulnerable. The EU first agreed in 1972 to establish a currency 'snake'—an arrangement to keep EU currencies within 2.5 percent of one another within a broader 'tunnel' of exchange values. The snake disappeared in the fallout from the 1973 oil shock. The oil price rise fed an already inflationary environment, causing prices to jump rapidly. Efforts to fine-tune this problem contributed to the perplexing policy environment of 'stagflation'—simultaneous inflation and sluggish growth.

This was a turning point in Europe's post-war history. The boom was ending, growth levels declined and unemployment began to grow. From this point European economies would have great difficulty sustaining near-full employment, maintaining spending on social programmes and keeping their public finances in order. When EU member states initially improvised on old themes to cope, usually assuming that the new conditions were transitory, it made matters worse. Productivity, profit margins and investment levels declined and European industry began to lose competitive advantage. Europe's 1970s failures were constructed of the same national materials as earlier successes. The 1960s had deepened tendencies toward inflexible labour markets, inflation and statist economic management, creating patterns that shaped responses in the 1970s. Organized labor had a clear interest in protecting jobs and post-war reforms in industrial relations and social policy. The political left, whose strength was based largely on labor, had its own stake in post-war strategies. Capital had depended upon the national state for favours, protection and subsidies. Finally, state managers had their own interests to advance. Political structures and coalitions at the coming of the crisis therefore led national governments virtually everywhere towards accentuation of the specifically national developmental strategies that earlier had worked so successfully.

PROACTIVITY OR AN ACCIDENTAL APPROACH TO GLOBALIZATION? THE EU TO MAASTRICHT

By the end of the 1970s, EU members had begun to *need* 'more Europe.' Convinced, however, that the national development strategies which had worked so well during the post-war boom could be revitalized, most member states did not *want* more Europe. Policy divergence grew. International trade expanded less rapidly than it had and intra–EC trade expansion virtually stopped. The 'Common Market,' the EU's first stage, ultimately rose and fell as an instrument of a capitalist 'Europe of States.' Accounting for the renewal of European integration which came next constitutes an intriguing puzzle. Many in the globalization debate claim that it should be explained in terms of globalization—European nations returned to integration because changes in their international surroundings obliged them to. Another answer, one which I find more adequate, is that European nations, reacting to the collapse of their earlier efforts to conciliate national political economies with a more open trade setting through the Common Market, renewed European integration to cope with this collapse. In the process they probably promoted globalization rather more than responding to it.

'1992' and the Return of European Integration

First, however, we should review the story. In the mid-1980s an extraordinary turnaround began. The return of energetic European integration was part of a new strategy to de-emphasize the role of national states in economic life and create a regional economic bloc structured around a liberated single European market. The shift involved first of all an admission by European elites that post-war national models could no longer be sustained. The key moment came when France, which with Germany took the lead, abandoned its post–1981 strategy of 'social democracy in one country' in spring 1983. In the first half of 1984, under the French Presidency of the Council of Ministers, the dimensions of France's shift to a 'Europe option' became clearer. At Fontainebleau in spring 1984 Mitterrand began to untie the EU's knots, in particular the chronic dispute over the 'British Check.' This made fruitful discussion possible in other areas, in particular enlarging the Community to Portugal and Spain. Jacques Delors, a former French Minister of Finances, was appointed President of the European Commission.

It was the Delors European Commission which devised the new EU agenda in its 1985 White Paper on Completing the Internal Market. This, the '1992' programme, was a list of 279 measures to unify the EU's largely separate national markets into an 'area without internal boundaries in which the free movement of goods, persons, services and capital is ensured.' The White Paper also included a timetable which scheduled the sequencing of legislation over two consecutive Commission terms (eight years), hence '1992.' The European Council of June 1985 then agreed to call an 'intergovernmental conference' (IGC) which resulted in treaty changes called the Single European Act (SEA) which linked completing the Single Market to a change in EC decision-making procedures involving 'qualified majority' decisions in most White Paper areas and an extension of the amending powers of the European Parliament.[2] It also proposed an extended list of areas in which the EU could act, including regional development policy ('economic and social cohesion'), research and technological development, and the environment.

'1992' was a quick political success. Business liked it and this helped change a morose climate. Governments in the poorer parts of the EC/EU liked it because of the SEA's promise for increased development aid. Public opinion was benignly positive at first, largely because the Single Market policies were cost-free in the short run (since they would take considerable time to be legislated and come into effect and only then be felt). Organized labour, already taking a huge beating, was unhappier, worrying about the 'social dumping' implications of '1992,' but the Delors Commission tried hard to placate its anxieties. The most important source of support for the new Single Market policies, however, was good economic luck. At about the point when awareness emerged that something new was happening in Brussels, European economies started to turn up, investment and business confidence rose. This was as much coincidence as cause and effect, but Europe's new activism could then be associated with a renewal of growth, prosperity and job creation.

The '1992' programme brought a number of ambitious complementary programmes, facilitated by the newly promising setting created by Single Market enthusiasm. The first, perhaps most significant, came in the 'Delors Budgetary Package' of 1987. The 'reform of the Structural Funds,' in part a payoff to new Spanish and Portuguese EU members, brought significant commitment to redistribution between richer and poorer member states. Resources would be co-ordinated on a set of prior objectives, the budget for regional aid was to be doubled over the period through 1992, when it would amount to 25 per cent of Community spending and the use of these funds would be planned, mainly by the Commission.[3]

Proposals for Economic and Monetary Union (EMU) came next, in 1987. EMU, to include a common monetary policy, a powerful European Central Bank and a single European currency, was advertised as the logical culmination of the Single Market. Without EMU, currency fluctuations and monetary policy divergence could cause instability and tempt member states to back away from single market commitments. The new campaign began in 1987 with the commissioning of the Delors Report, which, when submitted in 1989, proposed a three-stage path toward EMU plus a new Intergovernmental Conference to redo the EU treaty to fit in EMU. The deeper logic of the EMU plan was political. Pooling monetary and portions of economic policy sovereignty would necessitate supranational control over a wide range of economic matters. The single currency, when it came, would completely remove the tool of currency revaluation from national policy makers.

Up to this point the overwhelming logic of the renewal of European integration was 'market building,' the elimination of barriers to trade and competition by deregulation and liberalization. Efforts made by various actors, in particular the Delors Commission, to promote 'spillover' into areas of market re-regulation at European level were relatively limited, with the one important exception of the reform of the structural funds. In particular, hopes that the redistributive effects of the new Single Market would facilitate new initiatives in Euro-level social policy fell rather flat. The May 1989 'Community Charter of Fundamental Social Rights,' or Social Charter, was a 'solemn commitment' on the part of member states—only eleven, given furious British opposition—to a set of wage-earner rights based on unfulfilled social promises the Community's treaty base already contained. The Commission quickly produced an action programme to implement it but unanimity decision rules meant that little beyond workplace health and safety proposals, decided by qualified majority, could get through. The Single European Act also included a new Article 118B stating that 'the Commission shall endeavour to develop the dialogue between management and labour at European level which could, if the two sides consider it desirable, lead to relations based on agreement.' The 'social dialogue' which followed did not produce many concrete results, however.

By 1991, the Maastricht negotiating year, the renewal of European integration had reached fever pitch. The Commission was producing unprecedented amounts of legislation to implement the '1992' programme, implementing the reform of regional policy and trying to innovate in social policy areas. The GATT Uruguay Round talks were reaching a critical point and the EU and the United States were staring one another down about the international trade effects of the CAP. The Community also had to respond to the end of the Cold War and German unification. Last, but not least, the member states had committed themselves to two new Intergovernmental Conferences to change the EU treaties. The climax came with the controversial Maastricht Treaty.[4]

At Maastricht, getting a deal on EMU was relatively easy because the 1989 Delors Report had set out a programme which the talks followed. Even the sticking points were predictable. The Germans, asked to give up the deutschmark, wanted EMU to provide iron-clad guarantees about price stability and financial responsibility. The British opposed EMU. The Spanish wanted commitment to more North-South redistribution. These hurdles were all overcome. Discussions on 'political union,' held separately, were another story. The idea of talking about political union—a common foreign and security policy, greater democratization of the Community, more efficient institutions and coherence in monetary, economic and political action—had emerged only in spring 1990. This gave very little time to make the careful preparations needed to make interstate negotiations orderly.

The Maastricht negotiations brought out classic disagreements about the desirable nature of European integration between 'federalists' and 'intergovern-mentalists' and between member states which wanted European integration in the political area and those which preferred minimalism. The proposed 'common foreign and security policy' divided 'Atlanticists' insisting upon the pre-eminence of NATO from those who desired independent European positions. How the EU might be given greater 'democratic legitimacy' was murky as well. The Germans wanted to give more power to the European Parliament. Others, including the French, wanted greater involvement for national parliaments. Finally, there were chronic differences between North and South over development help—the South wanted more and the North did not want to pay.

The final Maastricht document (135 pages, 17 'Protocols,' various addenda and 33 separate declarations) was difficult even for insiders to read. It was also problematic in a 'constitutional' sense, since it divided up essential matters among three 'pillars,' each with different decision rules. Its substance was the most prob-lematic matter of all, however. EMU would mean that member states would no longer control their currencies and monetary policies. Europe, or rather Europe's proposed new central banking system, would gain much of what the member states lost. Even before full EMU came they would no longer be able to adjust the value of their currencies, run large deficits, allow high levels of inflation and build up large debts, all techniques that had traditionally been useful to cushion domes-tic economies against changes coming from outside. The range of macroeconomic management instruments available to national states would be narrowed to direct taxation policies (indirect taxation being part of the Single Market and hence also guided from European levels). The political union results were less clear. What Maastricht said and what it led to were certain to be different since much of the treaty was vague and 'evolutive,' an EU word for vague and open-ended. The CFSP provisions left almost everything to future politicking. The defence area was an empty shell fraught with future disagreements. The ultimate meanings of other Maastricht provisions, the clauses on 'European citizenship,' for example, or the 'third pillar' on justice and internal affairs, were virtually impossible to foresee.

Globalization and Renewed European Integration: A False Correlation?

It is all too facile to argue from the present back to the mid-1980s and claim that renewed European integration was in response to globalization. In fact, the record shows that this is far from true. It is important to ask first about the motives of key European actors during this period. Did they think that they were responding to globalization? Or, alternatively, did they perceive themselves as anticipating globalizing trends proactively?

Jacques Delors, President of the European Commission, was clearly one such leader, and in this period he was wont to announce that rapid new European integration was a matter of 'survival or decline.' Without it Europe would soon be swamped by the Americans and the Japanese. The discourse which Delors most often used was significant. Completing the Single Market, EMU and the rest were, to Delors, proactive efforts to prepare Europe to respond effectively to changes in the transnational setting, but not to globalization as currently defined. Delors perceived the dangers facing Europe as coming from the other regions of the 'Triad,' primarily in terms of a growing disparity in competitiveness. To him Europe's economic performance was falling more and more behind other advanced capitalist regions. Renewing European integration was an appropriate response. Creating a Single European Market could set up an internally open European regional economy in which business and other actors would gain economies of scale, broader strategic vision and greater competitive challenge. The hope was that in consequence they would abandon parochial national outlooks and adopt new European identities and relationships. EMU was needed, first of all, because the Single Market would be precarious without it. In addition, it could help diminish Europe's vulnerability to inflation and monetary instability created by American inability and/or unwillingness to anchor the international monetary system.

There is considerable evidence that much of large European business shared Delors' perspectives. The other leading political actors had additional geostrategic motives, particularly the Franco-German 'couple.' French President François Mitterrand had strong domestic and foreign political reasons for pushing for more Europe. In need of a new strategy to substitute for the failure of his 1981 socialist programme, he decided that renewed European integration, particularly if it worked economically, might be useful. More Europe had the added advantage for Mitterrand of being an ideal way to 'exogenize' reforms that would be explosive if attempted purely within the French domestic scene. Mitterrand also believed that new Europeanization could lead to French centrality in the EU, giving France an international weight—*grandeur?*—beyond its objective capacities. The Germans could not lead, given their history. The British did not believe in Europe. Beyond this, Mitterrand had come of age in the years around World War Two and it was personally very important to him—and traditionally important to French diplomacy—to deepen the commitment of the Germans to the EU and keep them out of the continental mischief that had caused such trouble in the past. This particular concern became even more urgent as the Cold War ended. Finally, reinforced European integration might ultimately help France achieve its traditional Gaullist dream of a Europe freed from American domination.

The German leader, Helmut Kohl, shared Mitterrand's goal of grounding Germany in EU Europe, both because he understood Germany's past and because

Europe promised to provide political cover for growing German economic power that was needed to moderate anti-German feelings. Ultimately, however, Germany wanted more and better markets for its goods. British Prime Minister Margaret Thatcher, who ultimately lost out to the Franco-German couple, initially saw the Single Market as one route toward the deregulated quasi-free-trade zone of her Britannic dreams. Other key European leaders had their own domestic, geopolitical and economic interests. The Spanish and Portuguese saw Europe as an anchor for democratization, as a tool to change their economies and as a source of investment capital. The Italians, strongly European in most circumstances, shared many of these purposes. What was most interesting in all this, however, was that renewing European integration to confront some kind of abstract globalization was rarely considered at all.

There are no clear cases that globalization *per se* had priority, however globalization might be defined, in this list of leadership and elite preferences. To be sure, this cannot be taken to mean that globalizing changes played no role in structuring these preferences. But the review does demonstrate, at the very least, that leadership preferences and purposes in the renewal of European integration were many and varied. Globalization issues, when present, were usually combined with other priorities and concerns. At the very least, therefore, it is not particularly useful to draw causal arrows between globalizing processes as independent variables and new Europeanization. More important, the fact cannot be disregarded that the arrows run in the opposite direction from any theory of globalization as independent variable. Renewed European integration, in other words, might have had an important effect in promoting new globalization.

Finally, whatever the varying motives of central actors, what they *did* in responding to processes of difficult-to-decode change was profoundly 'path-dependent.' Despite the demoralization of the 'Eurosclerosis' years, deep European commitments, institutions, ways of problem-solving and customs already existed. 'Europeanizing' important matters was a habit for European elites built upon significant sunk costs. Thus, given new stimuli in the early 1980s, key European leaders did not really have an abstract choice between 'going it alone' nationally or going forward to 'more Europe.' More Europe provided a much more familiar and compelling course of action. This meant, however, that whatever the reasons for new elite actions—globalization or other—strong incentives towards European integrationist responses existed. The constraints created by this path dependency therefore biased European responses to economic change in central ways.

Path-dependent incentives existed in the choice of concrete policies. Completing the Single Market and EMU had been first broached much earlier (at the Hague Summit in 1969, in fact) as ways of carrying out the 'finalities' of the Rome Treaties after the first, Common Market, phase had been completed. Moreover, they had been discussed to the point of 'solemn commitment' before being shelved. When new circumstances emerged in the Eurosclerosis period of the later 1970s and early 1980s these already legitimated options, whose contents were already sketched, were there to invoke as precedents to follow. Thus when it became possible politically to renew European integration it was these options, rather than starting anew, which were chosen. The ideas, shapes and logics behind what happened in the later 1980s had thus been set out long before anyone had reflected about globalization.

GLOBALIZATION IN ONE REGION: THE TERRIBLE 1990S

The renewal of European integration should thus not be seen as either a reactive or proactive response to perceived 'globalization,' at least in the popular sense that the term globalization is now used. Much of what happened after the mid-1980s was meant to resolve problems that had little directly to do with globalization. Moreover, the precise forms of European integration which occurred in this period derived from path-dependent incentives whose logics had been set out long before globalization was a serious concern. These reflections lead to an intriguing, and seemingly perverse, query. Might it be that rather than responding to globalization, the renewal of European integration in the 1980s was significant in hastening globalization's coming? The possibility is worth exploring.

Does European Integration Promote Globalization?

Everyone agrees that enhanced international trade liberalization is one essential component of globalization. That the Single Market programme sought the particular liberalization of financial operations (the end of exchange controls, restrictions on capital movements, the creation of single markets for insurance and banks, etc.) can easily be interpreted as a contributing factor to the rapid intensification of transnational financial flows that is now apparent. Here there is obviously a chicken-and-egg problem, because it might just as easily be argued that financial liberalization in Europe was caused by these flows. Nonetheless, financial liberalization was clearly embedded in the Single Market idea, in the famous 'four freedoms of movement,' of goods, services, labour and capital, consecrated as the EU's purpose long before the term globalization became current. Whichever view one adopts, however, that Europe liberalized rather than maintained both internal and international restrictions is highly significant to the explosion of financial dealings we see in the 1990s.

One of the claims most often made for globalization is that it has led to a marked diminution in national policy capacities. Proponents of strong globalization theses most often see the central causal arrows as flowing from autonomous international changes into national contexts. Globalization is the independent variable, in other words, national contexts the intermediate variable, and specific losses in national policy capacities the consequences. Where doubt is permitted, at least for Europe, is in explaining why this has occurred. Take, first of all, one of the most significant losses of national capacity in the economic and monetary policy realms. The current setting for all capitalist societies is one where major constraints exist compelling any country to pursue price stability and avoid public deficits and indebtedness. In this area it may well be possible to speak of a new transnational anti-inflationary monetary 'regime' which has replaced its Keynesian predecessor. The causes of this regime may not be globalization *per se,* however. Renewed European integration made decisive contributions to its elaboration, which occurred in specific policy decisions by particular actors.

The U.S. Federal Reserve, the Reagan Administration and the new British Conservative government all turned to deflationary policies in 1979–80, together causing a huge recession. These decisions aligned the Americans and the British with the Germans, with their own long-standing commitment to price stability. All of this made French Socialist plans after 1981 much more difficult to pursue, leading to the policy shifts of 1983–84. It was at this point that French President Mitterrand decided to implement his new 'Europe option'. French commitment to price stability, judged a necessary complement to the Europe option (alignment of the franc and the DM were deemed important for establishing the credibility of other French European initiatives), created general policy alignment.

It was the institutionalization of this alignment in European monetary policy which turned a set of discrete policy choices into a regime. The EU further institutionalized the regime in its plans for EMU and, later, the 'convergence criteria' for creating EMU which constrained all potential EMU members to control inflation, debt, deficits, currency valuation and interests within very strict limits. The importance of all this for levels of employment in Europe needs also to be underlined. No doubt declining competitiveness and a certain degree (perhaps smaller than generally believed) of employment loss to parts of the developing world explain part of the growth in EU unemployment levels which, incidentally, coincided with renewed European integration. Constraints on rigid price stability and budget balancing account for a large part. Moreover, the creation of a regime was an important element in transferring veto power over economic policy to international financial markets.

The Single Market itself also contributed powerfully to removing capacities from EU states, as it was meant to do. The '1992' programme moved a wide range of policy prerogatives from national to European level while simultaneously 'marketizing' many of the same realms of policy. EU member states thus not only lost policy levers which had been central in the national development models that preceded the '1992' programme, but also these policy areas were largely removed from political determination altogether as they were Europeanized. The marketizing bias of EU treaties and prevailing diplomatic circumstances clearly limited any substantial relocation of regulatory activity to EU level. Studying the fate of the efforts made by the Delors Commissions and their member state supporters to broaden the EU's mandate into market regulating activities in social, regional, environmental and industrial policy is revelatory. Despite considerable goodwill the results turned out to be thin indeed.[5] From the point of view of European citizens, therefore, renewed European integration meant declining ability to constrain and shape markets to promote desirable public goals in social and industrial relations policies, for example. Moreover, the new setting created additional incentives for business to promote labour market and social policy deregulation in the interests of the 'flexibility' needed to cope.

Intentional Globalization on One Small Continent?

We have established that renewed European integration was a complex construction which flowed from multiple motives in response to a variety of pressing problems. It is hard to credit any strong version of globalization as the independent variable, or even as a powerful variable at all. Despite this, the EU is rapidly looking like an exercise in 'anticipatory globalization in one region.' What does this mean? Globalization is supposed to be a process which subordinates nations and their peoples to irresistible market flows beyond their control. In consequence these nations lose earlier capacities to shape economic life and their citizens lose considerable political power—democratic power?—to decide desirable outcomes, particularly distributive outcomes. Whether global trends have done this or not in general, and this remains an open question, the Single Market has simulated it for citizens of EU nations. These nations can no longer regulate economic exchanges within the Single Market. Indeed, given the marketization of most regulatory decisions, there is no one who can do this.

The implementation of Economic and Monetary Union, . . . [begun] on 1 January 1999, . . . greatly accentuated what has already happened. Decisions, taken largely on German insistence, at the Dublin European Council in December 1996 . . . [extended] the stringent Maastricht convergence criteria (in a 'stability and growth pact') well into the [current] century. Strong guidance and police mechanisms to enforce price stability and budgetary stringency will be backed by the threat of very large sanctions (penalties to miscreant nations of up to 0.5 per cent of GDP are possible).

All this means that the great pressures on governments to pursue rigid price stability and balance budgets, which have been closely correlated with rising unemployment in the 1990s, will be continued. EMU and . . . the single currency will in themselves remove any possibility of national governments adjusting to changed economic circumstances through the traditional monetary techniques of currency revaluation and interest rate shifts. This means that adjustments will have to be accomplished through changing price and wage levels and manipulating state spending, largely in social protection areas. The implications are clear.

EMU will act to exert strong pressures on European nations to 'Americanize' their labour markets and welfare states.

CONCLUSIONS: THE PRICE OF PRECOCIOUS GLOBALIZATION?

A social scientist named Karl Marx projected the 'heavy tendencies' of globalization 150 years ago. It would therefore be foolish indeed for us to deny that globalization is of consequence for modern European integration. But, as the invocation of Marx indicates, globalization must be seen as a long-term affair, beginning with the voyages of exploration, continuing with colonization and mercantilism, progressing through imperialism and neocolonialism to the present period when financial globalization is a fact, when transnational corporations do see large areas of the planet as their territory, when advanced capitalism has spread well beyond the North American and European regions where it began and when new regions of the world have been integrated into its labour and product markets. Moreover, it would stand to reason, to Marx at least, that globalization could not be seen as simply a process in which autonomous economic flows almost magically become 'global' from having earlier been 'national.' Capitalism had global dimensions, from its earliest points. Quite as important, capitalist globalization occurred, and continues to occur, because specific actors seek to resolve important strategic dilemmas by choices which move them outside earlier geographic parameters. What we now label as globalization may well be the unintended product of strategic choices meant to confront problems which had little or nothing to do with globalization.

At its origins European integration was meant to resolve European regional problems, not to promote globalization. Yet its creation was strongly conditioned by processes of globalization at work long before the concept was used in popular discourse, among them the reconfiguration of great power politics into a bipolar-planetary mode, the reconfiguration of the capitalist world's monetary and financial system to reflect US power and the success of American-style Fordist consumerism as a model for Europe and others to emulate. The irony in early European integration was that Europeanization, in the context of these globalizing processes, created a setting of strongly self-contained national political economies which moved from success to success for more than two decades. When 'crisis' arrived in the 1970s, brought less by globalization than by the discrete acts of oil producers and American administrations, European integration plunged into a dismal, and potentially disaggregating, *sauve qui peut* cycle in which EU members responded by accentuating national strategies at the price of increasing policy divergence in the EU more broadly. The renewal of European integration in the 1980s was caused less by globalization than by strategic choices by key European actors to accelerate integration rather than to continue these discrete national strategies. These choices were constructed around path-dependent constraints left by the earlier period of European integration before globalization was in the current vocabulary. The results, however, look today very much as if European leaders were trying to simulate globalization within the EU—whether or not it actually existed anywhere else. Whatever we make of this, it is clear that the largely unintended consequences of decisions to deepen European integration after 1985 have promoted globalization.

The problem is that these recent stages in the globalization process, whatever their causes, have encouraged massive hyperbole. All manner of claims have been made about the ineluctable decline of the nation-state, completely footloose capitalism and the rapid disappearance of national margins of manoeuvre in economic matters. The image we have used to illustrate this hyperbole is one in which a 'global economy,' floating free above continents, acts as an unrestrained and all-powerful independent variable obliging nations, peoples and individuals to respond. That significant change underlies these claims is clear, although it is doubtful, first of all, that reality corresponds to the rhetoric and, next, that causality is as simple as the rhetoric claims. There is another disturbing side to the globalization discourse. It is clearly tainted with interests when it is not directly 'interested.' Capital and conservative elites routinely use it to undercut the popular gains—the welfare state, civility in industrial relations, high wages—of the 'Golden Age' after the war. That social scientists should have bought into this rhetoric, often without serious examination, should lead us to doubt their claims to scientific detachment.

Another deep question is in order. Who can now know whether the forward movement of European integration taken in the last fifteen years of the twentieth century will turn out ultimately to have been an inadvertently proactive response to globalizing trends? In other words, even if the renewal of European integration was largely not to confront new indices of globalization, will it turn out to have been an appropriate response to globalization despite this? All we know now is that for a variety of reasons European leaders have pursued a course of action which has simulated what globalization is claimed to be doing everywhere, within the continental boundaries of the EU. Elite European actors have created huge structural constraints on what European governments can do, and these constraints seem certain to grow considerably in the near future. Other things being equal, European national governments have sacrificed many of their capacities to shape market flows, monetary policy and budgets. To what extent the effects of an EU Single Market, EMU and the projected Euro will sap and perhaps even reconfigure the 'European model of society' with its humane welfare states, civilized industrial relations procedures and negotiated settlements between groups remains to be seen. It is clear that new European integration has comforted the interests which would like to see change in all these areas. These interests disagree, however, on what kind of change should occur—reform or dismantling. It has become clear, as well, that the populations of Europe's nations do not particularly want what their leaders have designed for them. Were the Single Market and

EMU now submitted to referenda across the EU there can be little doubt that they would be rejected.

Inadvertent globalization in one region has dispossessed European peoples of many of the democratic prerogatives to which they had become accustomed, and to which many had been initiated, in the period after World War Two. It is no longer possible to influence the allocation of resources and the shape of distribution through public decisions nationally as it once was. The making of many of these fundamental social choices has been shifted from politics altogether, to the market. Others have remained 'public' but have been moved into delegated undemocratic decision arenas. EMU institutions and processes are illustrative of this. Central bankers, only very lightly constrained by politicians, will control policy areas vital to the welfare of ordinary Europeans. It is worth adding that many of the decisions which have gone into the construction of this new order were also made on the outer margins of democratic legitimacy, as has almost always been the case in the history of European integration. European national leaders opted for new Europeanization *in camera*, through diplomacy, using the extensive executive powers reserved to them in foreign affairs to change Europe fundamentally and, in many cases, also to 'exogenize' processes of change which they never could have implemented in their domestic political arenas. Moreover, to the extent to which the European Commission, whatever its good intentions, has pushed new Europeanization forward through the long-consecrated 'Monnet method' of promoting integration by stealth, convinced that it was doing good for European peoples behind their backs, similar remarks are in order.

European integration has most often been defended as a set of techniques to allow different European peoples, each with strong identities, to live together in peace. Centuries of bloody warfare attested to the need for this. Yet recent European integration has gone beyond its original purpose of knitting different nations together in tapestries of mutual exchange and confidence towards removing the control of important matters from the hands of the European peoples themselves. However much the world has changed in recent decades, it is undeniable that these peoples still maintain strong national identities and desires to shape their own national fates. It would be ironic indeed were European integration's simulation of globalization in one corner of one continent to lead to a re-stimulation of these identities and the rekindling of old and best-buried animosities. The various manifestations of intolerant populisms that one sees across the continent are probably less the issue than what is likely to occur as EMU comes into existence and ordinary Europeans are called upon to sacrifice even more than they already have on the altar of Europe. There may eventually be a very large bill to pay.

Notes

[1]The European Union came into being when the Maastricht Treaty was ratified in November 1993. 'Europe' (the politics and institutions of European integration) was

called the EEC (European Economic Community) or, colloquially, the 'Common Market' until the 1980s, when it became the EC (European Community). I shall use EU throughout, except when explicitly discussing the earliest years, but the reader should be aware of the anachronism.

[2]Only the most sensitive matters—fiscal policy, border controls concerning the movement of people and workers' rights—remained under unanimity rules.

[3]The structural fund priority objectives included aid to less developed regions in the EU (largely in the South), reconversion of deindustrialized areas, programmes to overcome long-term unemployment, help to enter the labour market for unemployed young people and, finally, development and structural adjustment aid in rural areas.

[4]Ross, *Jacques Delors and European Integration* (Cambridge: Polity Press, 1995), chs 3–6.

[5]On this topic see Stephan Leibfried and Paul Pierson (eds), *Social Europe* (Washington: Brookings, 1996), particularly the chapters by Martin Rhodes, Wolfgang Streeck and George Ross and the editors' conclusions.

STUDY AND DISCUSSION QUESTIONS

1. What are the three initial postwar forms of globalization? Why does Ross consider the third form, beginning with the formation of the European Economic Community (EEC), paradoxical?
2. What is the relationship between globalization and European integration?
3. Do you agree—or disagree—with Ross when he contends that the EU has misunderstood globalization and as a consequence imperiled the distinctive European social and economic model?

14

Europe in the New World Order

David P. Calleo

At least since the early 1990s, Europe and America have been operating on different geopolitical wavelengths. They have been divided over the use of force versus the advantages of diplomacy in achieving desirable foreign policy goals and at loggerheads over the virtues of multilateral organizations and international law. Europe and the United States have been embroiled in disputes over the war in Iraq. They have trouble staying on the same page when it comes to policy toward China and Taiwan, Iran, and North Korea.

Some have argued that these divisions are driven by fundamental differences in culture and perspective anchored in a huge power asymmetry.* According to this view, the United States has the preponderance of power and is prepared to use it, while the Europeans, lacking hard power, have succumbed to a psychology of weakness masked as international idealism. Hence, Europeans and Americans are divided by their different perspectives on the role of power in global politics, and are likely to remain divided.

In this selection, David Calleo takes a different approach, as he analyzes the emergence of Europe as a major geopolitical player. He suggests that the processes of European integration are likely to extend from the economic sphere to the realm of foreign affairs and collective security. Calleo looks beyond the relatively recent deterioration of transatlantic relations to anticipate an emerging world order—one that might lead to a rejuvenated Atlantic partnership on more equal footing and enhanced prospects for stability and peace.

How would a more united and powerful Europe fit within the likely global order of the twenty-first century? How it might fit depends not only on its own character but on the likely nature of the rest of the global system. A major question is whether that system will continue to be "unipolar"—dominated by the United States, the unique "indispensable nation." Certainly, no one else at the turn of the century seems in a position to supplant the United States—still the greatest military power by far and also endowed with a highly dynamic national economy, still the world's largest. But even if there is no new pretender to hegemony, the distribution of power and wealth may nevertheless be growing more "plural," and with significant consequences for global order. In any event, the strength of the United States may well be less enduring than it seems. Americans may be growing weary of hegemony and may no longer be disciplined enough politically to run the world successfully. America's superior military power may be less and less capable of being applied efficiently. The economic and military rise of Asian states may be making the world less manageable; a more independent European Union may portend a brewing geopolitical conflict within the

---

*Robert Kagan, *Of Paradise and Power: America and Europe in the New World Order* (New York: Knopf, 2003).

West itself. Or the world's economic life may be growing too complex and anarchical to be regulated by any state. This last consideration points to another familiar set of issues: the perennially tense relations between nation states and capitalism. Is globalized capitalism growing more impervious to political regulation? Is it also increasingly unstable?

Obviously, no one can answer such questions with any great assurance. We sense that Europe, America, Russia, and the Asian states are moving toward a new dispensation, within which old questions about hegemony, nation states, and capitalism may well need fresh answers. How should we now think about these questions? What can the past tell us about them?

AMERICAN HEGEMONY IN A UNIPOLAR WORLD?

Throughout the 1990s, Americans were still enjoying the Indian summer of their global hegemony. Balance as a precondition for world order was not a view strongly favored in Washington. The abrupt end of the Cold War had left behind a large bureaucracy and intellectual establishment, together with extensive economic interests—all oriented toward America's exercise of international power. After the Cold War, these elements were naturally disposed to see the world as unipolar and the United States as its unique and indispensable superpower. Events often conspired to confirm that perspective. European states were embarrassingly ineffective in the long Yugoslav crisis of the 1990s. And Europe's economies floundered while the American economy continued to steam ahead.

As a mood of military and economic triumphalism grew rampant in the American government, American policy often grew increasingly assertive and unilateral, loath to submit to multilateral decision making. American behavior in trade disputes grew increasingly imperious and quarrelsome, while projects to strengthen Europe in the world economy, like EMU, aroused widespread American suspicion and animosity. Militarily, the United States was also in an assertive mood. Within Europe, it pressed a maximalist view of NATO's future missions and membership and dragged its feet on internal reforms relaxing American hegemony. The United States was instead emphasizing its own predominance in Eurasian affairs. American military advisers, using the machinery of NATO's Partnership for Peace, were ubiquitous and active throughout Eastern Europe and Central Asia. In the Middle East, ten years after the Gulf War, the Clinton administration was still insisting on an embargo against Iraq, punctuated by desultory bombing and missile attacks, despite strong opposition among most of the European allies. Similarly, American diplomacy frowned on European efforts to return to more normal relationships with Iran. By the turn of the century, the United States was pressing strategic projects, in particular national missile defense, that seemed designed to perpetuate American military and technological

predominance, even at the cost of upsetting the world's underlying strategic stability. The Clinton administration, which had begun with a modest geopolitical
agenda and a determination to focus on domestic rejuvenation, ended up
bemused by a neo–Wilsonian globalist vision, with America the world's indispensable leader.

. . .

ANOTHER AMERICAN CENTURY?

It is difficult to look back over the 1990s without sensing a deterioration of
transatlantic relations, one manifested less in open confrontation than in quiet
mutual alienation. The deterioration continues. The prospect of a Europe growing stronger—economically, politically, and militarily—clashes with those visions
of a unipolar world popular with certain parts of America's political elites. Having had one American century, these elites are now preparing themselves for
another. This imperial American vision of the future is not very well founded. To
begin with, it misreads the nation's own basic character. Most Americans do not
see the United States as the Roman Empire reborn, nor does America's peacetime
political system easily adapt itself to a Roman future. The imperial vision also
misunderstands the sources of America's postwar success in Europe. America's
postwar strategy was not Roman. Its aim was not to annex Europe to America,
but to set Europe on its own feet as a partner rather than as a dependency.

That American strategy not only helped to restore Europe's pride but also
aroused America's own best instincts. Dragged into Europe's balance-of-power
system, the United States proved different from the typical European power at its
apogee. The United States did not act like a republican version of the Habsburgs
or the Bourbons, or even of the British Empire. America's greatest successes were
at the outset of the postwar era—from the Marshall Plan to the consolidation of
the German Federal Republic and the launching of the European Economic
Community. American leaders were notable in Europe not only for their stead-
fast resistance to the Soviets, but also for their reticence and restraint toward
their allies. American leaders succeeded not least because of their sophisticated
and generous sympathy with Europe and, in many cases, their capacity for genuine friendship with Europe's leaders.

It is interesting to speculate on the roots of this American better self—its
sympathy, generosity, and respect for other countries. History has perhaps been
kinder to the United States than to Europe's great powers. As a nation state, the
United States was planted in a bounteous, spacious, and isolated continent. It
united its polyglot and restless population around universal ideals of liberty,
opportunity, and equality before the law. It is pleasing to think that America's
idealism, diversity, and good fortune have produced a national character gener-

ous toward the outside world.[1] But, postwar America's better instincts toward its allies were undoubtedly helped by sharing with them a particularly sinister, threatening, and clumsy enemy. Ironically, the demise of that enemy seems to have brought forward a meaner and smaller America, a place where bombastic imperial visions mingle with dangerously moralistic, self-righteous, and simplistic views of past and future.

Tomorrow's global system, however, does not seem hospitable to facile imperial visions. The new Asia promises great turmoil, and Americans will almost inevitably be drawn deeply into trying to channel and accommodate its rising powers. For the United States, the Asian challenge in the new century is likely to be no less demanding than the European challenge in the last. Logically, this Asian challenge should make it in America's interest to have Europe be a serious ally rather than a costly dependency. In other words, the Asian challenge should encourage the United States to welcome a Europe that is strong and self-sufficient, one that is able to take the primary initiative for maintaining order in its own space, and one that engages generously and constructively with Russia. That sort of Europe is far more likely to be a positive world force than a fragmented Europe whose schizophrenic quarrels render it impotent and sullen, its pusillanimous nation states perennially attracted to free riding. Under the circumstances, triumphalist American diffidence toward European unity and independence in the 1990s was, for the longer term, a dysfunctional reaction for the Americans themselves. Fortunately, instead of discouraging the Europeans, it spurred them to greater efforts.

UNCONTROLLABLE CAPITALISM?

American triumphalism after the Cold War was not only military but economic. Throughout most of the 1990s, the huge American economy was almost uniquely successful among advanced nations. Nevertheless, many analysts were increasingly troubled by what seemed dangerous flaws in the economy's foundations: a basic disequilibrium evidenced by large and expanding trade and current account deficits, together with a low, even negative, rate of personal saving, heavy foreign borrowing, and a stock market whose values seemed crazily overvalued. These flaws, moreover, seem intimately related to basic problems of the world economy as a whole.

For most parts of the world economy, the 1990s were a troubled decade. The Soviet collapse at the outset was followed by a prolonged slump in Western Europe and a brutal deterioration of conditions in Japan. Most other Asian economies had fallen into severe trouble by 1998, with consequences that helped to blight the still fragile Russian recovery, then spread to Latin America and reverberated in the West itself. In this rolling global crisis, trouble began typically in currency and financial markets and then spread to production, trade, and employment. The common explanation combined the raucous volatility of world financial markets with the weakened condition of many financial institutions exposed to that volatility. In addition, a powerful deflationary trend in commodity prices, including oil, ran through much of the decade and depressed conditions in many countries, Russia included. A parallel deflationary tendency in manufactures, visible by 1996, also made trade competition increasingly sharp.

Dysfunctional legacies from the Cold War were often at the bottom of these difficulties. Arguably, the enormous pool of mobile capital that made it so easy to destabilize foreign-exchange and financial markets was a natural result of the decades of systematic monetary inflation and exploitation of the dollar, consequences related, in turn, to the West's chronic overspending for "guns and butter" and skewed burden sharing. The pitiful disarray of former Soviet economies reflected their own decades of malinvestment in war-oriented production. The later deflationary trends in manufactured goods were fed by large increases of production exported by countries with low costs and low consumption. Probably the greatest deflationary shock was the rapid entry of Chinese goods and labor into world markets in the 1980s, after decades of absence resulting from the warfare, chaos, and lunatic tyranny that had been China's fate throughout most of the twentieth century.

With Asian conditions so deflationary, the principal obstacle to a world depression lay, it seemed, in the capacity of the United States to go on absorbing the surplus products of others, while attracting foreign capital to finance its consequent very large trade deficits. By the later 1990s, American officials noted how the United States had become the world's "consumer of last resort," a major feature of America's lingering hegemonic role in the world economy. Initially, it was the outsized American appetite for imports that helped call into being the rapidly growing export industries of Asia's "little tigers" in the 1970s, just as it had greatly facilitated the rapid growth of Japanese exports earlier in the 1960s. America's trade and current account deficits grew still larger in the 1980s. By the 1990s, they were swelling to new records and, in the process, underwriting China's explosive entry into the global economy. With deflationist trends menacing the international economy, any serious improvement in America's trade balance threatened to collapse what was left of Asia's "export-led" growth and reinforce a spiral of deflation around the world.

America's ability to continue absorbing the rest of the world's surplus production depended on its own habitual high consumption and low saving, together with its capacity to finance the consequent current account deficits easily and cheaply. By the late 1990s, America's heavy consuming habits seemed to depend on the wealth effects of what many feared was an already vastly inflated stock market. At the same time, EMU's launching of the euro, fated to rival the dollar as a reserve currency, cast doubt on whether America's habitual easy financing of external deficits could continue indefinitely. Arguably, a global economy whose prosperity appeared to rest on such uncertain foundations needed serious structural adjustment. The old forms of American economic hegemony were no longer adequate.

From an American perspective, an obvious solution was for the EU to start absorbing a larger share of the world's bloated production. In 1997, for example, with a GDP roughly the same size as the American GDP, the EU's current account surplus was roughly $117 billion, and its trade with Asia was approximately in balance. The United States, by contrast, had an overall current account deficit close to $155 billion and a trade deficit with Asia of around $141 billion. With Europe's growth sluggish and its unemployment high, boosting its demand seemed an obvious prescription. Doing so would presumably stimulate not only domestic production and employment but also imports. Fear that such a course would lead to inflation seemed unreasonable; the EU's overall rate of price increases was low throughout most of the decade and well below 2 percent per annum by the end. Moreover, as U.S. practice seemed to demonstrate, opening trade with Asia was the best way to pursue a growth-oriented domestic policy while avoiding the inflationary consequences. More open Asian trade would not only keep down European prices but also pressure European governments, unions, and business firms to accelerate long-overdue reforms of the labor market. A more flexible labor market, as in the United States, would open the way to a rapid growth of employment in services, despite the increased importing of manufactures.

Europeans resisted this new version of "locomotive" economics, as they had resisted the old version in the late 1970s. With the EU's unemployment over 10 percent throughout most of the decade, governments were leery of actively promoting more imports from Asia, let alone of justifying such imports as a means of breaking resistance to labor market reform. In any event, it was not self-evident that Europe was more "protectionist" toward Asian imports than the United States. As for stimulating consumption in general, European governments shied away from a prescription that they feared would simply exchange one disequilibrium (unemployment) for another (a trade deficit). Instead, the EU was struggling to find its own combination of microeconomic structural reform and macroeconomic equilibrium that would permit low inflation, high employment, balanced trade, and reasonable growth—shared equitably throughout the population. To achieve these balanced aims would require not only reforming the labor markets but also sustaining the macroeconomic discipline that had been the fruit of achieving EMU.

European policies in the 1990s seemed informed by a fundamentally different economic worldview from American policies: Europeans seemed influenced by a more classic vision of economic balance. Instead of a world economy where one radical imbalance (the American deficit) sustains another (the Asian surplus), Europeans favored a global regime where all countries and regions stay in external equilibrium because they guard their own internal balances. A United States adopting such a regimen would cut its external deficit to manageable proportions. This reduction would presumably require restoring macroeconomic balance, a regimen broadly similar to what European states had adopted for EMU. Consumption would have to be reduced, savings increased, and excessive credit brought under control. Applied to Asia, the European perspective would prescribe drastically reducing dependence on Western markets by developing domestic markets. To do so, Asia should presumably imitate the West by enriching its own population, as opposed to relying on America's capacity to absorb cheap imports ad infinitum, thanks to inflated domestic demand and hegemonic forms of foreign borrowing. In other words, Asian economies should increase public and private consumption and reduce saving, or at least cut borrowing from abroad, in order to keep investment and growth to a rate sustainable without an outsized trade surplus. One obvious way to increase Asia's domestic and regional absorption is by improving public infrastructure and amenities and sharing more wealth with workers. Europe's enthusiasm for restoring a global system of stable exchange rates reflects a similar priority for domestic and regional equilibrium. To make a world with stable exchange rates, constituent units should converge on domestic policies conducive to equilibrium, as Europe did during its long struggle for EMU.

Behind these economic preferences are major philosophical differences that run all through modern culture. European policymakers in the 1990s hoped to unite their economies around a shared notion of equilibrium and how to maintain it. This was that pensée unique of German provenance that had come to dominate the imaginations of European policymakers in the 1970s, as they struggled with runaway inflation and welfare spending. By contrast, the United States was still boldly using its hegemonic power to impose American preferences on a malleable world. The preferences, often benevolent in intent, nevertheless presumed an indefinite continuation of America's unbalanced hegemonic habits. From the reigning European perspective, these habits represented a world order imposed by an alien and superior power rather than a natural and self-sustaining equilibrium based on rules applicable to all. America was, in truth, a "hyperpower." It was only a short step to regarding America as itself a menace to world order. But the fault lay as much with the unnatural weakness and dependency of Europe as with the excessive strength and aggressiveness of the Americans.

In the conditions of the 1990s, the American government felt little compulsion to take European views seriously. Discussions were mostly a dialogue of the deaf. Economic quarrels multiplied, and a basic erosion of transatlantic trust and cooperation was apparent. Europe's principal reaction was to press ahead with the Economic and Monetary Union. In a global system with shaky rules and precarious stability, Europe's states felt they needed a solid monetary and trading bloc to defend their own prosperity and social peace. If they succeeded, they might ultimately be able to force the Americans to negotiate more seriously about a stable global regime. In other words, achieving a better framework of global rules and balances would first require a global balance of power. A European bloc seemed the necessary precondition for such a global balance. In effect, Europeans were pursuing the global strategy List had foretold in the mid-nineteenth century and that the Imperial Germans, in their fashion, had proclaimed in World War I.

EMU was thus an implicit challenge to American economic hegemony; the advent of the euro was, in itself, a sign that the world economy was outgrowing the old patterns of the Pax Americana. This basic trend toward a more plural dispensation of wealth and power reflected not so much American failure as American success. For over half a century, a liberal world economy, inspired and largely managed by the Americans, had spread prosperity, investment, and growth throughout the world. One consequence had been predictable from the start: a more plural distribution of global wealth, power, and initiative. As a result, the Americans, by themselves, increasingly lacked the means, imagination, or will to dominate the system as a whole. In such a situation, the alternative to mounting chaos is either a fresh or renewed hegemony or a cooperative multilateral system, based on rules and with an effective balance of power to sustain those rules.

A new hegemon to replace the United States seems unlikely in the present state of the world. For the reasons I have been suggesting, clinging to the old postwar American hegemony is a policy also likely to fail. But while American global hegemony may show numerous signs of flagging, a balanced and cooperative plural system to replace it still seems far away. Ideally, such a system could be constructed from a group of major powers and regional blocs that, committed to stabilizing their own countries and regions, could also converge on rules for stabilizing the world system as a whole. Creating regional blocs and global structures requires effective multilateral institutions to encourage the search for common interests and perspectives. The twentieth century, of course, spawned many such regional and global institutions. Of these, the European Union was by far the most intensive and significant.

Perversely, taming Europe's own self-destructive power struggles might, in the end, lead to a new conflict between Europe and America. But Europe's new strength could also make possible a more efficacious form of cooperation across the Atlantic—one that results in a broad strengthening of the West in the world. Instead of quarreling over definitions of "burden sharing" that tend to presume a continuing special hegemonic exceptionalism for the United States, the two Western giants might work out a more balanced and comprehensive view of their global roles and responsibilities. And just as France and Germany have created a civilized form of joint hegemony for Europe, the EU and the United States may one day build a similar form of joint and balanced leadership for the emerging new global system.

The basis for renewed Western partnership will not be, we can hope, a shared determination to suppress the Asians for another century or two. Rich and liberal Western nations do, however, share a legitimate interest in avoiding self-destructive quarrels among themselves and bloody chaos in the rest of the world. And it is also in their interest to foster the sort of growth needed to reduce the desperate poverty that still afflicts a great proportion of the world's population. A rejuvenated Western partnership would, of course, draw on longstanding habits of institutionalized transatlantic cooperation, based initially on American hegemony and European need during the Cold War. A rebalancing of responsibility and power might prolong those ties indefinitely. Europe and America could re-create on a global scale the postwar accommodation of France and Germany on a regional scale. Both sides of the Atlantic would have learned enough from the past to avoid repeating the old mistake of refusing mutual accommodation.

Ideally, Europe would contribute not only its economic weight to a Western global partnership but also its "civilian" mentality. Europe, lacking America's legacy of oversized military power, should be more inclined toward conciliation than confrontation. In the recurring struggle between the worldviews of Herder and Hobbes, Europeans might be more naturally inclined to Herder—to the principle that nations and regions can live peacefully together and develop in their own ways, so long as they respect the right of others to do the same. Since time has made us sadder and wiser historians than Herder, we know that international harmony seldom comes without great effort—requiring both enlightened leadership and balanced power. A genuinely "Euro-American" form of global leadership should be more acceptable to the rest of the world than the American hyperpower. Euro-American leadership might be more efficacious in prompting the difficult adjustments that the twenty-first century's rapidly expanding global system will require. For ordering a new and more plural global economy, Europe's preference for economic equilibrium might prove a more durable and appealing intellectual foundation than the voluntarist and ad hoc economics popular in hegemonic America. As America came to rescue Europe in the twentieth century, a rejuvenated Europe may come to save the Pax Americana in the twenty-first.

Before such a balanced global system emerges in any reliable form, however, Europe must strengthen its own structures. In particular, the EU must adopt the constitutional reforms and achieve the security arrangements needed to consolidate a coherent European bloc. And the European Union must recast its relations with both the United States and Russia. A pan-European order that is genuinely tripolar, rather than hyper-American or hyper-European, seems the soundest long-term basis for Eurasian peace. Only within such a pan-European structure does it seem likely that Russia can be brought back into the European family and that the United States can be comfortably kept there. And only within such a frame can the European Union be saved from its own temptation toward Eurasian overstretch.

. . . [I]t is tempting to see a balanced and cohesive Europe as the harbinger not only of a more plural world—arguably a mixed blessing—but also of a world with reasonable hopes for peaceful stability. Europe may once more be ready to give political lessons to others. In the nineteenth century, the European nation state proved the best formula for reconciling the conflicting domestic needs of democratic Western societies. But in crowded, interdependent Europe, the nation state formula was unable to resolve the old problem of interstate order. Since World War II, Europe has pushed the nation state formula to a new confederal plane, one that preserves the accomplishments of the nation state while it seeks to overcome its limitations. Europe's hybrid confederacy is, in effect, a highly creative evolution of the nation state, a genuinely new political form. Thanks to it, European states have converted their interdependence into a strength rather than a liability. And with this new strength, Europeans have gone a long way toward reconciling the democratic politics of communitarian nation states and the efficiencies of international capitalism. With luck, Western Europe's experience may provide the inspiration for a stable order in Pan-Europe as well. And perhaps, just as Europe's nineteenth-century nation state became the political formula adopted throughout the world in the twentieth century, Europe's twentieth-century hybrid confederacy may become the model for the new regional systems needed elsewhere in the twenty-first century.

Dynamic and deeply rooted trends—military, political, cultural, and economic—are pushing European states to consolidate their union and take charge of their own collective security. In doing so, they will naturally recast the Atlantic relationship on a more plural basis. While nothing in such matters is reliably certain, the plural direction in the West itself seems part of an unfolding historical pattern across the globe. A contemporary Herder should rejoice in the new and richer palate of cultures and energies that such a world implies. But Herder's happy ending seems more likely if the West itself, managing its own maturity with grace and imagination, presents a rational model for the rest of the world. A strong, humane, and cohesive Europe—linked to Russia as well as America, and helping to give balance to both East and West—seems a vision of the future in harmony with the better parts of our nature and the most promising trends in our history.

Notes

[1]Early America's virtues coexisted with slavery, the dark side of the American heritage—a caution against assuming an exceptional virtue that somehow frees Americans from the baser tendencies that generally affect other powerful peoples, whenever their power is excessive and inadequately restrained.

STUDY AND DISCUSSION QUESTIONS

1. How does Calleo characterize America's geopolitical orientation since the early 1990s? Do you agree or disagree with his characterization?
2. Do you think that the United States and Europe can overcome their differences in power and perspectives to get on the same geopolitical wavelength?
3. How would Mearsheimer respond to Calleo's prediction (and hope) that dynamic trends in the global order—and enhanced European integration—are likely to stabilize the Atlantic alliance?

15

"We, the Peoples of Europe . . ."

Kalypso Nicolaïdis

In May 2004, the EU expanded to include eight Eastern and Central European countries. Cyprus and Malta joined the EU simultaneously, enlarging the Union from 15 to 25 members. In June 2004 the leaders of each of the member states approved a provisional constitutional treaty. A year later the French "non" shattered the constitutional project. How will the historic transformations of the EU heralded by enlargement and its constitution-building failure affect the prospects of Europe preserving its distinctive social and economic model and its unique institutional architecture? In this selection, Kalypso Nicolaïdis, an Oxford Lecturer, argues that the draft Constitution does much to advance the EU's core objectives which include the promotion of peace and social justice as well as full employment within the context of the "social market econ- omy" that describes Europe's distinctive economic and social model, which blends an efficient and competitive economy with generous wel- fare state benefits. He presents an intriguing vision of the EU as a new kind of political community, based on the mutual recognition of diverse European identities and institutional arrangements, the principles of multi-level governance, and the prospect that transnational projects can become the glue that will bind the Union.

A MORE PERFECT UNION

Political tremors are shaking the old continent. As the European Union's enlargement brings most of the continent under the same banner, Europeans, like their American cousins two centuries ago, are on the verge of treating themselves to a full-blown constitution. In June [2004] after more than two years of heated debate, EU heads of state settled on the text of the Treaty Establishing a Constitution for Europe. The treaty will not enter into force, however, until it is ratified by all 25 member states, through their national parliaments or popular referendums. And a single defection could spell the end of the entire exercise.

Was the June meeting Europe's Philadelphia? The text's drafters claim that it was. They argue that the constitution will give the EU a more effective government, better adapted to its greater size and ambitions, and make it a more democratic polity. The document's detractors, meanwhile, make one of two critiques. Some say the document is not bold enough, especially on the social front; others claim that it is a watershed but warn that it will blur the precious differences among the members' unique histories and identities, turning the EU into a monolithic "United States of Europe."

The EU's original sin may be that it was not built on a democratic foundation; its citizens were not asked to vet the union's creation. But that may also be the union's saving grace, as it allowed the war-torn continent to tackle integration more pragmatically. Eschewing grand visions of a regional democracy, the EU was founded on judicious power sharing. It put member states in the driver's seat by conducting most of its business through intense day-to-day diplomacy, while giving the European Commission, its law-initiating body, the task of balancing the interests of big states with a vision of the common good. An elected parliament was added only later for a bit of democratic flavor. As Jean Monnet, one of the EU's founders, rightly predicted, states then engaged in creative bargains and built ad hoc solidarities among cross-border constituencies.

By and large, this so-called community method has served Europeans well. It has enabled them to accommodate both social-democratic and conservative postwar ideologies and to balance the divergent interests of political parties, industries, trade unions, and nongovernmental organizations (NGOs) on issues ranging from food safety and banking regulation to immigration and global trade. But it is not a democratic model that Europeans can readily recognize. Who is accountable for what in the EU's bureaucratic maze? The EU does not have separate legislative and executive branches to speak of. The European Commission comprises nationals from every member state, but it is unelected and holds more power than any national administration. Ministers on the council must answer to their national constituencies, but they can easily claim to have been outvoted in Brussels. And the parliament, which is directly elected, can neither initiate laws nor control significant resources. Although some scholars have rightly argued that the EU does not exhibit nearly as many flaws as populist critics charge (and offers more safeguards against abuses of power than do many member states), the fact remains that Europeans cannot hold their politicians directly accountable for what the EU does.

By the turn of the millennium, the EU's powers had stretched to include prerogatives long associated with the nineteenth-century sovereign state: police, external boundaries, foreign policy, and regulating money. But, critics charged, this expansion came without any increase in accountability to European citizens. When over the course of the past decade the EU doubled in size, critics warned that, without reform, enlargement would spell the union's demise. So a constitutional convention was launched in early 2002, and for the first time in EU history, delegates other than diplomats were invited to debate the EU's foundation, goals, and methods. Central and eastern European states were invited to participate even before they had acceded. Discussions lasted more than a year, and after government representatives spent another one haggling over sensitive issues, a final blueprint was approved in June.

Despite the hopes of some delegates, this was no democratic baptism. And despite the full paraphernalia of Web casts and electronic forums, the constitutional process has not (yet) instilled in the hearts of Europeans a newfound faith in the European democracy. Still, given the wide spectrum of European political families and national sensitivities, it is remarkable that an agreement was reached at all.

The document offers much to advance the EU's core objectives. Member states have reached a sensible settlement about the division of powers between the union and themselves. The constitution incorporates the Charter of Human Rights, the most modern and ambitious document of its kind. It creates for the EU a post of foreign minister and gives the union a single legal personality. Decision-making will be simpler and more transparent. And Europeans will have a single statement of what their union is about. Thus, despite many imperfections, the constitution does manage to balance and so to celebrate the plurality of the EU's very diverse peoples.

THE DEMON IN THE DEMOS

Debates about the EU have often been perverted by the tyranny of oppositions: European superstate vs. union of states; superpower Europe vs. Europe of peace; European democracy vs. national democracies. At the start of the convention, two main camps emerged: intergovernmentalists and supranationalists—representing the ideological poles between which the EU has always swung. The intergovernmentalists, who included representatives of the French and British governments, wanted to make up the EU's democratic deficit by strengthening the council of state representatives, using unanimous voting on issues that pertain to state sovereignty, and strictly delineating power-sharing arrangements between the union and its members. The supranationalists, mostly smaller member states and European parliamentarians, wanted to protect the commission (the traditional advocate of weaker parties), strengthen democratic control by the European Parliament, extend majority voting, and generally expand EU powers. Although the issue seemed largely institutional, the two camps were really asking a fundamental philosophical question: if democracy requires a *demos*—a group of individuals who have enough in common to manage their affairs collectively—is there, or can there be, a single European *demos?*

Intergovernmentalists often subscribe to a form of sovereigntism, holding that nations, which are bound by a common language, culture, history, and often ethnicity, are the only credible foundations of polities. Being part of a nation is a precondition, they argue, for the basic compromise of representative democracy: agreeing to be in the minority one day with the expectation of being in the majority another. Intergovernmentalists defend national sovereignty not as a reactionary reflex but as the ultimate guarantee of democracy. Because Europe is the realm of agreements between states, its democracy must operate indirectly, through politicians in Brussels who are accountable to their electorate at home, rather than through direct links between citizens and European institutions.

Supranationalists, on the other hand, ultimately believe that it is both possible and desirable to aspire to a single European *demos*—and a European democracy—because the connection between the nation and democracy is a historical accident, not a necessity. They argue that a uniquely European identity can be forged and layered on top of older but equally artificial national ones. If civic education in the 1800s could turn peasants into Frenchmen, why could it not now turn them into Europeans or at least into Europeans of French origin? Having successfully reinvented themselves as a postnational, or antinationalist, community, the Germans tend to champion this view, as do the Italians and the Belgians. Visions of the European *demos* come in different shades, with some believing it was born on February 15, 2003—when Europe's population took to the streets to protest the U.S.-led war in Iraq—and others conceding that it is still in the making. But supranationalists agree that the EU must be perfected along traditional lines of representative democracy, by creating state-like institutions, such as legislative chambers and a prime minister position, at the European level.

THE THIRD WAY

For all their differences, traditional supranationalists and intergovernmentalists are really only two sides of the same coin: both owe allegiance to some version of the nation-state model. With their calls for a common flag, passport, and anthem, supranationalists are trying to recreate a national mystique on the European level. But in so doing, they are relying on the sovereigntist notion that a single *demos*—albeit one, in this case, that transcends the state—is necessary for a genuine political community of identity.

There is a third way to understand Europe. In the half-century since its creation, the EU has established itself as a new kind of political community: one that is defined not by a uniform identity—a *demos*—but by the persistent plurality of its peoples—its *demoi*. Intergovernmentalists must accept that the EU is a community of citizens, not only of states, and supranationalists must accept that democracy can exist among EU members without their merging into a single polity that expresses its will through traditional state-like institutions.

Yet the EU is not simply a halfway house between intergovernmentalism and supranationalism. It is more than a confederation of sovereign states; its peoples are also connected through the European Parliament and a regional civil society. But since these peoples are also organized into states, states remain at the core of the union. The EU is neither a union of democracies nor a union as democracy; it is a union of states and of peoples—a *"demoicracy"*—in the making. It appeals to a political philosophy of its own—transnational pluralism—rather than to some extended notion of the nation-state. And however paradoxical, recognizing that its different needs require a different model is in fact a way to honor the nation-state's role as a cornerstone of national democracy.

American constitutionalists might argue that this definition is just a fancy way of referring to a federal vision much like the one that dominated in the United States in the decades before the Civil War and before Franklin Roosevelt's presidency. Indeed, federalism stands in opposition to the notion of a homogeneous state. But the history of federalism is about the gradual subjugation of constituent units to a central power. That is the reason why sovereigntists in Europe (especially in the United Kingdom) saw the exclusion of the "f-word" from the EU draft constitution as a victory against superstate drift. Given the history of the United States and other federations, it would be difficult to persuade them that federalism does not ultimately mean "more" Europe and "less" nation-state, or that it is a mode of organization more compatible with *demoi* than with a single *demos*, or that it protects local differences from being erased. They would be right, because the EU should not become a federal state. (What sort of state would it be, with its tiny budget and administration, its rules negotiated and enforced by national authorities, and its role limited to tasks other than critical welfare functions?) On the other hand, they would be wrong not to understand the EU as a federal union.

To really celebrate the EU as a *demoicracy,* one must depart from mainstream constitutional thinking. And to do that requires making three conceptual shifts: seeking the mutual recognition of all of the members' identities rather than a common identity; promoting a community of projects, not a community of identity; and sharing governance horizontally, among states, rather than only vertically, between states and the union.

The first shift consists in recognizing that Europeans are part of "a community of others," who are somewhat at home anywhere in Europe. The European *demoicracy* is predicated on the mutual recognition of the many European identities—not on their merger. Not only does it promote respect for their differences, in a classic communitarian sense, it also urges engaging with each other and sharing cultural and political identities. In an apt metaphor, existing European treaties allow nationals of EU member states to use each other's consular services outside of the union. (A Spaniard's belonging to the EU allows her to be a bit Italian or a bit British when traveling outside the union.) In the same spirit, today's constitution does not call for a homogeneous community or for laws grounded on the will of a single European *demos*. Rather, it makes mutual respect for national identities and institutions one of its foremost principles.

If the European *demoicracy* is not predicated on a European identity, then it does not require that its citizens develop a singularly European public space; it asks only that they have an informed curiosity about the opinions and political lives of their neighbors. In time, multinational politics and citizenship will emerge from the confrontation, accommodation, and inclusion of Europe's varied political cultures. For that to happen, however, Europe's peoples must continue their critical reflection on their intertwined national pasts, as the constitution's preamble invites them to do with its opening nod to their bloody histories. They must also respect the importance of regional groups, such as the Basques or the Corsicans, in the European mosaic.

Thus, the glue that binds the EU together is not a shared identity; it is, rather, shared projects and objectives. This distinction is enshrined in the constitution's very first article, in which member states give the EU the power "to attain objectives they have in common." The members' sense of belonging and commitment to the union is based on what they accomplish together, not what they are together. Witness, for example, the EU's defining projects to date—the single market, the euro, and expansion—and the ambitious to-do list it sets out in the constitution—the promotion of peace, social justice, gender equality, and children's rights; sustainable development; a "highly competitive social market economy"; and full employment. Forging common projects is no less demanding than forging a common identity, but it is voluntary and differentiated rather than essentialist and holistic. Likewise, the constitution's proclamation of common European values, including the respect for human dignity and for the rule of law, should be read as a guide for action, not a definition of "Europeanness."

Finally, the European *demoicracy* should not be based on a hierarchical understanding of governance, with supranational institutions towering over national bureaucracies and European constitutional norms trumping national values. It ought to be premised on the horizontal sharing of sovereignty, and it ought to encourage dialogue between different authorities at different levels, such as national and European constitutional courts, national and European parliaments, and national and European executives. It must remain multicentered, with decisions made not by Brussels, but in Brussels and other European capitals. The EU is neither national nor supranational; it is transnational. It must strive to empower, not dominate, local actors; favor mutual recognition, not harmonization, of national laws and regulations; and ensure fair competition among them.

STUDY AND DISCUSSION QUESTIONS

1. What are most significant distinctions between the intergovernmentalist and the supranationalist models of the European Union?
2. How would you describe the third way model that Nicolaïdis offers to understand the European Union?
3. In the absence of a common sense of identity and shared fates among the peoples of EU Europe—and in light of the defeat of the constitution—do you think common transnational projects will be sufficient to sustain political community and bind the Union?

East Asia: The Paradox of State Power

16

The Politics of the Asian Economic Crisis

T. J. Pempel

For years, the Japanese economy had been struggling against severe and unrelenting stagnation. Also, by 1996 there were signs that the "tiger" economies* were becoming somewhat less fierce: there were signs of excess capacity in some sectors, earnings had peaked and were beginning to decline, exports were slowing. Perhaps most ominous, in light *of what was to come, there were growing indications that the "bubble economy" in Thailand's financial and real estate sectors was stretched too thin. Despite these ominous signs, few were prepared when the Asian financial and economic crisis erupted in July 1997. The crisis began with an enormous run on the Thai baht, which lost nearly half its value by the end of the year. A host of neighboring countries—South Korea, Indonesia, Singapore, and the Philippines—experienced much the same pattern.*

As T. J. Pempel explains in this selection, when the financial bubble burst, banks crumbled, jobs and savings were lost, and massive corruption and cronyism was revealed, a lot of political bubbles exploded as well. In Indonesia, the country after Thailand that was hardest hit by the Thai currency's collapse, as urban poverty and joblessness skyrocketed, massive demonstrations and political unrest scuttled the Suharto regime. As Pempel explains, the economic turmoil also helped sweep leaders from office in the Philippines and South Korea and triggered internecine battles with the government and street protests in Malaysia. Pempel paints one of the clearest pictures of the Asian economic crisis, presenting both the financial and the political developments at the national, regional, and international levels.

In July 1997, there was a massive run on the Thai baht. Despite a $26 billion effort by the Thai government, the currency lost 48.7 percent of its value over the next six months, triggering a sharp downturn in Thai assets and growth. Thailand's problems were quickly replicated, with variations, in several neighboring countries, most notably Malaysia, South Korea, Indonesia, Singapore, and the Philippines. Each experienced a tidal wave of troubles centering on the rapid outflow of foreign capital, 30 to 50 percent plunges in their stock markets, and significant declines in the exchange rates of their national currencies. Most also faced banking crises, problems of short-term debt repayment, recessions, sharp decelerations in their previously soaring economic growth rates, or some combination of these. Between July 1997 and April 1998, some 150 Asian financial institutions were shut down, suspended, nationalized, or placed under the care of a government restructuring agency. Another fifty announced plans to merge. Within several months, three of these countries—Thailand, Indonesia, and South

*The term "Asian tigers" was initially applied exclusively to four newly industrializing East Asian economies: the Republic of Korea (South Korea), Taiwan, Hong Kong, and Singapore, but has often been extended to include a set of Southeast Asian countries that pursued similar development strategies in the 1980s: Indonesia, Malaysia, and Thailand. Discussions of the East Asian financial or economic crises nearly always include the Southeast Asian countries as well as Japan and China.

Korea—had petitioned the IMF for complex financial assistance packages. Suddenly, many of Asia's most rapidly advancing countries found themselves sliding down the rungs of the hierarchical world income ladder instead of enjoying the steady climb up they had experienced for the previous decade or more.

Economic problems brought political repercussions. Massive street demonstrations forced the resignation of Indonesia's ruler of thirty-two years, President Suharto; power transfers overlaid by the economic turmoil took place in Thailand, the Philippines, and South Korea. Malaysia's finance minister and erstwhile prime-ministerial heir apparent, Anwar Ibraham, sought to set the country on a course of fiscal and monetary austerity, thereby threatening many Malay and Chinese business leaders who had been close supporters of Prime Minister Mahathir and the ruling party, UMNO. Mahathir eventually reversed Anwar's policy directions and introduced strict capital controls that effectively ended the international convertibility of the Malaysian ringgit. Simultaneously, sweeping criminal charges were leveled against Anwar, whose arrest and trial triggered street protests from his supporters, demanding sweeping governmental and economic reforms.

The rich tableau that surrounded these activities commanded months of worldwide attention. Headlines that for a decade or more had proclaimed the arrival of the "Asian miracle" were replaced with boldface blazonings about "the Asian economic crisis" or "the Asian flu." The speed and magnitude of Asia's collective stumble, the erosion of wealth, and the increases in poverty and social insecurity were the regional equivalent of the Great Depression of the 1930s (Wade 1998, 1–2).

These cascading events triggered a host of far-ranging debates about the roots of the problem, appropriate and inappropriate roles for investment capital, the desirability of competing models of political economy, the future of Asia, and the dangers of moral hazard. Explanations for the sudden outbreak of this regional epidemic of economic ill health ranged widely, as did, naturally enough, the prescriptions for its cure. Indeed, like economic meltdowns in earlier times and other locations, the web of events in Asia became an ideological Rorschach test onto which various and competing interpretations of a host of complex and normative issues have been projected.

MARKET ECONOMICS AND ASIA

The economics of the Asian crisis have been widely reported. Among the most frequently proffered explanations for Asia's sudden straits are exchange rate and currency misalignments, exorbitant credit expansion, asset bubbles in real estate and stocks, liquidity excesses, productive overcapacity, and trade-linked ripple effects throughout the region. All of these were compounded by panic, the effects of demonstrations, and other psychoeconomic contagions.

Woven through the macroeconomic technicalities are varying strands of criticisms tracing the Asian crisis to endogenous institutional debilities and "crony capitalism." To many, the problems centered on industrial policies predicated on excessively close government targeting of investment capital. To others, the principal flaws lay in political patronage and close personal connections between powerful politicians, bankers, regulators, and business people. In particular, these were said to have led to poor quality regulation within many Asian financial institutions. The result was a morally hazardous public guarantee for nominally private business transactions.

How to weigh these elements has generated considerable debate among professional economists inside and outside international financial institutions, but the bulk of the blame has been laid on a mélange of alleged shortcomings in Asian capitalism. East Asia, in this view, set itself up for problems because its financial systems were rife with corruption, insider trading, and weak corporate governance, or because Asian political and economic leaders operated in ways that interfered with the unfettered interplay of the two key macroeconomic principles of free markets—fear and greed. Certainly, there is no shortage of analyses, most powerfully from within the IMF, charging that Asia's economic problems should be attributed largely to Asian mistakes.

Tempting as it may be to place the blame solely on the borrower, the dual nature of any loan, as Radelet and Sachs (1998), for example, have pointed out, makes it hard to absolve the lender from all blame. If the borrower was so patently inept, ill advised, or evil, why did the lender provide the money in the first place? Important and regionally concentrated as the Asian crisis was in 1997, the world historically has had no shortage of financial crises. Indeed, Eichengreen and Fishlow (1998, 23) contend that periods of debt crises are perhaps more "normal" than are periods in which capital flows smoothly. Several regions suffered financial crises in the 1980s: Mexico had one in 1995; Brazil and Russia were beset by financial crises soon after that in Asia, albeit for different reasons. It is difficult to contend that Asia's problems were exclusively the result of debilities germinated in some "Asian" Petri dish and subsequently transmitted through "Asian contagion."

Without denying the importance of domestic flaws, Asia's problems were more complex than can be grasped by an exclusive focus on poor macroeconomic or structural arrangements in Thailand, Indonesia, and elsewhere. The other side of the problem involved excessive and poorly monitored foreign capital inflows coming primarily from the United States, Europe, and Japan. Only when the excesses of external funds collided with internal misallocations did Asia's meltdown occur. Ed Lincoln of the Brookings Institution has proffered one succinct and not untypical summary of such an analysis: "If a common thread weaves through most of Asia, it is a combination of weakly developed domestic banking systems exposed to deregulation of international capital flows" (1998, 4).

A MORE POLITICALLY
SENSITIVE PERSPECTIVE

. . . Unlike most economic explanations, which grow predominantly out of deductive reasoning and consequently are predisposed toward parsimony, those offered here stress inductive nuance and detail. They are concerned not with presenting one explanation for the crisis as a whole, but rather with explicating the various aspects of a broader mosaic.

Second, [the explanations here] stress the importance of politics. It is not that [I] believe economic factors were less important than the somehow more compelling political factors. This [essay] is not intended to be another fusillade in the ongoing disciplinary turf war—"my variables can swallow your variables"—between politics and markets. [The explanations offered here] continually engage in the exploration of problems of an economic nature. Yet, they share the belief that many of the most intriguing and puzzling aspects of the Asian crisis involve the kinds of power relationships and institutional configurations that are not subject to resolution through an exclusively economic analysis, which typically marginalizes those relationships and configurations as "externalities."

What happened in Asia, we argue, took place at the intersection of economics and politics. We thus . . . investigate the ways in which the problems that arose in Asia in 1997–98 involved not only property values, financial flows, loan portfolio makeup, and debt ratios, but also the power relationships that undergirded them. Rather than accepting generic generalizations about "rent seekers" or "crony capitalism," we try to unravel precisely which capitalists were whose cronies and why they got the rents they did—in short, what groups and institutions were most responsible for the ways in which the crisis played out.

We believe that politics and economics in Asia, as more generally, are locked in an ongoing dance in which actions by one partner are matched by responses from the other. One moves forward and the other moves back, only to be followed by turns and spins that shift direction and sometimes reverse the lead. For us, the national differences in how the economic crises played out suggest that different Asian dancers moved to distinctly different beats: the liquidity crisis cha-cha in South Korea was quite distinct from the rupiah rumba in Indonesia; in Taiwan, politics and economics spun together in a waltz that could remain rather gracefully oblivious to the crises elsewhere.

Moreover, to continue the metaphor, like Ginger Rogers and Fred Astaire, economics and politics often dance up and down various staircases and move across different levels. Here, we differ in a third way from many existing analyses. The problems in Asia had unquestionably domestic political and economic roots, but our analysis argues that such domestic underpinnings were interlaced with political and economic linkages at two other levels: international and regional.

. . . [We] suggest that a complicated multilevel dynamic between economics and politics was at play in the Asian crisis of 1997–98. The currency and financial problems that rocked a number of East Asian economies during 1997–98 had unquestionably endogenous roots—the kind of ontological bias built into terminology such as *the Asian crisis*. At the same time, we stress that many of the most powerful seismic repercussions rippling across Asia had epicenters well outside the region.

. . .

INTERNATIONAL AND REGIONAL POLITICS OF THE ASIAN CRISIS

In 1960, the richest fifth of the world's population held thirty times more of the world's income than did the poorest fifth. This ratio widened to 32 to 1 in 1970, 45 to 1 in 1980, and 59 to 1 in 1989. These and related data demonstrate the tremendous relative reallocation of wealth that has taken place between rich and poor countries over the last three decades. Despite absolute improvements in many parts of the world, relatively speaking, the world's rich have gotten richer and its poor have gotten poorer.

The stunningly rapid advance of most of the national economies in East Asia marked a substantial deviation from this broad trend. In 1960, Japan and Northeast Asia accounted for only 4 percent of world GNP, compared to 37 percent for the United States, Canada, and Mexico. By the early 1990s, the combined economies of Japan, South Korea, Taiwan, Hong Kong, the ASEAN countries, and Greater China contributed roughly 30 percent of world GNP, approximately the same share as that held by North America on the one hand and Western Europe on the other.

Except for the relatively short-term spurt in riches to the OPEC countries during the 1970s, East Asia's economic success marked the most meaningful reallocation of wealth between rich and poor countries since the end of World War II. And unlike the oil-producing countries, the nations of Asia enhanced their wealth through deep-seated structural changes in their national production profiles, rather than through the fortuities of natural resource endowment and the temporary production limits of an oil-producing cartel. Asia's successes thus garnered significantly larger shares in the production and export of the world's high-value-added manufactured goods.

As I have argued elsewhere (Pempel 1999), Asia's collective economic success was over-determined, politically constructed, and yet far from easy. Ultimately, it involved a complex mixture of politics and economics played out across three different levels—international, regional, and national. A similarly complex interaction was involved in the Asian economic crisis.

The economic havoc that crystallized in the summer of 1997 was catalyzed by a witches' brew that contained at least four major ingredients largely external to the countries themselves. First, there were changes in the international and regional balance of power. Second, the once diffuse and separate national economies of Asia had become increasingly interconnected. Third, important changes occurred in the nature of corporate production processes. Fourth and finally, the size and speed of cross-national capital movements expanded geometrically. Together, these four provided a substantially altered international and regional context for Asia's national political economies. All four are closely connected. . . .

By the late 1980s and early 1990s, the collapse of communism and the end of the Cold War; the changing power balance in Asia; economic competitiveness from Japan, South Korea, and Taiwan; the economic integration of Europe and the formulation of NAFTA; and changing U.S. domestic politics combined to reduce America's indulgence of Asian trade policies. Although the military links between the United States and Japan, South Korea, and Taiwan changed very little, the predominant profiles of these latter three metamorphosed from unquestioned strategic allies into unscrupulous economic competitors.

In keeping with the prevalence of neoclassical economic thinking and a rising faith in monetarism, American policy makers turned increasingly to exchange rate policies in an effort to rectify bilateral trade imbalances with Asia. The Plaza and Louvre Accords, primarily between the United States and Japan, reduced the export prices of goods denominated in dollars while raising those denominated in yen, wón, or NT dollars. Subsequently, in an ad hoc agreement in April 1995, the United States and Japan cooperated to enhance the value of the dollar, thereby triggering much of the export slowdown and currency instability within Asian countries whose currencies were pegged to the dollar.

Currency realignments were important to a second major trend, namely the deepening of Asian regional ties. . . . [E]xchange rate recalibrations in the mid-1980s strengthened the national currencies of Japan, South Korea, and Taiwan, and these, along with changing domestic economic conditions and government policy shifts, stimulated the outflow of investment capital from all three countries to other parts of Asia. This new investment money, combined with a long-standing base of Japanese official assistance, fueled a surge in manufacturing production, national growth, and intra-Asian trade, particularly among the ASEAN countries. These in turn wove ever-denser webs of economic connections among the previously rather separated Asian economies. Initially, the results were increased production and growth through much of Asia; subsequently, however, excess capital led to the overproduction and asset bubbles that catalyzed the crisis of 1997.

. . .

Interestingly, and in contrast to the deeply institutionalized regionalism in Europe and even NAFTA and Mercosur, the regional ties linking Asia remained largely commercial in character. There was very little institutionalization of political authority (Katzenstein and Shiraishi 1997). . . . Asia has no equivalent of a Brussels secretariat issuing regionwide regulations on trucking or social welfare for the whole region. Instead, ASEAN, and to a large extent APEC, rely on *musyawarah mufakat,* the Indonesian phrase for simple consultation and consensus. The institutional focus has been on regional trade liberalization, and, to the extent that intraregional trade has increased, so has regionwide vulnerability to trade-induced contagions.

The commercial and nonpolitical character of Asian regionalism also eliminated the possibility of any authoritative Asia-wide response to the external tremors as they began to ripple across the Asian region. Instead, Asia's heightened commercial integration left a host of seemingly national economies highly vulnerable to the various contagions that swept across the region. Cross-border downturns raced forward with none of the buffering protections that might have come from regionwide political or financial institutions.

The cross-national capital flows that linked various national economies and production networks throughout Asia were simultaneously part of the fourth and final major international change: the geometric increases and changing character, particularly during the 1990s, in cross-national capital mobility. . . .

Capital flows now total more than seventy times the volume of world trade. Once the major flows of cross-border money involved government-to-government or bank-to-government transactions. Long-term capital and foreign aid projects such as factories, roads, harbors, hospitals, and schools were the result. The new monies, in contrast, are increasingly composed of private capital. Such capital has the enhanced ability to move quickly and autonomously, subject to political restraints from neither host government nor home government.

By the early 1990s, these private capital flows were rising throughout the developing world, going not only into Asia but into Latin America and central and eastern Europe as well (Kahler 1998, 1). In 1995, private capital accounted for three-fourths of all investment resources to the developing world. Much of this new investment money involved "hot money" such as short-term loans and portfolio investments. Eighty percent of net global foreign exchange transactions now have a maturity date of seven days or less (Wade 1998, 3).

From the 1990s onward, Japan presented one important source of such "hot money." Huge amounts of new money entered Asia as a consequence of Japanese domestic monetary policies seeking to bail out the Japanese banks and financial institutions from upward of $1 trillion in bad debt accumulated during the "bubble economy". The Japanese government reduced its official discount rate to virtually zero, giving Japanese banks attractive incentives to borrow yen cheaply and lend it at higher rates to Asia's eagerly expanding firms and banks. By mid-1997, Japanese banks accounted for more than one-third of the total outstanding commercial bank debt in the five ASEAN member countries (with 54 percent of the loans in Thailand). Moreover, while Japanese banks were lending at such low rates, U.S. and European banks were able to borrow yen in Japan and lend it throughout Asia and elsewhere in what was known as the *carry trade*.

Equally important as a source of "hot money" was new portfolio investment capital, particularly, but not exclusively, from the United States. In the United States, an explosion of middle-aged savers worried about their retirement prospects deposited huge pools of capital into an ever-expanding number of privately managed mutual funds. The search for ever-higher rates of return led many of these funds to invest in the growing economies of East Asia. As of 1994, nineteen U.S. closed-end funds with assets of $4.2 billion specialized in East Asia; twelve had been established since 1990. These included several country funds investing exclusively in South Korea, Malaysia, Indonesia, and Thailand. Another $1.8 billion was held in open-ended East Asian funds. For each fund launched in the United States during 1990 and 1991, seven others were formed in other countries, including, importantly, Hong Kong and Singapore. . . .

Portfolio capital . . . rose from just 2 percent of total net financial capital flows to developing countries in 1987 to nearly 50 percent by 1996. The bulk of this staggering sum is in the hands of fewer than one hundred developing-markets fund managers operating out of financial centers within Asia but also across the world.

The first "Asian contagion" was a contagion of unfettered optimism in the investment decisions of portfolio managers and short-term lenders. A herding instinct led most to sprinkle ever-expanding amounts of portfolio money and short-term loans liberally across rapidly growing Asian markets, convinced that past growth (and not a little bit of cronyism) would ensure that the new monies would be uniformly safe, take seed, and generate consistently high returns and expanding multiples. Ultimately, much of this money generated overproduction or found its way into bubble-prone property markets and thinly traded stocks.

. . .

Just as an optimistic "Asian contagion" involved the failure by many lenders to differentiate among individual Asian borrowers, when the crisis began, the contagion of pessimism was often insensitive to national borders. The first whiff of economic problems in one country led outside investors to question the economic underpinnings of its neighbors. . . . [O]nce crisis struck, unrelated markets fell as investors sold securities or redeemed loans to maintain their overall risk profiles or to raise cash to cover losses elsewhere. . . . [G]eneric doubts about "Asia" swept through the Philippines, Taiwan, South Korea, Hong Kong, Singapore, and Malaysia despite the widely differing economic conditions and political structures in each.

International politics also played a role . . . in the changing character of the IMF and its analysis of what had happened in Asia. American responses to the crisis in different countries were quite different. . . . The United States was anxious to assist South Korea, where it had thirty-five thousand troops and where its American-based banks had substantial exposure, in contrast to its much less animated response to the problems in Indonesia, which had no U.S. bases and limited U.S. banking exposure.

With time, the importance of intra-Asian differences became apparent. . . . Discrete national political biases and institutional configurations created highly differentiated levels of vulnerability and resistance to investment withdrawals, currency attacks, and debt repayment demands. In short, just as international and regional politics were vital ingredients in the outbreak of the economic havoc, so individual countries demonstrated varying degrees of vulnerability or inoculation against their worst effects.

POLITICS OF NATIONAL RESPONSES

A generic phrase such as *the Asian crisis* masks the widely varied experiences of different countries, both in the impact of the crisis and in responses to it. Although some countries were hard hit, others, notably Taiwan, China, and Singapore, escaped with only minor damage. Some countries, such as South Korea, responded with official efforts at greater capital integration, but others, such as Malaysia and Hong Kong, opted for restrictions on capital movement and monetary flexibility. Such differences reflected the specific market economics and policy choices of individual countries. Yet, . . . neither economic fundamentals nor policy choices were created within a political vacuum. On the contrary, they were fundamentally the consequences of the intranational divisions of power and the nationally differentiated institutional arrangements that reflected these divisions.

For purposes of analysis, these political forces can be said to have played out during two rather separate periods. At first, there were differences in the degree of vulnerability to the various short-term capital and currency movements. Then, individual countries demonstrated widely disparate political biases in their efforts to make adjustments, once the first waves of the crisis had rolled over them.

Initial vulnerabilities were undeniably tied to a nation's financial openness. Which individual Asian economies were most shocked by, or immune to, the currency speculations, short-term capital withdrawals, and liquidity crises that swept through much of Asia was the direct result of how they were, or were not, "plugged in" to international capital markets. Countries such as Burma, Vietnam, China, and, to a lesser extent, Taiwan, stood at one pole, with only minimal connection to the international capital grid. Investment in Taiwan, . . . was sharply constricted by government regulations and CBC policy oversights, particularly over portfolio investment. . . . [T]he PRC attracted substantial sums of fdi, [but] its communist government retained restrictions over capital flows, foreign trade, and currency convertibility that were among the most severe in the region. As a consequence of such insulation, these countries were largely immune to short-term property and stock bubbles, currency speculations, and "hot money" outflows.

In contrast, South Korea had recently qualified for membership in the OECD, thereby incurring that organization's requirement to open its capital markets. Singapore, . . . also had a deeply institutionalized commitment to relative capital openness through a monetary regime predicated on the managed float of exchange rates. Hong Kong, although generally open, retained a currency board that restricted free-floating exchange rates. Between these two extremes, but having undergone varying degrees of financial liberalization over the previous decade or two, were countries such as Thailand, Indonesia, Malaysia, and the Philippines.

Choices about currency convertibility and openness to short-term foreign capital movements, however, were clearly politically rooted. Taiwan, for example, had an ever-narrowing circle of strategic allies in its dealings with a hostile China. KMT leaders thus opted for policy mechanisms designed to ensure high levels of monetary and financial stability and fiscal balance. Economic stability became a foreign policy weapon critical to Taiwan's international acceptance and external security. To retain maximum political control over the process, financial liberalization in Taiwan gave priority to deregulation of the domestic capital market rather than to foreign participation.

In their efforts to restrict openness to international capital, the government was greatly aided by the fact that Taiwanese business was fragmented into numerous small and medium-sized industries, rather than being dominated by highly capitalized mega-corporations such as Japan's *keiretsu* or Korea's *chaebŏl* or by huge, internationally sensitive financial institutions. Taiwan's few large industrial complexes were almost exclusively under the politically safe control of the KMT itself. The end result was an economy that was highly buffered politically from the worst excesses of international capital movement.

Rather a different picture emerges for South Korea. Close ties among the government bureaucracy, the political parties, and the large and primarily family-owned *chaebŏl* gave the latter a virtual public guarantee for their highly leveraged borrowing practices (Wade 1990; Woo 1991). Serious credit analysis was frowned on. Instead, intra-*chaebŏl* loan guarantees became a way of life that allowed Korean and foreign banks to soften their exposure. As Woo-Cumings has suggested, the idea was that the loan guarantee turned the entire *chaebŏl* group into a gigantic chunk of collateral. This system came under political attack with Korea's democratization and internationalization as early as 1993, but the institutionalized power of the *chaebŏl* left the excess borrowing highly resistant to change. As a result, the Korean private sector remained highly vulnerable to the short-term liquidity crisis it eventually confronted in 1997. Yet Korea's crisis of short-term debt was quite different from the currency and investment outflows that hit Thailand, Indonesia, and Malaysia. And in an additional twist of political fate, it was the crisis and the subsequent IMF assistance package that allowed the new government of Kim Dae Jung to force through policies designed to break up the long-standing and cozy ties among the *chaebŏl*, the government, the banks, and the previously governing parties that were Kim's political enemies.

Finally, and in contrast to the banking reforms being carried out in South Korea, stands the Philippines. . . . [F]or that country, simple openness or closedness of capital markets and investment opportunities were hardly unilateral determinants of the amounts of outside money flowing into countries.

Far more important, there as elsewhere, were the politics behind government monetary policies. Banking in the Philippines epitomized "crony capitalism": throughout the late 1980s and early 1990s, the government provided selected banks with high-interest, low-risk treasury bills that became "a major pot of gold" for the few chosen banks. . . . This lucrative intranational deal allowed Philippine banks to earn high levels of profits with low risk and hence to avoid the temptation to turn to international borrowings. When capital accounts were opened to foreign participation, the Philippines' long history of banking oligarchy, comparative macroeconomic disappointment, and high levels of political risk meant that the country initially attracted far smaller shares of outside fdi and portfolio money than did neighboring Thailand, Indonesia, Hong Kong, Singapore, and South Korea. Ironically, the country's lower economic elevation left it was far less vulnerable to the "hot money" outflows that affected so many of its neighbors.

In addition to such socioeconomic underpinnings of political power, institutional structures were also politically critical in the unfolding of the economic crisis within different countries. Thus . . . Indonesia and Thailand were both highly vulnerable to "hot money" flight, but for very different institutional reasons. Thailand, with its highly fragmented electoral and parliamentary system, had governments that found it impossible to make and carry out consistent policies. Investors were thus highly skittish of even the mildest short-term Thai economic problems. In contrast, Indonesia, with far better economic fundamentals, also proved to be vulnerable, but for precisely the opposite reason. Suharto's one-man rule made it relatively certain that his decisions would be carried out; but to the dismay of change-averse investors, his policy preferences zigged and zagged erratically in response to the unfolding crisis.

. . .

Interestingly, despite greater levels of electoral democracy in Malaysia, Prime Minister Mahathir enjoyed much the same autocratic power as did Indonesia's Suharto, and Mahathir too spooked foreign investors. For Malaysia, however . . . the problem was hardly uncertainty. Instead, it was outright hostility.

Foreign investors had little incentive to keep capital in a country whose prime minister made unending pronouncements about the dangers of an international Jewish conspiracy and of foreign investors, and who issued nationalistic warnings that IMF assistance would carry strings binding Malaysian assets inflexibly to foreign controls.

Singapore's far more deeply institutionalized commitments to open markets, free capital flows, and integration with the world economy allowed it to do far better, after the first wave of problems, than many of its neighbors. Singapore was able both to hold on to much invested capital and to re-attract it quickly after the meltdown. Indeed, . . . after the crisis of 1997 foreign fund managers were given incentives by Singapore's government to establish operations there, to manage portions of the government's huge CPF, and, against the objections of Hong Kong, the Singapore exchange (SIMEX) began trading Hong Kong index futures.

. . .

The Asian crisis of 1997–98 raises a host of important and complicated questions. . . . But as I have tried to highlight in this [essay], what happened in Asia can be at best only partially understood by focusing exclusively on domestic macroeconomic forces. The crisis was the result of a complicated interweaving of economics and politics; a sensitivity to these political forces is vital to understanding why the crisis began and how it unfolded.

References

Eichengreen, Barry, and Albert Fishlow. 1998. Contending with capital flows: What is different about the 1990s? In *Capital flows and financial crises*. Ed. Miles Kahler. Ithaca: Cornell University Press, 1998, 23–68.

Kahler, Miles, ed. 1998. *Capital flows and financial crises*. Ithaca: Cornell University Press.

Katzenstein, Peter J., and Takashi Shiraishi. 1997. *Network power: Japan and Asia*. Ithaca: Cornell University Press.

Lincoln, Edward J. 1998. Exploring the Asian financial crisis. *Brookings Review* (summer): 4–5.

Pempel, T. J. 1999. The developmental regime in a changing world economy. In *The developmental state*. Ed. Meredith Woo-Cumings. Ithaca: Cornell University Press.

Radelet, Steven, and Jeffrey Sachs. 1998. The East Asian financial crisis: Diagnosis, remedies, prospects. Harvard Institute for International Development unpublished paper, 20 April.

Wade, Robert. 1990. *Governing the market: Economic theory and the role of government in East Asian industrialization*. Princeton: Princeton University Press.

———. 1998. The Asian crisis and the global economy: Causes, consequences and cure. *Current History* (October): 1–15.

Woo, Jung-en [Meredith Woo-Cumings]. 1991. *Race to the swift: State and finance in Korean industrialization*. New York: Columbia University Press.

STUDY AND DISCUSSION QUESTIONS

1. How would you describe the Asian financial and economic crisis?
2. What were the key political sources of the crisis?
3. What explains the different national responses—and what was there about Asian regionalism that inhibited an effective Asia-wide response to the crisis?

17

State Power and the Asian Crisis

Linda Weiss

What are the implications of the East Asian miracle, the crisis, and the recovery for understanding the interactive effects of globalization and state power? The Asian financial crisis revitalized the debate about state power in Asian economic development. This selection by Linda Weiss represents an important contribution to that debate.

Weiss argues that state power—understood as the capacity of the state to respond strategically and effectively to a changed external environment—is a key part of the explanation of why some states (such as Korea) proved to be more vulnerable than others (such as Taiwan).

South Korea has been called a "strong state": a state that can effectively interact with social forces and act with effect, discretion, and a degree of autonomy. But as the crisis approached, the effectiveness and capacity of the Korean state had receded. Hence when the crisis hit, Korea was extremely vulnerable. As Weiss argues, a gradual weakening of the institutional capacities of the state opened the door to high-risk borrowing strategies and over-investment in chaebols,* which in turn exposed the country to capital flight and financial disruptions. Not so in Taiwan, where peculiar geopolitical circumstances—the exclusion from the IMF and the World Bank (since 1978), the ever-present potential of economic sanctions instigated by the PRC, and the incessant diplomatic tension—created a determination to institutionalize an extensive capacity *to absorb external shocks. The goals and institutional capacities of the Taiwanese state remained intact into the 1990s and the pressures to embrace economic liberalism were kept at arms length.*

The comparative study of state power and the Asian crisis by Weiss provides important evidence that globalization does not uniformly weaken states, but rather creates a set of challenges to which states must respond—and they do so in particular ways with varying success depending, in large part, on the institutionalized capacities they can marshal to respond to the external challenges of globalization.

The Asian financial crisis has re-opened the debate about the role of the state in the region's industrialisation. Just when there seemed to be growing acknowledgement across the economic and political disciplines that certain kinds of state involvement were vital to the rapid upgrading of the Northeast Asian economies, and that understanding what made states effective or ineffective was a crucial issue, along came the financial hurricane. Profound disarray of an economic and social nature has been the most immediate and important consequence of this watershed event. Theoretical disarray has followed closely in its path. This article seeks to inject some theoretical rigour into the discussion of the Asian crisis. State power in the Asian setting—whether and in what way the state's transformative capacity is weak or robust—and how it relates to the impact of international markets is central to the argument that follows.

THE ARGUMENT: THE TWO FACES
OF THE ASIAN CRISIS

Although commentators disagree about the fundamental causes of the crisis, explanatory efforts by and large have taken one of two different tacks. One focuses on variables inside the nation-state, giving primacy to domestic weaknesses (i.e. flawed policies or institutions or some combination of the two). The other directs the analytical focus outward, attributing most weight to international and global financial markets (i.e. investor panic).

Rather than appraising the respective merits of an 'outside' or an 'inside' approach, we can move to a more fruitful starting point. We begin with the observation that this particular crisis has two faces, not one: a 'normal' or ordinary aspect and an 'abnormal' one.

---

*The *chaebol* is an extensive conglomerate of many companies clustered around one parent company, which does business under integrated financial and managerial control in multiple markets, and often exhibits a considerable degree of family control.

To say that there is a normal aspect to the crisis is to make the simple but important point that there is little novelty to financial crises. Although they occur suddenly and unexpectedly, and at times perhaps even arbitrarily, they do so with great regularity. Although the latest crisis is always viewed as the most compelling, such events as we have witnessed in Asia, at least before the crisis deepened— including falling asset prices, plunging currency values and weakened banks— have a long history. Whether one's perspective is that of 15 years or 150 years, it appears that the history of capitalism is strewn with financial crises of one form or another. Their recurrence over a very long period suggests that crashes, panics and manias are endemic to modern capitalism.[1]

The implication is that no country can be considered immune. This does not mean, of course, that all countries are equally susceptible to financial crises. Rather, in a world of volatile capital flows, *some* countries may become *more* vulnerable to crisis than others. What makes them so? Students of financial crises suggest that vulnerability is a function of some domestic weakness or weaknesses which before the crisis were regarded as benign. Generally speaking, then, the normal face of the Asian crisis directs analytic attention to national-level variables. These are examined below.

But we cannot leave the analysis at this point. No matter which domestic 'weaknesses' are singled out, the very act of highlighting them runs the strong risk of overstatement and distortion. The afflicted economies were not basket cases, but reasonably sound, generally with moderate if not striking prospects for improvement. Most of them enjoyed high savings, balanced budgets, strong private sector investment, low inflation, a relatively egalitarian income distribution and a strong export drive. 'Vulnerability' therefore needs to be placed in perspective: it is, after all, merely a condition, not a cause of the upheaval that ensued. It cannot be emphasised too often that, regardless of one's theoretical perspective, there is a real danger in the temptation to make overly coherent—and thus apparently inevitable—an outcome which remains, in several important respects, genuinely confounding.

Separating out for special explanatory treatment the abnormal aspect of the crisis is one way of guarding against this tendency. In so doing, I propose to explain why a problem that should have been transient and quite quickly rectified, like so many others before it, turned into a full-blown disaster.

To emphasise the 'abnormal' face of the crisis is to draw attention to its deepening and its severity, and thus to highlight what was special about the Asian experience. Abnormality in this context refers to outcomes far in excess of what one could reasonably anticipate or justify in the light of what is known about pre-crisis conditions of the affected economies. Domestic weaknesses may explain country vulnerability, but such weaknesses are unlikely to be lethal—that is, they are unlikely to explain the way the bursting of the property bubble in Thailand, for example, turned into full-blown capital flight. There is, in short, much about the Asian crisis—its timing, its pattern of contagion and, above all, its magnitude—that has only a tenuous connection with the state of the real economy of the countries in question. Many have remarked on the peculiar depth and severity of the phenomenon. Few have attempted to theorise it. To do so, I shall turn again to political power variables, but this time (in the second part of the article) to those originating *outside* the nation-states in question.

I propose, then, a two-pronged approach to the issue. If we take this duality seriously, it stands to reason that monocausal approaches will not take us far. Rather than adding to the steady stream of monocausal explanations that presently compete for attention, a different tack is required. A state power framework enables one to address the question of the sources and evolution of the crisis with a degree of theoretical rigour, while at the same time giving due weight to national and international factors.

We have then two central questions: why were some East Asian countries much more vulnerable than others to financial meltdown—i.e. why was the crisis so *uneven* in its occurrence (thus, for example, Korea proving more vulnerable than Taiwan); and why was it so *severe* in the Asian setting (i.e. 'severe' relative to economic fundamentals and to earlier crises elsewhere)?

FINANCIAL MARKETS, DOMESTIC INSTITUTIONS, INTERNATIONAL POWER ACTORS

The general argument is that, while global financial markets somewhat obviously and directly produced the outcomes commonly labelled as the Asian crisis (by way of speculative runs and sudden withdrawal of funds—so-called investor panic or herding), they were not the primary determining factor. For financial markets to have wrought their effects in the first place (and in differential measure), two less obvious variables had to be present. The first—a 'normal' pull factor—is some sort of domestic vulnerability in the real economy, in this case, I shall argue, one whose common denominator is weak or decomposing institutional capacities. These, in turn, depending on the context, considerably exacerbated real economy vulnerabilities such as falling exports, rising current account deficits and surplus capacity.

The second variable—an 'abnormal' push factor—consists in vulnerability which is externally induced or intensified. The common denominator of this second-order vulnerability is the strong external power of a leading state (the USA) pursuing its own national economic agenda (with a strong input from its domestic financial interests), partly on its own and partly in concert with the International Monetary Fund (IMF).

Thus two theses are advanced. Both implicate state power. The more general thesis is that the relative weakness of state capacity (in Southeast Asia), and its marked if incomplete decomposition (in Korea), made these economies more prone to speculative investment (in the Korean case, over-investment), asset bubbles and current account deficits, and consequently more vulnerable to financial upheaval. In the Korean case, it was not institutionalised weakness *per se* but the gradual decomposition of core capacities that paved the way for the high-risk borrowing strategies and over-investment of the *chaebol,* which then exposed Korea to sudden downturns and capital flight. In the Asian episode at least, one can generalise that, by virtue of both limited and decomposing state capacities, certain economies became significantly more vulnerable than others to investor pull-out (triggered in the first instance by the bursting of the property bubble in Thailand). But, in saying this, one is merely drawing attention to the ordinary, 'normal' face of financial crisis.

The second, more specific thesis is that it was an outside force, namely, the relative strength of US international state power which, partly through its own independent actions and partly through the auspices of the IMF, helped to deepen the crisis, turning an otherwise ordinary event (that is to say, transient and quickly repaired) into an unusually severe and protracted phenomenon.

NATIONAL INSTITUTIONS AND ECONOMIC VULNERABILITY

Domestic Power and the Asian Crisis

In what way, then, is state power at issue in the crisis? When commentators invoke the state's role to explain the crisis, they typically draw on one of two quite different interpretations. By far the most common is the 'state interventionism' or 'too much state power' thesis.

(1) **Too much state intervention.** If there is an 'official' version of the Asian crisis, this is it. It views the crisis as a demonstration of the folly of state intervention in the economy. The 'too much power' conclusion is that 'interventionist' states have brought the Asian economies down by distorting market processes. For, if states had not been so 'interventionist' in their economies in the first place, there would be fewer distortions (viz. corruption, cronyism and other forms of rent-seeking) blocking efficient resource allocation. For proponents of this view, state interventionism shades ineluctably into cronyism; both are typically equated with the 'Japanese model' of state-guided capitalism (a.k.a. the 'Asian model'), and the crisis is seen as proof of its failure. As an expression of this understanding, consider the following statement celebrating, somewhat prematurely, the triumph of the US model in Asia:

> *There is an emerging consensus on both sides of the Pacific that the Japanese model has failed. Countries up and down the Pacific Rim are embracing market oriented reforms in the wake of an economic crisis widely blamed upon Japanese style institutions.*

For all the crude overtones replaying the fruitless 'state-versus-market' dichotomy, this is probably the most popular view of what has gone wrong in Asia. It is favoured by the IMF, by top officials in the US Treasury and the Federal Reserve, and by liberal economists more generally. If state involvement is seen as a recipe for unstable economic foundations, this is because in most such reasoning it is virtually inseparable from rent-seeking, political favouritism and straightforward corruption. However, to the extent that such practices are the norm rather than the exception, they may be seen as symptoms of *weak*, not robust, state capacity; to this extent, evidence of their pervasiveness in the troubled economies is more likely to support than to refute the argument advanced here.

(2) **Too little regulation.** For others, however, the problem of state power is one of inadequate regulation or too little state control rather than too much. These commentators propose that state weakness (in a regulatory sense) helped to create the crisis. As Joseph Stiglitz, chief economist and vice president of the World Bank, puts it, 'the crisis was caused in part by too little government regulation (or perverse or ineffective government regulation)'.[2] The 'too little' proponents are chiefly concerned with the laxity of regulatory control over capital inflows consequent upon financial liberalisation (hence overexposure to unhedged, short-term debt). This is undoubtedly important. After all, the opening of the capital account is central to the whole story of what has gone wrong in Asia. It resulted in massive amounts of short-term capital (in foreign denominated currency) coming in to service long-term investments (at pegged exchange rates). From this perspective, the cause of the Asian crisis was straightforward: if the state had been a stronger regulator—preventing dangerous inflows—there would have been no crisis, end of story. So the weak regulation of the capital account 'caused' the problem: for what comes in can go out; and very quickly it did go. This thesis has much to recommend it. But there is more at issue than regulatory capacity, as we shall see in the next section.

Indeed, the real intellectual challenge would seem to lie elsewhere. It is twofold: the first task is to explain why capital flowed in in such massive amounts in the first place. In other words, what was the capital being used for and how did that use reflect underlying institutional weaknesses and exacerbate economic vulnerability? This is the focus here. The second task is to explain why capital went out in a seemingly unstoppable haemorrhage—to the point where Indonesia, as the worst case, became totally disconnected from the international banking community. This is the focus of part two.

As indicated earlier, there would seem to be a good case for arguing that some economies may be more vulnerable to financial crisis than others. Identifying weaknesses in the 'real economy' is not too difficult in the Asian experience. Most analysts agree on what they are: falling export growth—the main cause of the ballooning current account deficits—was common to all the affected countries in the two years before the crisis. Falling exports in the troubled economies can be explained in a number of different ways,[3] but two common underlying conditions for the loss of markets can be identified. One is institutional inability or slowness to upgrade skills, products and technology, and thus an over-reliance on the highly price-sensitive goods that are also being produced by new competitors down market (e.g. pre-crisis Thailand). The other is the tendency to produce surplus capacity (resulting from what the Japanese call 'excessive competition'), caused in part by the absence of an institutional discipline for investment coordination and in part by the absence of an external or institutional pressure to upgrade (exemplified by the Korean experience).

Where this analysis differs from existing accounts on the vulnerability issue is in going deeper to trace its institutional sources. I propose that the sources of vulnerability in the real economy lie in the relatively limited or weakened transformative powers of the state in the most affected countries (Thailand, Indonesia and South Korea). The more limited transformative capacities of Thailand and Indonesia (above all, the failure to coordinate investment into productive sectors of the economy and to hasten upgrading of skills and technology) paved the way for high levels of speculative investment (notably in real estate), falling export growth and rising current account deficits. In Southeast Asia, the flipside of this institutional failing was increased foreign indebtedness by private corporations and financial institutions in order to fund the deficits, massive investment in nontradeables and ultimately property bubbles which burst, triggering the first phase of the crisis.

In Korea, on the other hand, where state capacities had been gradually decomposing, excessive foreign borrowing by private companies and extensive 'over-investment' in leading export sectors (steel, petrochemicals, cars, semiconductors) resulted in oversupply, falling exports, interest repayment difficulties and a spate of corporate collapses, thus triggering the first phase of the crisis in Korea.

From Weak Transformative Capacity to 'Real Economy' Vulnerability and Weak Regulatory Control

My account therefore takes a different tack, though one that is complementary, to the Stiglitz approach ('too little regulatory control'). For in all the troubled economies we are confronted with another kind of institutional debility: that is, limited or—in the case of Korea—weakened 'transformative capacity'. I use this term to refer to national contexts where the sociopolitical project of government and the organisation of state-society relations are biased towards improvement of the production regime. In such contexts the goal of trading at ever higher levels of skill and technology (sectoral transformation) has priority over that of maximising consumer welfare, and the state—rather than the market alone—is viewed as an important means of achieving it.[4]

Transformative capacity is important for at least two reasons. The first and most immediate consequence of low (or weakened) transformative capacity is economic vulnerability in the form of falling export growth, rising current account deficits and excess investment. For investors, current account deficits in particular are among the most important indicators of a nation's economic prospects. On the eve of the crisis, current account deficits (most marked in Thailand) soared as exports slowed and as borrowed capital was invested in non-tradeables (especially real estate). As the current account deficits ballooned, the demand grew for foreign capital to sustain them. Attracting such capital meant raising domestic interest rates, which in turn resulted in a dramatic fall in real estate prices, thus bursting the bubble economy. Thailand manifested in exaggerated form the problem common to the Southeast Asian economies: a consumption boom, stock and property bubbles, and asset price inflation. These were the immediate source of its increasing current account deficits. At a more fundamental level, however, these outcomes were ensured by the fact that Thailand had ceased to be a low-cost producer, yet remained poorly equipped to supply more sophisticated, less price-sensitive goods. In short, the move to upgrade the industrial portfolio—and thus move up-market of the cheaper producers in China and Vietnam—had been much delayed. This contrasts with the high-growth phase of Taiwan and Korea, where the drive to trade at higher levels of technology was orchestrated by way of a selective industrial policy which linked credit allocation and tax incentives to investment in specific sectors of the economy. As one might anticipate, in the absence of the more consistent regime priorities and dedicated institutional arrangements of their Northeast Asian neighbours, the Southeast Asian countries were much less predisposed to coordinating industrial investment and upgrading. The end result for Thailand has been massive capital inflows whose composition and destination the state has appeared neither able nor willing to shape. Below I indicate the ways in which Southeast Asian states failed to institutionalise such powers for sustainable development and show how the gradual unravelling of Korea's powers quickened in the 1990s. Ironically, as we shall see, only in one area has 'too much' state power been of relevance. This concerns the international arena and the role of the USA as 'opportunistic hegemon', whose interests and actions have deepened, and in turn been served by, the Asian crisis.

The second consequence of transformative weakness in the Asian industrial arena has to do with financial regulation. Where transformative capacity is limited or reduced, this appears to underpin or pave the way for weak regulatory control in the financial sector. Conversely, where transformative orientations and organisational capacities remain robust—as in Taiwan, Japan and Singapore—the approach to financial liberalisation has tended to affirm rather than remove state control over capital flows. Korea and Taiwan illustrate these differences in the way each went about the task of liberalising the corporate bond market.

Whichever way we look at it, the fact remains that, in the six or seven years before the Asian meltdown, the Korean authorities were much 'less guarded' than Taiwan's about the level of short-term inflows. Was it simply an error that led the Koreans to require that only foreign loans of more than one-year maturity be registered? There is some evidence to suggest that it was more a calculated policy choice, aimed at giving the *chaebol* access to affordable credit in a period marked not only by deteriorating economic performance, but also by state withdrawal from credit control and industrial policy. Rising wages and declining productivity in the first half of the 1990s made Korea less attractive to foreign lenders, thus placing a premium on long-term interest rates. As a result, long-term foreign loans became more expensive, harder to obtain, and recorded a net outflow as loan repayments continued. It was in this context that Ministry of Finance officials took the decision to relax controls to allow the *chaebol* greater access to short-term portfolio investment. The result was a surge in the inflow of foreign capital, most of it portfolio investment, exceeding a cumulative total of US$27 billion between 1991–94 alone. The contrast with Taiwan's deregulation of the corporate bond market in 1993 is instructive. The Central Bank (CBC) for the first time allowed Taiwanese companies to remit the proceeds of overseas bond issues for domestic use. However, this was accompanied by new rules that all such foreign currency remittances be invested in plant expansion and that the total or national aggregate for all such inflows not exceed US$3 billion. Moreover, the CBC backs up the regulations with close monitoring, intervening under its emergency powers when it suspects foreign inflows are not being used for designated purposes.

One might speculate that the Korean government was less guarded than the Taiwanese about raising the level of short-term inflows because it was subject to greater pressure from big business. But even if such pressure could be demonstrated, it would not contradict a more fundamental point: Korean business would most probably find itself pushing against an open door in the 1990s in so far as state actors had been working for over a decade to relinquish financial control, wind down credit activism and advance the *chaebol*'s financial autonomy— in short, to dismantle the state's transformative capacity. In the preceding decade growing ideological divisions within the state elite helped to reorient ideas about the role and scope of the state in industrial governance; and by 1993, with the Cold War behind them and the election of the first wholly civilian government under Kim Young Sam, the newly empowered neoliberals in the bureaucracy voted to dismantle their key transformative agency, the Economic Planning Board (EPB). Consequently, when the Koreans approached the task of liberalising the capital account in the 1990s, they did so with a view to preparing the ground for further dismantling state control over the economy—not maintaining it.

This contrasted with the approach taken in Taiwan where the goals and organisational arrangements of state actors (and thus what I have called their transformative capacity) remained largely intact in the period leading up to financial liberalisation. That legacy ensured a different approach to financial reform, one which would deploy the new rules as a means of securing state involvement in national economic management. In spite of the growing importance of liberal economic ideas in Taiwan's public discourse, it is likely that the continuing geopolitical threat (the China question), together with Taiwan's peculiar diplomatic isolation, served as important countervailing pressures that tempered and moderated the domestic push to embrace economic liberalism. As a result, state actors in Taiwan by and large continued to view the state both as an important goal setter for the national economy and as an indispensable means of sustaining an internationally competitive industry. Accordingly, as Taiwanese authorities went about internationalising the financial system in the 1990s, they did so with a view to complementing and maintaining the state's powers of coordination.

To the extent that the Korea-Taiwan differences suggest different routes to liberlisation, Korea appears to have moved in a more state-minimising, market-enhancing (neoliberal?) direction, while Taiwan, like Japan, has chosen a more state-enhancing path via re-regulation. In each case, the outcome appears to be shaped by the pre-existing constellation of ideas and institutions regarding the state-market relationship.

The question of prime movers in state disengagement and financial deregulation is a separate and far from simple story which cannot be adequately recounted here. Suffice to say that the popular perception emphasises international forces bearing down on the Korean government, especially US pressures for economic liberalisation. But the nature and timing of those external pressures (most effective in the early 1990s as Korea sought OECD membership) need closer scrutiny, as does the domestic momentum for reform. In the Korean setting, the first great step towards state disengagement and financial deregulation occurred in the early 1980s. Domestic political crisis and intra-elite divisions over the state's role in economic change provided much of the impetus for change in this period. Push turned to pull in the 1990s as Korea's quest for OECD membership was made conditional upon greater opening of its capital account. It is not hard to appreciate that Korea's desire to be part of the rich countries' club (something unavailable to Taiwan) would not only have 'intensified external pressure to liberalise the economy', but also made such pressure more effective. But to claim that external pressure was the primary driving force behind Korea's efforts to reconfigure the state-finance-industry relationship and to dismantle some of the more elaborate machinery of state control would be misleading. For that reorientation had been underway throughout the 1980s, and that shift is inexplicable without reference to domestic pressures. In sum, there is no shortage of external pressure for liberalisation, especially after 1989 and the cessation of Cold-War politics. But it may be easy to overstate its importance in a context where the internal pressures for liberalisation were far from weak. One can imagine insistent prodding from the USA for financial deregulation making some impression; one can *expect* it to make a mark when it dovetails with the agenda of pro-liberalisation supporters within the financial bureaucracy and government-sponsored think-tanks like the Korean Development Institute. These same Korean bureaucrats and economists, not the Americans, were the ones who pressed for complete dismantling of the EPB, the 'central coordinating intelligence' which had presided over Korea's rapid transformation.

There is, however, a larger point to be made, which dovetails with the argument being advanced here. By the early 1990s, having already ceded a large chunk of its transformative capacity—including its sectoral investment coordination and upgrading role—to a private sector enthusiastic for independence (but ambivalent about state withdrawal from industrial credit), it was merely a short step for the Korean government to relinquish control over the financial system. To say—as indeed many have—that liberalisation took place in a 'flawed' manner, that is, without accompanying regulatory controls, may be somewhat beside the point. For, as I have indicated, the Korean authorities appear to have undertaken liberalisation with a view to further dismantling, not securing, the state's core capacities. In the process, of course, they relinquished much more than they bargained for.

It is important to be clear about the causal logic of the present argument. It is not proposed that robust transformative capacity is always essential for effective regulatory control. Clearly countries do not require the elaborate underpinnings of state capacity in order to engage in regulatory control. Effective efforts to control the level and composition of capital flows can also evolve as a form of institutional learning in response to the experience of severe financial crisis, as for example in the case of Chile. Thus firm regulatory control of finance may sit alongside institutional arrangements which are far less elaborate than those entailed by transformative capacity. On the other hand, it is proposed that loose regulatory control is in some significant sense associated with limited or weakened transformative capacity. The proposition, then, is that governments tend to 'choose' a form of regulatory regime that matches up with their fundamental orientations and organisational arrangements. If, for instance, securing a strong and competitive industry is viewed as a basic economic goal and the role of the state is perceived as important to its achievement, one would expect reasonably strong complementarity between this (transformative) industrial orientation and the (closely managed) type of regulatory regime found in Taiwan, Singapore and Japan. If, on the other hand, the state's role is deemed of decreasing importance in achieving the economic goal (as in Korea), or the economic goal itself is inconsistent or uncertain (as, for example, in Thailand and Indonesia), one would expect a similar symmetry between weaker transformative orientation and regulatory looseness. So, while on the surface it may appear that Korea's current problems have more to do with the state's failure to manage financial liberalisation than with its declining commitment to and capacity for transformative projects, the import of my argument is that the two are inextricably linked. In so far as transformative capacity calls for greater coordination of investment flows and upgrading efforts, such a commitment entails more careful oversight of volatile capital flows and thus a degree of prudential regulation. This at least is the story for Taiwan.

This section has proposed that transformative capacity is significant for two reasons. First, it paved the way for economic weaknesses such as falling export growth, rising current account deficits and excess capacity. Second, it contributed to regulatory weakness, thus enabling uncontrolled speculative and short-term inflows. Let us see how this argument applies to the main crisis-stricken economies.

Southeast Asia: In Search of the Effective State

The fast growth of the Southeast Asian economies has tempted many to assume a fundamental similarity in the political economies of Southeast and Northeast Asia (hence the widely touted notion of an 'Asian model'). One consequence of this geographical elision is the tendency to see state involvement in the economy as all of a piece, the state's role in the Indonesian or Thai economy being considered much the same as for Korea or Taiwan. The result, say the same sources, is 'crony capitalism', a normative rather than analytical term to suggest that close ties between government and business are harmful to economic performance, in so far as they produce decisions based on non-economic criteria and are therefore market-subverting.

It is, of course, one thing to note the existence of cronyism, another to establish its causal role in the events culminating in the Asian crisis. Thus far, however, that case has not been established and any serious attempt to do so should bear in mind two important points. First, among economists it is now recognised that so-called cronyism comes in different guises, some forms playing a positive developmental role. Which forms prevailed in the East Asian setting on the eve of the crisis? We lack the necessary evidence but, considering the decent economic performance of the stricken economies in the pre-crisis period, one may presume that at least some aspects of cronyism were growth-enhancing. Second, although the term has been used mostly by Western analysts to describe Asian practices, cronyism is equally at home in Western settings, at times central to the operation of a country's core institutions. For example, financial institutions in the City of London operated principally through such networks up until the 1960s. Thus the presence of cronyism *per se* may offer little explanatory insight. It may be growth-enhancing, -retarding or neutral; and it may constitute a core organising principle in even the most liberal free-market contexts. It is therefore possible to draw at least one interim conclusion: whatever the extent of cronyist practices in Southeast Asia in particular, or the region more generally, they are not the distinguishing building blocks of developmental states.

Indeed Malaysia, Thailand and Indonesia, in spite of the frequent rhetoric of growth *über alles,* have never institutionalised 'developmental market economies' of the kind found in Japan, Korea and Taiwan. If one takes the high-growth period of each country, the differences between first- and second-generation industrialisers in fundamental national orientations, in state architecture and in coordinating capabilities seem to undermine, rather than justify, the notion of a unified 'Asian model'. While government-business ties have often been close, they have rarely approached the 'governed interdependence' model of Northeast Asia, whereby a competent, relatively insulated economic bureaucracy institutionalises a negotiating relationship with organised industrial groups in order to pursue sectoral industrial policies based on well publicised criteria. This is not to suggest that the Southeast Asian states are unremittingly weak. These countries have undergone considerable 'structural transformation', involving the shift from a largely agrarian and primary commodity-export base to an increasingly industrial one. There is no doubt that state capacity building has advanced considerably compared to most Third World countries; but the process of 'sectoral transformation' appears to have stalled, as I argue below. This process tends to demand a more elaborate set of capacities as well as consistent economic priorities.

In Malaysia, where the bureaucracy for the past two decades has been preoccupied with ethnic redistribution, what passes for industrial policy has been appraised by analysts as a tool for resource redistribution rather than an instrument of industrial transformation.[5] The story for Indonesia is one similarly at odds with the transformative capacity of developmental states. While ethnic distance has given the state some autonomy from the dominant (Chinese) entrepreneurial group, and while the state in the Suharto era has been surprisingly insulated from organised societal pressures, the overall picture is one of a relatively weak bureaucracy unable to monitor and enforce policy preferences. In his study of the politics of credit activism in the Suharto period, Andrew MacIntyre concluded that, notwithstanding the development of an elaborate system of preferential credit (relatively little of it targetted to industry), official policy preferences were routinely subverted by a 'patrimonially based allocation of rent-taking opportunities within the state elite'.[6] Strong interventionism plus autonomy from societal pressures may describe important features of the Indonesian state; but such features do not amount to a state that is developmentally oriented and configured.

A similar conclusion applies to Thailand. In contrast with Indonesia, where oil exports have played a dominant role in economic expansion, Thailand's rapid growth since the 1980s has had a stronger base in manufacturing exports. Yet, like Indonesia, Thailand's growth appears to owe little to a state-coordinated industrial strategy. This may imply that Thailand, like Malaysia and Indonesia, has developed successfully without a developmental state, thus questioning the 'governed market' arguments developed to account for Northeast Asia's rapid transformation. An altogether different interpretation, however, may be more plausible: the absence of developmental institutions in each of the Southeast Asian countries may give rise to systemic weakness and incomplete transformative capacity, thus heightening economic vulnerability. Some aspects of the Thai experience are consistent with this argument. For, in spite of expanding manufacturing exports since the mid 1980s (heavily skewed towards electronics fabricated in Japanese plants), on the eve of the crisis Thailand appeared trapped at the lower end of technology, pursuing what neoclassical economists would consider a key plank of economic success: static comparative advantage based on access to cheap labour and raw materials. Whatever the precise basis of its rapid growth, Thailand, it seems, has been relatively slow to upgrade skills and technology, for its capacity to shift skills and technology upmarket is still relatively weak. This is reflected in very low high-school completion rates, in the underdevelopment of the domestic production of capital goods and in real labour costs rising faster than real productivity. It is also reflected to some extent in the comparative rankings of state funding of research and development in 1998. Thus, for example, while Taiwan ranked 24th out of 53 industrialised and major developing nations worldwide, Thailand, at 48th place, was located at the lower end of the scale along with Malaysia (42nd) and Indonesia (53rd) at the bottom. Recent moves by the Thai government since the Asian crisis suggest there is some substance to the 'transformative weakness' argument being advanced here, for it has identified inadequate upgrading as a serious problem demanding a coordinated national effort.

On the eve of the crisis, the chief problem for Thailand was not simply soaring current account deficits (7.9 per cent of GNP in 1996), but the fact that its prospects for rectifying them were relatively low, since the national industrial structure was not being adjusted fast enough to absorb the rise in labour costs engendered by rapid economic growth. Given the weakening state of Thailand's manufacturing export sector, coupled with the absence of a national upgrading effort, it was unlikely that the huge capital inflows would find productive outlets of their own accord. Moreover, far from overseeing capital flows, the state failed to ensure that capital was invested productively and earning foreign currency to service the debt.

Without wishing to overstate the differences which distinguish Southeast Asian countries like Thailand from first-generation industrialisers to the north, it is nevertheless important to highlight them. More generally, while there may be considerable 'embeddedness'[7] of Southeast Asian states in their surrounding societies (whether via ethnically structured, patrimonially linked or interest-based networks), the findings of several area and comparative studies indicate that there has been much less 'insulation' of relevant state agencies where transformative projects can be pursued at some remove from particularistic interest politics. Where investment and financial flows are concerned, for example, this institutional weakness has been reflected less in the absence of relevant rules (inadequate regulation) or the proliferation of errors (policy mistakes) than in an inability to ensure policy implementation. In Thailand, for example, even before the rules were changed—when the purchase of real estate and foreign securities by residents required approval from the Bank of Thailand—the Bank and Ministry of Finance remained vulnerable to political intervention. In comparison with the Northeast Asian experience, the interdependence of government and business in the Southeast Asian economies, at least during their high-growth phase, has been governed much more weakly by transformative goals and institutional arrangements and, in consequence, public policy has more often been captured by particular interests jostling for favour in the political process.

Korea: Revenge of the International Market Against the Transformative State?

In Korea, what began as a banking crisis was precipitated by a series of corporate collapses throughout 1997, beginning with the Hanbo group in January. Indeed the *chaebol* loom large as the villains of the Korean débacle. If one is seeking a common denominator in these events, it was not that of weak-state cronyism, or even of a strong state overriding efficient market logic. Rather, it was one of private sector excesses: uncoordinated over-investment exacerbated by state retreat, that is, massive private borrowing for investments in sectors not only already well supplied by other *chaebol* (e.g. petrochemicals, steel, semiconductors) but also subject to cyclical downturn.

This was a pattern that became increasingly marked in the decade before the financial meltdown, as government gradually abandoned its long-standing role of coordinating industrial investment. First under Roh Tae Woo's presidency, then finally under Kim Young Sam's, policy loans were phased out and financial liberalisation speeded up. Ironically, it was a pattern that marked the *loosening* of the business-government relationship and gradual decline of transformative capacity in Korea. There can be no clearer symbol of this change than that offered by the definitive dismantling of the Economic Planning Board, which was merged with the Ministry of Finance in 1993. Although their explanatory aims may differ, many studies allude to the state's declining willingness and ability to operate a formal industrial policy and to oversee *chaebol* investments by the early 1990s. 'So what?' economists might retort. Why should government be any better than business in deciding where to invest? Why indeed! Yet, posed like this, the question misses the point. Like the Japanese, both the Korean and Taiwanese authorities have long emphasised the benefits of limiting what they refer to as 'excessive competition', whether through licensing, credit control, producer cartels or some combination of these. In spite of state encouragement, however, producer cartels have been much less successful in Korea than in Japan, highlighting industry's weak capacity for self-governance. Licensing and credit control are further instruments of industrial policy that can function to limit 'excessive competition' and its consequences (viz. over-investment and surplus capacity). But, once the state had retreated from industrial policy, and its efforts to encourage industrial self-governance among the *chaebol* had failed, the market did not take over to produce an optimum result, nor did the *chaebol* seek collectively to advance their well-being.

Whether one ponders this outcome theoretically in terms of market failure, prisoner's dilemma, the logic of collective action or some such hypothesis, it is hard to avoid the conclusion that some form of central coordination might have helped to mitigate the excessive, overlapping investments of the *chaebol* and, by the same token, have served to concentrate *chaebol* efforts on the process of industrial upgrading. Instead, decomposing political capacity unleashed a frenzied scramble for market share among the *chaebol* (especially among middle-level conglomerates seeking expansion), resulting in over-investment and high-risk borrowing strategies. As government-business 'interdependence' became steadily 'ungoverned', the *chaebol* tended to take the easier course of expansion rather than upgrading, pursuing growth rather than innovation. This pattern became a hallmark of the Korean industrial landscape in the democratisation decade.

But the Korean pattern of over-investment and massive foreign borrowing was far from fatal. It was certainly not Korea's first encounter with economic downturn, difficulties of foreign debt repayment or even IMF intervention. Because of its massively leveraged conglomerates, Korea has always been vulnerable to external shocks, leading in 1980 to a 6 per cent loss in GNP. Such shocks, however, had proved more containable in the past. So why was it so uncontainable now? What was new? Was it the composition of external debt, or perhaps its level or provenance? Surely not, for even in a more protected financial system, Korea managed to scale the heights of foreign indebtedness and was no stranger to repayment difficulties. (Large debts of short-term maturity prompted Korea's first major crisis of 1971–72; and the debt-*cum*-oil crisis of 1979–82 involved difficulties servicing a huge foreign debt. Yet these problems were overcome with much less upheaval compared with the 1990s.)

To understand what was new about the 1997 experience, we need to consider the role of external factors in turning a run-of-the-mill debt crisis into an over-the-top financial crash. One thing had altered fundamentally—the geopolitical landscape. Since the end of the Cold War, the USA–Korea security relationship had gradually weakened. Consequently, Korea in the 1990s was no longer a special case whose deviation from the free-market norm could be tolerated for larger political goals. Thus, far from seeking to buttress the Korean state as it had done in other times of difficulty, the USA was now prepared to stand back and let the crisis rip through the institutional fabric it so wished to tear apart.

INTERNATIONAL POWER ACTORS
AND DEEPENING FINANCIAL CRISIS

When Crisis Turned to Tragedy

I have argued that weak or weakened transformative capacity rendered some economies more vulnerable to economic turmoil. But the fact remains that vulnerabilities of various kinds do not necessarily produce a banking or currency crisis. Moreover, the kind of weakness identified here is far from lethal. It is certainly no candidate for explaining the scope or depth of the crisis—in short, why it turned abnormal.

To the question of why the crisis was so much worse than it was supposed to be, several authorities have answered that it was because of investor panic, self-fulfilling expectations and sheer 'herd' behaviour, whereby everyone withdraws from the market simply because that is what everyone else is doing. But what nurtured and sustained the panic? It may well be that the herding phenomenon is more prevalent in a global environment where the world's money is controlled by fund managers who feel most secure when they follow everyone else. However, to invoke panic, herding and similar behavioural metaphors is to provide not so much an explanation as a restatement of the problem. Why was capital flight so massive, so relentless and thus so damaging? To answer this, we must look outside the nation-states in question to the role of external power actors which coalesce around and within the US federal administration.

The explanation thus requires that we turn our attention to the exercise of state power (and the constellation of interests embedded therein), but this time state power which is being applied externally by the world's most powerful nation-state. It has been proposed in another context that (externally oriented) state power can in certain limited cases—the USA being the exemplary case—provide a (temporary) substitute for domestic capacity by forcing other nation-states to relinquish their internal transformative powers.

Today, the most vivid illustration of that proposition can be seen in the extraordinary behaviour of the USA in the Asian region in exploiting the financial crisis to force systemic change in the troubled economies. Acting externally to bring about structural change has been a persistent pattern in the postwar US experience. That pattern shows how a leading power, apparently weak in domestic transformative capacity, but powerful externally, may seek to compensate for relative domestic weakness by attempting to force change upon others and, if possible, conformity with its own system. In the troubled 1980s, when debate turned on the industrial decline of the United States, such power inversion invoked the idea of the USA as an 'opportunistic' great power with a free-riding strategy: shifting the costs of change on to others more readily than adapting its own institutions. In the triumphalist 1990s, it would seem more evocative of an 'intellectual' hegemon convinced of the economic superiority and global applicability of its own system.

The Role of the US Treasury–Wall Street–IMF Complex

Of the three international power actors involved in deepening the crisis, it has been the US Treasury–finance nexus that has been the least visible yet the most damaging. While the IMF is also implicated in the unfolding drama, its role has differed on two counts: its interventions have neither enjoyed the level of autonomy displayed by the other actors (though independence is strongly desired by the Fund), nor deployed their more calculated self-interest. The key proposition is that the US administration has not merely used the crisis as a leveraging opportunity to prise open markets once closed to foreign financial institutions; it has played a critical role in deepening the crisis in the first place. The impact of external power sources coalescing around the US administration can be seen in three main ways, as elaborated below.

(1) **Shutting the door after the horse has bolted.** The main point can be summarised thus: the US government did not act with due speed to contain the panic, indeed it appeared also to prevent containment, intervening only after the situation had deteriorated to an alarming degree. This is important because—if one takes earlier crises as the norm—early intervention would in all probability have circumvented investor panic, curbed capital flight and brought the crisis to a swift resolution. Even a slight familiarity with earlier financial crises indicates that, when the foreign exchange turmoil struck Korea, the primary need was clear and straightforward. It was to maintain liquidity and thus to persuade foreign creditors to maintain lending by rolling over existing loans as they came due. That could be done without IMF guarantees, simply by ensuring that lenders understood that Korea's problem of inadequate reserves was a temporary problem of liquidity, not insolvency. Above all, Korea needed workouts, not bailouts: 'coordinated action by creditor banks to restructure its short-term debts, lengthening their maturity and providing additional temporary credits to help meet the interest obligations.'[8] But it was not until Korea's reserves were almost depleted and *after the major damage had already been done* that the US government—in January 1998—took the steps that would earlier have averted the 'deep' crisis, namely, bringing together the major players to coordinate a programme of debt restructuring and short-term loan rollovers.

The key proposition therefore has to do with actions of the US administration, which entailed both calculated non-intervention as well as prevention of intervention. The unwillingness to intervene in a timely manner to stem the degradation of the currency poses a striking contrast with US action in earlier such episodes in Europe and Latin America (where recovery was relatively quick). For instance, when sovereign debt led Mexico to the brink of bankruptcy in 1982, and twice more in 1994 and 1995 in response to massive capital flight and the peso crisis, the USA moved quickly to coordinate a rescue plan. In the recent peso crisis, the US government and the IMF took early action to rescue the currency, first with a credit line of US$6 billion, finally orchestrating a rescue fund of US$50 billion, engineering a massive international loan which restored investor confidence. This is not to say that the Mexican and Korean crises were similar; they were not. The point is that timely intervention was at hand in the Mexican case—and it worked. As Kindleberger has remarked, the strategy 'proved persuasive'. The haemorrhaging stopped, capital returned.[9] As studies of financial crises indicate, whenever international cooperation or even a lender of last resort has come to the rescue—and such instances appear to be the rule, not the exception—the business depression that follows financial crisis is momentary, slowing the economy only briefly; recovery after the panic is swift, without deeper significance.

By not intervening, it could be argued that the USA was merely bringing policy into alignment with the new geopolitical reality. In a post–Cold-War environment, there was no longer the significant national (security) interest in protecting Asia that in the past would so often have overridden the economic interest of opening Korean markets to US goods and finance. Should one therefore leave it at that: calculated inaction occurred because it was not in US interests to intervene? It could be argued, for instance, that the US government acted swiftly to support Mexico, but not Korea, because of strong political pressures for intervention by domestic firms with high levels of direct investment in the Latin American region. With much less direct investment in East Asia, US firms were unlikely to form a strong constituency for timely intervention in the Korean crisis.

Such negative considerations surely played a part. But, more positively, one might also argue that it was now very much in US interests *not* to intervene. Greater leverage over the stricken—and thus over market access—was the ultimate payoff. A number of top-level officials conceded as much in public statements as the IMF was called in by the Koreans. In a now widely publicised statement, Deputy Treasury Secretary Lawrence Summers proclaimed in February 1998 that 'the IMF has done more to promote America's trade and investment agenda in Korea than 30 years of bilateral trade talks'.

Certainly no-one anticipated quite how stricken the Asian economies would become, but that does not weaken the proposition that there was an element of calculation involved in the 'failure' to intervene. While it is highly plausible that the US administration could not have anticipated just how devastating the impact of the crisis would be, it is implausible to suggest complete ignorance of the seriousness of the situation. It is implausible for at least one good reason. The Japanese authorities had declared themselves prepared to intervene relatively early in the crisis—as early as August–September 1997—with the establishment of a US$100 billion bailout fund. That proposal (effectively laid to rest by the US administration) would surely have conveyed some sense of the gravity of the situation unfolding.

It is, of course, notoriously difficult to mount a convincing case for the sort of calculated behaviour that leaders are usually at pains to conceal. But we can add two further pieces of evidence in support of the proposition that, in failing to intervene in a timely manner, US power actors were mindful of the benefits to themselves (rather than the costs to others). First, as already intimated, the US government also acted to prevent intervention by another nation-state. When Japan stepped forward in August 1997 with a formal offer of funds to redeem some of its neighbours' debts, and a proposal to create a new multinational financial institution which would offer credit facilities to the ailing economies in the region, the Americans quickly scuttled the plan.[10] Perhaps, as Johnson suggests, the worry was that the Japanese would begin to deploy their surplus capital for the benefit of Asian countries, thus withdrawing this capital from the world's largest debtor nation (close to US$350 billion of Japanese money was invested in US Treasury bonds). Perhaps, more simply, Japan's proposal was rejected because of the fear that a contender to the IMF would not impose US-friendly conditions on those seeking its assistance. Whatever the precise mix of motives, it is surely not far fetched to anticipate a very different outcome had the USA supported, rather than undermined, the Japanese proposal.

Finally, in November and December 1997 the Koreans themselves were making frantic behind-the-scenes efforts to enlist US support in their plans for crisis management—and thus staving off calling in the IMF. The Korean government appealed to Washington and to Wall Street for financial support in a bid to raise US$15 billion to replenish foreign exchange reserves. As to why Korea's funding plans failed, Ministry of Finance officials—in a report submitted to the Korean National Assembly's special committee on currency crisis management—have claimed that the US government stood in the way of Korea's crisis management efforts. Whether such allegations are true, they seem of a piece with the US administration's earlier response to the Japanese proposal.

How then is one to interpret calculated non-intervention—as a matter of indifference or of national interest, or perhaps some combination of the two? The geopolitical argument leans towards indifference: 'if we don't help the Koreans it won't impact negatively on our security interests'. The interest argument leans towards positive benefits: 'if we don't help the Koreans this time it may just help to advance our economic interests that little bit further'. Attributing motives, even in the best of circumstances, is an exercise fraught with imprecision. It is especially difficult when consensus among the key decision makers is hard to discern. The real issue is: 'could the US Treasury and the Federal Reserve have intervened earlier to prevent the crisis deepening, as they had on other occasions?' If the answer is yes, as I have proposed, then, regardless of the precise mix of political motives for the absence of timely intervention, the devastating consequences of their inaction have been all too clear.

(2) **Screaming 'fire' in the theatre.** The second way in which external power deepened the crisis has to do with the imposition of a US trade and investment agenda in the IMF agreements. The latter have already received wide discussion, so let us simply note two points. First, the documents leave little doubt as to the embeddedness of the US Treasury in the financial interests which dominate Wall Street. (While the IMF is no mere instrument of US interests, seeking to maintain an independent role, it nevertheless depends on US support and is inescapably drawn into a close relationship with the world's leading nation-state and 'its' finance capital.) The IMF plan for Korea, for example, imposes as a condition of funding a series of institutional makeovers which have nought to do with dousing the fire or even making the structure fireproof. These include the opening of capital markets to enable hostile takeovers and foreign (majority) ownership of Korean firms, as well as greater access for foreign banks and insurance companies. It should be noted, however, that in Korea's case some aspects of structural reform included in the IMF agreements—notably the restructuring of its giant industrial groups—had been sought and pursued unsuccessfully by governments for at least a decade. According to official thinking, under the authority of the agreements, corporate reform might at last go forward. To this extent, the crisis was being hailed by some policy makers as a 'blessing in disguise'—allowing more foreign ownership of Korean assets, at least in the short term, but also restoring balance to the government-business relationship by granting state authorities the power to force long overdue streamlining of the conglomerates.

In some cases, the reform measures were sound but poorly sequenced. Thus, for example, the IMF's insistence that the Indonesian government take tough action to clean up its banking system led, on 1 November 1997, to the sudden closure of 16 banks with links to the Suharto family, which in turn precipitated a run on deposits that became a haemorrhage. This is because the closure was undertaken before Indonesia had established a system of deposit insurance. A stunned populace, faced with the prospect of a massive bank collapse, rushed to withdraw its savings. A similarly abrupt imposition of conditionality measures had occurred two months earlier in Thailand with the freezing of several financial institutions. This precipitated a rush for the exit among investors, thus giving rise to the image of an IMF whose actions—to use Jeffrey Sachs's vivid imagery—amounted to 'screaming "fire" in the theatre'.[11]

But the main outcome of the IMF agreements was the unintended one of inviting panic by undermining investor confidence. 'Lenders who listened to the IMF could not be blamed for concluding that Korea would be unable to service its debts unless its economy had a total overhaul. Unsurprisingly, after the program was announced, the bond rating agencies downgraded Korean debt to junk bond status.'[12] By emphasising the need for major structural overhaul, the IMF prescriptions suggested to investors a systemic weakness that did not exist, thus fuelling further investor panic resulting in currency plunges and capital outflows. In this way, by shouting 'fire' in the theatre, the IMF helped engineer the very outcome that it was supposed to have prevented.

(3) **Striking the fallen.** There is a third aspect to the 'external power' story, which has attracted the widest commentary and discussion. This concerns the uncalculated but significant harm wrought by standard IMF austerity measures, such as the imposition of high interest rates in highly inappropriate circumstances. These measures exacerbated the liquidity problem, thereby helping to kill off sick and healthy companies alike. In the Indonesian setting, in particular, IMF measures often had the most perverse results, threatening to kill off the patient whose health they were designed to restore. (The case of the sudden bank closures mentioned earlier provides a powerful illustration.)

As for the standard IMF policies of high interest rates and reduced public spending, these certainly added significantly to the economic and social hardship (and indeed were scaled back considerably by the second half of 1998). But the IMF measures have had less causal impact than the other two areas of US intervention. This is not simply because they were quickly watered down in some settings, but rather because they were introduced after the main damage had been done: in short, capital had already left—and this is after all our main explanatory target in this context.

Let us be clear about the argument as it applies to crisis deepening. I am not claiming that the US government or American financial institutions, or even the IMF, set out to deepen the crisis. What I am proposing is that *some* of their actions (including their absence of action) were critical in deepening the crisis, that some of these actions were calculated to further US interests, that in so doing they were more cognisant of the benefits to the US than of the costs to the East Asians—and that they had the unintended consequence of exacerbating a situation that could and should have been quite quickly repaired.

CONCLUSION

We have, then, a two-pronged approach to the Asian meltdown: why Asia became embroiled in financial turmoil in the first place, and why it turned so savage. Institutional weaknesses (e.g. in the orientation and organisation of state actors) contributed to real economy vulnerabilities, which then acted as flashpoints to investors as other events, above all the actions of external power actors, helped to precipitate full-scale panic (that is, the deep crisis). I have argued that, far from East Asia being at the mercy of global financial markets, the impact of global finance depends, in the first instance, on core coordinating capacities of domestic political institutions, and ultimately on the strength and cooperation of leading (international) power actors. This is a state-capacity (though non-statist) explanation. It is able to encompass both domestic and international variables while at the same time making power relations—particularly those connected with state power—the focal point of analysis. In sum, global markets were a key (if somewhat obvious) factor in the Asian financial crisis, but not in a primary determining sense. For financial markets to have had such a dramatic impact on the economies in question, two critical if less obvious variables had to be present: a pull factor in the form of domestic vulnerability—in this case afforded by either relatively limited or decomposing state capacities; and a push factor in the form of a strong external impulse which served, directly and indirectly, to deepen that vulnerability—in this case, the organised expression of US economic power.

Thus the Asian crisis offers support for a state power argument in two ways. First, it suggests how relatively low domestic transformative capacity can increase vulnerability to international shocks like financial crises. This contradicts a widespread perception according to which the Asian crisis was able to strike hardest where countries had adopted Japanese-style institutions of economic governance. But institutional analyses offer little evidence to suggest that the Southeast Asian countries have been guided by development states pursuing structural change as a national priority. From this perspective, it is not the strength but the limited nature of their developmentalism (both as orientation and institutional complex) that appears the more salient. Having more limited transformative goals and organisational capacities has left Thailand and Indonesia not only less effective in the game of technological catch-up, but in some respects less guarded about capital inflows and more vulnerable to financial volatility. By contrast, South Korea—once a powerful example of state-guided capitalism—has seen its developmental orientations contested and its coordinating powers unravel. This began with a slow process of ideological osmosis in the 1980s, as economic liberalism took hold in the upper ranks of the bureaucracy, and culminated in the virtual dismantling of the country's pilot agency soon after 1993. In this process, outside pressures to prise open Korean markets tended to make most impact when they coincided with the domestic agenda and internal struggles for reform. Although certain legacies of guided capitalism persist in Korea's half-way house of economic management (viz. strong resistance to direct foreign investment), the resulting changes have meant a virtual abandonment of control over both the sectoral flow of credit (enabling 'excessive competition' and over-investment) and the composition of capital inflows (enabling soaring indebtedness of short-term maturity). The relevant contrast is with Taiwan, where geopolitical particularities and political continuities helped to offset the influence of neoliberal ideas, leaving transformative orientations and institutions largely intact.

Second, the Asian crisis illustrates how the 'transformative' role of state power applied externally can exploit vulnerability and deepen the effect of international shocks. The pre-eminent example offered here is that of the 'opportunistic' behaviour of the USA, which had the unintended effect of helping, both directly and indirectly, to deepen and extend the crisis, turning the historically 'normal' face of financial crisis into something 'abnormal' and extraordinary.

As to what all this means for the so-called replacement of capitalist diversity in Asia with free-market liberalism or with some variant of the Anglo-American model of capitalism, one thing can be said with some confidence. While 'global' and 'national' are commonly portrayed as antithetical, mutually exclusive principles of organisation and interaction, 'Asia in crisis' has shown that they are in fact in critical respects interdependent and mutually reinforcing. The important point is that globalisation is able to make of the state only what the state is able to make of globalisation. Thus the extent and sustainability of financial liberalisation will continue to depend on the solidity of domestic structures. Where these structures are weak, global networks merely end up undermining their own conditions of existence. The extreme case is that of Indonesia, where domestic collapse has gone hand in hand with the country's involuntary detachment from the global financial system. At the other extreme lies the Malaysian response of voluntary semi-detachment from global finance, ostensibly in an effort to build and strengthen its institutional capabilities. Somewhere between these two extremes, others like Hong Kong, Taiwan and Singapore are drawing lessons from the crisis by tightening and improving capital controls (or, in the more acceptable language of high finance, engaging in 'prudential regulation'). Above all, 'Asia in crisis' vividly illustrates the implausibility of a world economy sustained by unlimited global flows and draws attention instead to the underlying (institutional) limits to liberalisation. Based on the variety of national-level responses, and not least on the strength of the intellectual arguments by pre-eminent economists calling for re-regulation of global finance, is it plausible to anticipate that post-crisis Asia will edge more closely towards neoliberal American ways than those of state-guided Japan?

Notes

[1] Charles Kindleberger, *Manias, Panics and Crashes: A History of Financial Crises* (John Wiley, 1996).

[2] Joseph Stiglitz, 'The Role of International Financial Institutions in the Current Global Economy', Address to the Chicago Council on Foreign Relations, Chicago, 27 February 1998, p. 2.

[3] See, for example, Robert Wade, 'From "Miracle" to "Cronyism": Explaining the Great Asian Slump', *Cambridge Journal of Economics,* Vol. 22, No. 6 (1998), pp. 693–707.

[4] Linda Weiss, *The Myth of the Powerless State* (Cornell University Press/Polity Press, 1998).

[5] K. S. Jomo, *Southeast Asia's Misunderstood Miracle* (Westview, 1997), pp. 105–7.

[6]Andrew J. MacIntyre, 'The politics of finance in Indonesia: command, confusion, and competition', in: S. Haggard *et al.* (Eds), *The Politics of Finance in Developing Countries* (Cornell University Press, 1993), pp. 151, 161.

[7]For a discussion of the concept and its significance, see Peter Evans, *Embedded Autonomy: States and Industrial Transformation* (Princeton University Press, 1995).

[8]M. Feldstein, 'Refocusing the IMF,' *Foreign Affairs,* Vol. 77, No. 2 (1998), pp. 25–6, 31.

[9]*Ibid.,* p. 187.

[10]Chalmers Johnson, 'Economic Crisis in East Asia: The Clash of Capitalisms', *Cambridge Journal of Economics,* Vol. 22, No. 6 (1998), pp. 653–62.

[11]'The IMF and the Asian Flu,' *The American Prospect,* No. 37 (1998), pp. 16–21.

[12]Feldstein, 'Refocusing the IMF,' p. 31.

STUDY AND DISCUSSION QUESTIONS

1. What does Weiss mean by the transformative capacity of states?
2. Why is state power (understood this way) so critical to explaining why some countries were able to contain the disruptive effects of the crisis— and others were not?
3. Compare and contrast the experiences of Korea and Taiwan. Why, according to Weiss, was Korea more vulnerable?

18

The End of Complacency

Claude Smadja

As Claude Smadja explains, not only did globalization create a set of problems for the Asian economies, but the Asian financial crisis, in turn, presented a set of challenges to policy-makers and political leaders around the world. In this contribution, written while the worldwide reverberations of the crisis were still playing out in countries such as Brazil and Russia, the author cautions against the complacency of a response in Washington or Brussels that "it couldn't happen here." He argues that the economic crisis of 1997 is not simply a bad case of the Asian flu, the result of crony capitalism and mismanagement by East Asian governments, although ineffective institutions and poor government oversight certainly played a role. On the contrary, argues Smadja, the crisis underscores a more general problem: the destabilizing potential of short-term capital flows (Friedman's electronic herds), which create volatility in every region of the world.

Smadja concludes that the crisis should inspire a healthy dose of skepticism about all ideological models about how the global economy should be governed, including the American version of unfettered capitalism, which makes regulation a dirty word. He calls for an effort to strengthen the global financial institutions such as the IMF and the World Bank and, in an argument reminiscent of Stiglitz, calls for a "G-something" (including developing countries) to replace the G-7 so that the interests and perspectives of a far more diverse set of countries, not just great economic powers, will be represented around the table when it is time for states to roll up their sleeves and take on the challenges posed by globalization.

Globalization has not run into a brick wall. Instead, today's financial crisis is the result of the complacency and arrogance of leaders in the developed countries who assumed that the world could be organized around one single model: their own. For years, Japan and the Asian tigers derided the stagnant economic growth of the West and extolled the virtues of "Asian values" and "Confucian capitalism." More recently, the United States proved that it could give as well as it could get, arguing that it had stumbled on the secret of perpetual economic growth, all the while chortling over Europe's skyrocketing unemployment rates and the collapse of Asia's so-called crony capitalism. In the last few years, the hyping of the American version of free market capitalism reached its peak, and its prescription as a universal panacea became all too common.

One global crisis later, this cycle of arrogance has come to an abrupt end. America's attempt to remake the world in the image of Wall Street seems less promising in the aftermath of the Russian meltdown. Mismanagement by East Asian governments undeniably played a role in creating the distortions and structural imbalances that led to the decline of their economies. At the same time, it had become quite obvious by the end of 1998 that the global malaise was more than a bad case of the Asian flu. Rather, it was the first systemic crisis of a world economy where financial capitalism had overtaken industrial capitalism. The truth of the matter is that nobody fully understands how this new economy functions.

If the international community is to have any hope of anticipating how such crises spread and intensify, it must be prepared to forsake long-held ideological preconceptions. One of the key issues facing us today is how to deal with the destabilizing volatility of massive short-term capital flows without simultaneously destroying the market. Unfortunately, complacency has blinded many policymakers, business leaders, and commentators to the true underlying causes of the current turmoil. Case in point: The same individuals who criticized the lack of transparency in East Asia's banking and financial systems chose to ignore the complete opaqueness under which hedge funds operate. Such behavior is difficult to understand given that the capability for hedge funds to wreak havoc in the global economy is much higher than the breakdown of the entire banking system of, say, Indonesia or Thailand. It took the near collapse of Long Term Capital Management, a U.S. hedge fund—and the fact that the individuals running this firm were considered to be among the best and brightest in the financial community—to shake everybody out of the illusion that these kinds of accidents happen only in immature markets.

In the last few years, regulation has become a dirty word among free market fundamentalists. Not anymore. The events of the past year have made it obvious that the key economic players must establish appropriate structures and processes to monitor and regulate hedge funds, derivative transactions, and other types of highly leveraged short-term financial flows. The challenge is how to monitor and regulate without recreating bureaucratic straitjackets. Complacency is no longer an option: A sound economy is no defense against speculators who succumb to the kind of frenzy and herd instinct that we have seen at play during the past year. As the case of Hong Kong demonstrated, when even the most free market-minded society is faced with an onslaught of hedge fund operators, there are only two choices: Either submit to economic oblivion or manipulate the market in such a way that you can fend off the invaders and make them think twice about a second attack. The risk of economic collapse is simply too high a price to pay for the sake of an ideological orthodoxy that considers capital controls and government intervention to be heresy.

Developed countries must therefore shed themselves of the delusion that as soon as the emerging economies put their macroeconomic house in order, we will return to an era of global economic bliss. By the same token, however, emerging economies in Asia and Latin America would do well to draw a few lessons from this crisis. They must undertake reforms that will restructure their banking and financial sectors, operate under rules of genuine transparency, and reinforce an institutional framework that supports open markets. These local reforms would be most successful when implemented in tandem with global reforms. Consider, for example, the recent East Asia Economic Summit of the World Economic Forum in Singapore where business executives, government leaders, and regional experts participated in two simulation exercises that arrived at identical conclusions: The optimal strategies for East Asian recovery are those that combine economic restructuring and the recapitalization of the banking sector with international measures aimed at reducing the volatility of short-term capital flows. Of course, a new and more effective role for global financial institutions is also a main precondition for recovery. There is apparent consensus on the need to reengineer the international financial institutions. But there is considerably less clarity on how to increase the accountability and transparency of these institutions and a great deal of disagreement on the nature of their governance—in other words, who is to wield effective control. Until satisfactory answers are discovered to these questions, the world will have to live with an unnecessarily high level of systemic financial risk.

It is also worth pointing out that the global crisis was precipitated by the collapse of several Asian economies whose cumulative gross domestic product (GDP) barely equals that of New York State. This noteworthy statistic is yet another indicator of how globalization has had a "humbling" effect on the world's economic powerhouses: Gross domestic product is no longer a reliable measure of a country's economic clout. In a world where the United States and Europe now rely on policymakers in Brazil or China to head off a worldwide recession, it seems safe to say that exclusive "wealthy-nation" organizations such as the Group of Seven (G-7) are of limited relevance (if not completely obsolete) in dealing with contemporary global crises. In an increasingly integrated world, the resilience of the global economy is only as strong as the weakest of its components.

Consequently, the time has come to create a "G-something" structure that would comprise not only the eurozone countries, Japan, and the United States, but also pivotal economies such as Brazil and China. (The Group of Twenty-two meeting in Washington last September was a promising development in that respect.) The European Union, Japan, and the United States would want to keep open the option to consult and coordinate with one another on macroeconomic- and monetary-policy issues within a trilateral framework. But that does not in any way reduce the need for a larger structure that monitors developments in the global economy, allows for the sharing of views and analyses, and coordinates actions as soon as the need arises.

The global financial crisis also warns against complacency of another sort—the belief that the end of the Cold War and the rise of free market capitalism are the only necessary and sufficient conditions to guarantee a future of peace and stability and that the role of governments is becoming increasingly obsolete. In fact, globalization increases the role of government. Its role may be different than in the past, but it nonetheless remains crucial. The hiccups in the globalization process and darkening of the world's economic outlook have brought to the fore concerns that many Western countries, especially the United States, had thought relegated to history. The social chaos in Russia has reopened the issue of stability on the European continent. East Asia, a region beset by a potential nuclear-arms race and chronic political discord, must now also confront the specter of frictions that had abated in the last 15 years.

During the Cold War, if an entire region had suddenly fallen into economic disarray, the Western democracies would have rushed to find some sort of solution, fearing that social turmoil would pave the way for communist expansionism. This past year when entire regions fell into economic turmoil, the first instinct of the United States and Europe was to pat themselves on the back for their supposedly superior economic models.

To be candid, what has now been put into question is the pronounced tendency—most notably in Washington, the G-7, and the International Monetary Fund—to view globalization solely as a process to make the world safe for Wall Street. Just because the American blueprint for free market capitalism has proved successful in ensuring an unprecedented period of economic expansion does not mean that the global economy should function as a magnified picture of the U.S. economy. The attempt to equate globalization with the "Wall Streetization" of the international system has created a backlash against globalization.

We now know that the process of globalization needs to be elevated beyond any attempt to impose a single economic model, a scenario where only the strong shall survive. The challenge of globalization is to attain a synthesis that is acceptable for every region—and, above all else, develop a system that takes into account cultural and historical specificities; one that is agreed upon, not one that is imposed.

STUDY AND DISCUSSION QUESTIONS

1. According to Smadja, what were the key factors that contributed to the Asian economic and financial crisis of 1997?
2. What lessons have policy-makers and political leaders taken from the crisis?
3. What other lessons should they consider more seriously than they have? If you had one piece of advice to give to G-7 leaders on the basis of Smadja's argument, what would it be?

CHAPTER 4

Post–9/11: Terror, War, and Empire

Through much of the 1990s, the most profound question about globalization concerned the yawning chasm between rich and poor—the fear that the diffusion of trade, investment, production, and communication technologies had done nothing to close the gap between the developed world of Europe, America, and a powerful East Asian trading bloc on the one side, and the rest of the developing world on the other. The financial and economic crisis in East Asia in 1997 and 1998 and its rapid global diffusion seemed to intensify concerns about the dislocating effects of economic globalization, as did the tumultuous protests at the 1999 WTO ministerial meetings in Seattle.

At the same time, brutal brushfire wars and ethnic conflagrations—the bloody street fighting between Somali warlords and UN peacekeeping forces in Somalia in 1993 leading to brutal killing of 18 American soldiers, the Rwandan genocide launched in 1994—began to capture the world's attention. Looked at from this perspective, the attacks of September 11, 2001, and the fears, threats, and experiences of terrorism ever since—whether in Jerusalem, Jakarta, Riyadh, Madrid, or Beslan—seem of a piece with the political violence that greeted the intensified combat over the state during the implosion of post-communist and post-colonial regimes in the 1990s. Against this backdrop of violence and terror, although the development gap remains very much in focus, attention has naturally turned to concerns about security, war, vulnerabilities in the face of a widening circle of terrorist assaults, and the implications of a new hard power American empire.

Enduring questions about how America and the world can—and must—meet the security threats of the post–9/11 world have risen to the very top of the agenda of global politics. We can no longer separate the study of globalization and state power from the explicit consideration of terrorism and the use of force.

242

Nor can we ignore the obvious transformation that 9/11 has wrought with reference to America's geopolitical strategy. The selections in Chapter 4 will consider two themes in turn: globalization, terror and the use of force; and, globalization, empire, and America's geopolitical strategy.

STUDY AND DISCUSSION QUESTIONS

1. How should the United States and the international community define and prosecute the war on terrorism?
2. What are the lessons of the war in Iraq for the role of the Security Council in authorizing the use of force—and what reforms should now be given more serious consideration?
3. What are the implications of the new American empire for understanding globalization and its consequences for state power?

Globalization, Terror, and the Use of Force

19

Behind the Curve:
Globalization and International Terrorism

Audrey Kurth Cronin

In this powerful contribution, Audrey Kurth Cronin argues that terrorism must be counted among the consequences of globalization and that the American response to the terror threats has been hamstrung by bureaucratic mindsets and theoretical paradigms that have limited the effectiveness of its responses to terror from non-state actors such as Al-Qaeda. Military action in Afghanistan (and the war in Iraq, which was launched after this selection was written) demonstrates that the United States knows how to apply power to destroy states and their armed forces. But, as the author observes, America has been far less impressive when it comes to the more subtle instruments of statecraft, such as the use of intelligence, the building of coalitions, and the application of principles of international law to defeat enemies in the age of globalized terrorism.

Trends in terrorist activity since the 1990s, which have been acutely underscored by the attacks of September 11, 2001, suggest the increased incidence of religiously inspired attacks as well the increased focus of attacks on the United States. Terrorists have employed new means associated with globalization such as the Internet and the ends have changed as well, with increasing emphasis put on violence intended to signify a lashing out against U.S.-led globalization. Cronin concludes with a warning that the globalization of terror may well be the greatest threat to stability in the twenty-first century, but that globalization at the same time creates new opportunities for more effective international responses to terrorist threats.

The coincidence between the evolving changes of globalization, the inherent weaknesses of the Arab region, and the inadequate American response to both ensures that terrorism will continue to be the most serious threat to U.S. and Western interests in the twenty-first century. There has been little creative thinking, however, about how to confront the growing terrorist backlash that has been unleashed. Terrorism is a complicated, eclectic phenomenon, requiring a sophisticated strategy oriented toward influencing its means and ends over the long term. Few members of the U.S. policymaking and academic communities, however, have the political capital, intellectual background, or inclination to work together to forge an effective, sustained response. Instead, the tendency has been to fall back on established bureaucratic mind-sets and prevailing theoretical paradigms that have little relevance for the changes in international security that became obvious after the terrorist attacks in New York and Washington on September 11, 2001.

The current wave of international terrorism, characterized by unpredictable and unprecedented threats from nonstate actors, not only is a reaction to globalization but is facilitated by it; the U.S. response to this reality has been reactive and anachronistic. The combined focus of the United States on state-centric threats and its attempt to cast twenty-first-century terrorism into familiar strategic terms avoids and often undermines effective responses to this nonstate phenomenon. The increasing threat of globalized terrorism must be met with flexible, multifaceted responses that deliberately and effectively exploit avenues of globalization in return; this, however, is not happening.

As the primary terrorist target, the United States should take the lead in fashioning a forward-looking strategy. As the world's predominant military, economic, and political power, it has been able to pursue its interests throughout the globe with unprecedented freedom since the breakup of the Soviet Union more than a decade ago. Even in the wake of the September 11 terrorist attacks on the World Trade Center and the Pentagon, and especially after the U.S. military action in Afghanistan, the threat of terrorism, mostly consisting of underfunded and ad hoc cells motivated by radical fringe ideas, has seemed unimportant by comparison. U.S. strategic culture has a long tradition of downplaying such atypical concerns in favor of a focus on more conventional state-based military power. On the whole, this has been an effective approach: As was dramatically demonstrated in Afghanistan, the U.S. military knows how to destroy state governments and their armed forces, and the American political leadership and public have a natural bias toward using power to achieve the quickest results. Sometimes it is important to show resolve and respond forcefully.

The United States has been far less impressive, however, in its use of more subtle tools of domestic and international statecraft, such as intelligence, law enforcement, economic sanctions, educational training, financial controls, public diplomacy, coalition building, international law, and foreign aid. In an ironic twist, it is these tools that have become central to the security of the United States and its allies since September 11. In an era of globalized terrorism, the familiar state-centric threats have not disappeared; instead they have been joined by new (or newly threatening) competing political, ideological, economic, and cultural concerns that are only superficially understood, particularly in the West. An examination of the recent evolution of terrorism and a projection of future developments suggest that, in the age of globalized terrorism, old attitudes are not just anachronistic; they are dangerous.

Terrorism as a phenomenon is not new, but for reasons explained below, the threat it now poses is greater than ever before. The current terrorist backlash is manifested in the extremely violent asymmetrical response directed at the United States and other leading powers by terrorist groups associated with or inspired by al-Qaeda. This backlash has the potential to fundamentally threaten the international system. Thus it is not just an American problem. Unless the United States and its allies formulate a more comprehensive response to terrorism, better balanced across the range of policy instruments, the results will be increasing international instability and long-term failure.

. . .

KEY TRENDS IN MODERN TERRORISM

By the late 1990s, four trends in modern terrorism [were] apparent: an increase in the incidence of religiously motivated attacks, a decrease in the overall number of attacks, an increase in the lethality per attack, and the growing targeting of Americans.

Statistics show that, even before the September 11 attacks, religiously moti-vated terrorist organizations were becoming more common. The acceleration of this trend has been dramatic: According to the RAND–St. Andrews University Chronology of International Terrorism, in 1968 none of the identified interna-tional terrorist organizations could be classified as "religious"; in 1980, in the aftermath of the Iranian Revolution, there were 2 (out of 64), and that number had expanded to 25 (out of 58) by 1995.

Careful analysis of terrorism data compiled by the U.S. Department of State reveals other important trends regarding the frequency and lethality of terrorist attacks. The good news was that there were fewer such attacks in the 1990s than in the 1980s: Internationally, the number of terrorist attacks in the 1990s aver-aged 382 per year, whereas in the 1980s the number per year averaged 543. But even before September 11, the absolute number of casualties of international ter-rorism had increased, from a low of 344 in 1991 to a high of 6,693 in 1998. The jump in deaths and injuries can be partly explained by a few high-profile inci-dents, including the bombing of the U.S. embassies in Nairobi and Dar-es-Salaam in 1998, but it is significant that more people became victims of terrorism as the decade proceeded. More worrisome, the number of people killed per incident rose significantly, from 102 killed in 565 incidents in 1991 to 741 killed in 274 incidents in 1998. Thus, even though the number of terrorist attacks declined in the 1990s, the number of people killed in each one increased.

Another important trend relates to terrorist attacks involving U.S. targets. The number of such attacks increased in the 1990s, from a low of 66 in 1994 to a high of 200 in the year 2000. This is a long-established problem: U.S. nationals consistently have been the most targeted since 1968. But the percentage of inter-national attacks against U.S. targets or U.S. citizens rose dramatically over the 1990s, from about 20 percent in 1993–95 to almost 50 percent in 2000. This is perhaps a consequence of the increased role and profile of the United States in the world, but the degree of increase is nonetheless troubling.

The increasing lethality of terrorist attacks was already being noticed in the late 1990s, with many terrorism experts arguing that the tendency toward more casualties per incident had important implications. First it meant that, as had been feared, religious or "sacred" terrorism was apparently more dangerous than the types of terrorism that had predominated earlier in the twentieth century. The world was facing the resurgence of a far more malignant type of terrorism, whose lethality was borne out in the larger death toll from incidents that increas-ingly involved a religious motivation. Second, with an apparent premium now apparently placed on causing more casualties per incident, the incentives for ter-rorist organizations to use chemical, biological, nuclear, or radiological (CBNR) weapons would multiply. The breakup of the Soviet Union and the resulting increased availability of Soviet chemical, biological, and nuclear weapons caused experts to argue that terrorist groups, seeking more dramatic and deadly results, would be more drawn to these weapons. The 1995 sarin gas attack by the Japanese cult Aum Shinrikyo in the Tokyo subway system seemed to confirm that worry. More recently, an examination of evidence taken from Afghanistan and Pakistan reveals al-Qaeda's interest in chemical, biological, and nuclear weapons.

In addition to the evolving motivation and character of terrorist attacks, there has been a notable dispersal in the geography of terrorist acts—a trend that is likely to continue. Although the Middle East continues to be the locus of most terrorist activity, Central and South Asia, the Balkans, and the Transcaucasus have been growing in significance over the past decade. International connections themselves are not new: International terrorist organizations inspired by common revolutionary principles date to the early nineteenth century; clandestine state use of foreign terrorist organizations occurred as early as the 1920s (e.g., the Mussolini government in Italy aided the Croat Ustasha); and complex mazes of funding, arms, and other state support for international terrorist organizations were in place especially in the 1970s and 1980s. During the Cold War, terrorism was seen as a form of surrogate warfare and seemed almost palatable to some, at least compared to the potential prospect of major war or nuclear cataclysm. What has changed is the self-generating nature of international terrorism, with its diverse economic means of support allowing terrorists to carry out attacks sometimes far from the organization's base. As a result, there is an important and growing distinction between where a terrorist organization is spawned and where an attack is launched, making the attacks difficult to trace to their source.

Reflecting all of these trends, al-Qaeda and its associated groups (and individuals) are harbingers of a new type of terrorist organization. Even if al-Qaeda ceases to exist (which is unlikely), the dramatic attacks of September 2001, and their political and economic effects, will continue to inspire similarly motivated groups—particularly if the United States and its allies fail to develop broad-based, effective counterterrorist policies over the long term. Moreover, there is significant evidence that the global links and activities that al-Qaeda and its associated groups perpetuated are not short term or anomalous. Indeed they are changing the nature of the terrorist threat as we move further into the twenty-first century. The resulting intersection between the United States, globalization, and international terrorism will define the major challenges to international security.

THE UNITED STATES, GLOBALIZATION, AND INTERNATIONAL TERRORISM

Whether deliberately intending to or not, the United States is projecting uncoordinated economic, social, and political power even more sweepingly than it is in military terms. Globalization, in forms including Westernization, secularization, democratization, consumerism, and the growth of market capitalism, represents an onslaught to less privileged people in conservative cultures repelled by the fundamental changes that these forces are bringing—or angered by the distortions and uneven distributions of benefits that result. This is especially true of the Arab world. Yet the current U.S. approach to this growing repulsion is colored by a kind of cultural naïveté, an unwillingness to recognize—let alone appreciate or take responsibility for—the influence of U.S. power except in its military dimension. Even doing nothing in the economic, social, and political policy realms is still doing something, because the United States is blamed by disadvantaged and alienated populations for the powerful Western-led forces of globalization that are proceeding apace, despite the absence of a focused, coordinated U.S. policy. And those penetrating mechanisms of globalization, such as the internet, the media, and the increasing flows of goods and peoples, are exploited in return. Both the means and ends of terrorism are being reformulated in the current environment.

The Means

Important changes in terrorist methods are apparent in the use of new technologies, the movement of terrorist groups across international boundaries, and changes in sources of support. Like globalization itself, these phenomena are all intertwined and overlapping but, for ease of argument, they are dealt with consecutively here.

First, the use of information technologies such as the internet, mobile phones, and instant messaging has extended the global reach of many terrorist groups. Increased access to these technologies has so far not resulted in their widely feared use in a major cyberterrorist attack: In Dorothy Denning's words, terrorists "still prefer bombs to bytes."[1] Activists and terrorist groups have increasingly turned to "hacktivism"—attacks on internet sites, including web defacements, hijackings of websites, web sit-ins, denial-of-service attacks, and automated email "bombings"—attacks that may not kill anyone but do attract media attention, provide a means of operating anonymously, and are easy to coordinate internationally. So far, however, these types of attacks are more an expense and a nuisance than an existential threat.

Instead the tools of the global information age have led to enhanced efficiency in many terrorist-related activities, including administrative tasks, coordination of operations, recruitment of potential members, communication among adherents, and attraction of sympathizers. Before the September 11 attacks, for example, members of al-Qaeda communicated through Yahoo email; Mohammed Atta, the presumed leader of the attacks, made his reservations online; and cell members went online to do research on subjects such as the chemical-dispersing powers of crop dusters. Although not as dramatic as shutting down a power grid or taking over an air traffic control system, this practical use of technology has significantly contributed to the effectiveness of terrorist groups and the expansion of their range. Consider, for example, the lethal impact of the synchronized attacks on the U.S. embassies in 1998 and on New York and Washington in 2001, neither of which would have been possible without the revolution in information technology. When he was arrested in 1995, Ramzi Yousef, mastermind of the 1993 World Trade Center attack, was planning the simultaneous destruction of eleven airliners.

The internet has become an important tool for perpetuating terrorist groups, both openly and clandestinely. Many of them employ elaborate list serves, collect money from witting or unwitting donors, and distribute savvy political messages to a broad audience online. Groups as diverse as Aum Shinrikyo, Israel's Kahane Chai, the Popular Front for the Liberation of Palestine, the Kurdistan Worker's Party, and Peru's Shining Path maintain user-friendly official or unofficial websites, and almost all are accessible in English. Clandestine methods include passing encrypted messages, embedding invisible graphic codes using steganography,[2] employing the internet to send death threats, and hiring hackers to collect intelligence such as the names and addresses of law enforcement officers from online databases. All of these measures help to expand and perpetuate trends in terrorism that have already been observed: For example, higher casualties are brought about by simultaneous attacks, a diffusion in terrorist locations is made possible by internet communications, and extremist religious ideologies are spread through websites and videotapes accessible throughout the world.

More ominous, globalization makes [chemical, biological, nuclear and radiological] (CBNR) weapons increasingly available to terrorist groups. Information needed to build these weapons has become ubiquitous, especially through the internet. Among the groups interested in acquiring CBNR (besides al-Qaeda) are the PLO, the Red Army Faction, Hezbollah, the Kurdistan Workers' Party, German neo-Nazis, and the Chechens.

Second, globalization has enabled terrorist organizations to reach across international borders, in the same way (and often through the same channels) that commerce and business interests are linked. The dropping of barriers through the North American Free Trade Area and the European Union, for instance, has facilitated the smooth flow of many things, good and bad, among countries. This has allowed terrorist organizations as diverse as Hezbollah, al-Qaeda, and the Egyptian al-Gama'at al-Islamiyya to move about freely and establish cells around the world. Movement across borders can obviously enable terrorists to carry out attacks and potentially evade capture, but it also complicates prosecution if they are apprehended, with a complex maze of extradition laws varying greatly from state to state. The increased permeability of the international system has also enhanced the ability of nonstate terrorist organizations to collect intelligence (not to mention evade it); states are not the only actors interested in collecting, disseminating, and/or acting on such information. In a sense, then, terrorism is in many ways becoming like any other international enterprise—an ominous development indeed.

Third, terrorist organizations are broadening their reach in gathering financial resources to fund their operations. This is not just an al-Qaeda phenomenon, although bin Laden's organization—especially its numerous business interests—figures prominently among the most innovative and wealthy pseudocorporations in the international terrorist network. The list of groups with global financing networks is long and includes most of the groups identified by the U.S. government as foreign terrorist organizations, notably Aum Shinrikyo, Hamas, Hezbollah, and the Tamil Tigers. Sources of financing include legal enterprises such as non-profit organizations and charities (whose illicit activities may be a small or large proportion of overall finances, known or unknown to donors); legitimate companies that divert profits to illegal activities (such as bin Laden's large network of construction companies); and illegal enterprises such as drug smuggling and production (e.g., the Revolutionary Armed Forces of Colombia—FARC), bank robbery, fraud, extortion, and kidnapping (e.g., the Abu Sayyaf group, Colombia's National Liberation Army, and FARC). Websites are also important vehicles for raising funds. Although no comprehensive data are publicly available on how lucrative this avenue is, the proliferation of terrorist websites with links or addresses for contributions is at least circumstantial evidence of their usefulness.

The fluid movement of terrorists' financial resources demonstrates the growing informal connections that are countering the local fragmentation caused elsewhere by globalization. The transit of bars of gold and bundles of dollars across the border between Afghanistan and Pakistan as U.S. and allied forces were closing in on the Taliban's major strongholds is a perfect example. Collected by shopkeepers and small businessmen, the money was moved by operatives across the border to Karachi, where it was transferred in the millions of dollars through the informal *hawala* or *hundi* banking system to the United Arab Emirates. There it was converted into gold bullion and scattered around the world before any government could intervene. In this way, al-Qaeda preserved and dispersed a proportion of its financial resources. In addition to gold, money was transferred into other commodities—such as diamonds in Sierra Leone and the Democratic Republic of Congo, and tanzanite from Tanzania—all while hiding the assets and often making a profit, and all without interference from the sovereign governments that at the time were at war with al-Qaeda and the Taliban.

As this example illustrates, globalization does not necessarily require the use of high technology: It often takes the form of traditional practices used in innovative ways across increasingly permeable physical and commercial borders. Terrorist groups, whose assets comparatively represent only a small fraction of the amount of money that is moved by organized crime groups and are thus much more difficult to track, use everything from direct currency transport (by couriers) to reliance on traditional banks, Islamic banks, money changers (using accounts at legitimate institutions), and informal exchange. . . .

This is by no means a comprehensive presentation of global interpenetration of terrorist means, and some of the connections described above have existed for some time and in other contexts. The broad strategic picture, however, is of an increasing ability of terrorist organizations to exploit the same avenues of communication, coordination, and cooperation as other international actors, including states, multinational corporations, nongovernmental organizations, and even individuals. It would be naïve to assume that what is good for international commerce and international communication is not also good for international terrorists—who are increasingly becoming opportunistic entrepreneurs whose "product" (often quite consciously "sold") is violence against innocent targets for a political end.

The Ends

The objectives of international terrorism have also changed as a result of globalization. Foreign intrusions and growing awareness of shrinking global space have created incentives to use the ideal asymmetrical weapon, terrorism, for more ambitious purposes.

The political incentives to attack major targets such as the United States with powerful weapons have greatly increased. The perceived corruption of indigenous customs, religions, languages, economies, and so on are blamed on an international system often unconsciously molded by American behavior. The accompanying distortions in local communities as a result of exposure to the global marketplace of goods and ideas are increasingly blamed on U.S.-sponsored modernization and those who support it. The advancement of technology, however, is not the driving force behind the terrorist threat to the United States and its allies, despite what some have assumed. Instead, at the heart of this threat are frustrated populations and international movements that are increasingly inclined to lash out against U.S.-led globalization.

As Christopher Coker observes, globalization is reducing tendencies toward instrumental violence (i.e., violence between states and even between communities), but it is enhancing incentives for expressive violence (or violence that is ritualistic, symbolic, and communicative). The new international terrorism is increasingly engendered by a need to assert identity or meaning against forces of homogeneity, especially on the part of cultures that are threatened by, or left behind by, the secular future that Western-led globalization brings.

According to a report recently published by the United Nations Development Programme, the region of greatest deficit in measures of human development—the Arab world—is also the heart of the most threatening religiously inspired terrorism. Much more work needs to be done on the significance of this correlation, but increasingly sources of political discontent are arising from disenfranchised areas in the Arab world that feel left behind by the promise of globalization and its assurances of broader freedom, prosperity, and access to knowledge. The results are dashed expectations, heightened resentment of the perceived U.S.-led hegemonic system, and a shift of focus away from more proximate targets within the region.

Of course, the motivations behind this threat should not be oversimplified: Anti-American terrorism is spurred in part by a desire to change U.S. policy in the Middle East and Persian Gulf regions as well as by growing antipathy in the developing world vis-à-vis the forces of globalization. It is also crucial to distinguish between the motivations of leaders such as Osama bin Laden and their followers. The former seem to be more driven by calculated strategic decisions to shift the locus of attack away from repressive indigenous governments to the more attractive and media-rich target of the United States. The latter appear to be more driven by religious concepts cleverly distorted to arouse anger and passion in societies full of pent-up frustration. To some degree, terrorism is directed against the United States because of its engagement and policies in various regions. Anti-Americanism is closely related to antiglobalization, because (intentionally or not) the primary driver of the powerful forces resulting in globalization is the United States.

Analyzing terrorism as something separate from globalization is misleading and potentially dangerous. Indeed globalization and terrorism are intricately intertwined forces characterizing international security in the twenty-first century. The main question is whether terrorism will succeed in disrupting the promise of improved livelihoods for millions of people on Earth. Globalization is not an inevitable, linear development, and it can be disrupted by such unconventional means as international terrorism. Conversely, modern international terrorism is especially dangerous because of the power that it potentially derives from globalization—whether through access to CBNR weapons, global media outreach, or a diverse network of financial and information resources.

PROSPECTS FOR THE FUTURE

Long after the focus on Osama bin Laden has receded and U.S. troops have quit their mission in Afghanistan, terrorism will be a serious threat to the world community and especially to the United States. The relative preponderance of U.S. military power virtually guarantees an impulse to respond asymmetrically. The lagging of the Arab region behind the rest of the world is impelling a violent redirection of antiglobalization and antimodernization forces toward available targets, particularly the United States, whose scope and policies are engendering rage. Al-Qaeda will eventually be replaced or redefined, but its successors' reach may continue to grow via the same globalized channels and to direct their attacks against U.S. and Western targets. The current trajectory is discouraging, because as things currently stand, the wellspring of terrorism's means and ends is likely to be renewed: Arab governments will probably not reform peacefully, and existing

Western governments and their supporting academic and professional institutions are disinclined to understand or analyze in depth the sources, patterns, and history of terrorism.

Terrorism is a by-product of broader historical shifts in the international distribution of power in all of its forms—political, economic, military, ideological, and cultural. These are the same forms of power that characterize the forces of Western-led globalization. At times of dramatic international change, human beings (especially those not benefiting from the change—or not benefiting as much or as rapidly from the change) grasp for alternative means to control and understand their environments. If current trends continue, widening global disparities, coupled with burgeoning information and connectivity, are likely to accelerate—unless the terrorist backlash, which is increasingly taking its inspiration from misoneistic religious or pseudoreligious concepts, successfully counters these trends. Because of globalization, terrorists have access to more powerful technologies, more targets, more territory, more means of recruitment, and more exploitable sources of rage than ever before. The West's twentieth-century approach to terrorism is highly unlikely to mitigate any of these long-term trends.

[T]he ad hoc and purportedly benign intentions of the preponderant, secular West do not seem benign at all to those ill served by globalization. To frustrated people in the Arab and Muslim world, adherence to radical religious philosophies and practices may seem a rational response to the perceived assault, especially when no feasible alternative for progress is offered by their own governments. This is not to suggest that terrorists should be excused because of environmental factors or conditions. Instead, Western governments must recognize that the tiny proportion of the population that ends up in terrorist cells cannot exist without the availability of broader sources of active or passive sympathy, resources, and support. Those avenues of sustenance are where the center of gravity for an effective response to the terrorist threat must reside. The response to transnational terrorism must deal with the question of whether the broader enabling environment will increase or decrease over time, and the answer will be strongly influenced by the policy choices that the United States and its allies make in the near future.

CONCLUSIONS AND POLICY PRESCRIPTIONS

The characteristics and causes of the current threat can only be analyzed within the context of the deadly collision occurring between U.S. power, globalization, and the evolution of international terrorism. The U.S. government is still thinking in outdated terms, little changed since the end of the Cold War. It continues to look at terrorism as a peripheral threat, with the focus remaining on states that in many cases are not the greatest threat. The means and the ends of terrorism are changing in fundamental, important ways; but the means and the ends of the strategy being crafted in response are not.

Terrorism that threatens international stability, and particularly U.S. global leadership, is centered on power-based political causes that are enduring: the weak against the strong, the disenfranchised against the establishment, and the revolutionary against the status quo. Oversimplified generalizations about poverty and terrorism, or any other single variable, are caricatures of a serious argument. The rise in political and material expectations as a result of the information revolution is not necessarily helpful to stability, in the same way that rising expectations led terrorists to take up arms against the czar in Russia a century ago. Indeed the fact that so many people in so many nations are being left behind has given new ammunition to terrorist groups; produced more sympathy for those willing to take on the United States; and spurred Islamic radical movements to recruit, propagandize, and support terrorism throughout many parts of the Muslim world. The al-Qaeda network is an extremist religious terrorist organization, its Taliban puppet regime was filled with religious zealots, and its suicide recruits were convinced that they were waging a just holy war. But the driving forces of twenty-first-century terrorism are power and frustration, not the pursuit of religious principle. To dismiss the broad enabling environment would be to focus more on the symptoms than the causes of modern terrorism.

The prescriptions for countering and preventing terrorism should be twofold: First, the United States and other members of the international community concerned about this threat need to use a balanced assortment of instruments to address the immediate challenges of the terrorists themselves. Terrorism is a complex phenomenon; it must be met with short-term military action, informed by in-depth, long-term, sophisticated analysis. Thus far, the response has been virtually all the former and little of the latter. Second, the United States and its counterterrorist allies must employ a much broader array of longer-term policy tools to reshape the international environment, which enables terrorist networks to breed and become robust. The mechanisms of globalization need to be exploited to thwart the globalization of terrorism.

In the short term, the United States must continue to rely on capable military forces that can sustain punishing air strikes against terrorists and those who harbor them with an even greater capacity for special operations on the ground. This requires not only improved stealthy, long-range power projection capabilities but also agile, highly trained, and lethal ground forces, backed up with greater intelligence, including human intelligence supported by individuals with language skills and cultural training. The use of military force continues to be important as one means of responding to terrorist violence against the West, and there is no question that it effectively preempts and disrupts some international terrorist activity, especially in the short term.

Over time, however, the more effective instruments of policy are likely to remain the nonmilitary ones. Indeed the United States needs to expand and deepen its nonmilitary instruments of power such as intelligence, public diplomacy, cooperation with allies, international legal instruments, and economic assistance and sanctions. George Kennan, in his 1947 description of containment, put forth the same fundamental argument, albeit against an extremely different enemy.[3] The strongest response that the United States can muster to a serious threat has to include political, economic, and military capabilities—in that order; yet, the U.S. government consistently structures its policies and devotes its resources in the reverse sequence.

The economic and political roots of terrorism are complex, increasingly worrisome, and demanding of as much breadth and subtlety in response as they display in their genesis. The United States must therefore be strategic in its response: An effective grand strategy against terrorism involves planning a global campaign with the most effective means available, not just the most measurable, obvious, or gratifying. It must also include plans for shaping the global environment after the so-called war on terrorism has ended—or after the current political momentum has subsided.

The United States, working with other major donor nations, needs to create an effective incentive structure that rewards "good performers"—those countries with good governance, inclusive education programs, and adequate social programs—and works around "bad performers" and intervenes to assist so-called failed states. Also for the longer term, the United States and its allies need to project a vision of sustainable development—of economic growth, equal access to basic social needs such as education and health, and good governance—for the developing world. This is particularly true in mostly Muslim countries whose populations are angry with the United States over a perceived double standard regarding its long-standing support for Israel at the expense of Palestinians, policies against the regime of Saddam Hussein at the expense of some Iraqi people, and a general abundance of American power, including the U.S. military presence throughout the Middle East. Whether these policies are right or wrong is irrelevant here; the point is that just as the definition of terrorism can be subjective and value laden, so too can the response to terrorism take into account perceptions of reality. In an attempt to craft an immediate military response, the U.S. government is failing to put into place an effective long-term grand strategy.

. . .

The globalization of terrorism is perhaps the leading threat to long-term stability in the twenty-first century. But the benefit of globalization is that the international response to terrorist networks has also begun to be increasingly global, with international cooperation on law enforcement, intelligence, and especially financial controls being areas of notable recent innovation. If globalization is to continue—and there is nothing foreordained that it will—then the tools of globalization, including especially international norms, the rule of law, and international economic power, must be fully employed against the terrorist backlash. There must be a deliberate effort to move beyond the current episodic interest in this phenomenon: Superficial arguments and short attention spans will continue to result in event-driven policies and ultimately more attacks. Terrorism is an unprecedented, powerful nonstate threat to the international system that no single state, regardless of how powerful it may be in traditional terms, can defeat alone, especially in the absence of long-term, serious scholarship engaged in by its most creative minds.

Notes

[1]See Dorothy Denning, "Activism, Hacktivism, and Cyberterrorism: The Internet as a Tool for Influencing Foreign Policy," paper presented at Internet and International Systems: Information Technology and American Foreign Policy Decision-making Workshop at Georgetown University, http://www.nautilus.org/info-policy/workshop/papers/denning.html (accessed January 5, 2003).

[2]Steganography is the embedding of messages usually in pictures, where the messages are disguised so that they cannot be seen with the naked eye.

[3]George F. Kennan, "The Sources of Soviet Conduct," *Foreign Affairs,* Vol. 25, No. 4 (July 1947), pp. 575–576.

STUDY AND DISCUSSION QUESTIONS

1. How has globalization transformed both the means and the aims of terrorism?
2. According to Cronin, why is the United States failing to meet the challenges of global terrorism as effectively as it could?
3. What would you consider Cronin's single most important policy prescription?

20

The National Security Strategy of the United States of America

President George W. Bush

Has the Bush doctrine (for better or worse) fundamentally transformed the principles that govern American foreign policy, the most powerful country not only able but willing to advance its national interests and exert state power to secure desirable outcomes autonomously—without regard to the preferences of key allies and at the expense of their capacities to exercise power?

This view that something fundamental has changed in U.S. foreign policy—that it has jettisoned more than 50 years of what Ikenberry characterized as strategic restraint—gained force with the appearance of the new National Security Strategy of the United States of America (NSS) in September 2002, reproduced here from the official White House website. The document crystallized Bush's signature on foreign affairs and codified the beginnings of a distinctive doctrine. It was then catapulted to the status of a dominant paradigm with the invasion of Iraq, which so vividly illustrated the doctrine and which symbolized (depending on your opinion of the war in Iraq) what was either good or bad about America's new more aggressive and unilateralist security and geopolitical strategy.

The document argues that new dangers at the "crossroads of radicalism and technology" require a new strategic posture. The National Security Strategy justifies what was termed "preemption" by asserting that September 11 created a new kind of threat that could not be met by the now anachronistic Cold War doctrines of deterrence and containment. Many have argued that it also reflects the classic realpolitik rationale for preventive war that uses the post–9/11 security threats to justify America's assertion of the hegemonic right to lock in the benefits of overwhelming military superiority.

The great struggles of the twentieth century between liberty and totalitarianism ended with a decisive victory for the forces of freedom—and a single sustainable model for national success: freedom, democracy, and free enterprise. In the twenty-first century, only nations that share a commitment to protecting basic human rights and guaranteeing political and economic freedom will be able to unleash the potential of their people and assure their future prosperity. People everywhere want to be able to speak freely; choose who will govern them; worship as they please; educate their children—male and female; own property; and enjoy the benefits of their labor. These values of freedom are right and true for every person, in every society—and the duty of protecting these values against their enemies is the common calling of freedom-loving people across the globe and across the ages.

Today, the United States enjoys a position of unparalleled military strength and great economic and political influence. In keeping with our heritage and principles, we do not use our strength to press for unilateral advantage. We seek instead to create a balance of power that favors human freedom: conditions in which all nations and all societies can choose for themselves the rewards and challenges of political and economic liberty. In a world that is safe, people will be able to make their own lives better. We will defend the peace by fighting terrorists and tyrants. We will preserve the peace by building good relations among the great powers. We will extend the peace by encouraging free and open societies on every continent.

Defending our Nation against its enemies is the first and fundamental commitment of the Federal Government. Today, that task has changed dramatically. Enemies in the past needed great armies and great industrial capabilities to endanger America. Now, shadowy networks of individuals can bring great chaos and suffering to our shores for less than it costs to purchase a single tank. Terrorists are organized to penetrate open societies and to turn the power of modern technologies against us.

To defeat this threat we must make use of every tool in our arsenal—military power, better homeland defenses, law enforcement, intelligence, and vigorous efforts to cut off terrorist financing. The war against terrorists of global reach is a global enterprise of uncertain duration. America will help nations that need our assistance in combating terror. And America will hold to account nations that are compromised by terror, including those who harbor terrorists—because the allies of terror are the enemies of civilization. The United States and countries cooperating with us must not allow the terrorists to develop new home bases. Together, we will seek to deny them sanctuary at every turn.

The gravest danger our Nation faces lies at the crossroads of radicalism and technology. Our enemies have openly declared that they are seeking weapons of mass destruction, and evidence indicates that they are doing so with determination. The United States will not allow these efforts to succeed. We will build defenses against ballistic missiles and other means of delivery. We will cooperate with other nations to deny, contain, and curtail our enemies' efforts to acquire dangerous technologies. And, as a matter of common sense and self-defense, America will act against such emerging threats before they are fully formed. We cannot defend America and our friends by hoping for the best. So we must be prepared to defeat our enemies' plans, using the best intelligence and proceeding with deliberation. History will judge harshly those who saw this coming danger but failed to act. In the new world we have entered, the only path to peace and security is the path of action.

As we defend the peace, we will also take advantage of an historic opportunity to preserve the peace. Today, the international community has the best chance since the rise of the nation-state in the seventeenth century to build a world where great powers compete in peace instead of continually prepare for war. Today, the world's great powers find ourselves on the same side—united by common dangers of terrorist violence and chaos. The United States will build on these common interests to promote global security. We are also increasingly united by common values. Russia is in the midst of a hopeful transition, reaching for its democratic future and a partner in the war on terror. Chinese leaders are discovering that economic freedom is the only source of national wealth. In time, they will find that social and political freedom is the only source of national greatness. America will encourage the advancement of democracy and economic openness in both nations, because these are the best foundations for domestic stability and international order. We will strongly resist aggression from other great powers—even as we welcome their peaceful pursuit of prosperity, trade, and cultural advancement.

Finally, the United States will use this moment of opportunity to extend the benefits of freedom across the globe. We will actively work to bring the hope of democracy, development, free markets, and free trade to every corner of the world. The events of September 11, 2001, taught us that weak states, like Afghanistan, can pose as great a danger to our national interests as strong states. Poverty does not make poor people into terrorists and murderers. Yet poverty, weak institutions, and corruption can make weak states vulnerable to terrorist networks and drug cartels within their borders.

The United States will stand beside any nation determined to build a better future by seeking the rewards of liberty for its people. Free trade and free markets have proven their ability to lift whole societies out of poverty—so the United States will work with individual nations, entire regions, and the entire global trading community to build a world that trades in freedom and therefore grows in prosperity. The United States will deliver greater development assistance through the New Millennium Challenge Account to nations that govern justly, invest in their people, and encourage economic freedom. We will also continue to lead the world in efforts to reduce the terrible toll of HIV/AIDS and other infectious diseases.

In building a balance of power that favors freedom, the United States is guided by the conviction that all nations have important responsibilities. Nations that enjoy freedom must actively fight terror. Nations that depend on international stability must help prevent the spread of weapons of mass destruction. Nations that seek international aid must govern themselves wisely, so that aid is well spent. For freedom to thrive, accountability must be expected and required.

We are also guided by the conviction that no nation can build a safer, better world alone. Alliances and multilateral institutions can multiply the strength of freedom-loving nations. The United States is committed to lasting institutions like the United Nations, the World Trade Organization, the Organization of American States, and NATO as well as other long-standing alliances. Coalitions of the willing can augment these permanent institutions. In all cases, international obligations are to be taken seriously. They are not to be undertaken symbolically to rally support for an ideal without furthering its attainment.

Freedom is the non-negotiable demand of human dignity; the birthright of every person—in every civilization. Throughout history, freedom has been threatened by war and terror; it has been challenged by the clashing wills of powerful states and the evil designs of tyrants; and it has been tested by widespread poverty and disease. Today, humanity holds in its hands the opportunity to further freedom's triumph over all these foes. The United States welcomes our responsibility to lead in this great mission.

George W. Bush
The White House,
September 17, 2002

I. OVERVIEW OF AMERICA'S INTERNATIONAL STRATEGY

"Our Nation's cause has always been larger than our Nation's defense. We fight, as we always fight, for a just peace—a peace that favors liberty. We will defend the peace against the threats from terrorists and tyrants. We will preserve the peace by building good relations among the great powers. And we will extend the peace by encouraging free and open societies on every continent."

President Bush
West Point, New York
June 1, 2002

The United States possesses unprecedented—and unequaled—strength and influence in the world. Sustained by faith in the principles of liberty, and the value of a free society, this position comes with unparalleled responsibilities, obligations, and opportunity. The great strength of this nation must be used to promote a balance of power that favors freedom.

For most of the twentieth century, the world was divided by a great struggle over ideas: destructive totalitarian visions versus freedom and equality.

That great struggle is over. The militant visions of class, nation, and race which promised utopia and delivered misery have been defeated and discredited. America is now threatened less by conquering states than we are by failing ones. We are menaced less by fleets and armies than by catastrophic technologies in the hands of the embittered few. We must defeat these threats to our Nation, allies, and friends.

This is also a time of opportunity for America. We will work to translate this moment of influence into decades of peace, prosperity, and liberty. The U.S. national security strategy will be based on a distinctly American internationalism that reflects the union of our values and our national interests. The aim of this strategy is to help make the world not just safer but better. Our goals on the path to progress are clear: political and economic freedom, peaceful relations with other states, and respect for human dignity.

And this path is not America's alone. It is open to all. To achieve these goals, the United States will:

- champion aspirations for human dignity;
- strengthen alliances to defeat global terrorism and work to prevent attacks against us and our friends;
- work with others to defuse regional conflicts;
- prevent our enemies from threatening us, our allies, and our friends, with weapons of mass destruction;
- ignite a new era of global economic growth through free markets and free trade;
- expand the circle of development by opening societies and building the infrastructure of democracy;
- develop agendas for cooperative action with other main centers of global power; and
- transform America's national security institutions to meet the challenges and opportunities of the twenty-first century.

II. CHAMPION ASPIRATIONS FOR HUMAN DIGNITY

"Some worry that it is somehow undiplomatic or impolite to speak the language of right and wrong. I disagree. Different circumstances require different methods, but not different moralities."

President Bush
West Point, New York
June 1, 2002

In pursuit of our goals, our first imperative is to clarify what we stand for: the United States must defend liberty and justice because these principles are right and true for all people everywhere. No nation owns these aspirations, and no nation is exempt from them. Fathers and mothers in all societies want their children to be educated and to live free from poverty and violence. No people on earth yearn to be oppressed, aspire to servitude, or eagerly await the midnight knock of the secret police.

America must stand firmly for the nonnegotiable demands of human dignity: the rule of law; limits on the absolute power of the state; free speech; freedom of worship; equal justice; respect for women; religious and ethnic tolerance; and respect for private property.

These demands can be met in many ways. America's constitution has served us well. Many other nations, with different histories and cultures, facing different circumstances, have successfully incorporated these core principles into their own systems of governance. History has not been kind to those nations which ignored or flouted the rights and aspirations of their people.

America's experience as a great multi-ethnic democracy affirms our conviction that people of many heritages and faiths can live and prosper in peace. Our own history is a long struggle to live up to our ideals. But even in our worst moments, the principles enshrined in the Declaration of Independence were there to guide us. As a result, America is not just a stronger, but is a freer and more just society.

Today, these ideals are a lifeline to lonely defenders of liberty. And when openings arrive, we can encourage change—as we did in central and eastern Europe between 1989 and 1991, or in Belgrade in 2000. When we see democratic processes take hold among our friends in Taiwan or in the Republic of Korea, and see elected leaders replace generals in Latin America and Africa, we see examples of how authoritarian systems can evolve, marrying local history and traditions with the principles we all cherish.

Embodying lessons from our past and using the opportunity we have today, the national security strategy of the United States must start from these core beliefs and look outward for possibilities to expand liberty.

Our principles will guide our government's decisions about international cooperation, the character of our foreign assistance, and the allocation of resources. They will guide our actions and our words in international bodies. We will:

- speak out honestly about violations of the nonnegotiable demands of human dignity using our voice and vote in international institutions to advance freedom;
- use our foreign aid to promote freedom and support those who struggle non-violently for it, ensuring that nations moving toward democracy are rewarded for the steps they take;

- make freedom and the development of democratic institutions key themes in our bilateral relations, seeking solidarity and cooperation from other democracies while we press governments that deny human rights to move toward a better future; and
- take special efforts to promote freedom of religion and conscience and defend it from encroachment by repressive governments.

We will champion the cause of human dignity and oppose those who resist it.

III. STRENGTHEN ALLIANCES TO DEFEAT GLOBAL TERRORISM AND WORK TO PREVENT ATTACKS AGAINST US AND OUR FRIENDS

"Just three days removed from these events, Americans do not yet have the distance of history. But our responsibility to history is already clear: to answer these attacks and rid the world of evil. War has been waged against us by stealth and deceit and murder. This nation is peaceful, but fierce when stirred to anger. The conflict was begun on the timing and terms of others. It will end in a way, and at an hour, of our choosing."

President Bush
Washington, D.C. (The National Cathedral)
September 14, 2001

The United States of America is fighting a war against terrorists of global reach. The enemy is not a single political regime or person or religion or ideology. The enemy is terrorism—premeditated, politically motivated violence perpetrated against innocents.

In many regions, legitimate grievances prevent the emergence of a lasting peace. Such grievances deserve to be, and must be, addressed within a political process. But no cause justifies terror. The United States will make no concessions to terrorist demands and strike no deals with them. We make no distinction between terrorists and those who knowingly harbor or provide aid to them.

The struggle against global terrorism is different from any other war in our history. It will be fought on many fronts against a particularly elusive enemy over an extended period of time. Progress will come through the persistent accumulation of successes—some seen, some unseen.

Today our enemies have seen the results of what civilized nations can, and will, do against regimes that harbor, support, and use terrorism to achieve their political goals. Afghanistan has been liberated; coalition forces continue to hunt down the Taliban and al-Qaida. But it is not only this battlefield on which we will engage terrorists. Thousands of trained terrorists remain at large with cells in North America, South America, Europe, Africa, the Middle East, and across Asia.

Our priority will be first to disrupt and destroy terrorist organizations of global reach and attack their leadership; command, control, and communications; material support; and finances. This will have a disabling effect upon the terrorists' ability to plan and operate.

We will continue to encourage our regional partners to take up a coordinated effort that isolates the terrorists. Once the regional campaign localizes the threat to a particular state, we will help ensure the state has the military, law enforcement, political, and financial tools necessary to finish the task.

The United States will continue to work with our allies to disrupt the financing of terrorism. We will identify and block the sources of funding for terrorism, freeze the assets of terrorists and those who support them, deny terrorists access to the international financial system, protect legitimate charities from being abused by terrorists, and prevent the movement of terrorists' assets through alternative financial networks.

However, this campaign need not be sequential to be effective, the cumulative effect across all regions will help achieve the results we seek. We will disrupt and destroy terrorist organizations by:

- direct and continuous action using all the elements of national and international power. Our immediate focus will be those terrorist organizations of global reach and any terrorist or state sponsor of terrorism which attempts to gain or use weapons of mass destruction (WMD) or their precursors;

- defending the United States, the American people, and our interests at home and abroad by identifying and destroying the threat before it reaches our borders. While the United States will constantly strive to enlist the support of the international community, we will not hesitate to act alone, if necessary, to exercise our right of selfdefense by acting preemptively against such terrorists, to prevent them from doing harm against our people and our country; and

- denying further sponsorship, support, and sanctuary to terrorists by convincing or compelling states to accept their sovereign responsibilities. We will also wage a war of ideas to win the battle against international terrorism. This includes:

- using the full influence of the United States, and working closely with allies and friends, to make clear that all acts of terrorism are illegitimate so that terrorism will be viewed in the same light as slavery, piracy, or genocide: behavior that no respectable government can condone or support and all must oppose;

- supporting moderate and modern government, especially in the Muslim world, to ensure that the conditions and ideologies that promote terrorism do not find fertile ground in any nation;
- diminishing the underlying conditions that spawn terrorism by enlisting the international community to focus its efforts and resources on areas most at risk; and
- using effective public diplomacy to promote the free flow of information and ideas to kindle the hopes and aspirations of freedom of those in societies ruled by the sponsors of global terrorism.

While we recognize that our best defense is a good offense, we are also strengthening America's homeland security to protect against and deter attack. This Administration has proposed the largest government reorganization since the Truman Administration created the National Security Council and the Department of Defense. Centered on a new Department of Homeland Security and including a new unified military command and a fundamental reordering of the FBI, our comprehensive plan to secure the homeland encompasses every level of government and the cooperation of the public and the private sector.

This strategy will turn adversity into opportunity. For example, emergency management systems will be better able to cope not just with terrorism but with all hazards. Our medical system will be strengthened to manage not just bioterror, but all infectious diseases and mass-casualty dangers. Our border controls will not just stop terrorists, but improve the efficient movement of legitimate traffic.

While our focus is protecting America, we know that to defeat terrorism in today's globalized world we need support from our allies and friends. Wherever possible, the United States will rely on regional organizations and state powers to meet their obligations to fight terrorism. Where governments find the fight against terrorism beyond their capacities, we will match their willpower and their resources with whatever help we and our allies can provide.

As we pursue the terrorists in Afghanistan, we will continue to work with international organizations such as the United Nations, as well as non-governmental organizations, and other countries to provide the humanitarian, political, economic, and security assistance necessary to rebuild Afghanistan so that it will never again abuse its people, threaten its neighbors, and provide a haven for terrorists.

In the war against global terrorism, we will never forget that we are ultimately fighting for our democratic values and way of life. Freedom and fear are at war, and there will be no quick or easy end to this conflict. In leading the campaign against terrorism, we are forging new, productive international relationships and redefining existing ones in ways that meet the challenges of the twenty-first century.

IV. WORK WITH OTHERS
TO DEFUSE REGIONAL CONFLICTS

"We build a world of justice, or we will live in a world of coercion. The magnitude of our shared responsibilities makes our disagreements look so small."

President Bush
Berlin, Germany
May 23, 2002

Concerned nations must remain actively engaged in critical regional disputes to avoid explosive escalation and minimize human suffering. In an increasingly interconnected world, regional crisis can strain our alliances, rekindle rivalries among the major powers, and create horrifying affronts to human dignity. When violence erupts and states falter, the United States will work with friends and partners to alleviate suffering and restore stability.

No doctrine can anticipate every circumstance in which U.S. action—direct or indirect—is warranted. We have finite political, economic, and military resources to meet our global priorities. The United States will approach each case with these strategic principles in mind:

- The United States should invest time and resources into building international relationships and institutions that can help manage local crises when they emerge.
- The United States should be realistic about its ability to help those who are unwilling or unready to help themselves. Where and when people are ready to do their part, we will be willing to move decisively.

The Israeli-Palestinian conflict is critical because of the toll of human suffering, because of America's close relationship with the state of Israel and key Arab states, and because of that region's importance to other global priorities of the United States. There can be no peace for either side without freedom for both sides. America stands committed to an independent and democratic Palestine, living beside Israel in peace and security. Like all other people, Palestinians deserve a government that serves their interests and listens to their voices. The United States will continue to encourage all parties to step up to their responsibilities as we seek a just and comprehensive settlement to the conflict.

The United States, the international donor community, and the World Bank stand ready to work with a reformed Palestinian government on economic development, increased humanitarian assistance, and a program to establish, finance, and monitor a truly independent judiciary. If Palestinians embrace democracy, and the rule of law, confront corruption, and firmly reject terror, they can count on American support for the creation of a Palestinian state.

Israel also has a large stake in the success of a democratic Palestine. Permanent occupation threatens Israel's identity and democracy. So the United States continues to challenge Israeli leaders to take concrete steps to support the emergence of a viable, credible Palestinian state. As there is progress towards security, Israel forces need to withdraw fully to positions they held prior to September 28, 2000. And consistent with the recommendations of the Mitchell Committee, Israeli settlement activity in the occupied territories must stop. As violence subsides, freedom of movement should be restored, permitting innocent Palestinians to resume work and normal life. The United States can play a crucial role but, ultimately, lasting peace can only come when Israelis and Palestinians resolve the issues and end the conflict between them.

In South Asia, the United States has also emphasized the need for India and Pakistan to resolve their disputes. This Administration invested time and resources building strong bilateral relations with India and Pakistan. These strong relations then gave us leverage to play a constructive role when tensions in the region became acute. With Pakistan, our bilateral relations have been bolstered by Pakistan's choice to join the war against terror and move toward building a more open and tolerant society. The Administration sees India's potential to become one of the great democratic powers of the twenty-first century and has worked hard to transform our relationship accordingly. Our involvement in this regional dispute, building on earlier investments in bilateral relations, looks first to concrete steps by India and Pakistan that can help defuse military confrontation.

Indonesia took courageous steps to create a working democracy and respect for the rule of law. By tolerating ethnic minorities, respecting the rule of law, and accepting open markets, Indonesia may be able to employ the engine of opportunity that has helped lift some of its neighbors out of poverty and desperation. It is the initiative by Indonesia that allows U.S. assistance to make a difference.

In the Western Hemisphere we have formed flexible coalitions with countries that share our priorities, particularly Mexico, Brazil, Canada, Chile, and Colombia. Together we will promote a truly democratic hemisphere where our integration advances security, prosperity, opportunity, and hope. We will work with regional institutions, such as the Summit of the Americas process, the Organization of American States (OAS), and the Defense Ministerial of the Americas for the benefit of the entire hemisphere.

Parts of Latin America confront regional conflict, especially arising from the violence of drug cartels and their accomplices. This conflict and unrestrained narcotics trafficking could imperil the health and security of the United States. Therefore we have developed an active strategy to help the Andean nations adjust their economies, enforce their laws, defeat terrorist organizations, and cut off the supply of drugs, while—as important—we work to reduce the demand for drugs in our own country.

In Colombia, we recognize the link between terrorist and extremist groups that challenge the security of the state and drug trafficking activities that help finance the operations of such groups. We are working to help Colombia defend its democratic institutions and defeat illegal armed groups of both the left and right by extending effective sovereignty over the entire national territory and provide basic security to the Colombian people.

In Africa, promise and opportunity sit side by side with disease, war, and desperate poverty. This threatens both a core value of the United States—preserving human dignity—and our strategic priority—combating global terror. American interests and American principles, therefore, lead in the same direction: we will work with others for an African continent that lives in liberty, peace, and growing prosperity. Together with our European allies, we must help strengthen Africa's fragile states, help build indigenous capability to secure porous borders, and help build up the law enforcement and intelligence infrastructure to deny havens for terrorists.

An ever more lethal environment exists in Africa as local civil wars spread beyond borders to create regional war zones. Forming coalitions of the willing and cooperative security arrangements are key to confronting these emerging transnational threats.

Africa's great size and diversity requires a security strategy that focuses on bilateral engagement and builds coalitions of the willing. This Administration will focus on three interlocking strategies for the region:

- countries with major impact on their neighborhood such as South Africa, Nigeria, Kenya, and Ethiopia are anchors for regional engagement and require focused attention;
- coordination with European allies and international institutions is essential for constructive conflict mediation and successful peace operations; and
- Africa's capable reforming states and sub-regional organizations must be strengthened as the primary means to address transnational threats on a sustained basis.

Ultimately the path of political and economic freedom presents the surest route to progress in sub-Saharan Africa, where most wars are conflicts over material resources and political access often tragically waged on the basis of ethnic and religious difference. The transition to the African Union with its stated commitment to good governance and a common responsibility for democratic political systems offers opportunities to strengthen democracy on the continent.

V. PREVENT OUR ENEMIES FROM THREATENING US, OUR ALLIES, AND OUR FRIENDS WITH WEAPONS OF MASS DESTRUCTION

"The gravest danger to freedom lies at the crossroads of radicalism and technology. When the spread of chemical and biological and nuclear weapons, along with ballistic missile technology—when that occurs, even weak states

and small groups could attain a catastrophic power to strike great nations. Our enemies have declared this very intention, and have been caught seeking these terrible weapons. They want the capability to blackmail us, or to harm us, or to harm our friends—and we will oppose them with all our power."

President Bush
West Point, New York
June 1, 2002

The nature of the Cold War threat required the United States—with our allies and friends—to emphasize deterrence of the enemy's use of force, producing a grim strategy of mutual assured destruction. With the collapse of the Soviet Union and the end of the Cold War, our security environment has undergone profound transformation.

Having moved from confrontation to cooperation as the hallmark of our relationship with Russia, the dividends are evident: an end to the balance of terror that divided us; an historic reduction in the nuclear arsenals on both sides; and cooperation in areas such as counterterrorism and missile defense that until recently were inconceivable.

But new deadly challenges have emerged from rogue states and terrorists. None of these contemporary threats rival the sheer destructive power that was arrayed against us by the Soviet Union. However, the nature and motivations of these new adversaries, their determination to obtain destructive powers hitherto available only to the world's strongest states, and the greater likelihood that they will use weapons of mass destruction against us, make today's security environment more complex and dangerous.

In the 1990s we witnessed the emergence of a small number of rogue states that, while different in important ways, share a number of attributes. These states:

- brutalize their own people and squander their national resources for the personal gain of the rulers;
- display no regard for international law, threaten their neighbors, and callously violate international treaties to which they are party;
- are determined to acquire weapons of mass destruction, along with other advanced military technology, to be used as threats or offensively to achieve the aggressive designs of these regimes;
- sponsor terrorism around the globe; and
- reject basic human values and hate the United States and everything for which it stands.

At the time of the Gulf War, we acquired irrefutable proof that Iraq's designs were not limited to the chemical weapons it had used against Iran and its own people, but also extended to the acquisition of nuclear weapons and biological agents. In the past decade North Korea has become the world's principal purveyor of ballistic missiles, and has tested increasingly capable missiles while developing its own WMD arsenal. Other rogue regimes seek nuclear, biological, and chemical weapons as well. These states' pursuit of, and global trade in, such weapons has become a looming threat to all nations.

We must be prepared to stop rogue states and their terrorist clients before they are able to threaten or use weapons of mass destruction against the United States and our allies and friends. Our response must take full advantage of strengthened alliances, the establishment of new partnerships with former adversaries, innovation in the use of military forces, modern technologies, including the development of an effective missile defense system, and increased emphasis on intelligence collection and analysis.

Our comprehensive strategy to combat WMD includes:

- *Proactive counterproliferation efforts.* We must deter and defend against the threat before it is unleashed. We must ensure that key capabilities—detection, active and passive defenses, and counterforce capabilities—are integrated into our defense transformation and our homeland security systems. Counterproliferation must also be integrated into the doctrine, training, and equipping of our forces and those of our allies to ensure that we can prevail in any conflict with WMD-armed adversaries.
- *Strengthened nonproliferation efforts to prevent rogue states and terrorists from acquiring the materials, technologies, and expertise necessary for weapons of mass destruction.* We will enhance diplomacy, arms control, multilateral export controls, and threat reduction assistance that impede states and terrorists seeking WMD, and when necessary, interdict enabling technologies and materials. We will continue to build coalitions to support these efforts, encouraging their increased political and financial support for nonproliferation and threat reduction programs. The recent G-8 agreement to commit up to $20 billion to a global partnership against proliferation marks a major step forward.
- *Effective consequence management to respond to the effects of WMD use, whether by terrorists or hostile states.* Minimizing the effects of WMD use against our people will help deter those who possess such weapons and dissuade those who seek to acquire them by persuading enemies that they cannot attain their desired ends. The United States must also be prepared to respond to the effects of WMD use against our forces abroad, and to help friends and allies if they are attacked.

It has taken almost a decade for us to comprehend the true nature of this new threat. Given the goals of rogue states and terrorists, the United States can no longer solely rely on a reactive posture as we have in the past. The inability to deter a potential attacker, the immediacy of today's threats, and the magnitude of potential harm that could be caused by our adversaries' choice of weapons, do not permit that option. We cannot let our enemies strike first.

In the Cold War, especially following the Cuban missile crisis, we faced a generally status quo, risk-averse adversary. Deterrence was an effective defense. But deterrence based only upon the threat of retaliation is less likely to work against leaders of rogue states more willing to take risks, gambling with the lives of their people, and the wealth of their nations.

- In the Cold War, weapons of mass destruction were considered weapons of last resort whose use risked the destruction of those who used them. Today, our enemies see weapons of mass destruction as weapons of choice. For rogue states these weapons are tools of intimidation and military aggression against their neighbors. These weapons may also allow these states to attempt to blackmail the United States and our allies to prevent us from deterring or repelling the aggressive behavior of rogue states. Such states also see these weapons as their best means of overcoming the conventional superiority of the United States.
- Traditional concepts of deterrence will not work against a terrorist enemy whose avowed tactics are wanton destruction and the targeting of innocents; whose so-called soldiers seek martyrdom in death and whose most potent protection is statelessness. The overlap between states that sponsor terror and those that pursue WMD compels us to action.

For centuries, international law recognized that nations need not suffer an attack before they can lawfully take action to defend themselves against forces that present an imminent danger of attack. Legal scholars and international jurists often conditioned the legitimacy of preemption on the existence of an imminent threat—most often a visible mobilization of armies, navies, and air forces preparing to attack.

We must adapt the concept of imminent threat to the capabilities and objectives of today's adversaries. Rogue states and terrorists do not seek to attack us using conventional means. They know such attacks would fail. Instead, they rely on acts of terror and, potentially, the use of weapons of mass destruction—weapons that can be easily concealed, delivered covertly, and used without warning.

The targets of these attacks are our military forces and our civilian population, in direct violation of one of the principal norms of the law of warfare. As was demonstrated by the losses on September 11, 2001, mass civilian casualties is the specific objective of terrorists and these losses would be exponentially more severe if terrorists acquired and used weapons of mass destruction.

The United States has long maintained the option of preemptive actions to counter a sufficient threat to our national security. The greater the threat, the greater is the risk of inaction—and the more compelling the case for taking anticipatory action to defend ourselves, even if uncertainty remains as to the time and place of the enemy's attack. To forestall or prevent such hostile acts by our adversaries, the United States will, if necessary, act preemptively.

The United States will not use force in all cases to preempt emerging threats, nor should nations use preemption as a pretext for aggression. Yet in an age where the enemies of civilization openly and actively seek the world's most destructive technologies, the United States cannot remain idle while dangers gather. We will always proceed deliberately, weighing the consequences of our actions. To support preemptive options, we will:

- build better, more integrated intelligence capabilities to provide timely, accurate information on threats, wherever they may emerge;
- coordinate closely with allies to form a common assessment of the most dangerous threats; and
- continue to transform our military forces to ensure our ability to conduct rapid and precise operations to achieve decisive results.

The purpose of our actions will always be to eliminate a specific threat to the United States or our allies and friends. The reasons for our actions will be clear, the force measured, and the cause just.

VI. IGNITE A NEW ERA OF GLOBAL ECONOMIC GROWTH THROUGH FREE MARKETS AND FREE TRADE

"When nations close their markets and opportunity is hoarded by a privileged few, no amount—no amount—of development aid is ever enough. When nations respect their people, open markets, invest in better health and education, every dollar of aid, every dollar of trade revenue and domestic capital is used more effectively."

President Bush
Monterrey, Mexico
March 22, 2002

A strong world economy enhances our national security by advancing prosperity and freedom in the rest of the world. Economic growth supported by free trade and free markets creates new jobs and higher incomes. It allows people to lift their lives out of poverty, spurs economic and legal reform, and the fight against corruption, and it reinforces the habits of liberty.

We will promote economic growth and economic freedom beyond America's shores. All governments are responsible for creating their own economic policies and responding to their own economic challenges. We will use our economic engagement with other countries to underscore the benefits of policies that generate higher productivity and sustained economic growth, including:

- pro-growth legal and regulatory policies to encourage business investment, innovation, and entrepreneurial activity;
- tax policies—particularly lower marginal tax rates—that improve incentives for work and investment;
- rule of law and intolerance of corruption so that people are confident that they will be able to enjoy the fruits of their economic endeavors;
- strong financial systems that allow capital to be put to its most efficient use;
- sound fiscal policies to support business activity;
- investments in health and education that improve the well-being and skills of the labor force and population as a whole; and
- free trade that provides new avenues for growth and fosters the diffusion of technologies and ideas that increase productivity and opportunity.

The lessons of history are clear: market economies, not command-and-control economies with the heavy hand of government, are the best way to promote prosperity and reduce poverty. Policies that further strengthen market incentives and market institutions are relevant for all economies—industrialized countries, emerging markets, and the developing world.

A return to strong economic growth in Europe and Japan is vital to U.S. national security interests. We want our allies to have strong economies for their own sake, for the sake of the global economy, and for the sake of global security. European efforts to remove structural barriers in their economies are particularly important in this regard, as are Japan's efforts to end deflation and address the problems of non-performing loans in the Japanese banking system. We will continue to use our regular consultations with Japan and our European partners—including through the Group of Seven (G-7)—to discuss policies they are adopting to promote growth in their economies and support higher global economic growth.

Improving stability in emerging markets is also key to global economic growth. International flows of investment capital are needed to expand the productive potential of these economies. These flows allow emerging markets and developing countries to make the investments that raise living standards and reduce poverty. Our long-term objective should be a world in which all countries have investment-grade credit ratings that allow them access to international capital markets and to invest in their future.

We are committed to policies that will help emerging markets achieve access to larger capital flows at lower cost. To this end, we will continue to pursue reforms aimed at reducing uncertainty in financial markets. We will work actively with other countries, the International Monetary Fund (IMF), and the private sector to implement the G-7 Action Plan negotiated earlier this year for preventing financial crises and more effectively resolving them when they occur.

The best way to deal with financial crises is to prevent them from occurring, and we have encouraged the IMF to improve its efforts doing so. We will continue to work with the IMF to streamline the policy conditions for its lending and to focus its lending strategy on achieving economic growth through sound fiscal and monetary policy, exchange rate policy, and financial sector policy.

The concept of "free trade" arose as a moral principle even before it became a pillar of economics. If you can make something that others value, you should be able to sell it to them. If others make something that you value, you should be able to buy it. This is real freedom, the freedom for a person—or a nation—to make a living. To promote free trade, the Unites States has developed a comprehensive strategy:

- *Seize the global initiative.* The new global trade negotiations we helped launch at Doha in November 2001 will have an ambitious agenda, especially in agriculture, manufacturing, and services, targeted for completion in 2005. The United States has led the way in completing the accession of China and a democratic Taiwan to the World Trade Organization. We will assist Russia's preparations to join the WTO.
- *Press regional initiatives.* The United States and other democracies in the Western Hemisphere have agreed to create the Free Trade Area of the Americas, targeted for completion in 2005. This year the United States will advocate market-access negotiations with its partners, targeted on agriculture, industrial goods, services, investment, and government procurement. We will also offer more opportunity to the poorest continent, Africa, starting with full use of the preferences allowed in the African Growth and Opportunity Act, and leading to free trade.
- *Move ahead with bilateral free trade agreements.* Building on the free trade agreement with Jordan enacted in 2001, the Administration will work this year to complete free trade agreements with Chile and Singapore. Our aim is to achieve free trade agreements with a mix of developed and developing countries in all regions of the world. Initially, Central America, Southern Africa, Morocco, and Australia will be our principal focal points.
- *Renew the executive-congressional partnership.* Every administration's trade strategy depends on a productive partnership with Congress. After a gap of 8 years, the Administration reestablished majority support in the Congress for trade liberalization by passing Trade Promotion Authority and the other market opening measures for developing countries in the Trade Act of 2002. This Administration will work with Congress to enact new bilateral, regional, and global trade agreements that will be concluded under the recently passed Trade Promotion Authority.
- *Promote the connection between trade and development.* Trade policies can help developing countries strengthen property rights, competition, the

rule of law, investment, the spread of knowledge, open societies, the efficient allocation of resources, and regional integration—all leading to growth, opportunity, and confidence in developing countries. The United States is implementing The Africa Growth and Opportunity Act to provide market-access for nearly all goods produced in the 35 countries of sub-Saharan Africa. We will make more use of this act and its equivalent for the Caribbean Basin and continue to work with multilateral and regional institutions to help poorer countries take advantage of these opportunities. Beyond market access, the most important area where trade intersects with poverty is in public health. We will ensure that the WTO intellectual property rules are flexible enough to allow developing nations to gain access to critical medicines for extraordinary dangers like HIV/AIDS, tuberculosis, and malaria.

- *Enforce trade agreements and laws against unfair practices.* Commerce depends on the rule of law; international trade depends on enforceable agreements. Our top priorities are to resolve ongoing disputes with the European Union, Canada, and Mexico and to make a global effort to address new technology, science, and health regulations that needlessly impede farm exports and improved agriculture. Laws against unfair trade practices are often abused, but the international community must be able to address genuine concerns about government subsidies and dumping. International industrial espionage which undermines fair competition must be detected and deterred.

- *Help domestic industries and workers adjust.* There is a sound statutory framework for these transitional safeguards which we have used in the agricultural sector and which we are using this year to help the American steel industry. The benefits of free trade depend upon the enforcement of fair trading practices. These safeguards help ensure that the benefits of free trade do not come at the expense of American workers. Trade adjustment assistance will help workers adapt to the change and dynamism of open markets.

- *Protect the environment and workers.* The United States must foster economic growth in ways that will provide a better life along with widening prosperity. We will incorporate labor and environmental concerns into U.S. trade negotiations, creating a healthy "network" between multilateral environmental agreements with the WTO, and use the International Labor Organization, trade preference programs, and trade talks to improve working conditions in conjunction with freer trade.

- *Enhance energy security.* We will strengthen our own energy security and the shared prosperity of the global economy by working with our allies, trading partners, and energy producers to expand the sources and types of global energy supplied, especially in the Western Hemisphere, Africa,

Central Asia, and the Caspian region. We will also continue to work with our partners to develop cleaner and more energy efficient technologies.

Economic growth should be accompanied by global efforts to stabilize greenhouse gas concentrations associated with this growth, containing them at a level that prevents dangerous human interference with the global climate. Our overall objective is to reduce America's greenhouse gas emissions relative to the size of our economy, cutting such emissions per unit of economic activity by 18 percent over the next 10 years, by the year 2012. Our strategies for attaining this goal will be to:

- remain committed to the basic U.N. Framework Convention for international cooperation;
- obtain agreements with key industries to cut emissions of some of the most potent greenhouse gases and give transferable credits to companies that can show real cuts;
- develop improved standards for measuring and registering emission reductions;
- promote renewable energy production and clean coal technology, as well as nuclear power—which produces no greenhouse gas emissions, while also improving fuel economy for U.S. cars and trucks;
- increase spending on research and new conservation technologies, to a total of $4.5 billion—the largest sum being spent on climate change by any country in the world and a $700 million increase over last year's budget; and
- assist developing countries, especially the major greenhouse gas emitters such as China and India, so that they will have the tools and resources to join this effort and be able to grow along a cleaner and better path.

VII. EXPAND THE CIRCLE OF DEVELOPMENT BY OPENING SOCIETIES AND BUILDING THE INFRASTRUCTURE OF DEMOCRACY

"In World War II we fought to make the world safer, then worked to rebuild it. As we wage war today to keep the world safe from terror, we must also work to make the world a better place for all its citizens."

President Bush
Washington, D.C. (Inter-American Development Bank)

A world where some live in comfort and plenty, while half of the human race lives on less than $2 a day, is neither just nor stable. Including all of the world's poor in an expanding circle of development—and opportunity—is a moral imperative and one of the top priorities of U.S. international policy.

Decades of massive development assistance have failed to spur economic growth in the poorest countries. Worse, development aid has often served to prop up failed policies, relieving the pressure for reform and perpetuating misery. Results of aid are typically measured in dollars spent by donors, not in the rates of growth and poverty reduction achieved by recipients. These are the indicators of a failed strategy.

Working with other nations, the United States is confronting this failure. We forged a new consensus at the U.N. Conference on Financing for Development in Monterrey that the objectives of assistance—and the strategies to achieve those objectives—must change.

This Administration's goal is to help unleash the productive potential of individuals in all nations. Sustained growth and poverty reduction is impossible without the right national policies. Where governments have implemented real policy changes, we will provide significant new levels of assistance. The United States and other developed countries should set an ambitious and specific target: to double the size of the world's poorest economies within a decade.

The United States Government will pursue these major strategies to achieve this goal:

- *Provide resources to aid countries that have met the challenge of national reform.* We propose a 50 percent increase in the core development assistance given by the United States. While continuing our present programs, including humanitarian assistance based on need alone, these billions of new dollars will form a new Millennium Challenge Account for projects in countries whose governments rule justly, invest in their people, and encourage economic freedom. Governments must fight corruption, respect basic human rights, embrace the rule of law, invest in health care and education, follow responsible economic policies, and enable entrepreneurship. The Millennium Challenge Account will reward countries that have demonstrated real policy change and challenge those that have not to implement reforms.

- *Improve the effectiveness of the World Bank and other development banks in raising living standards.* The United States is committed to a comprehensive reform agenda for making the World Bank and the other multilateral development banks more effective in improving the lives of the world's poor. We have reversed the downward trend in U.S. contributions and proposed an 18 percent increase in the U.S. contributions to the International Development Association (IDA)—the World Bank's fund for the poorest countries—and the African Development Fund. The key to raising living standards and reducing poverty around the world is increasing productivity growth, especially in the poorest countries. We will continue to press the multilateral development banks to focus on activities that increase economic productivity, such as improvements in education, health, rule of law, and private sector development. Every project, every loan, every grant must be judged by how much it will increase productivity growth in developing countries.

- *Insist upon measurable results to ensure that development assistance is actually making a difference in the lives of the world's poor.* When it comes to economic development, what really matters is that more children are getting a better education, more people have access to health care and clean water, or more workers can find jobs to make a better future for their families. We have a moral obligation to measure the success of our development assistance by whether it is delivering results. For this reason, we will continue to demand that our own development assistance as well as assistance from the multilateral development banks has measurable goals and concrete benchmarks for achieving those goals. Thanks to U.S. leadership, the recent IDA replenishment agreement will establish a monitoring and evaluation system that measures recipient countries' progress. For the first time, donors can link a portion of their contributions to IDA to the achievement of actual development results, and part of the U.S. contribution is linked in this way. We will strive to make sure that the World Bank and other multilateral development banks build on this progress so that a focus on results is an integral part of everything that these institutions do.
- *Increase the amount of development assistance that is provided in the form of grants instead of loans.* Greater use of results-based grants is the best way to help poor countries make productive investments, particularly in the social sectors, without saddling them with ever-larger debt burdens. As a result of U.S. leadership, the recent IDA agreement provided for significant increases in grant funding for the poorest countries for education, HIV/AIDS, health, nutrition, water, sanitation, and other human needs. Our goal is to build on that progress by increasing the use of grants at the other multilateral development banks. We will also challenge universities, nonprofits, and the private sector to match government efforts by using grants to support development projects that show results.
- *Open societies to commerce and investment. Trade and investment are the real engines of economic growth.* Even if government aid increases, most money for development must come from trade, domestic capital, and foreign investment. An effective strategy must try to expand these flows as well. Free markets and free trade are key priorities of our national security strategy.
- *Secure public health.* The scale of the public health crisis in poor countries is enormous. In countries afflicted by epidemics and pandemics like HIV/AIDS, malaria, and tuberculosis, growth and development will be threatened until these scourges can be contained. Resources from the

developed world are necessary but will be effective only with honest governance, which supports prevention programs and provides effective local infrastructure. The United States has strongly backed the new global fund for HIV/AIDS organized by U.N. Secretary General Kofi Annan and its focus on combining prevention with a broad strategy for treatment and care. The United States already contributes more than twice as much money to such efforts as the next largest donor. If the global fund demonstrates its promise, we will be ready to give even more.

- *Emphasize education.* Literacy and learning are the foundation of democracy and development. Only about 7 percent of World Bank resources are devoted to education. This proportion should grow. The United States will increase its own funding for education assistance by at least 20 percent with an emphasis on improving basic education and teacher training in Africa. The United States can also bring information technology to these societies, many of whose education systems have been devastated by HIV/AIDS.

- *Continue to aid agricultural development.* New technologies, including biotechnology, have enormous potential to improve crop yields in developing countries while using fewer pesticides and less water. Using sound science, the United States should help bring these benefits to the 800 million people, including 300 million children, who still suffer from hunger and malnutrition.

VIII. DEVELOP AGENDAS FOR COOPERATIVE ACTION WITH THE OTHER MAIN CENTERS OF GLOBAL POWER

"We have our best chance since the rise of the nation-state in the 17th century to build a world where the great powers compete in peace instead of prepare for war."

President Bush
West Point, New York
June 1, 2002

America will implement its strategies by organizing coalitions—as broad as practicable—of states able and willing to promote a balance of power that favors freedom. Effective coalition leadership requires clear priorities, an appreciation of others' interests, and consistent consultations among partners with a spirit of humility.

There is little of lasting consequence that the United States can accomplish in the world without the sustained cooperation of its allies and friends in Canada and Europe. Europe is also the seat of two of the strongest and most able international institutions in the world: the North Atlantic Treaty Organization (NATO), which has, since its inception, been the fulcrum of transatlantic and inter-European security, and the European Union (EU), our partner in opening world trade.

The attacks of September 11 were also an attack on NATO, as NATO itself recognized when it invoked its Article V self-defense clause for the first time. NATO's core mission—collective defense of the transatlantic alliance of democracies—remains, but NATO must develop new structures and capabilities to carry out that mission under new circumstances. NATO must build a capability to field, at short notice, highly mobile, specially trained forces whenever they are needed to respond to a threat against any member of the alliance.

The alliance must be able to act wherever our interests are threatened, creating coalitions under NATO's own mandate, as well as contributing to mission-based coalitions. To achieve this, we must:

- expand NATO's membership to those democratic nations willing and able to share the burden of defending and advancing our common interests;
- ensure that the military forces of NATO nations have appropriate combat contributions to make in coalition warfare;
- develop planning processes to enable those contributions to become effective multinational fighting forces;
- take advantage of the technological opportunities and economies of scale in our defense spending to transform NATO military forces so that they dominate potential aggressors and diminish our vulnerabilities;
- streamline and increase the flexibility of command structures to meet new operational demands and the associated requirements of training, integrating, and experimenting with new force configurations; and
- maintain the ability to work and fight together as allies even as we take the necessary steps to transform and modernize our forces.

If NATO succeeds in enacting these changes, the rewards will be a partnership as central to the security and interests of its member states as was the case during the Cold War. We will sustain a common perspective on the threats to our societies and improve our ability to take common action in defense of our nations and their interests. At the same time, we welcome our European allies' efforts to forge a greater foreign policy and defense identity with the EU, and commit ourselves to close consultations to ensure that these developments work with NATO. We cannot afford to lose this opportunity to better prepare the family of transatlantic democracies for the challenges to come.

The attacks of September 11 energized America's Asian alliances. Australia invoked the ANZUS Treaty to declare the September 11 was an attack on Australia itself, following that historic decision with the dispatch of some of the world's finest combat forces for Operation Enduring Freedom. Japan and the Republic of Korea provided unprecedented levels of military logistical support within weeks of the terrorist attack. We have deepened cooperation on counterterrorism with our alliance partners in Thailand and the Philippines and received invaluable assistance from close friends like Singapore and New Zealand.

The war against terrorism has proven that America's alliances in Asia not only underpin regional peace and stability, but are flexible and ready to deal with new challenges. To enhance our Asian alliances and friendships, we will:

- look to Japan to continue forging a leading role in regional and global affairs based on our common interests, our common values, and our close defense and diplomatic cooperation;
- work with South Korea to maintain vigilance towards the North while preparing our alliance to make contributions to the broader stability of the region over the longer term;
- build on 50 years of U.S.-Australian alliance cooperation as we continue working together to resolve regional and global problems—as we have so many times from the Battle of the Coral Sea to Tora Bora;
- maintain forces in the region that reflect our commitments to our allies, our requirements, our technological advances, and the strategic environment; and
- build on stability provided by these alliances, as well as with institutions such as ASEAN and the Asia-Pacific Economic Cooperation forum, to develop a mix of regional and bilateral strategies to manage change in this dynamic region.

We are attentive to the possible renewal of old patterns of great power competition. Several potential great powers are now in the midst of internal transition—most importantly Russia, India, and China. In all three cases, recent developments have encouraged our hope that a truly global consensus about basic principles is slowly taking shape.

With Russia, we are already building a new strategic relationship based on a central reality of the twenty-first century: the United States and Russia are no longer strategic adversaries. The Moscow Treaty on Strategic Reductions is emblematic of this new reality and reflects a critical change in Russian thinking that promises to lead to productive, long-term relations with the Euro-Atlantic community and the United States. Russia's top leaders have a realistic assessment of their country's current weakness and the policies—internal and external— needed to reverse those weaknesses. They understand, increasingly, that Cold War approaches do not serve their national interests and that Russian and American strategic interests overlap in many areas.

United States policy seeks to use this turn in Russian thinking to refocus our relationship on emerging and potential common interests and challenges. We are broadening our already extensive cooperation in the global war on terrorism. We are facilitating Russia's entry into the World Trade Organization, without lowering standards for accession, to promote beneficial bilateral trade and investment relations. We have created the NATO-Russia Council with the goal of deepening security cooperation among Russia, our European allies, and ourselves. We will continue to bolster the independence and stability of the states of the former Soviet Union in the belief that a prosperous and stable neighborhood will reinforce Russia's growing commitment to integration into the Euro-Atlantic community.

At the same time, we are realistic about the differences that still divide us from Russia and about the time and effort it will take to build an enduring strategic partnership. Lingering distrust of our motives and policies by key Russian elites slows improvement in our relations. Russia's uneven commitment to the basic values of free-market democracy and dubious record in combating the proliferation of weapons of mass destruction remain matters of great concern. Russia's very weakness limits the opportunities for cooperation. Nevertheless, those opportunities are vastly greater now than in recent years—or even decades.

The United States has undertaken a transformation in its bilateral relationship with India based on a conviction that U.S. interests require a strong relationship with India. We are the two largest democracies, committed to political freedom protected by representative government. India is moving toward greater economic freedom as well. We have a common interest in the free flow of commerce, including through the vital sea lanes of the Indian Ocean. Finally, we share an interest in fighting terrorism and in creating a strategically stable Asia.

Differences remain, including over the development of India's nuclear and missile programs, and the pace of India's economic reforms. But while in the past these concerns may have dominated our thinking about India, today we start with a view of India as a growing world power with which we have common strategic interests. Through a strong partnership with India, we can best address any differences and shape a dynamic future.

The United States relationship with China is an important part of our strategy to promote a stable, peaceful, and prosperous Asia-Pacific region. We welcome the emergence of a strong, peaceful, and prosperous China. The democratic development of China is crucial to that future. Yet, a quarter century after beginning the process of shedding the worst features of the Communist legacy, China's leaders have not yet made the next series of fundamental choices about the character of their state. In pursuing advanced military capabilities that can threaten its neighbors in the Asia-Pacific region, China is following an outdated path that, in the end, will hamper its own pursuit of national greatness. In time, China will find that social and political freedom is the only source of that greatness.

The United States seeks a constructive relationship with a changing China. We already cooperate well where our interests overlap, including the current war on terrorism and in promoting stability on the Korean peninsula. Likewise, we have coordinated on the future of Afghanistan and have initiated a comprehensive dialogue on counterterrorism and similar transitional concerns. Shared health and environmental threats, such as the spread of HIV/AIDS, challenge us to promote jointly the welfare of our citizens.

Addressing these transnational threats will challenge China to become more open with information, promote the development of civil society, and enhance individual human rights. China has begun to take the road to political openness, permitting many personal freedoms and conducting village-level elections, yet remains strongly committed to national one-party rule by the Communist Party. To make that nation truly accountable to its citizen's needs and aspirations, however, much work remains to be done. Only by allowing the Chinese people to think, assemble, and worship freely can China reach its full potential.

Our important trade relationship will benefit from China's entry into the World Trade Organization, which will create more export opportunities and ultimately more jobs for American farmers, workers, and companies. China is our fourth largest trading partner, with over $100 billion in annual two-way trade. The power of market principles and the WTO's requirements for transparency and accountability will advance openness and the rule of law in China to help establish basic protections for commerce and for citizens. There are, however, other areas in which we have profound disagreements. Our commitment to the self-defense of Taiwan under the Taiwan Relations Act is one. Human rights is another. We expect China to adhere to its nonproliferation commitments. We will work to narrow differences where they exist, but not allow them to preclude cooperation where we agree.

The events of September 11, 2001, fundamentally changed the context for relations between the United States and other main centers of global power, and opened vast, new opportunities. With our long-standing allies in Europe and Asia, and with leaders in Russia, India, and China, we must develop active agendas of cooperation lest these relationships become routine and unproductive.

Every agency of the United States Government shares the challenge. We can build fruitful habits of consultation, quiet argument, sober analysis, and common action. In the long-term, these are the practices that will sustain the supremacy of our common principles and keep open the path of progress.

IX. TRANSFORM AMERICA'S NATIONAL SECURITY INSTITUTIONS TO MEET THE CHALLENGES AND OPPORTUNITIES OF THE TWENTY-FIRST CENTURY

"Terrorists attacked a symbol of American prosperity. They did not touch its source. America is successful because of the hard work, creativity, and enterprise of our people."

President Bush
Washington, D.C. (Joint Session of Congress)
September 20, 2001

The major institutions of American national security were designed in a different era to meet different requirements. All of them must be transformed.

It is time to reaffirm the essential role of American military strength. We must build and maintain our defenses beyond challenge. Our military's highest priority is to defend the United States. To do so effectively, our military must:

- assure our allies and friends;
- dissuade future military competition;
- deter threats against U.S. interests, allies, and friends; and
- decisively defeat any adversary if deterrence fails.

The unparalleled strength of the United States armed forces, and their forward presence, have maintained the peace in some of the world's most strategically vital regions. However, the threats and enemies we must confront have changed, and so must our forces. A military structured to deter massive Cold War-era armies must be transformed to focus more on how an adversary might fight rather than where and when a war might occur. We will channel our energies to overcome a host of operational challenges.

The presence of American forces overseas is one of the most profound symbols of the U.S. commitments to allies and friends. Through our willingness to use force in our own defense and in defense of others, the United States demonstrates its resolve to maintain a balance of power that favors freedom. To contend with uncertainty and to meet the many security challenges we face, the United States will require bases and stations within and beyond Western Europe and Northeast Asia, as well as temporary access arrangements for the long-distance deployment of U.S. forces.

Before the war in Afghanistan, that area was low on the list of major planning contingencies. Yet, in a very short time, we had to operate across the length and breadth of that remote nation, using every branch of the armed forces. We must prepare for more such deployments by developing assets such as advanced remote sensing, long-range precision strike capabilities, and transformed maneuver and expeditionary forces. This broad portfolio of military capabilities must also include the ability to defend the homeland, conduct information operations, ensure U.S. access to distant theaters, and protect critical U.S. infrastructure and assets in outer space.

Innovation within the armed forces will rest on experimentation with new approaches to warfare, strengthening joint operations, exploiting U.S. intelligence advantages, and taking full advantage of science and technology. We must also transform the way the Department of Defense is run, especially in financial management and recruitment and retention. Finally, while maintaining near-term readiness and the ability to fight the war on terrorism, the goal must be to provide the President with a wider range of military options to discourage aggression or any form of coercion against the United States, our allies, and our friends.

We know from history that deterrence can fail; and we know from experience that some enemies cannot be deterred. The United States must and will maintain the capability to defeat any attempt by an enemy—whether a state or non-state actor—to impose its will on the United States, our allies, or our friends. We will maintain the forces sufficient to support our obligations, and to defend freedom. Our forces will be strong enough to dissuade potential adversaries from pursuing a military build-up in hopes of surpassing, or equaling, the power of the United States.

Intelligence—and how we use it—is our first line of defense against terrorists and the threat posed by hostile states. Designed around the priority of gathering enormous information about a massive, fixed object—the Soviet bloc—the intelligence community is coping with the challenge of following a far more complex and elusive set of targets.

We must transform our intelligence capabilities and build new ones to keep pace with the nature of these threats. Intelligence must be appropriately integrated with our defense and law enforcement systems and coordinated with our allies and friends. We need to protect the capabilities we have so that we do not arm our enemies with the knowledge of how best to surprise us. Those who would harm us also seek the benefit of surprise to limit our prevention and response options and to maximize injury.

We must strengthen intelligence warning and analysis to provide integrated threat assessments for national and homeland security. Since the threats inspired by foreign governments and groups may be conducted inside the United States, we must also ensure the proper fusion of information between intelligence and law enforcement.

Initiatives in this area will include:

- strengthening the authority of the Director of Central Intelligence to lead the development and actions of the Nation's foreign intelligence capabilities;
- establishing a new framework for intelligence warning that provides seamless and integrated warning across the spectrum of threats facing the nation and our allies;
- continuing to develop new methods of collecting information to sustain our intelligence advantage;
- investing in future capabilities while working to protect them through a more vigorous effort to prevent the compromise of intelligence capabilities; and
- collecting intelligence against the terrorist danger across the government with allsource analysis.

As the United States Government relies on the armed forces to defend America's interests, it must rely on diplomacy to interact with other nations. We will ensure that the Department of State receives funding sufficient to ensure the success of American diplomacy. The State Department takes the lead in managing our bilateral relationships with other governments. And in this new era, its people and institutions must be able to interact equally adroitly with non-governmental organizations and international institutions. Officials trained mainly in international politics must also extend their reach to understand complex issues of domestic governance around the world, including public health, education, law enforcement, the judiciary, and public diplomacy.

Our diplomats serve at the front line of complex negotiations, civil wars, and other humanitarian catastrophes. As humanitarian relief requirements are better understood, we must also be able to help build police forces, court systems, and legal codes, local and provincial government institutions, and electoral systems. Effective international cooperation is needed to accomplish these goals, backed by American readiness to play our part.

Just as our diplomatic institutions must adapt so that we can reach out to others, we also need a different and more comprehensive approach to public information efforts that can help people around the world learn about and understand America. The war on terrorism is not a clash of civilizations. It does, however, reveal the clash inside a civilization, a battle for the future of the Muslim world. This is a struggle of ideas and this is an area where America must excel.

We will take the actions necessary to ensure that our efforts to meet our global security commitments and protect Americans are not impaired by the potential for investigations, inquiry, or prosecution by the International Criminal Court (ICC), whose jurisdiction does not extend to Americans and which we do not accept. We will work together with other nations to avoid complications in our military operations and cooperation, through such mechanisms as multilateral and bilateral agreements that will protect U.S. nationals from the ICC. We will implement fully the American Servicemembers Protection Act, whose provisions are intended to ensure and enhance the protection of U.S. personnel and officials.

We will make hard choices in the coming year and beyond to ensure the right level and allocation of government spending on national security. The United States Government must strengthen its defenses to win this war. At home, our most important priority is to protect the homeland for the American people.

Today, the distinction between domestic and foreign affairs is diminishing. In a globalized world, events beyond America's borders have a greater impact inside them. Our society must be open to people, ideas, and goods from across the globe. The characteristics we most cherish—our freedom, our cities, our systems of movement, and modern life—are vulnerable to terrorism. This vulnerability will persist long after we bring to justice those responsible for the September 11 attacks. As time passes, individuals may gain access to means of destruction that until now could be wielded only by armies, fleets, and squadrons. This is a new condition of life. We will adjust to it and thrive—in spite of it.

In exercising our leadership, we will respect the values, judgment, and interests of our friends and partners. Still, we will be prepared to act apart when our interests and unique responsibilities require. When we disagree on particulars, we will explain forthrightly the grounds for our concerns and strive to forge viable alternatives. We will not allow such disagreements to obscure our determination to secure together, with our allies and our friends, our shared fundamental interests and values.

Ultimately, the foundation of American strength is at home. It is in the skills of our people, the dynamism of our economy, and the resilience of our institutions. A diverse, modern society has inherent, ambitious, entrepreneurial energy. Our strength comes from what we do with that energy. That is where our national security begins.

STUDY AND DISCUSSION QUESTIONS

1. What rationale does the NSS provide for a new security and foreign policy doctrine?
2. How does the NSS link the requirements for security in the post–9/11 world to a hegemonic project?
3. What part of the NSS is likely to be most appealing to allies? Most worrisome?

21

A Grand Strategy of Transformation

John Lewis Gaddis

In this selection, John Lewis Gaddis argues that the national security strategy (NSS) issued in 2002—the first after the attacks of September 11, 2001—represents the most far-reaching changes in America's military and geopolitical strategy since the start of the Cold War. Gaddis argues that the NSS sets forth a grand strategy which is likely to remain controversial. He adds to the controversy by suggesting that the success of the doctrine, which Gaddis interprets as being more multilateral than do many, is likely to depend on the welcomes given it by allies (and perhaps also enemies) around the world.

According to Gaddis, the Bush strategy argues that preemption requires hegemony, a hegemony potentially rendered acceptable to other great powers because it is built on shared principles and designed to foster democracy. Gaddis applauds the candid language of the NSS, while noting that it does not include the not-so-hidden agenda articulated by President Bush in his January 2002 State of the Union Address, that America will bring to account the "axis of evil" (Iraq, Iran, and North Korea). Writing before the war in Iraq, Gaddis is exceptionally acute in explaining the rationale for Bush's assault on Saddam Hussein as well as the difficulties in executing the plan effectively. He concludes by warning that the NSS strategy is fraught with dangers, but right on target in confronting the high-risk post–9/11 security environment.

President George W. Bush's national security strategy could represent the most sweeping shift in U.S. grand strategy since the beginning of the Cold War. But its success depends on the willingness of the rest of the world to welcome U.S. power with open arms.

It's an interesting reflection on our democratic age that nations are now expected to publish their grand strategies before pursuing them. This practice would have surprised Metternich, Bismarck, and Lord Salisbury, though not Pericles. Concerned about not revealing too much, most great strategists in the past have preferred to concentrate on implementation, leaving explanation to historians. The first modern departure from this tradition came in 1947 when George F. Kennan revealed the rationale for containment in Foreign Affairs under the inadequately opaque pseudonym "Mr. X," but Kennan regretted the consequences and did not repeat the experiment. Not until the Nixon administration did official statements of national security strategy became routine. Despite his reputation for secrecy, Henry Kissinger's "State of the World" reports were remarkably candid and comprehensive—so much so that they were widely regarded at the time as a clever form of disinformation. They did, though, revive the Periclean precedent that in a democracy even grand strategy is a matter for public discussion.

That precedent became law with the Goldwater-Nichols Department of Defense Reorganization Act of 1986, which required the president to report regularly to Congress and the American people on national security strategy (NSS). The results since have been disappointing. The Reagan, Bush, and Clinton administrations all issued NSS reports, but these tended to be restatements of existing positions, cobbled together by committees, blandly worded, and quickly forgotten. None sparked significant public debate.

George W. Bush's report on "The National Security Strategy of the United States of America," released on September 17, 2002, has stirred controversy, though, and surely will continue to do so. For it's not only the first strategy statement of a new administration; it's also the first since the surprise attacks of September 11, 2001. Such attacks are fortunately rare in American history—the only analogies are the British burning of the White House and Capitol in 1814 and the Japanese attack on Pearl Harbor in 1941—but they have one thing in common: they prepare the way for new grand strategies by showing that old ones have failed. The Bush NSS, therefore, merits a careful reading as a guide to what's to come.

WHAT THE NSS SAYS

Beginnings, in such documents, tell you a lot. The Bush NSS, echoing the president's speech at West Point on June 1, 2002, sets three tasks: "We will defend the peace by fighting terrorists and tyrants. We will preserve the peace by building good relations among the great powers. We will extend the peace by encouraging free and open societies on every continent." It's worth comparing these goals with the three the Clinton administration put forth in its final NSS, released in December 1999: "To enhance America's security. To bolster America's economic prosperity. To promote democracy and human rights abroad."

The differences are revealing. The Bush objectives speak of defending, preserving, and extending peace; the Clinton statement seems simply to assume peace. Bush calls for cooperation among great powers; Clinton never uses that term. Bush specifies the encouragement of free and open societies on every continent; Clinton contents himself with "promoting" democracy and human rights "abroad." Even in these first few lines, then, the Bush NSS comes across as more forceful, more carefully crafted, and—unexpectedly—more multilateral than its immediate predecessor. It's a tip-off that there're interesting things going on here.

The first major innovation is Bush's equation of terrorists with tyrants as sources of danger, an obvious outgrowth of September 11. American strategy in the past, he notes, has concentrated on defense against tyrants. Those adversaries required "great armies and great industrial capabilities"—resources only states could provide—to threaten U.S. interests. But now, "shadowy networks of individuals can bring great chaos and suffering to our shores for less than it costs to purchase a single tank." The strategies that won the Cold War—containment and deterrence—won't work against such dangers, because those strategies assumed the existence of identifiable regimes led by identifiable leaders operating by identifiable means from identifiable territories. How, though, do you contain a shadow? How do you deter someone who's prepared to commit suicide?

There've always been anarchists, assassins, and saboteurs operating without obvious sponsors, and many of them have risked their lives in doing so. Their actions have rarely shaken the stability of states or societies, however, because the number of victims they've targeted and the amount of physical damage they've caused have been relatively small. September 11 showed that terrorists can now inflict levels of destruction that only states wielding military power used to be able to accomplish. Weapons of mass destruction were the last resort for those possessing them during the Cold War, the NSS points out. "Today, our enemies see weapons of mass destruction as weapons of choice." That elevates terrorists to the level of tyrants in Bush's thinking, and that's why he insists that preemption must be added to—though not necessarily in all situations replace—the tasks of containment and deterrence: "We cannot let our enemies strike first."

The NSS is careful to specify a legal basis for preemption: international law recognizes "that nations need not suffer an attack before they can lawfully take action to defend themselves against forces that present an imminent danger of attack." There's also a preference for preempting multilaterally: "The United States will constantly strive to enlist the support of the international community." But "we will not hesitate to act alone, if necessary, to exercise our right of self-defense by acting preemptively against such terrorists, to prevent them from doing harm against our people and our country."

Preemption in turn requires hegemony. Although Bush speaks, in his letter of transmittal, of creating "a balance of power that favors human freedom" while forsaking "unilateral advantage," the body of the NSS makes it clear that "our forces will be strong enough to dissuade potential adversaries from pursuing a military build-up in hopes of surpassing, or equaling, the power of the United States." The West Point speech put it more bluntly: "America has, and intends to keep, military strengths beyond challenge." The president has at last approved, therefore, Paul Wolfowitz's controversial recommendation to this effect, made in a 1992 "Defense Planning Guidance" draft subsequently leaked to the press and then disavowed by the first Bush administration. It's no accident that Wolfowitz, as deputy secretary of defense, has been at the center of the new Bush administration's strategic planning.

How, though, will the rest of the world respond to American hegemony? That gets us to another innovation in the Bush strategy, which is its emphasis on cooperation among the great powers. There's a striking contrast here with Clinton's focus on justice for small powers. The argument also seems at odds, at first glance, with maintaining military strength beyond challenge, for don't the weak always unite to oppose the strong? In theory, yes, but in practice and in history, not necessarily. Here the Bush team seems to have absorbed some pretty sophisticated political science, for one of the issues that discipline has been wrestling with recently is why there's still no anti-American coalition despite the overwhelming dominance of the United States since the end of the Cold War.

Bush suggested two explanations in his West Point speech, both of which most political scientists—not all—would find plausible. The first is that other great powers prefer management of the international system by a single hegemon as long as it's a relatively benign one. When there's only one superpower, there's no point for anyone else to try to compete with it in military capabilities. International conflict shifts to trade rivalries and other relatively minor quarrels, none of them worth fighting about. Compared with what great powers have done to one another in the past, this state of affairs is no bad thing.

U.S. hegemony is also acceptable because it's linked with certain values that all states and cultures—if not all terrorists and tyrants—share. As the NSS puts it: "No people on earth yearn, to be oppressed, aspire to servitude, or eagerly await the midnight knock of the secret police." It's this association of power with universal principles, Bush argues, that will cause other great powers to go along with whatever the United States has to do to preempt terrorists and tyrants, even if it does so alone. For, as was the case through most of the Cold War, there's something worse out there than American hegemony.

The final innovation in the Bush strategy deals with the longer term issue of removing the causes of terrorism and tyranny. Here, again, the president's thinking parallels an emerging consensus within the academic community. For it's becoming clear now that poverty wasn't what caused a group of middleclass and reasonably well-educated Middle Easterners to fly three airplanes into buildings and another into the ground. It was, rather, resentments growing out of the absence of representative institutions in their own societies, so that the only outlet for political dissidence was religious fanaticism.

Hence, Bush insists, the ultimate goal of U.S. strategy must be to spread democracy everywhere. The United States must finish the job that Woodrow Wilson started. The world, quite literally, must be made safe for democracy, even those parts of it, like the Middle East, that have so far resisted that tendency. Terrorism—and by implication the authoritarianism that breeds it—must become as obsolete as slavery, piracy, or genocide: "behavior that no respectable government can condone or support and that all must oppose."

The Bush NSS, therefore, differs in several ways from its recent predecessors. First, it's proactive. It rejects the Clinton administration's assumption that since the movement toward democracy and market economics had become irreversible in the post–Cold War era, all the United States had to do was "engage" with the rest of the world to "enlarge" those processes. Second, its parts for the most part interconnect. There's a coherence in the Bush strategy that the Clinton national security team—notable for its simultaneous cultivation and humiliation of Russia—never achieved. Third, Bush's analysis of how hegemony works and what causes terrorism is in tune with serious academic thinking, despite the fact that many academics haven't noticed this yet. Fourth, the Bush administration, unlike several of its predecessors, sees no contradiction between power and principles. It is, in this sense, thoroughly Wilsonian. Finally, the new strategy is candid. This administration speaks plainly, at times eloquently, with no attempt to be polite or diplomatic or "nuanced." What you hear and what you read is pretty much what you can expect to get.

WHAT THE NSS DOESN'T SAY

There are, however, some things that you won't hear or read, probably by design. The Bush NSS has, if not a hidden agenda, then at least one the administration isn't advertising. It has to do with why the administration regards tyrants, in the post–September 11 world, as at least as dangerous as terrorists.

Bush tried to explain the connection in his January 2002 State of the Union address when he warned of an "axis of evil" made up of Iraq, Iran, and North Korea. The phrase confused more than it clarified, though, since Saddam Hussein, the Iranian mullahs, and Kim Jong Il are hardly the only tyrants around, nor are their ties to one another evident. Nor was it clear why containment and deterrence would not work against these tyrants, since they're all more into survival than suicide. Their lifestyles tend more toward palaces than caves.

Both the West Point speech and the NSS are silent on the "axis of evil." The phrase, it now appears, reflected overzealous speechwriting rather than careful thought. It was an ill-advised effort to make the president sound, simultaneously, like Franklin D. Roosevelt and Ronald Reagan, and it's now been given a quiet burial. This administration corrects its errors, even if it doesn't admit them.

That, though, raises a more important question: Why, having buried the "axis of evil," is Bush still so keen on burying Saddam Hussein? Especially since the effort to do so might provoke him into using the weapons of last resort that he's so far not used? It patronizes the administration to seek explanations in filial obligation. Despite his comment that this is "a guy that tried to kill my dad," George W. Bush is no Hamlet, agonizing over how to meet a tormented parental ghost's demands for revenge. Shakespeare might still help, though, if you shift the analogy to Henry V. That monarch understood the psychological value of victory—of defeating an adversary sufficiently thoroughly that you shatter the confidence of others, so that they'll roll over themselves before you have to roll over them.

For Henry, the demonstration was Agincourt, the famous victory over the French in 1415. The Bush administration got a taste of Agincourt with its victory over the Taliban at the end of 2001, to which the Afghans responded by gleefully shaving their beards, shedding their burkas, and cheering the infidels—even to the point of lending them horses from which they laser-marked bomb targets. Suddenly, it seemed, American values were transportable, even to the remotest and most alien parts of the earth. The vision that opened up was not one of the clash among civilizations we'd been led to expect, but rather, as the NSS puts it, a clash "inside a civilization, a battle for the future of the Muslim world."

How, though, to maintain the momentum, given that the Taliban is no more and that al Qaeda isn't likely to present itself as a conspicuous target? This, I think, is where Saddam Hussein comes in: Iraq is the most feasible place where we can strike the next blow. If we can topple this tyrant, if we can repeat the Afghan Agincourt on the banks of the Euphrates, then we can accomplish a great deal. We can complete the task the Gulf War left unfinished. We can destroy whatever weapons of mass destruction Saddam Hussein may have accumulated since. We can end whatever support he's providing for terrorists elsewhere, notably those who act against Israel. We can liberate the Iraqi people. We can ensure an ample supply of inexpensive oil. We can set in motion a process that could undermine and ultimately remove reactionary regimes elsewhere in the Middle East, thereby eliminating the principal breeding ground for terrorism. And, as President Bush did say publicly in a powerful speech to the United Nations on September 12, 2002, we can save that organization from the irrelevance into which it will otherwise descend if its resolutions continue to be contemptuously disregarded.

If I'm right about this, then it's a truly grand strategy. What appears at first glance to be a lack of clarity about who's deterrable and who's not turns out, upon closer examination, to be a plan for transforming the entire Muslim Middle East: for bringing it, once and for all, into the modern world. There's been nothing like this in boldness, sweep, and vision since Americans took it upon themselves, more than half a century ago, to democratize Germany and Japan, thus setting in motion processes that stopped short of only a few places on earth, one of which was the Muslim Middle East.

CAN IT WORK?

The honest answer is that no one knows. We've had examples in the past of carefully crafted strategies failing: most conspicuously, the Nixon-Kissinger attempt, during the early 1970s, to bring the Soviet Union within the international system of satisfied states. We've had examples of carelessly improvised strategies succeeding: The Clinton administration accomplished this feat in Kosovo in 1999. The greatest theorist of strategy, Carl von Clausewitz, repeatedly emphasized the role of chance, which can at times defeat the best of designs and at other times hand victory to the worst of them. For this reason, he insisted, theory can never really predict what's going to happen.

Does this mean, though, that there's nothing we can say? That all we can do is cross our fingers, hope for the best, and wait for the historians to tell us why whatever happened was bound to happen? I don't think so, for reasons that relate, rather mundanely, to transportation. Before airplanes take off—and, these days, before trains leave their terminals—the mechanics responsible for them look for cracks, whether in the wings, the tail, the landing gear, or on the Acela the yaw dampers. These reveal the stresses produced while moving the vehicle from where it is to where it needs to go. If undetected, they can lead to disaster. That's why inspections—checking for cracks—are routine in the transportation business. I wonder if they ought not to be in the strategy business as well. The potential stresses I see in the Bush grand strategy—the possible sources of cracks—are as follows:

Multitasking Critics as unaccustomed to agreeing with one another as Brent Scowcroft and Al Gore have warned against diversion from the war on terrorism if the United States takes on Saddam Hussein. The principle involved here—deal with one enemy at a time—is a sound one. But plenty of successful strategies have violated it. An obvious example is Roosevelt's decision to fight simultaneous wars against Germany and Japan between 1941 and 1945. Another is Kennan's strategy of containment, which worked by deterring the Soviet Union while reviving democracy and capitalism in Western Europe and Japan. The explanation, in both instances, was that these were wars on different fronts against the same enemy: authoritarianism and the conditions that produced it.

The Bush administration sees its war against terrorists and tyrants in much the same way. The problem is not that Saddam Hussein is actively supporting al Qaeda, however much the Bush team would like to prove that. It's rather that authoritarian regimes throughout the Middle East support terrorism indirectly by continuing to produce generations of underemployed, unrepresented, and therefore radicalizable young people from whom Osama bin Laden and others like him draw their recruits.

Bush has, to be sure, enlisted authoritarian allies in his war against terrorism—for the moment. So did Roosevelt when he welcomed the Soviet Union's help in the war against Nazi Germany and imperial Japan. But the Bush strategy has long-term as well as immediate implications, and these do not assume indefinite reliance on regimes like those that currently run Saudi Arabia, Egypt, and Pakistan. Reliance on Yasir Arafat has already ended.

The welcome These plans depend critically, however, on our being welcomed in Baghdad if we invade, as we were in Kabul. If we aren't, the whole strategy collapses, because it's premised on the belief that ordinary Iraqis will prefer an American occupation over the current conditions in which they live. There's no evidence that the Bush administration is planning the kind of military commitments the United States made in either of the two world wars, or even in Korea and Vietnam. This strategy relies on getting cheered, not shot at.

Who's to say, for certain, that this will or won't happen? A year ago, Afghanistan seemed the least likely place in which invaders could expect cheers, and yet they got them. It would be foolish to conclude from this experience, though, that it will occur everywhere. John F. Kennedy learned that lesson when, recalling successful interventions in Iran and Guatemala, he authorized the failed Bay of Pigs landings in Cuba. The trouble with Agincourts—even those that happen in Afghanistan—is the arrogance they can encourage, along with the illusion that victory itself is enough and that no follow-up is required. It's worth remembering that, despite Henry V, the French never became English.

Maintaining the moral high ground It's difficult to quantify the importance of this, but why should we need to? Just war theory has been around since St. Augustine. Our own Declaration of Independence invoked a decent respect for the opinions of humankind. Richard Overy's fine history of World War II devotes an entire chapter to the Allies' triumph in what he calls "the moral contest." Kennedy rejected a surprise attack against Soviet missiles in Cuba because he feared losing the moral advantage: Pearl Harbor analogies were enough to sink plans for preemption in a much more dangerous crisis than Americans face now. The Bush NSS acknowledges the multiplier effects of multilateralism: "no nation can build a safer, better world alone." These can hardly be gained though unilateral action unless that action itself commands multilateral support.

The Bush team assumes we'll have the moral high ground, and hence multilateral support, if we're cheered and not shot at when we go into Baghdad and other similar places. No doubt they're right about that. They're seeking U.N. authorization for such a move and may well get it. Certainly, they'll have the consent of the U.S. Congress. For there lies behind their strategy an incontestable moral claim: that in some situations preemption is preferable to doing nothing. Who would not have preempted Hitler or Milosevic or Mohammed Atta, if given the chance?

Will Iraq seem such a situation, though, if we're not cheered in Baghdad? Can we count on multilateral support if things go badly? Here the Bush administration has not been thinking ahead. It's been dividing its own moral multipliers though its tendency to behave, on an array of multilateral issues ranging from the Kyoto Protocol to the Comprehensive Test Ban Treaty to the International Criminal Court, like a sullen, pouting, oblivious, and overmuscled teenager. As a result, it's depleted the reservoir of support from allies it ought to have in place before embarking on such a high-risk strategy.

There are, to be sure, valid objections to these and other initiatives the administration doesn't like. But it's made too few efforts to use diplomacy—by which I mean tact—to express these complaints. Nor has it tried to change a domestic political culture that too often relishes having the United States stand defiantly alone. The Truman administration understood that the success of containment abroad required countering isolationism at home. The Bush administration hasn't yet made that connection between domestic politics and grand strategy. That's its biggest failure of leadership so far.

The Bush strategy depends ultimately on not standing defiantly alone—just the opposite, indeed, for it claims to be pursuing values that, as the NSS puts it, are "true for every person, in every society." So this crack especially needs fixing before this vehicle departs for its intended destination. A nation that sets itself up as an example to the world in most things will not achieve that purpose by telling the rest of the world, in some things, to shove it.

WHAT IT MEANS

Despite these problems, the Bush strategy is right on target with respect to the new circumstances confronting the United States and its allies in the wake of September 11. It was sufficient, throughout the Cold War, to contain without seeking to reform authoritarian regimes: we left it to the Soviet Union to reform itself. The most important conclusion of the Bush NSS is that this Cold War assumption no longer holds. The intersection of radicalism with technology the world witnessed on that terrible morning means that the persistence of authoritarianism anywhere can breed resentments that can provoke terrorism that can do us grievous harm. There is a compellingly realistic reason now to complete the idealistic task Woodrow Wilson began more than eight decades ago: the world must be made safe for democracy, because otherwise democracy will not be safe in the world.

The Bush NSS report could be, therefore, the most important reformulation of U.S. grand strategy in over half a century. The risks are great—though probably no more than those confronting the architects of containment as the Cold War began. The pitfalls are plentiful—there are cracks to attend to before this vehicle departs for its intended destination. There's certainly no guarantee of success—but as Clausewitz would have pointed out, there never is in anything that's worth doing.

We'll probably never know for sure what bin Laden and his gang hoped to achieve with the horrors they perpetrated on September 11, 2001. One thing seems clear though: it can hardly have been to produce this document, and the new grand strategy of transformation that is contained within it.

STUDY AND DISCUSSION QUESTIONS

1. Why does Gaddis consider the NSS a grand transformation of American geopolitical and military strategy?
2. What are the most innovative aspects of the Bush security doctrine?
3. How—by what it says and what it leaves unsaid—does the NSS provide the rationale for the war in Iraq and for the potential use of force against Iran and North Korea?

22

Self-Defense in an Imperfect World

Chris Brown

In a world in which absolute security is unattainable and security threats are all too common, what rules should govern the right to preemptive use of force enshrined in the new national security strategy (NSS) of the United States? This selection, which was written by LSE international relations professor Chris Brown as a contribution to the pre-war debate about regime change in Iraq, examines the distinction between preemptive and preventive use of force and the validity of regime change without Security Council authorization.

As Brown explains, we have to reckon with a world in which global institutions for governance and security are seldom effective or legitimate (and almost never both at the same time)—and yet predatory states and those that harbor terror networks must be deterred. Under these circumstances, argues Brown, nonpredatory states may have to act unilaterally or outside the official institutional structure of the United Nations charter system, which he would like to see reformed and strengthened.

But in a radically imperfect world where the instinctive response to security threats is national as are the military delivery systems and where the rule of law is held hostage to great power politics, the opportunities for reform, although present, are limited. In this context, Brown argues that states should nonetheless behave to the extent possible in a way that would produce more effective institutions. They should also pay far greater attention to the rights of individuals as distinct from the rights of states.

In his address at West Point on June 1, 2002, President George W. Bush appeared to be signaling America's willingness to regard the mere possession of weapons of mass destruction (WMD) by potential enemies as grounds for an anticipatory war.[1] Historically, however, a clear distinction has been drawn between preemptive and preventive, or anticipatory, war, with the latter regarded as illegitimate. The National Security Strategy announced by the president on September 20, 2002, was more conventional in its approach to preemption, but doubts remain as to whether the old distinction can be preserved. And this discussion is taking place in the context of a specific problem, namely the apparent desire of Iraq to obtain WMD and the determination of the United States, and, less clearly expressed, the UN Security Council, to prevent this from happening.[2] At the time of writing (November 2002) this matter remains unresolved, but preemption has not received the attention it deserves. It is not only the United States that may engage in preemptive action; the possibility exists in other parts of the world and with respect to other conflicts, most noticeably on the Indo-Pakistani border.

The distinction between preemption and prevention is made by reference to the notion of an immediate threat.[3] States, it is presumed, do not have an unqualified right to use force in international relations, but they do have the right to defend themselves—a right established in customary international law and reaffirmed in the UN Charter—and, crucially, are under no obligation to allow an aggressor to strike first. The right to preempt is thus an extension of the right of self-defense, if, and only if, it is indisputably the case that there is an imminent threat of an unprovoked aggression.

Prevention, on the other hand, involves action in response to some putative future rather than immediate threat and is not legitimate. The assumption is that states have other ways of responding to such potential threats, and the presumption against being the first to use force, which is enshrined in the UN Charter and based on agreements such as the 1928 Kellogg-Briand Pact and the 1945 Charter of the International Military Tribunal at Nuremberg, applies. Less often expressed, but equally compelling, is that in a world environment that is by its very nature insecure, a strategy of meeting all possible future threats is simply not viable; sufficient unto the day is the evil thereof.[4]

THE IDEAL DISTINCTION

To illustrate the distinction between preemption and prevention, Israel's strike against the Egyptian air force that began the Six Day War of 1967 was accepted by many to have been a preemptive act because, it is said, the Israelis had good reason to believe they were about to be subjected to an attack that might have been fatal had the enemy been allowed to strike first. Alternatively, it might be argued that the closure of the Straits of Tiran might have been seen as tantamount to a declaration of war against Israel.[5] On the other hand, the Israeli strike on the Iraqi reactor at Osirak in 1981 was widely seen as not meeting the criteria for a legitimate act of preemption. The reactor was in the process of construction and could not be seen as an immediate threat.[6] Both these judgments could, of course, be contested, but, in any case, the distinction aimed at is clearly visible.

From this distinction some obvious problems arise of both a prudential and a normative nature. How can states really know that an attack is imminent? How certain do they have to be before they may properly act? Are they obliged to justify their risk assessment, and if so, to whom? These are good questions, but they rest upon some unspoken assumptions about the way the world works. They assume that a quite strong domestic analogy holds, and that a state's exercise of its right to self-defense can be judged in much the same way that the violent behavior of an individual might be judged in a domestic dispute, in which self-defense is usually qualified in terms of the nature of the threat and appropriateness of the response. This domestic analogy in turn rests upon a particular and contestable reading of the current state of international law and organization.

Suppose we lived in a world with a fully developed legal framework governing the use of force in international relations and outlawing its use as an instrument of foreign policy, and in which there were an international body charged with the maintenance of peace and security that possessed legitimate and effective decision-making procedures and the capacity to enforce its judgments. In such a world, the distinction between preemption and prevention would be clear-cut and of critical importance. Preventive war would be totally illegitimate because if one state believed that developments in another might threaten its security, it could refer the matter to the international body, where it would be investigated and dealt with appropriately. On the other hand, the possibility of the legitimate preemptive use of force remains as a theoretical concomitant of the residual right of self-defense. If a surprise attack were genuinely imminent and certain, and if there were insufficient time to refer the matter to the world body, since states are entitled to defend themselves, a state would be under no obligation to allow the aggressor to strike first. Given the assumptions made above, this is an unlikely scenario, but it would not be impossible.

The problem is that we do not live in this world. There is indeed an international legal order governing the use of force and a body charged with the maintenance of international peace and security, but the legal order is radically imperfect, as is the United Nations. Moreover, within the actual contemporary system states differ radically in terms of power, their commitment to the rule of law domestically and internationally, and in the responsibility and accountability of their governments.

International law condemns acts of aggression, but there is no court or other body with the power to rule on all disputes, and no international police force to preserve law and order. The UN Security Council is charged with the maintenance of international peace and security, but the veto power of the five permanent members means that even a wide consensus on a particular problem may not lead to action. The structure of the UN General Assembly is equally undemocratic, although in a somewhat different direction. The one state, one vote rule in the General Assembly allows a two-thirds majority to be constructed out of well under 10 percent of the world's population. Moreover, many, perhaps a majority of, UN members do not have democratic internal decision-making structures, and the elites who control their UN votes may well be motivated by concerns that have nothing to do with the issue at hand. Usually the rich and powerful are able to buy votes without too much difficulty. Sadly, there is no reason to think that anyone—the P-5, the nonpermanent members of the Security Council, or the members of the General Assembly—is likely to approach matters of peace and security in a fair-minded way. Partly for this reason, when resolutions are actually passed they are quite frequently ignored, especially if they go against the interests of the rich and powerful.

What all this means is that whereas there is a legal order that makes a clear distinction between preemption and prevention, unfortunately there can be no guarantee that the ideal substitute for preventive war—effective action by a legitimate international body—can be achieved. Here we approach the heart of the problem: In an imperfect world, how should states act with respect to potential threats to their security?

THE CHIMERA OF ABSOLUTE SECURITY

In the absence of an ideal international political framework that could restrain states in all but those few cases in which a preemptive attack was truly necessary, three propositions should guide the preemptive use of force. First, it might be assumed that it would be good to live in a world with an effective legal order and effective and legitimate global institutions, where the kind of existential insecurity of the present world no longer existed. Second, since this is not the case, it would be unwise and imprudent for states to behave as if it were. Given that there are some predatory states, and that it cannot be assumed that the existing international institutional structure is capable of handling the problems they pose, it may sometimes be necessary for nonpredatory states to act unilaterally or outside the official institutional structure. Third, states should, as far as possible, try to act in such a way that they encourage the transformation of the world into one in which effective institutions do exist, or at a minimum do not make such a transformation more difficult.

States have a strong self-interest in preserving a clear distinction between preemption and prevention and in making it clear that the latter is rejected as a national strategy. Based on the above propositions, states should not allow themselves to pursue the chimera of absolute security. The fact that a state might pose a threat in the foreseeable future should be seen as a reason to construct defenses against it, to pursue a containment strategy, because to attempt instead to eliminate all such threats is to commit to an endless series of wars to end all wars. States should as far as possible involve the United Nations and other institutional structures in the process of containment, although it must be acknowledged that sometimes this will be impossible. In the same vein, states must be aware of the possibility of a sudden act of aggression on the part of predatory states and must be prepared to react in such circumstances. Reaction in this case could involve preemption if the information that an attack is imminent is sufficiently reliable. States cannot, in the last resort, delegate the task of deciding on the reliability of this information to some other body. If a state has reasonable grounds for believing itself to be in danger of being the victim of aggression, it has the right to act in self-defense. This right would be strengthened if the state in question had rejected prevention as a general strategy because cases in which preemptive action was genuinely necessary would then be less likely to be misinterpreted.

In the extreme, states cannot be expected to delegate to others the decision of whether sufficient grounds exist to justify preemption, but they should be obliged to explain their reasoning in public and to seek wide approval for their actions. However imperfect the existing institutional structure may be, it is the only one there is, and there is no possibility that it will become more effective if it is ignored in a crisis or treated with contempt by those who have the power to act alone. What is important in this context is not the formal legal implication of particular votes, but the search for approval and consent. For example, the fact that NATO was unable to achieve a UN Security Council resolution endorsing its action in Kosovo in 1999 is perhaps less significant than the fact that a motion condemning its actions was defeated by twelve votes to three, the twelve including countries such as Malaysia and Argentina, on whose support NATO cannot always rely. The veto power of Russia and China prevented a positive vote, but NATO was able, nonetheless, to claim a degree of legitimacy for its action.[7] A technically positive vote by the UN Security Council may be no more important than the political legitimacy that stems from a more general sense of approval for one's actions. Legitimacy should be an issue. It is best if states behave prudently, and in extreme circumstances they will act as judges in their own cause. But they must justify themselves to the wider world through all available channels.

HUMANITARIAN INTERVENTION

How does this translate into a consideration of potential action against Iraq? By the time this article appears it is likely to have been overtaken by events, but the principles that apply can still be set down. As of now, the United States and the United Kingdom have presented ample evidence that the current Iraqi regime poses a serious threat to the security of the region, its own people, and thus, indirectly, the world. Twice in the last quarter century Saddam Hussein has launched unprovoked acts of aggression against his neighbors, and well over a million people have died as a result. Should Iraq come into possession of serious stocks of WMD the possibility of another such act of aggression is quite high, as is the possibility that such stocks could be transferred to third parties. The world should respond to this potential danger, as the UN Security Council has recognized in Resolution 1441. What is less clear is that the present strategy of containment has failed. If it is accepted that insecurity is an inherent feature of the current international order, and that the search for total security is chimerical, then good reasons are required to reject the policy of containment in favor of immediate action. So far such reasons have not been provided.

There is, however, one argument that is not usually employed by those who wish to see preemptive action but which is quite compelling. Even though it is probably not the case that the often-quoted figure of half a million Iraqi children killed by sanctions is anywhere near accurate—all such figures come ultimately from the Iraqi regime, even if they are given credence by other bodies—and although the responsibility for civilian suffering can be laid at the door of the Iraqi regime itself rather than at that of the United Nations, the main victims of containment have been innocent Iraqis and not the regime itself.[8] Nonmilitary sanctions almost always involve attacking the interests and sometimes the lives of "soft" targets—women, children, civilians—and policies of containment that rely on them are morally suspect. The fact that such sanctions are so often regarded as morally superior to acts of violence that target the regime itself and its military defenders is a striking commentary on the inability of many progressively minded Westerners to think clearly on this subject. That the innocent are suffering is usually presented by the antiwar movement as a reason for abandoning the sanctions regime on which containment is based, but it can equally, and much more sensibly, be seen to provide the best available justification for moving away from containment and employing force to bring about a change in the Iraqi regime.

An overthrow in this case would involve a particular kind of humanitarian intervention, and the politics and ethics of humanitarian intervention are rarely seen in the same context as discussions of preemptive war. In both cases preemption is involved, but on a different moral basis. Normally, preemption is discussed in the context of a potential act of aggression, that is, an immediate threat to state sovereignty, the assumption being that the territorial integrity and political independence of the sovereign state are the supreme values protected by any international order. However, for the last fifty years such sovereignty norms have been accompanied by a growing body of norms that challenges the right of sovereign states to do whatever they like to their own people, summarized by the idea of universal human rights.[9] This development should change the nature of the discussion. Just as preemptive action may sometimes be necessary to protect state sovereignty, so military action is sometimes required to protect a people from their sovereign. If a legitimate policy of containment designed to prevent aggression has the unintended consequence of imposing great suffering on the innocent Iraqi people—suffering the regime has done nothing to alleviate and may be promoting for propaganda reasons—that may provide a reason for moving to a more active policy.

There are prudential issues involved here and the costs of carrying out a forcible change of the regime may rule out action in this or similar cases, in the same way that a policy of anticipatory war to prevent the development of WMD might prove unviable. The point of raising a forcible change of regime in this context is not to advocate a humanitarian intervention but to widen the range of considerations that ought to be addressed and to challenge the compartmentalization that leads to the isolation and privileging of the rights and interests of sovereign states. In any practical case in which preemptive or anticipatory action is proposed, the rights and interests of individuals ought to enter into the equation, and it cannot be assumed that these rights are subsumed by the rights of states.

Notes

[1]"Remarks by the President at the 2002 Graduation Exercise of the United States Military Academy," June 1, 2002; available at www.whitehouse.gov/news/releases/2002/06/20020601-3.html.

[2]"The National Security Strategy of the United States of America September 2002"; available at www.whitehouse.gov/nsc/nss.pdf. (See selection 20 in this volume).

[3]Michael Walzer, *Just and Unjust Wars,* 2nd ed. (New York: Basic Books, 1992), presents this distinction with great clarity.

[4]See David C. Hendrickson, "Towards Universal Empire: The Dangerous Quest for Absolute Security," *World Policy Journal* (Fall 2002), pp. 1–10.

[5]For a judicious recent discussion, see Michael Oren, *Six Days of War: June 1967 and the Making of the Modern Middle East* (New York: Oxford University Press, 2002).

[6]See the strong condemnation contained in UN Security Council Resolution 487, June 19, 1981.

[7]There is a large literature on the Kosovo case. See, e.g., Ken Booth, ed., *The Kosovo Tragedy: The Human Rights Dimensions* (London: Frank Cass, 2000).

[8]See Robert Fisk, "The Dishonesty of This So-Called Dossier," Independent, September 25, 2002, for an uncritical presentation of the charge that "we" have killed half a million Iraqi children; available at www.commondreams.org/views02/0925-03.htm. The British government has vigorously contested this interpretation. See, e.g., Tony Blair, "Prime Minister's Iraq Statement to Parliament," September 24, 2002; available at www.number-10.gov.uk/output/Page5.asp.

[9]For a general discussion of this issue, see Chris Brown, *Sovereignty, Rights and Justice* (Cambridge: Polity Press, 2002).

STUDY AND DISCUSSION QUESTIONS

1. What is the distinction Brown develops between preemption and prevention?
2. In a world dominated by great power politics and weak international institutions, what conduct does Brown urge generally in the face of predatory action by states?
3. How convincing is his argument that military action is sometimes required to "protect a people from their sovereign"?

23

The Responsibility to Protect: The Way Forward

International Commission on Intervention and State Sovereignty

Since the 1990s, a widening circle of international non-governmental organizations, member states, and the last three Secretaries-General have argued that a mandate to intervene in the face of gross human rights violations should trump the sovereign rights of a state to assert exclusive jurisdiction and control over anything that occurs inside its borders. In cases such as the Rwandan genocide or the ethnic cleansing in Bosnia, the United Nations was criticized for doing too little, too late, not for doing too much.

For much of his term as Secretary-General Kofi Annan has labored to achieve a consensus in favor of a set of principles that would govern humanitarian intervention—and would, at the same time, enhance the authority of the Security Council by reversing the trend toward enforcement through coalitions of the willing and thereby revitalize direct Security Council control over the use of force. This would be no mean feat, since the debate over humanitarian intervention is fierce and unrelenting, pitting progressive advocates of human rights who come disproportionately from the North (the likely interveners) against the stalwart defenders of state sovereignty who come disproportionately from the South (the likely targets of humanitarian intervention).

Against this backdrop, the International Commission on Intervention and State Sovereignty (ICISS), sponsored by the Canadian government and reporting to the Secretary-General in December 2001, represents a landmark effort to reconceptualize the terrain of humanitarian intervention and break this deadlock. The report was influential in devising a new conceptual framework—the "responsibility to protect"—which has helped advance a productive debate that hopes to transcend North/South divisions. If the responsibility of states to protect their citizens is not met, then that responsibility (in accordance with strictly specified criteria) is transferred to the international community, which then

*has the duty to act. This selection, an excerpt from the ICISS Report,
summarizes the key findings of the Commission and presents an action
program for implementing the responsibility to protect.*

FROM ANALYSIS TO ACTION

This report has been about compelling human need, about populations at risk of slaughter, ethnic cleansing and starvation. It has been about the responsibility of sovereign states to protect their own people from such harm—and about the need for the larger international community to exercise that responsibility if states are unwilling or unable to do so themselves.

Past debates on intervention have tended to proceed as if intervention and state sovereignty were inherently contradictory and irreconcilable concepts—with support for one necessarily coming at the expense of the other. But in the course of our consultations this Commission has found less tension between these principles than we expected. We found broad willingness to accept the idea that the responsibility to protect its people from killing and other grave harm was the most basic and fundamental of all the responsibilities that sovereignty imposes—and that if a state cannot or will not protect its people from such harm, then coercive intervention for human protection purposes, including ultimately military intervention, by others in the international community may be warranted in extreme cases. We found broad support, in other words, for the core principle identified in this report, the idea of the responsibility to protect.

The most strongly expressed concerns that the Commission did hear in the course of our year-long consultations around the world went essentially to the political and operational consequences of reconciling the principle of shared responsibility with that of non-intervention. These concerns were of three different kinds. They might be described, respectively, as concerns about process, about priorities, and about delivery, with a cross-cutting concern about competent assessment of the need to act.

As to *process,* the main concern was to ensure that when protective action is taken, and in particular when there is military intervention for human protection purposes, it is undertaken in a way that reinforces the collective responsibility of the international community to address such issues, rather than allowing opportunities and excuses for unilateral action. The Commission has sought to address these concerns by focusing, above all, on the central role and responsibility of the United Nations Security Council to take whatever action is needed. We have made some suggestions as to what should happen if the Security Council will not act but the task, as we have seen it, has been not to find alternatives to the Security Council as a source of authority, but to make it work much better than it has.

As to *priorities*, the main concern was that attention in past debates and policy making had focused overwhelmingly on reaction to catastrophe—and in particular reaction by military intervention—rather than trying to ensure that the catastrophe did not happen in the first place. The Commission has tried to redress this imbalance by emphasizing over and again the integral importance of prevention in the intervention debate, and also by pointing out the need for a major focus on post-conflict peace building issues whenever military intervention is undertaken. We have argued that the responsibility to protect embraces not only the responsibility to react, but the responsibility to prevent, and the responsibility to rebuild.

As to *delivery*, we found the most widespread concern of all. There were too many occasions during the last decade when the Security Council, faced with conscience-shocking situations, failed to respond as it should have with timely authorization and support. And events during the 1990s demonstrated on too many occasions that even a decision by the Security Council to authorize international action to address situations of grave humanitarian concern was no guarantee that any action would be taken, or taken effectively. The Commission has been conscious of the need to get operational responses right, and part of our report has been devoted to identifying the principles and rules that should govern military interventions for human protection purposes.

But it is even more important to get the necessary political commitment right, and this is the issue on which we focus in this chapter. It remains the case that unless the political will can be mustered to act when action is called for, the debate about intervention for human protection purposes will largely be academic. The most compelling task now is to work to ensure that when the call goes out to the community of states for action, that call will be answered. There must never again be mass killing or ethnic cleansing. There must be no more Rwandas.

MOBILIZING DOMESTIC POLITICAL WILL

The key to mobilizing international support is to mobilize domestic support, or at least neutralize domestic opposition. How an issue will play at home—what support or opposition there will be for a particular intervention decision, given the significant human costs and financial costs that may be involved, and the domestic resources that may need to be reallocated—is always a factor in international decision making, although the extent to which the domestic factor comes into play does, however, vary considerably, country by country and case by case.

Contextual factors like size and power, geography, and the nature of the political institutions and culture of the country concerned are all important in this respect. Some countries are just more instinctively internationalist, and more reflexively inclined to respond to pleas for multilateral cooperation, than others: really major powers tend never to be as interested in multilateralism as middle powers and small powers, because they don't think they have to be. Geographic proximity comes into play, simply because what happens nearby is more likely to endanger nationals, to raise significant security concerns, and to result in refugees, economic disruptions and unwanted political spillovers—and to capture media attention and generate demands for action accordingly. By contrast, cultural affinity can mean particular concern for the plight of co-religionists, or fellow language speakers, even in small countries far away. Again, an extremely inward-looking political culture, by contrast, can find it hard to accommodate any external supporting role; many political systems disproportionately reward political actors whose focus and commitments are wholly domestic in character, leaving quite isolated those willing to stand up for international engagement.

Particular caution is also routinely to be expected from those countries in possession of the military, police, economic and other assets that are most in demand in implementing intervention mandates. Given the magnitude of continuing operations in the Balkans (more than 50,000 troops), as well as the shrinking military budgets of most countries in the post–Cold War era, there are real constraints on how much spare capacity exists to take on additional burdens. UN peacekeeping may have peaked in 1993 at 78,000 troops. But today, if both NATO and UN missions are included, the number of soldiers in international peace operations has soared by about 40 per cent to 108,000. Even states willing in principle to look at new foreign military commitments are being compelled to make choices about how to use limited and strained military capabilities.

In mobilizing political support for intervention for human protection purposes, as for anything else, a great deal comes down to the leadership of key individuals and organizations. Someone, somewhere has to pick up the case and run with it. Political leaders are crucial in this respect, but they are not the only actors: they are, for the most part, acutely responsive to the demands and pressures placed upon them by their various political constituencies, and the domestic media, and they are much influenced by what is put to them by their own bureaucracies. NGOs have a crucial and ever increasing role, in turn, in contributing information, arguments and energy to influencing the decision-making process, addressing themselves both directly to policy makers and indirectly to those who, in turn, influence them. The institutional processes through which decisions are made will vary enormously from country to country, but there are always those who are more responsible than others and they have to be identified, informed, stimulated, challenged, and held to account: if everyone is responsible, then no one is actually responsible.

The trouble with most discussions of "political will" is that more time is spent lamenting its absence than on analyzing its ingredients, and working out how to use them in different contexts. To reduce the issue to its bare essentials, what is necessary is a good understanding of the relevant institutional processes, as just mentioned, and good arguments. What constitutes a good argument will obviously depend on the particular context. But it is not too much of an oversimplification to say that, in most political systems around the world, pleas for international action of the kind we are dealing with in this report need to be supported by arguments having four different kinds of appeal: moral, financial, national interest and partisan.

As to *moral* appeal, preventing, averting and halting human suffering—all the catastrophic loss and misery that go with slaughter and ethnic cleansing and mass starvation—are inspiring and legitimizing motives in almost any political environment. Political leaders often underestimate the sheer sense of decency and compassion that prevails in their electorates, at least when people's attention is engaged (just as they also underestimate the public willingness, when well informed, to accept the risk of casualties in well designed military interventions aimed at alleviating that suffering). Getting a moral motive to bite means, however, being able to convey a sense of urgency and reality about the threat to human life in a particular situation. Unfortunately, this is always harder to convey at the crucial stage of prevention than it is after some actual horror has occurred.

The best *financial* argument is that earlier action is always cheaper than later action. If prevention is possible, it is likely to be cheaper by many orders of magnitude than responding after the event through military action, humanitarian relief assistance, postconflict reconstruction, or all three. In Kosovo, almost any kind of preventive activity—whether it involved more effective preventive diplomacy, or the earlier and sharper application of coercive preventive measures like the credible threat of ground-level military action—would have had to be cheaper than the $46 billion the international community is estimated to have committed at the time of writing in fighting the war and following up with peacekeeping and reconstruction.

National interest appeals can be made at many different levels. Avoiding the disintegration of a neighbour, with the refugee outflows and general regional security destabilization associated with it can be a compelling motive in many contexts. National economic interests often can be equally well served by keeping resource supply lines, trade routes and markets undisrupted. And whatever may have been the case in the past, these days peace is generally regarded as much better for business than war.

There is another dimension of the national interest which is highly relevant to intervention for human protection purposes: every country's national interest in being, and being seen to be, a good international citizen. There is much direct reciprocal benefit to be gained in an interdependent, globalized world where nobody can solve all their own problems: my country's assistance for you today in solving your neighbourhood refugee and terrorism problem, might reasonably lead you to be more willing to help solve my environmental or drugs problem tomorrow. The interest in being seen to be a good international citizen is simply the reputational benefit that a country can win for itself, over time, by being regularly willing to pitch into international tasks for motives that appear to be relatively selfless.

Making an argument with a *partisan* appeal for a government concerned about its political support at the ballot box or elsewhere is a more delicate matter. The point is simply that in any particular country, arguments which may not have a strong or sufficient appeal to the community at large may still have that appeal to a key section of the government's own particular support base, and be extremely influential for that reason. Governments often have to do things without knowing what is the majority view, and even when they know that the majority sentiment might be against the proposed action. What often matters more is that they have arguments that will appeal to, or at least not alienate, their immediate support base; and that they have arguments that they can use to deflate, or at least defend against, the attacks of their political opponents.

MOBILIZING INTERNATIONAL POLITICAL WILL

What happens in capitals is a crucial ingredient in international decision making. But it is only part of the story. International political will is more than just the sum of attitudes and policies of individual countries. What happens between states and their representatives in bilateral and multilateral contacts, and within intergovernmental organizations, is obviously also crucial. To get the right words uttered, and to turn them into deeds, requires—at international as at domestic level—the same kind of commitment and leadership, and the same kind of constant campaigning. Mobilizing support for specific instances of intervention is always a challenge, because there will always be a compelling rationale for inaction. The same strictures apply internationally as domestically about understanding where in the various processes responsibility for decision making actually lies, and how to pin it down. And it is just as important in the international arena as it is in the domestic to be able to produce arguments appealing to morality, resource concerns, institutional interests and political interests. This whole report is, in a sense, an expression of just such arguments in the context of intervention for human protection purposes.

An obvious starting point when looking for multilateral leadership on questions relating to intervention is the UN Secretary-General and senior officials in the Secretariat. Although the Secretary-General's formal role under Article 99 of the UN Charter could, as we have suggested, be further developed, his routine activities and interaction with the Security Council, and his international profile with governments and the media, give him a unique opportunity to mobilize international support; an important further part of his multilateral leadership role lies in constructing and maintaining the multinational coalitions which are an essential element in the contemporary implementation of UN-authorized peace operations. The Secretariat, particularly through its reports and recommendations to the Security Council, makes a major contribution to shaping the deliberations and determining the range of options considered. That contribution, it must be said again, can be negative as well as positive: Rwanda in 1994 involved a failure, not only by key member states, but in the leadership of the UN and in the effective functioning of the Secretariat as well.

Beyond the UN itself, including all the organs and agencies in the system beyond the Secretariat, there are multiple other international actors whose roles are immensely relevant to the intervention issue, in particular regional and sub-regional organizations, and international NGOs, and the media. We have mentioned the key institutional players throughout this report, and need not here do so again.

As to the media, there is no question that good reporting, well-argued opinion pieces and in particular real time transmission of images of suffering do generate both domestic and international pressure to act. The "CNN effect" can be almost irresistible, unbalanced in its impact though it may be, with similarly troubling crises not always receiving similar attention. On the other hand, by focusing attention on human suffering, media attention sometimes tends to divert policy makers from hard diplomatic and military decisions, with time pressures sometimes pushing them to become involved before serious analysis and planning can occur. That is perhaps a lesser sin than those of total inertia or excessive delay, but it can create problems nonetheless.

International NGOs have been significant advocates of cross-border human protection action, extending in some cases to military intervention, and their positive influence in stirring response—especially in the West—has been great. Yet they too, from the perspective of the decision makers they seek to influence, can have their limitations as advocates: they are seen often as lacking in policy making experience, frequently as unhelpfully divided over which precise policy course is optimal, and sometimes as reluctant publicly (as distinct from privately) to endorse coercive measures which may be necessary, but which are not easy for governments or intergovernmental institutions to deliver without overt support.

The goals of policy makers and humanitarian advocates are not so different from each other. Given that the application of deadly force should remain an option of last resort, there is still a range of choices between doing nothing and sending in the troops. There are always options to be considered before, during, and after lethal conflicts. Both policy makers and humanitarian advocates would like to see public policy succeed in tackling the most crucial issues of the day. One of the most pressing such issues is how to make good the responsibility to protect those facing the worst sort of horrors the contemporary world has to provide.

NEXT STEPS

The Commission's objective from the outset has been for our report to have a practical and concrete political impact, rather then simply provide additional stimulation to scholars and other commentators—though we hope to have done that as well. Consistent with our practical focus we have been mindful, through-out our work and consultations, of the need to ensure a solid foundation for the discussions that will take place at the United Nations and in other international forums after the presentation of the report, as well as within governments and among those who seek to influence them.

Our immediate hope is that by helping to clarify and focus the terms of the debate—not as a contest between sovereignty and intervention, but as involving "the responsibility to protect" as a common theme—a way forward will be found through the current polemics and present impasse in that debate. We want, above all, to strengthen the prospects for obtaining action, on a collective and principled basis, with a minimum of double standards, in response to conscience-shocking situations of great humanitarian need crying out for that action. If our report can help to stimulate support for such action by reminding states of their common responsibilities, then it will have made a very significant contribution indeed.

The principles of action around which we would like to see consensus develop are summarized in the Synopsis set out in the first pages of this report. What should happen next to advance them? There has been much discussion, at national, regional and international levels, on how best to approach the practical task of trying to embody any new consensus among states on the question of intervention for human protection purposes. Some suggest that the focus should be on drafting guidelines for the internal use of the Security Council; some sup-port the passing of a more formal resolution by the General Assembly; and oth-ers have gone so far as to suggest that work should begin on the drafting of a new international convention, or even an amendment to the UN Charter itself.

The Commission believes that it would be premature to make a judgement now as to what will ultimately prove possible if consensus around the idea of "the responsibility to protect" builds to the extent that we hope it will. The important thing now is to make a start, with member states working with the Secretary-General to give substantive and procedural content to the ideas we advance. There are major roles to be played by the Secretary-General himself, by the Secu-rity Council and by the General Assembly, and we make some suggestions in this respect in the following recommendations. The Commission makes no judgement as to the most appropriate sequence in which these steps should be taken.

The Commission recommends to the General Assembly:

That the General Assembly adopt a draft declaratory resolution embodying the basic principles of the responsibility to protect, and containing four basic elements:

- *an affirmation of the idea of sovereignty as responsibility;*
- *an assertion of the threefold responsibility of the international community of states—to prevent, to react and to rebuild—when faced with human protection claims in states that are either unable or unwilling to discharge their responsibility to protect;*
- *a definition of the threshold (large scale loss of life or ethnic cleansing, actual or apprehended) which human protection claims must meet if they are to justify military intervention; and*
- *an articulation of the precautionary principles (right intention, last resort, proportional means and reasonable prospects) that must be observed when military force is used for human protection purposes.*

The Commission recommends to the Security Council:

1. *That the members of the Security Council should consider and seek to reach agreement on a set of guidelines, embracing the "Principles for Military Intervention" summarized in the Synopsis, to govern their responses to claims for military intervention for human protection purposes.*
2. *That the Permanent Five members of the Security Council should consider and seek to reach agreement not to apply their veto power, in matters where their vital state interests are not involved, to obstruct the passage of resolutions authorizing military intervention for human protection purposes for which there is otherwise majority support.*

The Commission recommends to the Secretary-General:

That the Secretary-General give consideration, and consult as appropriate with the President of the Security Council and the President of the General Assembly, as to how the substance and action recommendations of this report can best be advanced in those two bodies, and by his own further action.

MEETING THE CHALLENGE

Throughout its deliberations, the Commission has sought to reconcile two objectives: to strengthen, not weaken, the sovereignty of states, and to improve the capacity of the international community to react decisively when states are either unable or unwilling to protect their own people. Reconciling these two objectives is essential. There is no prospect of genuine equality among peoples unless the sovereignty of states is respected and their capacity to protect their own citizens is enhanced. Equally, the very term "international community" will become a travesty unless the community of states can act decisively when large groups of human beings are being massacred or subjected to ethnic cleansing.

The Commission is optimistic that these dual objectives—enhancing the sovereign capacity of states and improving the ability of the international community to protect people in mortal danger—can be reconciled in practice. Our work reflects the remarkable, even historic, change that has occurred in the practice of states and the Security Council in the past generation. Thanks to this change, no one is prepared to defend the claim that states can do what they wish to their own people, and hide behind the principle of sovereignty in so doing. In the international community, just as there can be no impunity for unwarranted unilateral uses of force, nor can there be impunity for massacre and ethnic cleansing. No one who has perpetrated such horrors should ever be allowed to sleep easily.

This basic consensus implies that the international community has a responsibility to act decisively when states are unwilling or unable to fulfill these basic responsibilities. The Commission has sought to give clear articulation to this consensus, and calls on all members of the community of nations, together with non-governmental actors and citizens of states, to embrace the idea of the responsibility to protect as a basic element in the code of global citizenship, for states and peoples, in the 21st century.

Meeting this challenge is more than a matter of aspiration. It is a vital necessity. Nothing has done more harm to our shared ideal that we are all equal in worth and dignity, and that the earth is our common home, than the inability of the community of states to prevent genocide, massacre and ethnic cleansing. If we believe that all human beings are equally entitled to be protected from acts that shock the conscience of us all, then we must match rhetoric with reality, principle with practice. We cannot be content with reports and declarations. We must be prepared to act. We won't be able to live with ourselves if we do not.

STUDY AND DISCUSSION QUESTIONS

1. How does the doctrine of the responsibility to protect change the meaning of state sovereignty?
2. Does this doctrine provide a compelling case for humanitarian intervention?
3. Is the doctrine likely to convince great powers to intervene when their vital national interests are not at stake? Is it likely to reassure potential target states that great powers are not all too eager to trample the sovereignty of weaker states?

Globalization, Empire, and America's Geopolitical Strategy

24

The Empire Slinks Back

Niall Ferguson

Does the Bush doctrine herald the birth of a new American Empire, made possible—supporters would say made necessary—by the terror attacks on the World Trade Center and the Pentagon? Before 9/11, only critics of American foreign policy used the term empire with reference to the United States. But since 9/11, many neoconservative scholars and observers have celebrated the imperial exercise of U.S. power as a force for advancing liberty and democracy in the world, while defeating terrorism and fostering regime change in the Middle East, beginning with Iraq. What lessons will be learned about the prospects and consequences of a new American empire from the excruciating difficulties of bringing stability and democracy through the invasion and occupation of Iraq? Will the United States have the staying power and the capacity to transform the political geography of the Middle East?

The claim that America's post–9/11 geopolitical strategy is an imperial strategy has generated a far-reaching intellectual and public policy debate that has captured the popular imagination. In this selection Niall Ferguson, one of the leading figures in the empire debate and an unapologetic admirer of the British Empire, warns that the United States may not have the determination and staying power to achieve success in its global mission. He argues that the British Empire prospered because many of the best and the brightest were willing to spend their careers and much of their lives in Calcutta or Hong Kong or Cape Town. How many of their American counterparts today will be eager to take on long tours of duty in Kabul or Baghdad? Ferguson exhorts

*America to throw off its cultural reluctance to "do Empire" and put its
best and brightest into an enduring imperial project.*

Wheresoever the Roman conquers, he inhabits.—Seneca

Iraq has fallen. Saddam's statues are face down in the dust. His evil tyranny is at
an end.

So—can we, like, go home now?

You didn't have to wait long for a perfect symbol of the fundamental weakness at the heart of the new American imperialism—sorry, humanitarianism. I'm
talking about its chronically short time frame. I wasn't counting, but the Stars
and Stripes must have been up there on the head of that statue of Saddam for less
than a minute. You have to wonder what his commanding officer said to the
marine responsible, Cpl. Edward Chin, when he saw Old Glory up there. "Son,
get that thing down on the double, or we'll have every TV station from here to
Bangladesh denouncing us as Yankee imperialists!"

An echo of Corporal Chin's imperial impulse can be heard in the last letter
Cpl. Kemaphoom Chanawongse sent home before he and his Marine unit
entered Iraq. Chanawongse joked that his camp in Kuwait was like something
out of "M*A*S*H"—except that it would need to be called "M*A*H*T*S*F":
"marines are here to stay forever."

But the question raised by Corporal Chanawongse's poignant final joke—he
was killed a week later, when his amphibious assault vehicle was blown up in
Nasiriya—is, Are the marines in Iraq "to stay forever"? No doubt it is true, as
President Bush said, that the America will "honor forever" Corporal Chanawongse and the more than 120 other service personnel so far killed in the conflict. Honored forever, yes. But *there* forever? In many ways the biggest mystery
about the American occupation of Iraq is its probable duration. Recent statements by members of the Bush administration bespeak a time frame a lot closer
to ephemeral than eternal. As the president himself told the Iraqi people in a
television broadcast shortly after the fall of Baghdad: "The government of Iraq
and the future of your country will soon belong to you. . . . We will respect your
great religious traditions, whose principles of equality and compassion are
essential to Iraq's future. We will help you build a peaceful and representative
government that protects the rights of all citizens. *And then our military forces
will leave.*"

What the president didn't make entirely clear was whether the departing
troops would be accompanied by the retired Lt. Gen. Jay Garner and his "Office
of Reconstruction and Humanitarian Assistance," newspeak for what would
once have been called Omgus—the Office of Military Government (United
States). Nor was he very specific about when exactly he expected to see the han-
dover of power to the "peaceful and representative government" of Iraqis.

But we know the kind of time frame the president has in mind. In a prewar speech to the American Enterprise Institute, Bush declared, "We will remain in Iraq as long as necessary and not a day more." It is striking that the unit of measure he used was days. Speaking less than a week before the fall of Baghdad, Paul Wolfowitz, the deputy secretary of defense, suggested that Garner would be running Iraq for at least six months. Other administration spokesmen have mentioned two years as the maximum transition period. When Garner himself was asked how long he expected to be in charge, he talked about just three months.

If—as more and more commentators claim—America has embarked on a new age of empire, it may turn out to be the most evanescent empire in all history. Other empire builders have fantasized about ruling subject peoples for a thousand years. This is shaping up to be history's first thousand-day empire. Make that a thousand hours.

Let me come clean. I am a fully paid-up member of the neoimperialist gang. Twelve years ago—when it was not at all fashionable to say so—I was already arguing that it would be "desirable for the United States to depose" tyrants like Saddam Hussein. "Capitalism and democracy," I wrote, "are not naturally occurring, but require strong institutional foundations of law and order. The proper role of an imperial America is to establish these institutions where they are lacking, if necessary . . . by military force." Today this argument is in danger of becoming commonplace, at least among the set who read The National Interest, the latest issue of which is practically an American Empire Special Edition. Elsewhere, writers as diverse as Max Boot, Andrew Bacevich and Thomas Donnelly have drawn explicit (and in Boot's case, approving) comparisons between the pax Britannica of Queen Victoria's reign and the pax Americana they envisage in the reign of George II. Boot has gone so far as to say that the United States should provide places like Afghanistan and other troubled countries with "the sort of enlightened foreign administration once provided by self-confident Englishmen in jodhpurs and pith helmets."

I agree. The British Empire has had a pretty lousy press from a generation of "postcolonial" historians anachronistically affronted by its racism. But the reality is that the British were significantly more successful at establishing market economies, the rule of law and the transition to representative government than the majority of postcolonial governments have been. The policy "mix" favored by Victorian imperialists reads like something just published by the International Monetary Fund, if not the World Bank: free trade, balanced budgets, sound money, the common law, incorrupt administration and investment in infrastructure financed by international loans. These are precisely the things Iraq needs right now. If the scary-sounding "American empire" can deliver them, then I am all for it. The catch is whether or not America has the one crucial character trait without which the whole imperial project is doomed: stamina. The more time I spend here in the United States, the more doubtful I become about this.

The United States unquestionably has the raw economic power to build an empire—more, indeed, than the United Kingdom ever had at its disposal. In 1913, for example, Britain's share of total world output was 8 percent, while the equivalent figure for the United States in 1998 was 22 percent. There's "soft" power too—the endlessly innovative consumer culture that Joseph Nye argues is an essential component of American power—but at its core, as we have seen in Afghanistan and now in Iraq, American power is far from soft. It can be very, very hard. The trouble is that it is ephemeral. It is not so much Power Lite as Flash Power—here today, with a spectacular bang, but gone tomorrow.

Besides the presidential time frame—which is limited by the four-year election cycle—the most obvious symptom of its short-windedness is the difficulty the American empire finds in recruiting the right sort of people to run it. America's educational institutions excel at producing young men and women who are both academically and professionally very well trained. It's just that the young elites have no desire whatsoever to spend their lives running a screwed-up, sun-scorched sandpit like Iraq. America's brightest and best aspire not to govern Mesopotamia, but to manage MTV; not to rule Hejaz, but to run a hedge fund; not to be a C.B.E., or Commander of the British Empire, but to be a C.E.O. And that, of course, is one reason so many of the Americans currently in Iraq are first-generation immigrants to the United States—men like Cpl. Kemaphoom Chanawongse.

America's British allies have been here before. Having defeated the previous Ottoman rulers in the First World War, Britain ran Iraq as a "mandate" between 1920 and 1932. For the sake of form, the British installed one of their Arab clients, the Hashemite prince Faisal, as king. But there was no doubt who was really running the place. Nor did the British make any bones about why they were there. When two Standard Oil geologists entered Iraq on a prospecting mission, the British civil commissioner handed them over to the chief of police of Baghdad; in 1927 the British takeover paid a handsome dividend when oil was struck at Baba Gurgur, in the northern part of Iraq. Although they formally relinquished power to the ruling dynasty in 1932, the British remained informally in control of Iraq throughout the 1930's. Indeed, they only really lost their grip on Baghdad with the assassination of their clients Faisal II and his prime minister, Nuri es-Said, in the revolution of 1958.

The crucial point is this: when the British went into Iraq, they stuck around. To be precise, there were British government representatives, military and civilian, in Baghdad uninterruptedly for almost exactly 40 years.

And that brings up a simple question: Who in today's United States would like to be based in Baghdad as long as the British were—which would be from now until 2043?

"Don't even go there!" is one of those catch phrases you hear every day in New York. Somehow it sums up exactly what is flawed about the whole post–9/11 crypto-imperial project. Despite their vast wealth and devastating weaponry, Americans have no interest in the one crucial activity without which a true empire cannot enduringly be established. They won't actually go *there.*

A British counterexample. Gertrude Bell was the first woman to graduate from Oxford with a First Class degree. She learned to speak Arabic during an archaeological visit to Jerusalem in 1899 and, like T.E. Lawrence, became involved in British military intelligence. In 1920, she was appointed Oriental Secretary to the British High Commission in Baghdad. She died there in 1926, having scarcely visited England in the interim. "I don't care to be in London much," she wrote. "I like Baghdad, and I like Iraq. It's the real East, and it is stirring; things are happening here, and the romance of it all touches me and absorbs me."

Dotted all over the British Empire were thousands of "Orientalists" like Gertrude Bell—simultaneously enamored of the exotic "Other" and yet dominant over it. Her account of Faisal I's coronation in 1921 perfectly illustrates their mode of operation: "Then Saiyid Husain stood up and read Sir Percy's proclamation in which he announced that Faisal had been elected king by 96 percent of the people in Mesopotamia, long live the King! with that we stood up and saluted him, the national flag was broken on the flagstaff by his side and the band played 'God Save the King'—they have no national anthem yet."

The British regarded long-term occupation as an inherent part of their self-appointed "civilizing mission." This did not mean forever. The assumption was that British rule would end once a country had been sufficiently "civilized"—read: anglicized—to ensure the continued rule of law and operation of free markets (not to mention the playing of cricket). But that clearly meant decades, not days; when the British intervened in a country like Iraq, they simply didn't have an exit strategy. The only issue was whether to rule directly—installing a British governor—or indirectly, with a British "secretary" offering "advice" to a local puppet like Faisal.

In other words, the British did go there. Between 1900 and 1914, 2.6 million Britons left the United Kingdom for imperial destinations (by 1957 the total had reached nearly 6 million). Admittedly, most of them preferred to migrate to the temperate regions of a select few colonies—Canada, Australia, New Zealand and South Africa—that soon became semiautonomous "dominions." Nevertheless, a significant number went to the much less hospitable climes of Asia and Africa. At the end of the 1930's, for example, the official Colonial Service in Africa was staffed by more than 7,500 expat Brits. The substantial expatriate communities they established were crucial to the operation of the British Empire. They provided the indispensable "men on the spot" who learned the local languages, perhaps adopted some local customs—though not usually to the fatal extent of "going native"—and acted as the intermediaries between a remote imperial authority and the indigenous elites upon whose willing collaboration the empire depended.

Expat life was not all tiffin and gin. As Rudyard Kipling saw it, governing India was a hard slog: "Year by year England sends out fresh drafts for the first fighting-line, which is officially called the Indian Civil Service. These die, or kill themselves by overwork, or are worried to death or broken in health and hope." Yet this was a service that could confidently expect to attract the very brightest and best products of the elite British universities. Of 927 recruits to the Colonial Service between 1927 and 1929, nearly half had been to Oxford or Cambridge. The proportion in the Indian Civil Service was even higher.

Why were so many products of Britain's top universities willing to spend their entire working lives so far from the land of their birth, running infernally hot, disease-ridden countries? Why, to pick a typical example, did one Evan Machonochie, an Oxford graduate who passed the grueling Indian Civil Service exam, set off for Bengal in 1887 and spend the next 40 years in India? One clue lies in his Celtic surname. The Scots were heavily overrepresented not just in the colonies of white settlement, but also in the commercial and professional elites of cities like Calcutta and Hong Kong and Cape Town. The Irish too played a disproportionate role in enforcing British rule, supplying a huge proportion of the officers and men of the British army. Not for nothing is Kipling's representative Indian Army N.C.O. named Mulvaney. For young men growing up on the rainy, barren and poorer fringes of the United Kingdom, the empire offered opportunities.

Yet economics alone cannot explain what motivated Machonochie or Bell. The imperial impulse arose from a complex of emotions: racial superiority, yes, but also evangelical zeal; profit, perhaps, but also a sincere belief that spreading "commerce, Christianity and civilization" was not just in Britain's interest but in the interests of her colonial subjects too.

The contrast with today's "wannabe" imperialists in the United States—call them "nation-builders" if you prefer euphemism—could scarcely be more stark. Five points stand out.

First, not only do the overwhelming majority of Americans have no desire to leave the United States; millions of non-Americans are also eager to join them here. Unlike the United Kingdom a century ago, the United States is an *importer* of people, with a net immigration rate of 3.5 per 1,000 and a total foreign-born population of 32.5 million (more than 1 in 10 residents of the United States).

Second, when Americans do opt to reside abroad, they tend to stick to the developed world. As of 1999, there were an estimated 3.8 million Americans living abroad. That sounds like a lot. But it is a little more than a tenth the number of the foreign-born population in the United States. And of these expat Americans, almost three-quarters were living in the two other Nafta countries (more than one million in Mexico, 687, 700 in Canada) or in Europe (just over a million). Of the 294,000 living in the Middle East, nearly two-thirds were in Israel. A mere 37,500 were in Africa.

Third, whereas British imperial forces were mostly based abroad, most of the American military is normally stationed at home. Even the B-2 Stealth bombers that pounded Serbia into quitting Kosovo in 1999 were flying out of Knob Noster, Mo. And it's worth remembering that 40 percent of American overseas military personnel are located in Western Europe, no fewer than 71,000 of them in Germany. Thus, whereas the British delighted in building barracks in hostile territories precisely in order to subjugate them, Americans today locate a quarter of their overseas troops in what is arguably the world's most pacifist country.

Fourth, when Americans do live abroad they generally don't stay long and don't integrate much, preferring to inhabit Mini Me versions of America, ranging from military bases to five-star "international" (read: American) hotels. When I visited Lakenheath air base last year, one minute I was in the middle of rural Cambridgeshire, flat and ineffably English, the next minute, as I passed through the main gate, everything—right down to the absurdly large soft-drink dispensers—was unmistakably American.

The fifth and final contrast with the British experience is perhaps the most telling. It is the fact that the products of America's elite educational institutions are the people least likely to head overseas, other than on flying visits and holidays. The Americans who serve the longest tours of duty are the volunteer soldiers, a substantial proportion of whom are African-Americans (12.9 per cent of the population, 25.4 per cent of the Army Reserve). It's just possible that African-Americans will turn out to be the Celts of the American empire, driven overseas by the comparatively poor opportunities at home. Indeed, if the occupation of Iraq is to be run by the military, then it can hardly fail to create career opportunities for the growing number of African-American officers in the Army. The military's most effective press spokesman during the war, Brig. Gen. Vincent K. Brooks, exemplifies the type.

The British, however, were always wary about giving the military too much power in their imperial administration. Their parliamentarians had read enough Roman history to want to keep generals subordinate to civilian governors. The "brass hats" were there to inflict the Victorian equivalent of "shock and awe" whenever the "natives" grew restive. Otherwise, colonial government was a matter for Oxbridge-educated, frock-coated mandarins.

Now, ask yourself in light of this: how many members of Harvard's or Yale's class of 2003 are seriously considering a career in the postwar administration of Iraq? The number is unlikely to be very high. In 1998/99 there were 47,689 undergraduate course registrations at Yale, of which just 335 (less than 1 per cent) were for courses in Near Eastern languages and civilizations. There was just one, lone undergraduate senior majoring in the subject (compared with 17 doing film studies). If Samuel Huntington is right and we are witnessing a "clash of civilizations," America's brightest students show remarkably little interest in the civilization of the other side.

After graduation, too, the members of America's academic elite generally subscribe to the "Wizard of Oz" principle: "There's no place like home." According to a 1998 survey, there were 134,798 registered Yale alumni. Of these, little more than 5 percent lived outside the United States. A mere handful—roughly 70—lived in Arab countries.

Sure, the bolder products of the Kennedy School may be eager for "tours of duty" in postwar Baghdad. And a few of the star Harvard economists may want to do for Iraq what a couple of their professors did for post–Soviet Russia back in the early 90's. But what that means is flying back and forth, writing a bunch of papers on "transition economics," pocketing some fat consultancy fees and then heading for home.

As far as America's Ivy League nation-builders are concerned, you can set up an independent central bank, reform the tax code, liberalize prices and privatize the major utilities—and be home in time for the first reunion.

It can of course be argued that Americans' tendency to pay flying visits to their putative imperium—rather than settling there—is just a function of technology. Back in the 1870s, by which time the British had largely completed their global network of railways and steamships, it still took a minimum of 80 days to go around the world, as Jules Verne celebrated in the story of Phileas Fogg. Today it can be done in a day.

The problem is that with the undoubted advantages of modern technology comes the disadvantage of disconnection. For example, Secretary of State Colin Powell was criticized earlier this year for conducting his foreign policy by telephone. It was noted that Powell had traveled abroad twice in 2003 already, but one trip was to Davos, Switzerland (Jan. 25–26), and the other was to the Far East (Feb. 21–25). We can only guess at how much more Secretary Powell might have achieved if he had paid a visit to Paris—or Ankara—last month. And it is not just the big guns who seem happiest close to the Beltway. Recall, too, how after 9/11 the C.I.A. had to scour American colleges to find anyone capable of speaking fluent Pashto. It turned out that most C.I.A. officers preferred life in Virginia to what the British once called the North-West Frontier. (Have you seen the state of the restrooms up the Khyber Pass?)

One of this month's most disturbing pieces of news was that Garner's team at the Office of Reconstruction and Humanitarian Assistance would include people from the State Department and the U.S. Agency for International Development "who have worked in a similar capacity in the former Yugoslavia, in Haiti and in Somalia." Considering the pitifully short duration of American interventions in those countries, their dismal failure in two of three cases and the vast differences between Iraq and all three, this is scarcely encouraging. Even more surreal was the disclosure that the Office of Reconstruction and Humanitarian Assistance has been hiring British Gurkhas to provide security around their Kuwait base. A nice imperial touch, granted, but a bunch of Gurkhas are hardly going to blend in discreetly in downtown Baghdad.

What, then, about the much-vaunted role of nongovernmental organizations? Might they provide the men and women on the ground who are so conspicuously hard to find in government service?

It is true that a substantial number of Americans are currently working overseas for NGO's. An American friend of mine recently startled his friends—not to mention his wife—by quitting his artist's studio and his teaching job in London, where he has spent much of the last 20 years, to take a position with a French-run aid agency in one of the most dysfunctional of Central Africa's wretched republics. Perhaps he will find the new life he seeks there. But most Americans who do this kind of thing start younger and spend little more than a year overseas. For many it is not much more than a politically correct "gap year" before starting at graduate school.

Nor should we pin too much hope on the aid agencies that, like the missionaries of old, can be as much an irritant as a help to those trying to run a country like Iraq. It is one of the unspoken truths of the new imperialism that around every international crisis swarms a cloud of aid workers, whose efforts are seldom entirely complementary. If Garner's team successfully imposes law and order in Iraq, economic life will swiftly pick up and much aid will be superfluous. If it fails to impose order, aid workers will get themselves killed—as they frequently do in lawless Chechnya.

The dilemma is perhaps insoluble. Americans yearn for the quiet life at home. But since 9/11 they have felt impelled to grapple with rogue regimes in the hope that their overthrow will do something to reduce the threat of future terrorist attacks. The trouble is that if they do not undertake these interventions with conviction and commitment, they are unlikely to achieve their stated goals. Anyone who thinks Iraq can become a stable democracy in a matter of months—whether 3, 6 or 24—is simply fantasizing.

Where, then, is the new imperial elite to come from? Not, I hope, exclusively from the reserve army of unemployed generals with good Pentagon connections. The work needs to begin, and swiftly, to encourage American students at the country's leading universities to think more seriously about careers overseas—and by overseas I do not mean in London. Are there, for example, enough good scholarships to attract undergraduates and graduates to study Arabic? How many young men and women currently graduate with a functioning grasp of Chinese? That, after all, is the language of this country's nearest imperial rival, and the power President Bush urgently needs to woo if he is to deal effectively with North Korea.

After Kipling, John Buchan was perhaps the most readable writer produced by British imperialism. In his 1916 thriller "Greenmantle," he memorably personifies imperial Britain in the person of Sandy Arbuthnot—an Orientalist so talented that he can pass for a Moroccan in Mecca or a Pathan in Peshawar. Arbuthnot's antithesis is the dyspeptic American millionaire John Scantlebury Blenkiron: "a big fellow with a fat, sallow, clean-shaven face" and "a pair of full sleepy eyes, like a ruminating ox." These eyes have seen "nothing gorier than a presidential election," he tells Buchan's hero, Richard Hannay. The symbolism is a little crude, but it has something to it.

Well, now the Blenkirons have seen something gorier than an election. But will it whet their appetites for an empire in the British mode? Only, I think, if

Americans radically rethink their attitude to the world beyond their borders. Until there are more Americans not just willing but eager to shoulder the "nation-builder's burden," adventures like the current occupation of Iraq will lack a vital ingredient. For the lesson of Britain's imperial experience is clear: you simply cannot have an empire without imperialists—out there, on the spot—to run it.

Could Blenkiron somehow transform into Arbuthnot? Perhaps. After all, in the years after the Second World War, the generation that had just missed the fighting left Harvard and Yale with something like Buchan's zeal for global rule. Many of them joined the Central Intelligence Agency and devoted their lives to fighting Communism in far-flung lands from Cuba to Cambodia. Yet—as Graham Greene foresaw in "The Quiet American"—their efforts at what the British would have called "indirect rule" were constrained by the need to shore up the local potentates more or less covertly. (The low quality of the locals backed by the United States didn't help, either.) Today, the same fiction that underpinned American strategy in Vietnam—that the United States was not trying to resurrect French colonial rule in Indochina—is peddled in Washington to rationalize what is going on in Iraq. Sure, it may look like the resurrection of British colonial rule in Iraq, but honestly, all we want to do is give the Iraqi people democracy and then go home.

So long as the American empire dare not speak its own name—so long as it continues this tradition of organized hypocrisy—today's ambitious young men and women will take one look at the prospects for postwar Iraq and say with one voice, "Don't even go there."

Americans need to go there. If the best and brightest insist on staying home, today's unspoken imperial project may end—unspeakably—tomorrow.

STUDY AND DISCUSSION QUESTIONS

1. What rationale does Ferguson offer for being "a fully paid-up member of the neoimperialist gang"?
2. What lessons from the British Empire does he hope Americans will learn?
3. Do you think Ferguson is right to suggest that Americans are extremely reluctant imperialists? If so—is that a good thing or a bad thing?

25

Why Are We In Iraq?
(And Liberia? And Afghanistan?)

Michael Ignatieff

In this selection, Michael Ignatieff, Carr Professor of Human Rights Practice at Harvard's Kennedy School, and member of both the Independent International Commission on Kosovo and the International Commission on Intervention and State Sovereignty, begins with the observation that the war in Iraq must be placed in the broader context of American foreign interventions. The United States has never shrunk from foreign wars, he argues. However, since the end of the Cold War, no clear concept of national interest that would justify overseas engagements emerged at least until September 11, 2001. But even in the aftermath of the terror attacks, contends Ignatieff, the rules that justify "pre-emption" and American intervention, more generally, remain unclear.

In searching for a balance between the necessity of American leadership in the war against terror and his preference for multilateral solutions to the use of force, Ignatieff comes reluctantly to endorse what might be termed "empire-lite": intervention but not colonialism to advance human rights and nation-building under American leadership, preferably backed by the international community. He concludes with a last-ditch call for American leadership to revitalize the United Nations as an alternative to empire.

In the back alleys of Iraq, the soldiers from the 101st Airborne and First Armored Divisions are hot, dirty and scared. They want to go home, but instead they're pinned down, fighting off hit-and-run attacks and trying to stop sabotage on pipelines, water mains and electric grids. They were told they would be greeted as liberators, but now, many months later, they are an army of occupation, trying to save the reputation of a president who never told them—did he know himself?—what they were getting into. The Muslim fighters rushing to join the remnants of Saddam Hussein's loyalists in a guerrilla war to reclaim Iraq have understood all along what the war has been about—that it was never simply a matter of preventing the use of weapons of mass destruction; rather, it was about consolidating American power in the Arab world. Some in the administration no doubt understood this, too, though no one took the trouble to explain all their reasons for going to war to the American people or, for that matter, the rest of the world.

But now we know. Iraq may become for America what Afghanistan became for the Soviet empire: the place where its fight against Islamic jihad will be won or lost. Nor is the United States the only target. The suicide bomb that killed Sergio Vieira de Mello and decimated his team has drawn the United Nations into the vortex. The United Nations came to Baghdad to give American nation-building a patina of legitimacy. Now the world body has been targeted as an accomplice of occupation. If the United States fails in Iraq, so will the United Nations.

To see what is really unfolding in Iraq, we need to place it in the long history of American overseas interventions. It is worth remembering, for example, that when American soldiers have occupied countries before, for example Japan and Germany, the story started out much the same: not enough food, not enough electricity, not enough law and order (and, in Germany, ragtag Nazi fighters). And if this history is part of what drove us into Iraq, what doctrine, if any, has determined when and where Americans are sent to fight? Before the United States sends troops to any future front—Syria? North Korea? Iran?—it is crucial to ask: What does the history of American intervention teach us to hope and to fear? And how might the United States devise a coherent strategy of engagement suited for the perils—and possibilities—of the 21st century?

II.

From the very beginning, the American republic has never shrunk from foreign wars. A recent Congressional study shows that there has scarcely been a year since its founding that American soldiers haven't been overseas "from the halls of Montezuma to the shores of Tripoli," chasing pirates, punishing bandits, pulling American citizens out of harm's way, intervening in civil wars, stopping massacres, overturning regimes deemed (fairly or not) unfriendly and exporting democracy. American foreign policy largely consists of doctrines about when and where to intervene in other people's countries. In 1823, James Monroe committed the United States—militarily, if it came to that—to keeping foreign colonial powers out of the entire Western Hemisphere. In 1906, Theodore Roosevelt added a corollary giving the United States the right to send in troops when any of its Latin American neighbors engaged in "flagrant wrongdoing." Most Latin Americans, then and now, took that to mean that the United States would topple any government in the hemisphere that acted against American interests. Early in the last century, American troops went ashore to set up governments in Haiti and the Dominican Republic and chased Pancho Villa around Mexico. And this kind of intervention wasn't just confined to pushing around Latin Americans. Twelve thousand troops were sent to support the White armies fighting the Communists in the Russian Civil War that began in 1918. In the 1920's, during the civil war in China, there were 6,000 American soldiers ashore and a further 44 naval vessels in the China Sea protecting American interests. (Neither venture was much of a success. Both Russia and China eventually went Communist.)

Despite George Washington's call to avoid foreign entanglements and John Quincy Adams's plea that America should abjure slaying monsters abroad, splendid isolation has never proved to be a convincing foreign policy for Americans. First in 1917 and then again in 1941, American presidents thought they could keep America out of Europe's wars only to discover that isolation was not an option for a country wanting to be taken seriously as a world power—which, from the beginning, is precisely what America desired. Intervention required huge sacrifice—the haunting American graveyards in France are proof of this—but American soldiers helped save Europe from dictatorship, and their hard fighting turned America into the most powerful nation on earth.

Americans may think that their troops used to stay at home and that intervention and nation-building used to be rare. In fact, regime change is as old a story in American foreign policy, as is unilateralism. Until the United Nations came along in 1945, the United States did all this intervening without asking anyone's permission. But after watching America be dragged into world war because the League of Nations had been so weak, Franklin Roosevelt decided to back the creation of a muscular world body. He was even willing to hand over some authority over interventions to the United Nations Security Council, leaving it to the council to decide which threats to international peace and security gave states the right to send in military force. Cold-war deadlock on the council, however, frustrated the Roosevelt dream. Besides, a substantial body of American opinion has always questioned why the United States should ask the United Nations' permission to use force abroad.

After World War II, the boys may have wanted to come home, but Truman kept American soldiers on guard around the world to defend free governments from Communist overthrow. This meant shoring up the Greeks in 1947 and sending troops to prevent South Korea from going under in 1950. But anti-Communism had its limits. It did not mean going to the aid of the Hungarians when they rose up against Soviet domination in 1956. When the Soviet tanks rumbled into Budapest, Eisenhower turned a deaf ear as the Hungarians begged over the airwaves for American help. Like decided that intervention that risked conflict—perhaps nuclear conflict—with a great power was not worth the candle.

III.

Never pick on someone your own size, which in our time means someone with nuclear weapons: this has been Rule No. 1 of intervention since the end of the Second World War. Minor rogues, would-be tough guys like Saddam Hussein, perhaps, but never someone who can actually deliver a nuclear bomb. (We are about to see whether this rule holds with regard to North Korea.) Even the enormous American intervention in Vietnam took great care to avoid a direct clash with Russia and China.

When Lyndon Johnson sent half a million troops to Vietnam, he thought he was containing Communism in Asia (without threatening either the Chinese or Russian regimes that were financing North Vietnam's campaign). Johnson never realized his ultimate enemy was Vietnamese nationalism. The 58,000 names carved into the black granite of the Vietnam Memorial in Washington are the measure of Johnson's mistake. Rule No. 2 of American intervention evolved out of Vietnam: Never fight someone who is more willing to die than you are. (This is the rule now being tested by the hit-and-run attackers and suicide bombers in Iraq.) The Vietnam veterans who came to command the American military—led by Colin Powell—also settled on Rule No. 3, which remains much debated: Never intervene except with overwhelming force in defense of a vital national interest. (Thus this summer's gingerly approach to Liberia.)

But what has been the national interest once the cold war ended and the threat of a growing Communist empire evaporated? No clear national interest has emerged. No clear conversation about the national interest has emerged. Policy—if one can even speak of policy—has seemed to be mostly the prisoner of interventionist lobbies with access to the indignation machine of the modern media. America in the 1990's intervened to oust an invader (the first gulf war), to stop civil war (Bosnia), to stop ethnic cleansing (Kosovo), to feed the starving (Somalia) and to prevent a country from falling apart (Macedonia). America also dithered on the sidelines and watched 800,000 people die in three awful months in Rwanda, when airstrikes against the government sponsors of the genocide, coupled with reinforcement of the United Nations troops on the ground, might have stopped the horror. Rule No. 4: Never use force except as a last resort (sometimes turned into an alibi for doing nothing).

During the Clinton years, there were presidential directives that sought to define exactly what the Clinton doctrine on intervention might be. But no doctrine was ever arrived at. There was a guiding principle: reluctance to shed American blood. Thus, Rule No. 5 in American interventions: When force is used as a last resort, avoid American casualties. Since the Clinton administration's interventions were not of necessity to protect the national interest—whatever that was at the time—but matters of choice, this made a certain amount of sense, at least in terms of domestic politics.

The problem with Rule No. 5 is that it made force protection as important as mission accomplishment and may have sent the wrong signal to the enemy. By cutting and running after the botched intervention in Somalia in 1993, for instance, Clinton might have led Osama bin Laden to believe that Americans lacked the stomach for a fight. Ten years later, we may still be paying the price for that mistake.

By the end of the 1990s, conservative commentators were complaining that Clinton's intervention doctrine, such as it was, had lost touch with national interest and had degenerated into social work. The Bush campaign vowed that the 101st Airborne wouldn't be wasted escorting foreign children to school and promised to bring the boys home from Bosnia. (They remain.) As far as the Bush administration was concerned, too much intervention, where too little was at stake, was blunting the purpose of the military, which was to "fight and win the nation's wars." Of course, at the time he became president, the nation had no wars, and none loomed on the horizon.

Then came Sept. 11—and then came first Afghanistan and then Iraq. These two reversed Rule No. 4. (Only use force as a last resort.) Now the Bush administration was committing itself to use force as a first resort. But the Bush doctrine on intervention is no clearer than Clinton's. The Bush administration is committed to absolute military pre-eminence, but does anyone think that Clinton's military was less determined to remain the single—and overwhelming—superpower? The Bush doctrine is also burdened with contradiction. The president took office ruling out humanitarian interventions, yet marines did (finally) go ashore in war-torn Liberia. During the 2000 campaign, George Bush ruled out intervention in the cause of nation-building, only to find himself staking his presidency on the outcome of nation-building in Afghanistan and Iraq. Having called for a focused intervention strategy, he has proclaimed a war on terror that never clearly defines terrorism; never differentiates among terrorist organizations as to which explicitly threaten American interests and which do not; and never has settled on which states supporting or harboring terrorists are targets of American intervention. An administration whose supposed watchword is self-discipline regularly leaks to the press, for example, that its intervention list might include Syria or Iran—or might not, depending on the day of the week you ask. The administration, purposefully or not, routinely conflates terrorism and the nuclear threat from rogue nations. These are threats of a profoundly different order and magnitude. Finally, the administration promises swift and decisive interventions that will lead to victory. But as Afghanistan shows (and Iraq is beginning to show), this expectation is deluded. Taking down the state that sheltered Osama bin

Laden was easy; shutting down Al Qaeda has proved frustratingly difficult. Interventions don't end when the last big battle is won. In a war on terror, containing rather than defeating the enemy is the most you can hope for. Where is the doctrine acknowledging that truth?

The Bush administration, as no administration before it, has embraced "preemption." It's a strategy of sorts, but hardly a doctrine. Where is the definition of when pre-emption might actually be justified? The angry postwar debate about whether the American public (and the British public, too) were duped into the Iraq war is about much more than whether intelligence estimates were "sexed up" to make the threat from Hussein seem more compelling. It is about what level of threat warrants pre-emptive use of force. Almost 20 years ago, George P. Shultz, as Reagan's secretary of state, gave a speech warning that America would have to make pre-emptive intervention against terrorist threats on the basis of evidence that would be less than clear. Since Shultz, no one has clarified how intervention decisions are to be made when intelligence is, as it is bound to be, uncertain. As Paul Wolfowitz, the Bush administration's deputy secretary of defense, has candidly acknowledged, the intelligence evidence used to justify force in Iraq was "murky." If so, the American people should have been told just that. Instead, they were told that intervention was necessary to meet a real and imminent threat. Now the line seems to be that the war wasn't much of an act of pre-emption at all, but rather a crusade to get rid of an odious regime. But this then makes it a war of choice—and the Bush administration came to power vowing not to fight those. At the moment, the United States is fighting wars in two countries with no clear policy of intervention, no clear end in sight and no clear understanding among Americans of what their nation has gotten itself into.

IV.

There has always been an anti-intervention party in American politics, one that believes that the Republic should resist the temptations of empire and that democracy at home is menaced when force is used to export democracy abroad. During the war to annex the Philippines in 1898, the fine flower of the American intellectual and moral elite was dead set against the war: the humorist Mark Twain, the union leader Samuel Gompers, the multimillionaire Andrew Carnegie, the social critic and activist Jane Addams. From these luminaries of yesteryear to the luminaries of today—Norman Mailer, Noam Chomsky, the Dixie Chicks—intervention has been excoriated as an imperial misadventure, justified in the language of freedom and democracy but actually prosecuted for venal motive: oil, power, revenge, political advantage at home and nefarious designs abroad.

The anti-intervention party in American politics often captures the high moral ground but usually loses the war for public opinion. With the single exception of

Vietnam—where the sheer cost in blood made the exercise seem futile both to moralists and realists alike—the American public has never been convinced that the country would lose its soul in overseas wars. On the contrary, Americans have tended to get caught up in the adventure. They have also believed at times that intervention can serve their interests. When anti-interventionists in the months before the invasion of Iraq thundered, "No blood for oil!" many Americans no doubt thought, "If you won't fight to defend the oil supply, what will you fight for?"

Still, Americans want even this kind of interest backed by principle. Whether it is because America is a religious country at heart, ever concerned with the state of its soul, or just trying to set a better example than the nasty imperialists of old, its leaders have always justified intervention in righteous—or at least disinterested—terms. Teddy Roosevelt incessantly spoke of the restoration of civilized values when he laid hands on Cuba and the Philippines. His ulterior motives—guarding the sea lanes to the Panama Canal he planned to open, securing naval bases in the Pacific—were played down, lest they introduce a note of vulgar calculation into the proceedings. Likewise in Iraq, much mention was made of human rights and democracy and much less about the obvious fact that the operation was about oil, not in the callow sense of going to war for the sake of Halliburton but in the wider sense of America's consolidating its hegemonic role as the guarantor of stable oil supplies for the Western economy.

Yet oil is not the whole story, as capitalist interest has never been. From Teddy Roosevelt to George W. Bush, moral feeling has made a real difference to the timing and scope of interventions. Just compare Bush the father with Bush the son. The father is a cold-eyed realist. In 1991, he did not think the oppression of the Kurds and Shiites justified going all the way to Baghdad. His son is more a hotblooded moralist. Bringing freedom to the Iraqis seems to matter to him, which is why, perhaps, he rushed to Baghdad not caring whether he had a coalition behind him or not. This is not to say that this president's moralism is unproblematic or that it has gone unchallenged. When he went to the United Nations in September 2002 to make his case for action against Hussein, Amnesty International released a statement objecting to his citation of Hussein's abject human rights record as a ground for the use of force. Nothing makes human rights activists angrier than watching political leaders conscript human rights into a justification for aggression. Human Rights Watch and Amnesty International, both of which had denounced Hussein's tyranny for some 20 years with little or no support from successive American administrations, had good reason to be suspicious of the motives of a presidential Johnny-come-lately to the human rights cause. Nonetheless, this put human rights advocates in the curious position of denouncing Hussein but objecting when someone finally proposed to do something about him. To oppose an intervention that was bound to improve the human rights of Iraqis because the man leading that intervention was late to the cause would seem to value good intentions more than good consequences.

Some of the immediate consequences of the Iraq intervention have been good indeed: a totalitarian regime is no longer terrorizing Iraqis; Shiites marching in their hundreds of thousands to celebrate at their shrine at Karbala, along with professors, policemen and office workers demonstrating in the streets of Baghdad, are tasting freedom for the first time; Iraqis as a whole are discovering the truth about the torture chambers, mass graves and other squalid secrets of more than two decades of tyranny. The people may be using their freedom to demand an early exit of the troops who won it for them, but that is exactly how it should be. If the consequence of intervention is a rights-respecting Iraq in a decade or so, who cares whether the intentions that led to it were mixed at best? But it does matter that American intentions were never really spelled out and that the members of the Bush administration do not seem to have a clear intervention policy on Iraq or anywhere else. Establishing and sustaining a rights-respecting Iraq will depend, in part, on setting a policy and convincing the American people of it. And future interventions will depend on policy coherence, too.

Yet it is also true that if a rights-respecting regime is not the result in Iraq, blame cannot simply be laid on the Bush administration. Anti-interventionists assume that all the bad consequences of an intervention derive from ignoble American intentions, just as pro-interventionists tend to accord American good will miraculous power. In this, both sides mistake the true limits of American capacity to determine outcomes. The way things are going in Iraq, L. Paul Bremer III and his proconsuls in Baghdad must be fondly wishing that the reality of Iraq could be shaped by any American intentions at all.

The anti-interventionist party also charges that American good intentions in Iraq might be more credible if the United States defended human rights more consistently throughout the world—though how this might be brought about without sending in the troops from time to time is at best unclear. Tony Blair, whose human rights bona fides are not in much dispute—he had already dispatched British troops to prevent massacre and chaos in Sierra Leone before signing on for the Iraq invasion—says he thinks the demand to intervene consistently or not at all is an argument for sitting on your hands. In the early days of the Iraq war, when British opinion was still against him, Blair remarked to a journalist at 10 Downing Street: "What amazes me is how many people are happy for Saddam to stay. They ask why we don't get rid of Mugabe, why not the Burmese lot? Yes, let's get rid of them all. I don't because I can't, but when you can, you should." A lot of people who would call themselves defenders of human rights opposed intervention in Iraq for sound, prudential reasons—too risky, too costly, not likely to make America safer—but prudence also amounted to a vote for the status quo in the Middle East, and that status quo had at its heart a regime that tortured its citizens, used poison gas against its own population and executed people for the free exercise of religious faith.

Human rights could well be improved in Iraqi as a result of the intervention. But the Bush administration did not invade Iraq just to establish human rights.

Nor, ultimately, was this intervention about establishing a democracy or saving lives as such. And here we come to the heart of the matter—to where the Bush administration's interventions fit into America's long history of intervention. All such interventions have occurred because a president has believed going in that it would increase both his and his country's power and influence. To use Joseph S. Nye Jr.'s definition, "power is the ability to obtain the outcomes one wants." Presidents intervene because successful interventions enhance America's ability to obtain the outcomes it wants.

The Iraq intervention was the work of conservative radicals, who believed that the status quo in the Middle East was untenable—for strategic reasons, security reasons and economic reasons. They wanted intervention to bring about a revolution in American power in the entire region. What made a president take the gamble was Sept. 11 and the realization, with 15 of the hijackers originating in Saudi Arabia, that American interests based since 1945 on a presumed Saudi pillar were actually built on sand. The new pillar was to be a democratic Iraq, at peace with Israel, Turkey and Iran, harboring no terrorists, pumping oil for the world economy at the right price and abjuring any nasty designs on its neighbors.

As Paul Wolfowitz has all but admitted, the "bureaucratic" reason for war—weapons of mass destruction—was not the main one. The real reason was to rebuild the pillars of American influence in the Middle East. Americans may have figured this out for themselves, but it was certainly not what they were told. Nor were they told that building this new pillar might take years and years. What they were told—misleadingly and simplistically—was that force was justified to fight "terrorism" and to destroy arsenals of mass destruction targeted at America and at Israel. In fact, while Hussein did want to acquire such weapons, the fact that none have been found probably indicates that he had achieved nothing more than an active research program.

The manipulation of popular consent over Iraq—together with and tangled up with the lack of an intervention policy—is why the antiwar party is unresigned to its defeat and the pro-war party feels so little of the warm rush of vindication. Even those who supported intervention have to concede that in justifying his actions to the American people, the president was, at the least, economical with the truth. Because the casus belli over Iraq was never accurately set out for Americans, the chances of Americans hanging on for the long haul—and it will be a long haul—have been undercut. Also damaged has been the trust that a president will need from his people when he seeks their support for intervention in the future.

V.

Critics view Iraq as a perilous new step in the history of American intervention: unilateral, opposed by most of the world, an act of territorial conquest. The truth is we have been here before. The Iraq operation most resembles the conquest of the Philippines between 1898 and 1902. Both were wars of conquest, both were urged by an ideological elite on a divided country and both cost much more than anyone had bargained for. Just as in Iraq, winning the war was the easy part. The Spanish fell to Commodore Dewey even more quickly than Hussein's forces fell to Tommy Franks. But it was afterward that the going got rough. More than 120,000 American troops were sent to the Philippines to put down the guerrilla resistance, and 4,000 never came home. It remains to be seen whether Iraq will cost thousands of American lives—and whether the American public will accept such a heavy toll as the price of success in Iraq. The Philippines also provides a humbling perspective on nation-building in Iraq. A hundred years on, American troops are back in the Philippines, hunting down guerrillas, this time tied to Al Qaeda, and the democracy that Teddy Roosevelt sought to bring to that nation remains chronically insecure.

Roosevelt's "splendid little war" may not have done much for the Philippines, but it did a lot to make America a leading power in the Pacific. If Bush succeeds in Iraq, he will reap geostrategic benefit on the same scale. America's enemies understand this only too well. The current struggle in Iraq is much more than the death throes of the old Hussein regime. The foreign fighters who have crossed into Iraq from Syria, Iran and Palestine to join Hussein loyalists in attacks on American soldiers know how much is at stake. Bloodying American troops, forcing a precipitous withdrawal, destroying the chances for a democratic Iraq would inflict the biggest defeat on America since Vietnam and send a message to every Islamic extremist in the region: Goliath is vulnerable.

But the American Goliath recovers quickly from failure, and this keeps presidents throwing the interventionist dice. Nor is the risk of imperial overstretch—which kept the Romans and the British from battering every available barbarian rogue—a very real constraint on America's propensity to intervene. The occupation of Iraq is forcing the military to run at a high operational tempo, but still there appear to be enough troops to land in Liberia and garrison Bosnia and South Korea and all the other outposts of the imperium. Indeed, intervention is getting cheaper. The second gulf war cost half as much as the first gulf war and required about half the number of troops, and actual combat lasted a little more than half the time. If neither the risk of failure nor the cost of deployment is likely to restrain American use of force, what about the risk of casualties? While Clinton believed that Americans didn't want their sons and daughters dying in wars of choice, studies show that Americans are prepared for casualties in wars— if they understand them as wars of necessity. Besides, Americans count on precision missiles and stealth aircraft to deliver crushing lethality at low risk to American troops. Impunity lowers the threshold of risk for intervention. But that threshold does remain, and an army of occupation is particularly vulnerable. Nobody knows whether one of the president's Democratic opponents will manage to turn the deadly drip of bloodshed in Iraq into an electoral liability. Only one president—Lyndon Johnson—was brought down by a botched intervention, but no president since has been able to afford to ignore that warning.

VI.

If we take stock and ask what will curb the American appetite for intervention, the answer is, not much. Interventions are popular, and they remain popular even if American soldiers die. Even failure and defeat aren't much of a restraint: 30 years after Vietnam, America is intervening as robustly as ever. What Thomas Jefferson called "decent respect to the opinions of mankind" doesn't seem to exert much influence, either. About Iraq, the opinions of mankind told the Bush White House that the use of force was a dangerous and destabilizing adventure, but the intervention went ahead because the president believes that the ultimate authority over American decisions to intervene is not the United Nations or the world's opinion, but his constitutional mandate as commander in chief to "preserve, protect and defend" the United States. This unilateral doctrine alarms America's allies, but there is not a lot they can do about it. When Bush went to war, he set the timetable, and not even Tony Blair, who desperately needed more time to bring his domestic opinion with him, was able to stretch it out.

To date, the only factor that keeps the United States from intervening is if the country in question has nuclear weapons. One of the factors driving pre-emptive action in Iraq was the belief that were Hussein to acquire a nuclear or mass-casualty chemical or biological weapon, it would then be too late to use force. No wonder a Pakistani general is supposed to have remarked in 1999 that the chief lesson he drew from the display of American precision air power in Kosovo was for his country to acquire nuclear weapons as quickly as possible.

After Iraq, the key question is when the nuclear taboo will be broken. Already in 1994, over the last crisis with North Korea, the Clinton administration gamed out the possibilities of a conventional strike against a North Korean reactor where it believed nuclear weapons were being produced. Fortunately, it decided not to, realizing that any strike, either with conventional or the small precision nuclear weapons the United States is known to possess, might trigger horrendous military retaliation against South Korean or even Japanese cities.

There is actually a more daunting intervention possibility on the horizon. The United States recognizes one China but guarantees the security of Taiwan. Clinton sent the Navy into the China Sea in 1996 to make sure the Chinese respected that commitment. The freedom of Taiwan, one of the great success stories of American power in Asia, remains precarious. Were the Taiwanese to provoke the mainland, were the Americans to fail to hold them back or were the Chinese leadership to seek to divert attention from troubles at home with bellicose nationalism abroad, America might find itself having to decide how to confront a nuclear power of more than a billion people in defense of an imperative commitment to the freedom of 23 million. Doing so would require the president to break, or at least to threaten to break, the nuclear taboo that has restrained American intervention strategy since Hiroshima. Given American history, which seems to say that resolute use of force always pays dividends, it is difficult for the United States not to believe that it can get its way by relying on military force alone. Yet such a doctrine might end up endangering everyone, including itself.

VII.

For all its risks, Americans, by and large, still think of intervening as a noble act in which the new world comes to the rescue of the old. They remember the newsreels of G.I.'s riding into Rome in 1943 or driving through the lanes of northern Europe in 1944, kissing the girls and grabbing the bouquets and wine bottles held out to them by people weeping with gratitude at their liberation. All this has changed. There were few tearful embraces when the marines rode into Nasiriya, no bouquets and prayers of thanks when the Army rode into Baghdad. True, Iraq is not the first time an American intervention has been unpopular. Iranians were not happy that the C.I.A. engineered the overthrow of Mossadegh in 1953, Chilean democrats didn't like what was done to Allende and students the world over protested against Vietnam. But these occasions apart, and right through the Kosovo intervention in 1999, our allies kept faith with American good intentions. Now all that moral capital has been spent. Some Europeans actually think, to judge from a few polls, that George Bush is more of a threat to world peace than Osama bin Laden. This may be grotesque, but it makes it much harder for American interventions to find favor in world opinion.

Its allies wept with America after Sept. 11 and then swiftly concluded that only America was under attack. The idea that Western civilization had been the target was not convincing. While America and its allies stood shoulder to shoulder when they faced a common Soviet foe, Islamic terrorism seemed to have America alone in its sights. Why cozy up to a primary target, America's allies asked themselves, when it will only make you a secondary one? Indeed, after Sept. 11 an astonishing number of the United States' friends went further. They whispered, America had it coming. Aggrieved Americans were entitled to ask, For what? For guaranteeing the security of their oil supplies for 60 years? For rebuilding the European economy from the ruins of 1945? For protecting innumerable countries from Communist takeover? No matter, after Sept. 11, memories of American generosity were short, and the list of grievances against it was long.

As the Iraq debate at the United Nations showed so starkly, the international consensus that once provided America with coalitions of the willing when it used force has disappeared. There is no Soviet ogre to scare doubters into line. European allies are now serious economic rivals, and they are happy to conceal their absolute military dependence with obstreperously independent foreign policies.

Throughout the third world, states fear Islamic political opposition even more than American disapproval and are disposed to appease their Islamic constituencies with anti-American poses whenever they can get away with it.

There are those who think that the damage done by the Iraq debate at the United Nations can be repaired and that a coalition of the willing, at least one with more active players, might have been possible if the United States hadn't been so backhanded with its diplomacy. Yet the days when the United States intervenes as the servant of the international community may be well and truly over. When it intervenes in the future, it will very likely go it alone and will do so essentially for itself.

If this is the new world order, it will have costs that the rest of the world will have to accept: fewer humanitarian interventions on behalf of starving or massacred people in the rest of the world, fewer guarantees of other people's security against threat and invasion. Why bother with rescue and protection if you have to do everything alone? Why bother maintaining a multilateral order—of free trade, open markets and common defense—if your allies only use it to tie Gulliver down with leading strings?

American unilateralism will have costs for the United States too. The first gulf war was paid for by a coalition of the willing. The cost of the second one will be borne by the American taxpayer alone. The Bush administration affects not to care about the price tag of unpopularity abroad; foreigners don't vote. But Iraq has shown the costs, monetary and otherwise, that are added to the exercise of power when friends don't trust your intentions.

But can a war on terror be fought alone? The allies have intelligence networks and some good counterterrorist squads, and in a battle with Al Qaeda, the biggest breaks have come from the police work of specialists in Spain, Britain, Germany and Pakistan. In a war on terror, an isolated America whose military power awakens even the resistance of its friends may prove a vulnerable giant.

VIII.

There is a way out of this mess of interventionist policy, but it is also a route out of American unilateralism. It entails allowing other countries to have a say on when and how the United States can intervene. It would mean returning to the United Nations and proposing new rules to guide the use of force. This is the path that Franklin Roosevelt took in 1944, when he put his backing behind the creation of a new world organization with a mandate to use force to defend "international peace and security." What America needs, then, is not simply its own doctrine for intervention but also an international doctrine that promotes and protects its interests and those of the rest of the international community.

The problem is that the United Nations that F.D.R. helped create never worked as he intended. What passes for an "international community" is run by a Security Council that is a museum piece of 1945 vintage. Everybody knows that the Security Council needs reform, and everybody also knows that this is nearly impossible. But if so, then the United Nations has no future. The time for reform is now or never. If there ever was a reason to give Great Britain and France a permanent veto while denying permanent membership to Germany, India, Brazil or Japan, that day is over. The United States should propose enlarging the number of permanent members of the council so that it truly represents the world's population. In order to convince the world that it is serious about reform, it ought to propose giving up its own veto so that all other permanent members follow suit and the Security Council makes decisions to use force with a simple majority vote. As a further guarantee of its seriousness, the United States would commit to use force only with approval of the council, except where its national security was directly threatened.

All this is difficult enough, but the next step is tougher still. The United Nations that F.D.R. helped create privileged state sovereignty ahead of human rights: a world of equal states, equally entitled to immunity from intervention. One result has been that since 1945 millions more people have been killed by oppression, abuse, civil war and massacre inside their states than in wars between states. These have been the rules that made tyrants and murderers like Saddam Hussein members in good standing of the United Nations club.

This is the cruel reality of what passes for an "international community" and the comity of nations. United Nations member states will have to decide what the organization is actually for: to defend sovereignty at all costs, in which case it ends up defending tyranny and terror—and invites a superpower to simply go its own way, or to defend human rights, in which case, it will have to rewrite its own rules for authorizing the use of force.

So what rules for intervention should the United States propose to the international community? I would suggest that there are five clear cases when the United Nations could authorize a state to intervene: when, as in Rwanda or Bosnia, ethnic cleansing and mass killing threaten large numbers of civilians and a state is unwilling or unable to stop it; when, as in Haiti, democracy is overthrown and people inside a state call for help to restore a freely elected government; when, as in Iraq, North Korea and possibly Iran, a state violates the nonproliferation protocols regarding the acquisition of chemical, nuclear or biological weapons; when, as in Afghanistan, states fail to stop terrorists on their soil from launching attacks on other states; and finally, when, as in Kuwait, states are victims of aggression and call for help. These would be the cases when intervention by force could be authorized by majority vote on the Security Council.

Sending in the troops would remain a last resort. If the South Africans can persuade Mugabe to go into retirement, so much the better. If American diplomats can persuade the Burmese junta to cease harassing Aung San Suu Kyi, it would obviously be preferable to using force. But force and the threat of it are usually the only language tyrants, human rights abusers and terrorists ever understand. Terrorism and nuclear proliferation can be contained only by multilateral coalitions of the willing who are prepared to fight if the need arises.

These rules wouldn't require the United States to make its national security decisions dependent on the say-so of the United Nations, for its unilateral right of self-defense would remain. New rules for intervention, proposed by the United States and abided by it, would end the canard that the United States, not its enemies, is the rogue state. A new charter on intervention would put America back where it belongs, as the leader of the international community instead of the deeply resented behemoth lurking offstage.

Dream on, I hear you say. Such a change might lead to more American intervention, and the world wants a lot less. But we can't go on the way we are, with a United Nations Charter that has become an alibi for dictators and tyrants and a United States ever less willing to play by United Nations rules when trying to stop them. Clear United Nations guidelines, making state sovereignty contingent on good citizenship at home and abroad and licensing intervention where these rules were broken might actually induce states to improve their conduct, making intervention less, rather than more, frequent.

Putting the United States at the head of a revitalized United Nations is a huge task. For the United States is as disillusioned with the United Nations as the world is disillusioned with the United States. Yet it needs to be understood that the alternative is empire: a muddled, lurching America policing an ever more resistant world alone, with former allies sabotaging it at every turn. Roosevelt understood that Americans can best secure their own defense and pursue their own interests when they unite with other states and, where necessary, sacrifice unilateral freedom of action for a common good. The signal failure of American foreign policy since the end of the cold war has not been a lack of will to lead and to intervene; it has been a failure to imagine the possibility of a United States once again cooperating with others to create rules for the international community. Pax Americana must be multilateral, as Franklin Roosevelt realized, or it will not survive. Without clear principles for intervention, without friends, without dreams to serve, the soldiers sweating in their body armor in Iraq are defending nothing more than power. And power without legitimacy, without support, without the world's respect and attachment, cannot endure.

STUDY AND DISCUSSION QUESTIONS

1. Ignatieff argues that the United States has never shrunk from foreign wars. What lessons does he think this history of foreign intervention reveals?
2. According to Ignatieff, is the war in Iraq just another case of this history of foreign intervention—or does it have a different rationale and hold greater perils?

3. What alternative does Ignatieff offer as a way out of what he characterizes as a "mess of interventionist policy"?

26

Domination or Leadership

Zbigniew Brzezinski

*How can the United States make the most of its unrivalled hegemonic
power? In this selection, Zbigniew Brzezinski, a professor of foreign
policy at The John Hopkins University and the National Security Advi-
sor under President Carter, warns that America faces difficult choices.
The real choices, he argues, involve how the country should exercise its
hegemony—for domination or for leadership—and to what goals it
should dedicate its unrivalled power.*

*Brzezinski argues that security must come first, but that the
prospect of national security through the exercise of autonomous power
is a chimera. He contends that the tendency of the Bush administration
to make the war against terrorism appear to most of the world as the
exclusive focus of both domestic and international policy may be "politically captivating"—but is simplistic and short-sighted. Brzezinski
argues for an alternative approach. The United States should define its
central strategic challenge as the recognition of global turmoil—of
which terrorism and polarizing disparities in the human condition are
two dangerous symptoms—and apply its leadership to the task of forging a more humane globalization.*

American global hegemony is now a fact of life. No one, including America,
has any choice in the matter. Indeed, America would imperil its own existence were it somehow to decide—like China more than half a millennium ago—
to withdraw suddenly from the world. Unlike China, America would not be able
to isolate itself from the global chaos that would quickly ensue. But as in life, so

in political affairs: someday, everything must wane. A hegemony is a transient historical phase. Eventually, even if not soon, America's global dominance will fade. It is therefore not too early for Americans to seek to determine the shape of their hegemony's eventual legacy.

The real choices pertain to how America should exercise its hegemony, how and with whom that hegemony might be shared, and to what ultimate goals it should be dedicated. What is the central purpose of America's unprecedented global power? The answer will ultimately determine whether international consensus legitimates and reinforces American leadership, or whether American primacy relies largely on assertive domination based on might. Consensual leadership would increase America's supremacy in world affairs, with legitimacy enhancing America's status as the world's sole superpower; domination would require a greater expenditure of U.S. power, even if still leaving America in a uniquely preponderant position. In other words, as the former, America would be a Superpower Plus; as the latter, a Superpower Minus.

It almost goes without saying that America's own security has to be the first and foremost purpose of the exercise of national power. In the increasingly elusive global security environment, especially given the growing ability not only of states but of covert organizations to unleash massive lethality, the security of the American people must be the primary goal of America's global policy. But in our age, solitary national security is a chimera. The quest for security must include efforts to garner greater global support. Otherwise, international resentment and envy of America's primacy could turn into a rising security threat.

In some measure, that ominous trend has already begun. America emerged triumphant from the end of the Cold War, truly a Superpower Plus. A decade later, it risks becoming a Superpower Minus. In the two years since 9/11, the initial global solidarity with America has increasingly been transmuted into American solitude, while global sympathy has given way to widespread suspicion of the true motivations of the exercise of American power.

In particular, the militarily successful but internationally controversial invasion of Iraq produced a perplexing paradox: America's global military credibility has never been higher, yet its global political credibility has never been lower. It is universally recognized that the United States is the only power capable of mounting and winning a military operation anywhere in the world. But the justification for the war against Iraq—that Iraq was armed with weapons of mass destruction, a charge stated categorically as a fact by the president and his top officials—has turned out not to have been true. That has damaged America's global standing, not only among the frequently anti-American left but also among the right. Since international legitimacy in significant degree is derived from trust, the costs to America's global standing should not be viewed as negligible.

It is therefore all the more important how America defines for itself—and for the world as well—the central purposes of its hegemony. That definition has to capture and articulate the essential strategic challenge that America confronts and against which America seeks to mobilize the world. How it does so—with how much clarity and moral force, with what degree of comprehension of the needs and aspirations of others—will largely determine the effective scope and burdens of the exercise of America's power. In brief, it will determine whether America will be a Superpower Plus or a Superpower Minus.

Since 9/11, to much of the world it appears that the predominant emphasis of U.S. security policy, both domestically and internationally, is on "the war against terrorism with a global reach." Efforts to rivet public attention on that phenomenon have been the major public concern of the Bush administration. Terrorism—defined vaguely, reviled in largely theological or moralistic terms, castigated as unrelated to any regional conundrum though generally linked to Islam—is to be combated through ad hoc coalitions with like-minded partners who share (or expediently profess to share) a similar preoccupation with terrorism as the central security challenge of our time. The eradication of that scourge is thus presented as America's most urgent task, the success of which is expected to facilitate the more general promotion of global security.

The primary focus on terrorism is politically captivating in the short run. It has the advantage of simplicity. By demonizing an unknown enemy and exploiting vague fears, it can rally popular support. But as a longer-range strategy, it lacks staying power, can be internationally divisive, can breed intolerance of others ("he who is not with us is against us") and unleash jingoist emotions, and can serve as the point of departure for America's arbitrary designation of other states as "outlaws." Consequently, it poses the risk that America will be perceived abroad as self-absorbed and that anti-American ideologues will gain international credence by labeling the United States a self-appointed vigilante.

The three main strategic conclusions drawn from the definition of terrorism as the central threat to American security—that "he who is not with us is against us," that military preemption and prevention are equally justifiable and can be conflated into a single interchangeable proposition, and that enduring alliances may be supplanted by ad hoc coalitions—have prompted widespread concerns abroad. The first is viewed as dangerously polarizing, the second as inviting strategic unpredictability, and the third as politically unsettling. Cumulatively, they have contributed to the image of America as an increasingly arbitrary superpower.

An experienced European observer, comparing contemporary America to ancient Rome, noted perceptively that "World powers without rivals are a class unto themselves. They do not accept anyone as equal, and are quick to call loyal followers friends, or *amicus populi Romani*. They no longer know any foes, just rebels, terrorists, and rogue states. They no longer fight, merely punish. They no longer wage wars but merely create peace. They are honestly outraged when vassals fail to act like vassals."[1] (One is tempted to add, they do not invade other countries, they only liberate.) The author wrote before 9/11, but his comment strikingly captured the attitude some U.S. policymakers displayed during the UN debates surrounding the 2003 decision to go to war against Iraq.

The alternative approach to defining America's central strategic challenge is to focus more broadly on global turmoil in its several regional and social manifestations—of which terrorism is a genuinely menacing symptom—in order to lead an enduring and enlarging alliance of like-minded democracies in a comprehensive campaign against the conditions that precipitate that turmoil. To this end, the magnetic success of America's democracy and its outward projection through a humane definition of globalization would reinforce the effectiveness and legitimacy of America's power and enhance U.S. ability to overcome—together with others—both the consequences and the causes of global turmoil.

Global turmoil manifests itself in a variety of ways. It is intensified, though not entirely caused, by persistent mass poverty and social injustice. In some regions, it involves ethnic oppression; in others, tribal conflicts; elsewhere, religious fundamentalism. It is expressed through bursts of violence as well as pervasive disorder throughout the southern rim of Eurasia, the Middle East, much of Africa, and some portions of Latin America. It generates hate and envy of the dominant and prosperous and is likely to become more sophisticated in its lethality, especially with the proliferation of WMD. Some of that violence is much more indiscriminate than terrorism in its victims, with tens of thousands killed every year, hundreds of thousands maimed, and millions afflicted by primitive combat.

Recognition of global turmoil as the basic challenge of our time requires confronting complexity. That is the weakness of the issue insofar as the American political scene is concerned. It does not lend itself to sloganeering or rouse the American people as viscerally as terrorism. It is more difficult to personalize without a demonic figure like Osama bin Laden. Nor is it congenial to self-gratifying proclamations of an epic confrontation between good and evil on the model of the titanic struggles with Nazism and Communism. Yet not to focus on global turmoil is to ignore a central reality of our times: the massive worldwide political awakening of mankind and its intensifying awareness of intolerable disparities in the human condition.

The key issue for the future is whether that awakening will be seized and exploited by hate-mongering anti-American demagogues, or whether a compelling vision of a global community of shared interest will come to be identified with America's global role. To be sure, as with the narrower focus on terrorism, an effective response to global turmoil requires major reliance on American power as the essential prerequisite to global stability. But it also calls for a long-haul commitment, derived from a sense of moral justice as well as from America's own national interest, to progressively transform America's prevailing power into a co-optive hegemony—one in which leadership is exercised more through shared conviction with enduring allies than by assertive domination.

A global community of shared interest should not be confused with world government. A world government is not a practical goal at this stage of history. America certainly would not yield its sovereignty—nor should it—to a supranational authority in a world that lacks even the minimum of consensus needed for a common government. The only "world government" currently even remotely possible would be an American global dictatorship—and that would be an unstable and ultimately self-defeating enterprise. World government is either a pipe dream or a nightmare, but not a serious prospect for some generations to come.

A global community of shared interest, on the other hand, is not only possible and desirable but actually emerging. It is partially the outgrowth of a spontaneous process inherent in the dynamics of globalization and partially the consequence of more deliberate efforts, especially by the United States and the European Union, to weave together a broader fabric of binding and institutionalized international cooperation. Bilateral and multilateral free trade agreements, regional policy forums, and formal alliances all contribute to a web of interdependent relations, at this stage more on the regional level but increasingly also on the global. Cumulatively, they represent the natural evolution of interstate relations into an informal international governance structure.

That process needs to be encouraged, expanded, and institutionalized, so as to promote a growing awareness of the common destiny of mankind. Shared interest entails a balance of benefits and responsibilities, empowerment and not dictation. America is in a unique position to lead this process because it is both secure in its power and democratic in its governance. Since a selfish hegemony will inevitably breed its own antithesis but democracy breeds its own contagion, it is the commonsense dictate of hard-nosed realism that America should rise to this calling.

The practical issue of preserving its position thus pertains to the character of America's global leadership. Leadership entails a sense of direction that mobilizes others. Power for the sake of power, domination dedicated to the perpetuation of domination—these are not a formula for enduring success. Domination as an end in itself is a dead-end street. It eventually mobilizes countervailing opposition while its very arrogance produces self-deluding historical blindness. The ultimate destination of the globe, as argued in the preceding chapters, will be either steady movement over the next two decades or so toward a community of shared interest, or an accelerating plunge into global chaos. The acceptance of American leadership by others is the sine qua non for avoiding chaos.

In practice, wise leadership in world affairs calls, first of all, for a rational and balanced policy of self-protection in order to mitigate the most likely and most threatening risks to American society without stimulating a paranoiac sense of national insecurity. Second, it calls for a patient and protracted effort to pacify the more volatile regions of the globe, which generate much of the emotional hostility that fuels violence. Third, it requires a sustained effort to engage the most vital and friendly parts of the world in a joint framework to contain and, if possible, eliminate the likely sources of the greatest dangers. Fourth, it requires recognizing globalization as more than just an opportunity for enhanced trade and profit, but a phenomenon having a deeper moral dimension. And fifth, it requires fostering a domestic political culture that is actively aware of the complex responsibilities inherent in global interdependence.

The required co-optive global leadership calls for a conscious, strategically coherent, and intellectually demanding effort by whomever the American people choose to be their president. The president must do more than stir the American people; he must also educate them. The political education of a large democracy cannot be pursued by patriotic slogans, fear-mongering, or self-righteous arrogance. Every politician faces that temptation, and it is politically rewarding to yield to it. But harping on terrorism distorts the public's vision of the world. It breeds the risk of defensive self-isolation, fails to give the public a realistic understanding of the world's complexities, and furthers the fragmentation of the nation's strategic cohesion. America will be able to exercise global leadership over the long haul only if there is greater public understanding of the interdependence between U.S. national security and global security, of the burdens of global primacy, and of the resulting need for enduring democratic alliances to overcome the challenge of global turmoil.

The grand strategic choice facing America points to several specific implications. The foremost is the critical importance of a complementary and increasingly binding American-European global partnership. A mutually complementary if still asymmetrical Atlantic alliance with a global reach is clearly in the interest of both. With such an alliance, America becomes a Superpower Plus, and Europe can steadily unite. Without Europe, America is still preponderant but not globally omnipotent, while without America, Europe is rich but impotent. Some European leaders and nations may be tempted to pursue unity through an anti-American (or, rather, an anti-Atlanticist) self-definition, but both America and Europe itself would be the ultimate losers in the effort. As a Superpower Minus, America would find the costs of exercising its global leadership considerably higher, while Europe would then be even less likely to unite, because an anti-Atlanticist platform would not attract a majority of the EU members and prospective members.

Only the two sides of the Atlantic working together can chart a truly global course that may significantly improve the worldwide state of affairs. To do so, Europe must wake up from its current coma, realize that its security is even more inseparable from global security than is America's, and draw the inevitable practical conclusions. It cannot be secure without America, it cannot unite against America, and it cannot significantly influence America without being willing to act jointly with America. For some time to come, the much-discussed "autonomous" European political-military role outside of Europe will remain quite limited, largely because the European slogans about it outrun any determination to pay for it.

At the same time, America must resist the temptation to divide its most important strategic partner. There is no "old" or "new" Europe. That too is a slogan with no geographical or historical content. Moreover, the gradual unification of Europe does not threaten America; on the contrary, it can only benefit America by increasing the overall weight of the Atlantic community. A policy of *divide et impera,* even if tactically tempting for settling scores, would be shortsighted and counterproductive.

An important reality that also needs to be faced is that the Atlantic Alliance cannot be a perfectly balanced 50–50 partnership. The very idea of such a finely tuned and symmetrical equality is a political myth. Even in business, where shares can be precisely counted, a 50–50 arrangement is not workable. A demographically younger, more vigorous, and politically united America cannot be matched politically and militarily by a Europe of diverse and aging nation-states that are unifying but far from united. Nevertheless, each side of the Atlantic has assets the other needs. America will remain for some time to come the ultimate guarantor of global security even if Europe progressively enhances its still rather meager military capabilities. Europe can reinforce U.S. military power, while the combined economic resources of the United States and the EU would make the Atlantic community globally omnipotent.

The only real option, therefore, is not a European partner of equal weight, and even less a counterweight, but a European partner with weighty influence in the shaping and implementation of a shared global policy. The exercise of critically important influence, even if it does not involve exactly an equal share of decision-making, requires a willingness on both sides to act together when action is needed. It also means, when action is necessary, that the party with the greater means for action or greater interest in the outcome ultimately has the greater say. American primacy need not imply the automatic subordination of Europe, and partnership need not imply general paralysis in cases of initial disagreement. Both sides must foster the spirit of accommodation, nurture shared strategic perspectives, and promote additional Atlantic mechanisms for sustained global political planning.

Though Europe's economic unification will move more rapidly than political unification, it is not too early to consider some restructuring of NATO's decision-making in order to take into account the EU's slowly emerging political profile. As the EU's constitution becomes embedded in the fabric of European society, a common European political orientation will take shape. Given that the vast majority of NATO's members are also members of the EU, alliance procedures will have to reflect the fact that the alliance is becoming less a composite of twenty-six nation-states (one of them much more powerful than all the others) and more a two-pillar North American-European structure. To fail to take that reality into account would only encourage advocates of a separate and potentially duplicative European defense effort.

A transatlantic convention to discuss the implications of this emerging reality would be timely. It should consider not only the long-term strategic agenda for a redefined and perhaps restructured alliance but also the wider global implications of the fact that America and Europe together are genuinely omnipotent. Implicit in that fact is Europe's obligation to become more engaged in promoting global security. Europe's security perspective can no longer be limited to the continent and its periphery. With NATO already present in Afghanistan, indirectly also in Iraq, and soon perhaps along the Palestinian-Israeli frontier, the Atlantic Alliance's strategic scope eventually will have to include all of Eurasia.

A genuine U.S.-EU transatlantic alliance, based on a shared global perspective, must be derived from a similarly shared strategic understanding of the nature of our era, of the central threat that the world faces, and of the role and mission of the West as a whole. That calls for a serious and searching joint dialogue, and not mutual recriminations (often based on contrived argumentation that America and Europe are drifting in fundamentally divergent directions). The truth remains that the West as a whole has much to offer to the world, but it will be able to do so only if it articulates a common vision. The West's current deficit is neither in military power (America has a surfeit of it) nor in financial resources (Europe's match those of America). Rather, it is in the ability to transcend parochial concerns and narrow interests. At a time of unprecedented challenges to mankind's security and well-being, the leadership of the West often seems intellectually barren. A conscious strategic debate might inspire the needed global political innovation.

In any case, short of such an ambitious grand review, the transatlantic alliance needs to address a more specific agenda. In Europe, it involves the steady and complementary expansion of both the EU itself and NATO. That expansion is now entering its third phase. The first, the Warsaw round, involved coping with the immediate geostrategic legacy of the Cold War era by promptly admitting Poland, the Czech Republic, and Hungary into NATO; the second, the Vilnius round, pertained to the almost simultaneous and geographically largely overlapping decision to enlarge both NATO and the EU by seven and ten new states, respectively; the third and next (the Kyiv round?) looks further east, to Ukraine and maybe the Caucasus, and may even consider the eventual admission of Russia.

Outside of Europe itself, the Middle East is an area of strong American interest and of immediate concern to Europe. A roadmap for the Israeli-Palestinian peace—dependent in large part on joint and persistent efforts by America and Europe—is inseparable from a roadmap for Iraq's rehabilitation as a stable, independent, and democratizing state. Without both, peace in the region is not possible. Working together, the United States and the EU can also be more effective in avoiding a head-on collision between the West and Islam and in promoting the more positive tendencies within the world of Islam that favor its eventual incorporation into the modern and democratic world.

But joint pursuit of that goal requires also a subtle understanding of the contending forces within Islam, and Europe has the advantage over America in that regard. In addition, American sympathy for the security of the Israelis is balanced by European sympathy for the plight of the Palestinians. No peaceful outcome for the Israeli-Palestinian conflict is possible without both concerns being taken fully into account. A peaceful outcome will facilitate, in turn, the needed and much delayed internal transformation of the adjoining Arab societies and will reduce anti-American hostility. The unwillingness of several U.S. administrations to bite the bullet on this issue has been a major contributing factor in the rise of extremism in the region.

America also has a unique role to play in the promotion of democracy in the Arab world. For more than two centuries, America has been the cradle of liberty, the destination point for those who seek to live in freedom, and the source of inspiration for those who want to make their own countries as free as America itself. During the Cold War, it was America alone that clearly proclaimed—through Radio Free Europe—that it would not accept as permanent the subjugation of Central Europe to Moscow's control. It was America under President Carter that promoted the cause of human rights, thereby placing the Soviet Union on the ideological defensive. America thus propagated a shared aspiration; it did not seek to impose its own political culture.

It is important to recall this at a time when the now globally dominant America is publicly asserting its determination to democratize the Muslim countries. That goal is a noble one, and also practical in that the spread of democracy is generally congenial to global peace. But it is important not to lose sight of a basic lesson of history: any just cause, in the hands of fanatics, will degenerate into its antithesis. That is what happened when religious fervor in medieval Europe translated a uniquely compassionate and meek faith into the horror of the Inquisition. In more recent times, that is also what happened when the French Revolution, on behalf of "liberté-fraternité-égalité," came to be symbolized by the guillotine. The century that just ended experienced unprecedented human suffering because of the degeneration of the idealism of socialism into the inhuman totalitarianism of Leninism-Stalinism.

The promotion of democracy, if pursued with a fanatical zeal that ignores the historical and cultural traditions of Islam, could similarly produce democracy's very negation. The argument that America after World War II successfully imposed democracy upon both Germany and Japan ignores historically relevant facts. To cite but two: In 2003, Berlin celebrated the one hundredth anniversary of the victory of the German Socialist Party in its municipal elections—in the capital of imperial Germany, no less. Japanese compliance with U.S. postwar reforms gained social legitimacy because the Japanese emperor publicly endorsed them. In both cases, there were social foundations on which the United States after World War II was able to construct democratic constitutions.

There are some grounds, though more limited ones, for seeking the same outcome in the Middle East; but doing so will require historical patience and cultural sensitivity. The experience of several Muslim countries located on the periphery of the West—especially Turkey but also Morocco and (despite its fundamentalist veneer) Iran—suggests that, when democratization takes place through organic growth and not through dogmatic imposition by an alien force, Islamic societies also gradually absorb and assimilate a democratic political culture.

Given America's new prominence in the political life of the Arab Middle East in the aftermath of its occupation of Iraq, it is essential that U.S. policymakers not be seduced by doctrinaire advocates of an externally imposed and impatient democratization—a democratization "from above," so to speak. Sloganeering to that effect in some cases may reflect contempt for Islamic traditions. For others it may be tactical, rooted in the hope that the focus on democratization will provide a diversion from efforts to press both the Israelis and the Arabs to accept the compromises necessary for peace. Whatever the motivation, the fact is that genuine and enduring democracy is nurtured best in conditions that gradually foster spontaneous change and do not combine compulsion with haste. The former approach can indeed transform a political culture; the latter can only coerce a political correctness that is inherently unlikely to endure.

The strategic scope of the Atlantic agenda extends further east than the Middle East itself. The new Global Balkans—the arc of crisis ranging from the Persian Gulf to Xinjiang—will become less explosive if the resources of the three most successful regions of the world—the politically energetic America, the economically unifying Europe, and the commercially dynamic East Asia—are harnessed in a joint response to the security threat posed by turmoil in that large region. That threat is exacerbated by the acquisition of nuclear weaponry by two neighboring but hostile powers, India and Pakistan, each beset also by domestic tensions. Both America and Europe will need to keep pressing Japan and China, in particular, to become more engaged in joint efforts to contain disintegrative trends. Given that both of these states are already highly dependent on energy flows from the Persian Gulf and Central Asia—and becoming more so—they cannot remain bystanders in the face of a common challenge in this volatile area, which could become quicksand for America alone.

America has already greatly expanded its military involvement in Eurasia. It now has a continuing military presence in Afghanistan and in some of the newly independent Central Asian states. Given the growing Chinese commercial and political outreach to Central Asia, a zone until recently exclusively dominated by Russia, the need for wider international cooperation to cope with local instability has gained urgency. Both Japan and China should be pressed to become material participants in promoting the region's political and social stabilization.

How the power dynamics in the Far East are shaped by the interrelationship among America, Japan, and China will also affect global stability. The United States should seek to translate the emerging equilibrium among itself, Japan, and China into a more structured security relationship. Geopolitically, Asia roughly resembles Europe prior to World War I. America has stabilized Europe but it still faces a potential structural crisis in Asia, where several major powers still contend, though checked by America's peripheral strategic presence. That presence is anchored by the American-Japanese connection, but the rise of a regionally dominant China and the unpredictability of North Korea signal the need for a more active U.S. policy to promote, at a minimum, a triangular security relationship. As argued earlier, such a triangular equilibrium, to be enduring, will require a more internationally engaged Japan that will have gradually assumed a wider range of military responsibilities.

Creating this equilibrium might entail, in turn, fostering a trans-Eurasian multilateral security structure for coping with the novel dimensions of global security. Failure to engage China and Japan in at least a de facto security structure could eventually trigger a dangerous tectonic shift, perhaps involving the unilateral remilitarization of Japan, which already has the potential to very quickly become a nuclear power, in addition to the already grave challenge posed by North Korea's quest for a nuclear arsenal of its own. The need for a collective regional response to North Korea reinforces the more general point that only a co-optive American hegemony can cope effectively with the increasingly pervasive spread of weaponry of mass destruction, whether among states or extremist organizations.

America will have to cope with these dilemmas in the context of a historical marriage between U.S. global power and global interdependence in the age of instant communications. Striking a balance between an existential sovereign hegemony and an emerging global community, and between the values of democracy and the imperatives of global power, will continue to be America's major dilemma. Globalization, which America both favors and promotes, can help to dampen global turmoil—provided it does not disfranchise but empowers the poorer countries, and provided it is infused with humane concerns and not defined by economic self-interest alone. The U.S. attitude toward multilateral obligations, especially those that do not conveniently coincide with America's narrower and more immediate objectives, is thus a litmus test of its readiness to promote a globalization that genuinely advances equitable interdependence and not uneven dependence. The U.S. record in recent years regarding multilateral obligations has created a widespread perception that a level worldwide playing field is not its primary goal.

America must be more sensitive to the risk that its identification with an unjust version of globalization could prompt a worldwide reaction leading to the emergence of a new anti-American creed. Given that security depends not only on military power but also, in this age of global political awakening, on the foci of social passions and fanatical hatreds, how America defines and pursues globalization will bear directly on its long-term security.

Similarly, it behooves America to be sensitive to the unexpected political consequences of its unique worldwide cultural impact. America's globally seductive power has had the unanticipated effect of engendering singularly lofty expectations in the world's people. They hold America to a higher standard than they do other states, often including their own. Indeed, anti-Americanism has many trappings of betrayed affection. As a consequence, the dissatisfied of the world, because they expect more from America, tend to be especially outraged when they feel it is not doing enough to help them rectify their own deplorable circumstances. In effect, America's cultural seduction is politically destabilizing even as America seeks to promote global stability for its larger strategic interests. Thus only if America places a higher premium on a truly shared global cause will it derive any political benefit from the cultural revolution it is unleashing worldwide.

Since a critically important source of America's global appeal, and thus of its power, is the magnetic attraction of its democratic system, it is likewise essential for Americans to carefully preserve the delicate balance between their civil rights and the requirements of their national security. That is easier to do when wars are distant and their costs socially acceptable. But the intense public reactions to the crime of 9/11—reactions perhaps deliberately fanned for political reasons—could be leading to a more basic redefinition of that balance. A garrison-state mentality can poison any democracy. What regional hostility has been doing to Israel, fear fomented by worldwide hostility can do to America.

It follows that domestic security must be pursued in a manner that enhances both sovereign American power and the global legitimacy of that power. To repeat what was said earlier, America is now engaged in the third grand debate since its inception as an independent state regarding the requirements of its national defense. That debate is understandably focused on societal survivability in the novel setting of diffusion and diversification of weapons of mass destruction, percolating global turbulence, and widespread fear of terrorism.

That is a new historical condition for America. It creates an intimate interdependence between the security of the American homeland and the overall state of the world. Given its global security role and its extraordinary global ubiquity, America thus has the right to seek more security than other countries. It needs forces with a decisive worldwide deployment capability. It must enhance its intelligence (rather than waste resources on a huge homeland security bureaucracy) so that threats to America can be forestalled. It must maintain a comprehensive technological edge over all potential rivals in both its strategic and conventional forces. But it should also define its security in ways that help mobilize the self-interest of others. That comprehensive task can be pursued more effectively if the world understands that the trajectory of America's grand strategy is toward a global community of shared interest.

A fortress on a hill can only stand alone, casting a menacing shadow over all beneath. As such, America would become the focus of global hatred. A city on a hill, by contrast, could illuminate the world with the hope of human progress—but only in an environment in which that progress is both the focus of a vision and an attainable reality for all. "A city that is set on a hill cannot be hid. . . . Let your light so shine before men, that they may see your good works."[2] So let America shine.

Notes

[1]Peter Bender, "America: The New Roman Empire?" *Orbis* (Winter 2003), 155.
[2]Matthew 5:14–16.

STUDY AND DISCUSSION QUESTIONS

1. In Brzezinski's view, what paradox has resulted from the invasion of Iraq? How can it be resolved?
2. What should replace America's primary post–9/11 focus on terrorism? What should the United States consider its central strategic challenge?
3. How should the United States exercise its hegemonic power in Europe? In the Middle East? In Asia?

Credits

CHAPTER 1

1. "The New System," from *The Lexus and the Olive Tree,* by Thomas L. Friedman. Copyright © 1999, 2000 by Thomas L. Friedman. Reprinted by permission of Farrar, Strauss, and Giroux, LLC.
2. Reprinted with permission of Simon & Schuster Adult Publishing Group from *The Clash of Civilizations and the Remaking of World Order* by Samuel P. Huntington. Copyright © 1996 by Samuel P. Huntington.
3. "Broken Promises," from *Globalization and Its Discontents* by Joseph E. Stiglitz. Copyright © 2002 by Joseph E. Stiglitz. Used by permission of W. W. Norton & Company, Inc.
4. "Anarchy and the Struggle for Power," from *The Tragedy of Great Power Politics* by John Mearsheimer. Copyright © 2002 by John Mearsheimer. Used by permission of W. W. Norton & Company, Inc.
5. Saskia Sassen, "Global Cities and Survival Circuits," Barbara Ehrenreich and Arlie Russsell Hochschild, eds. *Global Woman: Nannies, Maids, and Sex Workers in the New Economy,* Metropolitan Books, 2002. Reprinted with permission.

CHAPTER 2

6. Stephen D. Krasner, *Sovereignty* © 1999 Princeton University Press. Reprinted by permission of Princeton University Press.
7. David Held, "Political Globalization," *Global Covenant,* Polity Press, 2004, pp. 73–88. Reprinted by permission of Polity Press.
8. From Paul Carmichael, "Briefing Paper: Multi-level Governance," *http://www.rpani.gov.uk/multilevel/index.htm*

CHAPTER 3

9. G. John Ikenberry, "Liberal Hegemony and the Future of the American Post-war Order," in T.V. Paul and John A. Hall, eds. *International Order and the Future of World Politics,* Cambridge University Press, pp. 123–145.

© Cambridge University Press 1999. Reprinted by permission of Cambridge University Press.

10. Robert Hunter Wade, "America's Empire Rules an Unbalanced World," *Counter Punch*, January 3, 2002. Reprinted with permission.

11. "Redefining the National Interest," from *The Paradox of American Power* by Joseph S. Nye, Jr. Used by permission of Oxford University Press, Inc.

12. Ivo H. Daalder and James M. Lindsay, *America Unbound: The Bush Revolution in Foreign Policy*, Brookings Institution Press, 2003, pp. 1–17. Reprinted by permission of Brookings Institution Press.

13. George Ross, "European Integration and Globalization," in Ronald Axtmann, ed. *Globalization and Europe* (London: Pinter, 1998), pp. 164–183. Reprinted with permission.

14. Calleo, David P., *Rethinking Europe's Future*. © 2001 The Century Foundation, published by Princeton University Press, 2003 paperback edition. Reprinted by permission of Princeton University Press.

15. Reprinted by permission of *Foreign Affairs*, 83: 6; November/December 2004. Copyright 2004 by the Council on Foreign Relations, Inc.

16. Reprinted from T. J. Pempel: *The Politics of the Asian Economic Crisis*, Copyright © 1999 by Cornell University. Used by permission of the publisher, Cornell University Press.

17. Linda Weiss, "State Power and the Asian Crisis," *New Political Economy*, Vol. 4, No. 3, 1999, pp. 317–342. Reprinted with permission.

18. Claude Smadja, "The End of Complacency," *Foreign Policy*, No. 113, Winter, 1998–1999), pp. 67–71. Claude Smadja is the President of "Smadja & Associates" Strategic Advisory. Reprinted with permission of the author.

CHAPTER 4

19. Audrey Kurth Cronin, "Behind the Curve: Globalization and International Terrorism," *International Security*, Vol. 27, No. 3, Winter 2002/2003, pp. 30–58. © 2003 by the President and Fellows of Harvard College and the Massachusetts Institute of Technology. Reprinted with permission.

20. The National Security Strategy of the United States of America, http://www.whitehouse.gov/nsc/print/nssall.html)

21. John Lewis Gaddis, "A Grand Strategy of Transformation," *Foreign Policy*, Nov/Dec 2002, pp. 50–58. Copyright 2002 by *Foreign Policy*. Reproduced with permission of *Foreign Policy* in the format textbook via Copyright Clearance Center.

22. This article originally appeared in *Ethics & International Affairs 17, No. 1* (2003). Reprinted by permission.

23. "The Responsibility to Protect: The Way Forward," *The Responsibility To Protect: Report of the International Commission on Intervention and State Sovereignty,* pp. 69–75., Department of Foreign Affairs and International Trade, December 2001. Reproduced with the permission of Her Majesty the Queen in Right of Canada, represented by the Minister of Foreign Affairs, 2005.

24. Niall Ferguson, "The Empire Slinks Back," *The New York Times Magazine,* April 27, 2003. Copyright © 2003 by Niall Ferguson, reprinted with the permission of The Wylie Adency, Inc.

25. Michael Ignatieff, "Why Are We In Iraq? (And Liberia? And Afghanistan?)," *The New York Times Magazine,* September 7, 2003. © 2003 Michael Ignatieff. Reprinted by permission.

26. From *The Choice: Global Domination or Global Leadership* by Zbigniew Brzezinski. Copyright © 2004 by Zbigniew Brzezinski. Reprinted by permission of Basic Books, a member of Perseus Books, L.L.C.